D0493161

The Performance Prism

The Performance Prism

The Scorecard for Measuring and Managing Business Success

Andy Neely,
Chris Adams
and Mike Kennerley

An imprint of **Pearson Education**

London · New York · Toronto · Sydney · Tokyo · Singapore · Hong Kong · Cape Town
New Delhi · Madrid · Paris · Amsterdam · Munich · Milan · Stockholm

PEARSON EDUCATION LIMITED

Edinburgh Gate
Harlow CM20 2JE
Tel: +44 (0)1279 623623
Fax: +44 (0)1279 431059
Website: www.pearsoned.co.uk

First published in Great Britain in 2002

ISBN-10: 0-273-65334-2
ISBN-13: 978-0-273-65334-9

British Library Cataloguing in Publication Data
A CIP catalogue record for this book can be obtained from the British Library

10 9 8 7 6

Typeset by Pantek Arts Ltd, Maidstone, Kent
Printed and bound in Great Britain by Henry Ling limited, at the Dorset Press, Dorchester, DT1 1HD

The Publishers' policy is to use paper manufactured from sustainable forests.

Purchase of this book entitles the purchaser to a single user licence for the CD of the Catalogue of Performance Measures. To purchase additional licences contact Dr Mike Kennerley at the Centre for Business Performance, Cranfield School of Management (m.kennerley@cranfield.ac.uk).

Contents

About the Authors

Andy Neely

Andy Neely is Director of the Centre for Business Performance at Cranfield School of Management, Professor of Operations Strategy and Performance and Managing Partner of The Performance Practice. Prior to joining Cranfield, Andy held a lecturing position at Cambridge University, where he was a Fellow of Churchill College. He has been researching and teaching in the field of business performance measurement and management since the late 1980s and also co-ordinates the Performance Management Association (PMA), an international network for those interested in the subject. Andy has authored over 100 books and articles, including *Measuring Business Performance*, published by *The Economist*. He is widely recognized as one of the world's leading authorities on performance measurement and brings a wealth of practical experience to his teaching and research, derived from his experiences as a consultant to numerous global organizations.

Chris Adams

Chris Adams is a Visiting Fellow at Cranfield School of Management's Centre for Business Performance and an independent consultant.

Until 2001 he worked at Accenture (formerly Andersen Consulting) for 13 years, providing strategy, process and capability performance improvement consultancy services to client organizations in a broad spectrum of industries. Latterly, he led the firm's Managing With Measures thought leadership development initiative – a joint venture with Cranfield School of Management.

With Professor Andy Neely he has co-authored a number of articles and white papers, illustrating the application of the Performance Prism framework – these include 'The Performance Prism Perspective', 'The Performance Prism in Practice', 'Measuring eBusiness Performance', 'Measuring Business Combinations and Alliances' and 'Managing with Measures in a Downturn'.

Prior to his consulting career, Chris gained 22 years of experience in industry with DuPont in a wide variety of customer service, logistics supply chain, quality management and internal support management roles.

Mike Kennerley

Mike Kennerley is a Research Fellow in Cranfield School of Management's Centre for Business Performance. His research and consulting interests are centred around business performance measurement, including the design, implementation and use of performance measurement systems.

Mike has been working in the field of performance measurement since the early 1990s. Since then he has undertaken collaborative research and consulting in business performance measurement, working with organizations from large multinationals to SMEs from a range of sectors. Mike has authored numerous academic publications and made conference presentations to academic and practitioner audiences.

Dr Kennerley's recent research has included investigation into the way in which measurement systems change over time and the development of the *Catalogue of Performance Measures*. This catalogue, aimed at helping practitioners to design and implement appropriate performance measures, forms a relevant and valuable appendix (in CD-ROM format) to this book.

Acknowledgments

Alun Evans, the associate partner who project managed much of the early development work within Accenture's Process Excellence Core Capability Group, was the first person to say that we should write this book back in 1998. However, through many twists and turns, it was not until a couple of years later that we actually started pressing our keyboards into action.

Accenture (then known as Andersen Consulting) sponsored the original 'Managing With Measures' joint venture initiative with the Centre for Business Performance at Cranfield School of Management (formerly at The Judge Institute, University of Cambridge). This work led to the creation of the Performance Prism framework and a range of white papers, articles and other 'spin-off' materials associated with it. And so our thanks are extended here first to the partners and associate partners who sponsored the development work. In particular, we should mention Alun Evans, Steve Shapiro, Mark McDonald, Peter Roberts and Mike Sutcliff. Of these, Steve deserves a special mention as the man who almost strangled the Performance Prism to death in its infancy! That was in September 1998, but it only served to make us all the more determined to develop the concept and by early 1999 we were back on track with an improved version. Steve subsequently became a convert and devotes substantial attention to the Performance Prism in Chapter 6, 'Innovation Through Measurement', of his own book *24/7 Innovation* (McGraw-Hill, 2001).

The Performance Prism framework itself was developed through a series of workshops and discussions. Numerous people have participated in these over the years. From Accenture they include Nick Lawrence, Dave Muthler, Neda Emami, Emma Dempsey, David Billingham, Laslo Moczy, Seema Malhotra, Neil Ramchandran, Tim Boole, Neil McTiffin and Neha Kapashi – all of whom worked directly with Chris Adams on the Accenture 'Managing With Measures' development project at various times. University colleagues from Cambridge and subsequently Cranfield who offered valuable comments and views include Mohammed Al Najjar, Mike Bourne, Jasper Hii, Bernard Marr, Ken Platts, Giovanni Schiuma, Angela Walters. Many others also helped us to develop the *application* of the Performance Prism. Thanks are due especially to Yasar Jarrar, Paul Crowe, Chris Smith, Naomi Maxwell Macdonald, Christos Andrakakos, Morgan Davies, Mark Haffner, Andy McGowan, Simon Crewe, Nicola Brown, Andrew McCaffer and Layo Osho, all of whom helped with opportunities and workshops to solve the challenges of making the theory work in practice.

Not least, we must also acknowledge some of the organizations that let us experiment on them with what was essentially a bunch of innovative concepts at the time. In particular, we should recognize executives of Ciba Specialty Chemicals, DHL International, London Youth, Williams Grand Prix Engineering, GKN Westland, House of Fraser, United Pan-Europe Communications, ASML (Netherlands) and Telewest Communications on all of whom we inflicted some of our formative ideas – but, on the whole, they seemed to enjoy it! And we certainly learned a lot about what works well and what not so well.

One particular acknowledgment also needs to be made. This goes to our co-author, Mike Kennerley. He was highly instrumental in developing and populating the Measures Catalogue, which accompanies this book and is structured around the Performance Prism framework. Financial support for this initiative was provided by the Engineering and Physical Sciences Research Council and Accenture, but without Mike's determination and dedication the catalogue would never have been completed.

Finally, and probably the most important acknowledgment of all, we would like to thank our families for their patience and support as we wrote this book. Their constant acceptance that Dad had to go back to the study yet again to work on the book was wonderful and much appreciated. Our special thanks then as well go to Liese, Lizzie, Ben, Tom and Emma; Jean, Graham and Georgina.

Introduction

The Performance Prism

Three fundamental premises underpin this book. First, it is no longer acceptable (or even feasible) for organizations to focus solely on the needs of one or two of their stakeholders – typically shareholders and customers – if they wish to survive and prosper in the long term. Second, an organization's strategies, processes and capabilities have to be aligned and integrated with one another if the organization is to be best positioned to deliver real value to all of its stakeholders. Third, organizations and their stakeholders have to recognize that their relationships are reciprocal. Stakeholders have to contribute to organizations, as well as expect something from them. These three fundamental premises not only underpin this book, but have also been incorporated into the performance measurement framework – The Performance Prism – that the book describes (see Figure 1.1). The Performance Prism sets out to be a holistic performance measurement framework. It builds on the best of the frameworks already in existence and in so doing seeks to address their shortcomings.

Fig 1.1 The Performance Prism

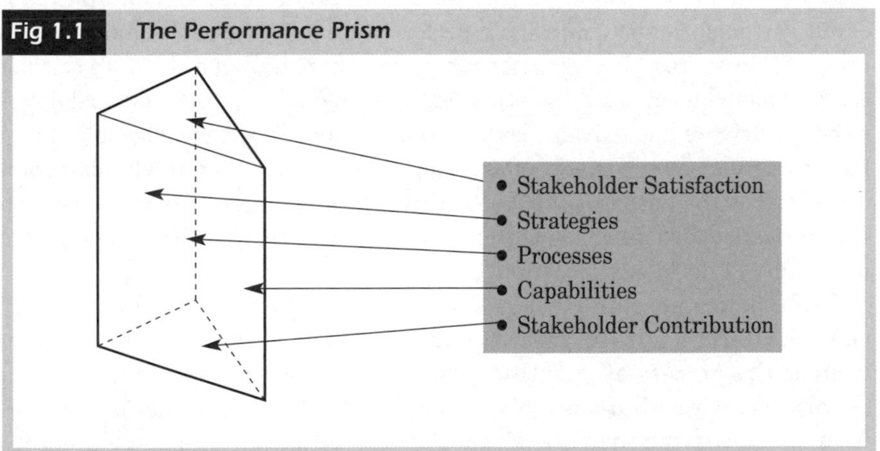

The Nature of the Problem

Why is this holistic performance measurement framework needed? Surely organizations today have sorted out their performance measurement systems? After all, everyone knows that 'you can't manage what you can't measure' and so it would seem reasonable to assume that anyone who is managing will have appropriate measures in place. And given that people have been managing organizations for years, then surely by now they must have sorted out their measurement systems?

Sadly, as in so many walks of life, theory does not reflect practice. The number of organizations with hopeless performance measures and measurement systems in place is immense. As we shall observe while we proceed through the book, examples abound of organizations that have introduced performance measures that quite simply drive entirely the wrong behaviours. There must be a better way.

The Performance Prism is not a cure-all. It won't solve all of the problems of performance measurement and it needs to be used intelligently to optimize its potential. However, we think that it does provide a robust and comprehensive framework through which to view and address the real problems and practical challenges of managing organizational performance.

The Fundamental Definitions

What exactly do we mean by performance measurement? This question is a fundamental one in that the language in the field of performance measurement complicates the subject because it is so confused. Commentators talk about key performance indicators, performance metrics, performance measures, critical success factors, without distinguishing between them. To this list could be added terms such as output and outcome measures, results and determinants, drivers and drivens, leading and lagging, and so on. The point is we have to strip away the superfluous terminology and focus on the fundamental concepts. For the purpose of this book then, we are going to rely principally on four terms: performance measurement, performance measure, performance metric and performance measurement system.

Performance measurement is a topic that is often discussed but rarely defined. Literally it is the process of quantifying past action, where measurement is the process of quantification and past action determines current performance. Organizations achieve their defined objectives – that is, they perform – by satisfying their stakeholders' and their own wants and needs with greater efficiency and effectiveness than their competitors. The terms efficiency and effectiveness are used precisely in this context. Effectiveness refers to the extent to which stakeholder requirements are met, while efficiency is a measure of how economically the firm's resources are utilized when providing a given level of stakeholder satisfaction.

This is an important distinction because it not only identifies the two fundamental dimensions of performance, but also highlights the fact that there can be internal as well as external reasons for pursuing specific courses of action. Take, for example, one of the quality-related dimensions of performance – product reliability. In terms of effectiveness, achieving a higher level of product reliability might lead to greater customer satisfaction. In terms of efficiency, it might reduce the costs incurred by the business through decreased field failure and warranty claims. Hence the level of performance a business attains is a function of the efficiency and effectiveness of the actions it has undertaken, and thus ***performance measurement*** *can be defined as the process of quantifying the efficiency and effectiveness of past action.* Once this definition has been established, then a second immediately follows. *A* ***performance measure*** *can be defined as a parameter used to quantify the efficiency and/or effectiveness of past action.*

A company or business unit may decide, for example, that the level of customer satisfaction with its products and services is a relevant and important performance measure. It is a frequently used business effectiveness measure. However, the aspects of customer satisfaction about which the company or business unit wishes to collect data – such as, say, the product in use, its packaging, its on-time delivery, its after-sales service, its value for money, and so on – are potential component parts of the measure and are its performance metrics. *A* ***performance metric*** *is the definition of the scope, content and component parts of a broadly-based performance measure.*

Defining what a performance measurement system constitutes, however, is not as straightforward. At one level, a performance measurement system is simply a set of performance measures which are used to quantify the efficiency and effectiveness of past actions. The shortcoming of this definition is that it ignores the fact that the performance measurement system encompasses a supporting infrastructure. Data have to be acquired, collated, sorted, analyzed and interpreted. If any of these data processing activities do not occur then the measurement process is incomplete and informed decisions and actions cannot subsequently take place. Thus a more complete definition is: ***a performance measurement system*** *enables informed decisions to be made and actions to be taken because it quantifies the efficiency and effectiveness of past actions through the acquisition, collation, sorting, analysis and interpretation of appropriate data.* In this context, the information processing activities – acquiring, collating, sorting, analyzing and interpreting – are defined as follows:

1 Data acquisition – the process of gathering raw facts.

2 Data collation – the process of compiling the raw facts into a single or integrated data-set.

3 Data sorting – the process of assigning the individual facts in the data-set to meaningful categories so that the data can be analyzed.
4 Data analysis – the process of searching for patterns that exist in the sorted data-set.
5 Data interpretation – the process of explaining the implications of any patterns that have been identified in the sorted data-set.

It is important to comprehend these definitions so that the reader will understand what we mean when we use these terms throughout the book.

The Book Navigator

We'll explore these and related themes and issues in much more detail in the chapters that follow, so all that remains for us to cover in this preface is a guide to the book and its structure. The book consists of three main parts. The first sets the scene by exploring the challenges facing managers today and establishing why a new performance measurement and management framework is needed. The second explains the Performance Prism framework and explores measures selection, stakeholder by stakeholder. The third explains how the Performance Prism framework can be implemented and used in practice.

If you just want to get an overview of the main themes and ideas in the book read Chapter 1 first and then dip into Chapters 4, 5 and 11, the last of which explains how the Performance Prism has been applied in the company DHL. Chapters 6 to 10 contain more detail and provide specific insights into how the Performance Prism framework can be used to identify appropriate measures. If you are looking to change your performance measurement and management systems, you should also read Chapter 3, as this provides practical hints and tips on implementing, using and refreshing performance measurement and management systems. Finally, if you are looking for specific measures, read Chapter 5 (which explains the Performance Prism framework) and then take a look at the CD-ROM appendix, which contains a catalogue of performance measures structured around the Performance Prism.[1] Towards the end of Chapters 6 to 10, there are also lists of typical measures relevant to each stakeholder group.

We recognize too that some readers might become frustrated by the fact that we do not really get into the 'meat' of fleshing out and applying the Performance Prism until Chapter 5 (and the rest of the book). The reason for this is that we believe that the context of the need for another performance measurement framework is important and necessary. Changes to the business landscape and emerging business issues were important factors in its development. Without that context, we suspect that readers might take a superficial or dismissive view about the relevance of this novel and innovative framework. So, if we're preaching to the already converted, then perhaps consider starting at Chapter 5 and reading on; but we recommend that you then check back to Chapter 3 afterwards for its implementation tips and traps.

Overall, we hope that you will enjoy reading the book. The Performance Prism is not meant to be a prescriptive framework. Instead it is a thinking aid. It seeks to integrate five related themes – stakeholder satisfaction, stakeholder contribution, strategies, processes and capabilities. It provides a structure that allows executives to think through the answers to the five fundamental questions that face them today:

- Who are our stakeholders and what do they want and need?
- What do we want and need *from* our stakeholders?
- What strategies do we need to put in place to satisfy these sets of wants and needs?
- What processes do we need to put in place to enable us to execute our strategies?
- What capabilities – bundles of people, practices, technology and infrastructure – do we need to put in place to allow us to operate our processes more effectively and efficiently?

Address these questions and, like the management team at DHL, you'll find you have a far better handle on the drivers of your organization's performance.

1 Measuring and Managing Performance in the 21st Century

Companies must try to understand better what their stakeholders' needs are and then deal with those needs ahead of time rather than learn about them later.

Marc J. Epstein • *distinguished research professor at the Jesse H. Jones Graduate School of Management, Rice University, Houston, USA.*[1]

The days when companies could survive and prosper by focusing on the wants and needs of one stakeholder – the shareholder – are long gone. The days when organizations could survive and prosper by focusing on the wants and needs of two stakeholders – the shareholders and the customers – are also numbered, if not yet already passed. Despite the fact that 'customer relationship management' is one of today's hot topics and 'customer focus' was the rallying cry for many of the management revolutions that swept the business world during the 1980s and 1990s – such as Just-In-Time, Total Quality Management and Business Process Re-engineering. Other worthy initiatives have tried to place greater emphasis on other individual stakeholders, such as Human Resource Management, for example, but have tended to lose sight of the broader picture.

The Stakeholder Revolution

Now – and increasingly in the future – the best way for organizations to survive and prosper in the long term will be to think about the wants and needs of all of their important stakeholders and endeavour to deliver value to each of them. Simply focusing on a subset of seemingly more influential stakeholders – typically the shareholders and customers – and ignoring the wants and needs of the rest is shortsighted and naïve in today's information-rich society. One only has to observe some of the recent experiences of global organizations to understand the impact that other stakeholders – consumers, employees, suppliers, regulators, legislators, activists and communities – can have. Here is a more or less random dozen international examples to illustrate the point.

- Caterpillar – world renowned for its products, also goes down in the history books for enduring one of the longest running strikes ever. In a bitter 17-month dispute with the Union of Auto Workers, the company lost some three million working days.
- Marks & Spencer – a French court ruled that the UK-based retailer had broken labour law in attempting to close 18 stores in France, throwing its restructuring plans into disarray. The judge also fined the company FF25,000 for what she described as a 'manifestly illegal trouble-making'.
- JCO Co. – workers at a Japanese uranium-reprocessing facility north of Tokyo set off a nuclear reaction in 1999 that resulted in two deaths and a further 439 being exposed to radiation fallout. An investigation revealed that the company was under pressure to cut costs and that an inadequate number of inspections had been conducted.
- Bridgestone/Firestone – carmaker Ford Motor Company has been waging a very public battle in the US with its Japanese-owned tyre supplier Bridgestone/Firestone. The spat has been about assigning responsibility – in other words, the blame – for tread separations on Ford's Explorer model that have been the cause of over 200 road deaths. Firestone attributes the cause primarily to vehicle design, Ford to faulty tyre production. The product recall and other associated costs, not least legal ones, are astronomic and, at the time of writing, still growing. Firestone, meanwhile, has severed its 95-year supply relationship with Ford.
- Mars – despite the adverse publicity, the confectioner was considered fortunate in 1998 when it was found not to have breached the UK's Food Safety Act after a mouse's head and shoulders were discovered in a Topic bar. A woman had eaten most of the bar before discovering what she described as 'a grey furry-looking object'. Mars said that the mouse parts had come from a consignment of hazelnuts from Turkey. In a separate incident, in 2001, the company was forced to destroy between two and three million Twix bars after beetles were found in its flour supply. Its quality control inspectors found black flecks in the popular snack's biscuit base.
- Sara Lee – the US consumer goods group pleaded guilty to selling hot dogs and meats that were contaminated with bacteria, which led to 15 deaths in 1998. It was forced to recall 15 million pounds of meat. The company took a $76 million charge in 1999 for the massive meat recall.
- Snow Brand Milk Products – Japan's largest dairy distributed contaminated milk in June 2000 and failed to notify the public for two days. During this time 14,500 people fell ill after drinking it.
- Sotheby's and Christie's – a grand jury in Manhattan indicted the chairmen of both Sotheby's and Christie's in May 2001 on criminal charges of

conspiring to fix prices in the art auction market. Separately, the two companies jointly agreed to pay $512 million to former customers to settle a class action lawsuit that stemmed from the scandal. Sotheby's has also been forced to pay a $45 million fine.

- Roche and BASF – Roche of Switzerland and BASF of Germany were fined a total of $725 million by the US Justice Department for indulging in antitrust cartel arrangements in their respective vitamins businesses. Executives also received fines and custodial sentences.
- Michelin – Europe's largest tyre manufacturer was ordered to pay a €19.7 million (£12 million) fine by the European Commission for anticompetitive behaviour and abusing its dominant position in France throughout the 1990s.
- Exxon-Mobil – campaigners from several hundred non-governmental organizations (NGOs) launched 'an international day of action' against the US oil company in July 2001. Protesters targeted offices and petrol stations around the world to highlight the firm's stance on issues ranging from climate change to human rights.
- McDonald's – the company may serve fast food, but it certainly takes its time in court. McDonald's has the somewhat dubious honour of being the litigant in the UK's longest ever libel trial, which lasted some two and a half years. With its annual income of over $30 billion, McDonald's took on two unemployed British protestors – David Morris, an ex-postman and Helen Steel, an ex-gardener, who between them earned some $12,000. The protestors decided to defend themselves. They kept McDonald's in court for a total of 313 days and had the chief executive over to give evidence. The legal fees alone are said to have cost McDonald's approximately $10m. Meanwhile the impact of the adverse press and publicity is immeasurable. Over 250 press reports, a book and a 60-minute documentary have all been produced, questioning why McDonald's ever decided to take the protestors to court in the first place. In addition, the original leaflet that first sparked the libel action has been published on the McSpotlight internet site. To date this site has been accessed by over 12 million people.[2]

Stakeholder Satisfaction

Increasingly, CEOs the world over recognize these issues. They understand intuitively the complexity inherent in the management of global organizations. They accept that today the way to protect and deliver long-term shareholder value is to find a way to deliver multiple stakeholder satisfaction. Speaking in September 2000, for example, Anders Dahvig, CEO of Ikea, the Swedish furnishings company, said:

> The world has changed enormously in the past decade ... All of us now act in ways we did not 10 years ago. Globalization means stakeholders and responsibilities everywhere, which have to be managed. It's quite a different level of complexity.[3]

In a similar vein, Chris Fay, Chairman and Chief Executive of Shell UK is quoted in the Institute of Chartered Accountants 21st Century Annual Report as saying:

> The days when companies were judged solely in terms of economic performance and wealth creation have long disappeared. Today, companies have far wider responsibilities to the environment, to local communities and to the broader society. These are not optional extras. They are not the 'icing on the cake'. I believe that Shell UK's wider social responsibilities form a fundamental and integral part of the way in which we do our business. They are vital to our long-term economic performance.[4]

Comments and views such as these have led to the emergence of new standards for corporate reporting. Shell, for example, now releases a supplement to their annual report entitled 'Profits and Principles', which explains what Shell is doing to ensure that it delivers value to society, as well as to its shareholders. The UK's Co-operative Bank has gone even further and reports how well the business has performed against the expectations of all of its stakeholders – shareholders, customers, staff and their families, suppliers, local communities, national and international society, past and future generations of 'co-operators' – in its annual Partnership Report. More formalized approaches to stakeholder accountability and reporting are being developed and documented. The Institute for Social and Ethical Accountability, an international membership organization based in the UK has been involved in the production of The Copenhagen Charter – A Guide to Stakeholder Reporting – and the development of the AA1000 stakeholder reporting framework.

These, and numerous other examples that we shall expand upon later, illustrate a growing trend – namely, that executives in organizations across the world recognize and accept that the business empires they manage have a broader role to play in the 21st century than simply delivering value to their shareholders. This is not to say that generating shareholder value is unimportant. Nor is it to suggest that shareholders should take their place at the back of the stakeholder queue. Indeed, quite the converse is true. Whereas some shareholders may not be pleased to learn that their interests seem to have been at least partially marginalized, that notion will only apply to the few (in value terms) that are short-term investors. Most long-term investors already realize that for companies to be successful over time they must address multiple constituencies. If companies do not give each of them the right level of focus, both their corporate reputation and their market capitalization are likely to suffer.

No one is immune from this trend. In 1999, Coca-Cola seemed to be at odds with all of its stakeholders. In the space of just 12 months, it managed to upset each constituent of its major stakeholder groups – its consumers, its retailers, its bottlers, its regulators (in several countries), its shareholders, its executives and, finally, its workforce. This was a pretty extraordinary performance for one of the world's most respected companies and led to the demise of its chairman and chief executive. See the box *Coca-Cola's Annus Horribilis* for details of the sequence of events.

Coca-Cola's Annus Horribilis

On 5 December 1999, the man who once said, 'I know how all the levers work, and I could generate so much cash I could make everybody's head spin,' fell on his sword and quit his job as chief executive of one of the world's biggest and most admired companies. After just two years at the helm as Chairman and Chief Executive of Coca-Cola, Douglas Ivester, was forced to resign after a series of mishaps that had a disastrous impact on the company's reputation and performance.

The reputedly data-driven and analytical former accountant and propounder of shareholder value, it seems, was using the wrong set of numbers to manage the business. Ivester's 12-month diary might read something like this:

February 1999	Profit for last year down from $4.1 billion to $3.5 billion – Far East and Russian problems. Fell out with UK retail customers over 10p per 2-litre bottle price increase.
March 1999	Nominated as America's second most admired company by Fortune.
May 1999	Forced to radically restructure $1.85 million Cadbury-Schweppes acquisition. Warned by European Commission that company faces heavy fines for not seeking clearance for the acquisition from the competition watchdog.
June 1999	Forced to recall and destroy 17 million cases of Coke in Belgium, France, the Netherlands and Luxembourg following contamination problem, when over 200 customers complained of illness. Company's response seen as tardy and unsympathetic. Reputation as a reliable and responsible company shaken. Coca-Cola Enterprises incurs $103 million additional cost.

July 1999	Following complaints from competitors, European Commission officials raided offices in Germany, Denmark, Austria and the UK in a probe into whether the company offered retailers and wholesalers incentives to increase sales volumes, carry full range of brands, or stop selling competitor's drinks through exclusivity deals.
	Coca-Cola Amatil under investigation by Australian Competition and Consumer Commission for alleged breaches of the country's Trade Practices Act. These relate to the company providing Coke at discounted prices to certain retail outlets on condition that they did not stock rival beverages.
August 1999	Accused by competition authorities in Italy of abusing dominant position, distorting competition rules through discounts and bonus system to wholesalers, and efforts to claim display space in supermarkets.
September 1999	Being sued in Atlanta by four black workers for racial discrimination.
	Market capitalization has fallen $34 billion in past three months.
October 1999	Pepsi suing in US over access to soda fountains, alleging unfair control of distribution.
November 1999	Ordered to cease a promotional campaign by Belgian court.
	Price of syrup to bottlers raised by 7.7 per cent (twice the rate of recent increases) – bottlers outraged.
	French government blocks FF4.7 billion revised offer to purchase Orangina from Pernod Ricard.
December 1999	Fined $16m in Italy for 'gravely' abusing dominant market position.
	Meeting in Chicago with major shareholders, including Warren Buffett.
	Resigned. Douglas Daft named as new CEO.
	Ironically, on the day following the announcement, the company nominated in the *Financial Times* as the world's third most respected company (for second successive year).

January 2000	Chilean antitrust commission investigating company's dominance of $800m-a-year soft drinks market.
	Coca-Cola's President for Northern Europe dismissed.
	Profits down 31 per cent last year.
	Announced plans to cut 21 per cent of workforce worldwide – 6,000 jobs lost.
February 2000	Dropped from *Fortune's* list of the Top 10 Most Admired Companies.

Could these stakeholder relations disasters have been avoided? We think so. A product recall can happen to almost any products company, but there is no excuse for handling it badly and there are many precedents for having the right policies and procedures in place to react quickly and decisively. There must also be something inherently wrong with the organisational culture for it to be accused of illegal practices in so many different countries. The arrogance demonstrated in believing that it is above the law in obtaining regulatory approvals for sizeable acquisitions is cultural in nature too, especially given that the press in several countries had already dubbed the invasion of US behemoths into their local markets as 'coca-colonialism'.

It is apparent that Coca-Cola has historically had an excellent grip of the financial numbers, its volume growth profile and its market shares around the world. However, it clearly did not have the 'radar systems' in place to adequately track either key components of its internal culture or external attitudes towards its business ethics. Too focused – to the point of overzealousness – on its business processes for demand generation, some vital capabilities of its fulfilment processes have been indelibly exposed (MBA students all over the world will surely be analysing the product recall episode for many years to come) as well as failures in its ability to effectively plan and manage the enterprise.

As Doug Ivester found out of course, and many other executives realize instinctively, not *all* the levers you have to pull are the financial ones. Hopefully, the company's new leadership has now rectified these pressing performance measurement and management issues.

The point is that the only sustainable way of delivering shareholder value in the 21st century is to deliver stakeholder value and this means enhancing, maintaining and defending the company's reputation on a broad range of fronts. The kind of corporate gaffs that we have described in this chapter (and will be described elsewhere in the book) illustrate just how difficult reputation is to manage. The level of media attention, though, has served to ensure that it is rapidly becoming one of the hottest of boardroom issues. Aon, the insurance company, regularly carries out a survey asking chief executives to name the greatest risk facing their business. They usually focus on issues such as fire or business interruption. In 2001, however, 'loss of reputation' topped the list of their concerns.

Furthermore, legislators (not always at the forefront of emerging trends) have already begun to recognize the climate change. Company law in Britain (the US is another matter – see Chapter 6) still enshrines the purpose of companies as 'formed and managed for the benefit of *shareholders*, but subject to safeguards for the benefit of actual and potential *creditors*'. However, the recently published British company law reform blueprint recommends a statutory statement of directors' duties, requiring them to take 'due account' of relations with employees, suppliers and customers, as well as shareholders.[5] So this phenomenon is not just another passing management fad, it is likely to become enshrined in company law. Indeed, some aspects of it already have – especially those related to competition law. It is these legal changes that have given regulators greater powers to deal with corporate transgressions, such as price fixing and the abuse of dominant market positions. Particularly in Europe, employment law is also moving increasingly towards protecting the rights of employees. In short, the face of capitalism is being changed permanently.

Stakeholder Contribution

So is it all a one-way street – more and more stakeholders making more and more demands? Not at all. Quite the opposite in fact. Organizations are becoming increasingly demanding of their stakeholders too. For example:

- *Investors* – capital for growth, greater risk-taking, long-term support.
- *Customers* – profitability, retention, loyalty, advocacy, feedback.
- *Intermediaries* – planning forecasts, forward demand visibility.
- *Employees* – flexibility, multi-skilling, antisocial hours, suggestions.
- *Suppliers* – more outsourcing, fewer vendors, total solutions, integration.
- *Regulators* – cross-border consistency, informal advice, early involvement.
- *Communities* – skilled employment pool, grants, support, integration.
- *Pressure Groups* – closer co-operation, shared research, co-branding.
- *Alliance Partners* – cross-selling, co-development, cost sharing.

These are just a few illustrations (and we shall explain them in greater detail later) of how organizations are making increased demands of their stakeholders. So, in effect, the interrelationship between stakeholder and organization is becoming an increasingly reciprocal one. Indeed, the very concept of stakeholder value itself should perhaps be quantified in terms of the strength of the interrelationship.

Strategies, Processes and Capabilities

Failing sufficiently to address the right stakeholders' wants and needs, plus the corresponding wants and needs of the organization *from* its stakeholders, is one performance management and measurement issue. Another is not aligning performance measures to the organization's strategies, processes and capabilities aimed at satisfying these two sets of wants and needs.

It is no good, for example, the sales and marketing department valiantly declaring that customer delivery service is the only thing that matters, when the poor guys in distribution are tasked with cost minimization – the hopeless task of trying to complete customer deliveries from a rickety cabin, using ancient information systems, a leaky warehouse and a clapped-out fleet of trucks that keep breaking down. Aligned measurement systems rely to a large extent on integrated organizational strategies across functions – in other words, in this case, right across the customer order fulfilment process.

Yet another common blunder is picking an internal process measure at random, but not making it part of an integrated set. When the wrong things are measured, or they are measured in the wrong way, then dysfunctional behaviours that are completely misaligned with the organization's strategy are likely to be the outcome. (For a typical example, see the box *Calais for a Quid*.)

Calais for a Quid

A ferry company introduced a new measure to address customer complaints – the time taken to respond to complaints. The company supplemented the measure with a target and declared that they would seek to respond to all customer complaints within ten working days.

Shortly after the introduction of this measure and target, the customer services department received a letter of complaint from two old ladies who had recently experienced the ferry company at its worst. They had dutifully collected vouchers from their newspaper that entitled them to a return trip to France for just £1. They had taken their trip shortly before Christmas, but had been forced to stay overnight in Calais as they had been unable to get a ferry home at the end of the day. The first ferry they tried to catch – the one they had been booked on – did not sail because of a mechanical fault. The second (and final ferry of the day) was so full, because no one had been able to get on the first, that there was not enough space. The customer services agent who received the letter reviewed the case, decided that the two old ladies had a valid complaint and sent them a reply – within ten working days – saying they would shortly be receiving a full refund, £1.

Is this service? Of course not. Does it address the customers' concern? Of course not. Will it satisfy the two old ladies? Of course not. Will it be counted as a success by the organization's measurement system? Yes! The customer services agent met the company target by responding to the complaint within ten working days. What a bizarre world we live in when managers think that this kind of service behaviour is acceptable to their customers.

People in organizations can deliver appalling service. They can completely fail to satisfy the customer and yet the measurement system that they are subject to can record their actions as perfectly acceptable. It would be fine if this were an isolated case, if it were an example of a single organization that had introduced an inappropriate measure. But regrettably it is not. We see and hear horror stories of poor measures selection and application such as this on a daily basis:

- A common performance measure in call centres is time taken to resolve customer queries. As an operator, how do you achieve a target of two minutes on average? Simple – cut the customer off after a minute and 50 seconds if the query has not been resolved.
- What happens when you measure branch profitability in a national or international service operation? Simple – branches compete with one another. How many companies do you know where you can encourage a price war between branches simply by telling the sales team in the second branch that the sales team in the first branch have made you a better offer? What happens when both of these branches are owned by the same parent company? The same thing. They battle it out to see who can offer the customer the best deal. Who loses? The business as a whole. Margin is given away by the business as it competes with itself!
- How do you maximize machine utilization in a manufacturing operation? Make for stock in large batches. Ignore what the customer wants, just keep those machines producing. There does not have to be a market for this output. As long as the machines keep producing, the utilization figures will look fine. This is supply chain 'push', not demand chain 'pull'.
- How do you hit the annual budget if you have had a bad year financially? Slash and burn. Cut all expenditure. Delay purchase of that new bit of capi-

tal equipment. Don't bother to send everyone on the training course so they understand how to use the latest piece of software. Don't go ahead with the final marketing campaign. Cut back R&D. Just batten down the hatches and meet this year's numbers. Next year may be someone else's problem.

- How do you hit the sales forecast targets if the customer orders aren't there? Stuff the demand chain full of inventory. Offer customers fantastic discounts and rebates if they order early – a malpractice known as trade loading – and hope that demand picks up next year.
- How do you incentivize sales staff? Pay them big bonuses. If each sales representative receives a bonus based on the level of sales to new customers, it will help to focus their attention on winning new business. It surely will. What it won't do, though, is focus their attention on winning *profitable* business with decent margins. They will sell at any price just to get their bonus up. It will also mean that existing customers are completely neglected.

Do you think that these things don't happen in organizations today? They do. The fact is that performance measurement is a mess in most organizations. Far too often performance measurement systems contain measures that are poorly defined, rarely integrated with one another or aligned to the organization's strategies, processes or capabilities. In essence, many measurement systems result in managers and employees destroying rather than creating value simply because they encourage dysfunctional behaviour.

Performance Measurement Frameworks

So why are we in such a mess with performance measurement? And even more importantly, what are we going to do about it? These have been perennial questions in recent years and between them have resulted in the development of a multi-million dollar industry. Consultants, academics, conference organizers and software vendors are providing the fuel for this, with a never-ending stream of measurement frameworks and methodologies, conferences and discussion forums, and of course, software products and services. In some ways this book is designed to add further fuel to this fire, since it presents yet another performance measurement framework. But we also hope that this book will serve to clarify some of the confusion that exists in and around performance measurement and management today.

While numerous measurement methodologies and frameworks have been proposed in recent years, there is a problem in that they appear to be inconsistent with one another. Take, for example, the balanced scorecard.[6] The traditional version of this – although some organizations have identified the need to adapt it – consists of four perspectives, which in turn allow executives to address four questions:

- Financial perspective – how do we look to our shareholders?
- Customer perspective – how do we look to our customers?
- Internal Process perspective – what must we excel at?
- Innovation and Learning perspective – how can we continue to innovate and create value?

No mention is made of end-users, or employees, or suppliers, or regulators, or pressure groups, or local communities. Yet all of these stakeholders can have a massive impact on the organization and on its ability to perform. If the workforce goes out on strike, for example, or the regulator closes a plant down, the organization cannot continue to operate and it can't deliver product and/or service to its customers. If the customers withhold payment, or the shareholders decide to withdraw their funds, then the organization will get strapped for cash and it won't be able to afford to pay its employees or suppliers. The point is that all of the different stakeholders in an organization interact within a kind of 'eco-system'. True, some stakeholders are more important than others. But to ignore any of the stakeholders in today's society can be extremely short-sighted and naïve. One only has to look at the web pages of 'Untied.com' or 'NorthWorstAir.org' or 'AirlinesSuck.com' to see the damage that frustrated stakeholders can do to organizations in a world where even individuals have massive communication power at their fingertips through the internet.

The balanced scorecard then can be criticized for not taking a broad enough view of the stakeholders who interact with an organization. It should be recognized, however, that it is now a decade old and the world has changed materially in that time. Nevertheless, to its credit, the balanced scorecard takes a far broader view than shareholder value or economic profit measurement techniques that effectively assume that the only stakeholder that matters is the shareholder. These approaches can be contrasted with another set of measurement methodologies, namely the self-assessment models, such as the Business Excellence Model and the Baldrige Award, which take a broader view of performance and include reference to a wider set of stakeholders, but also contain a host of dimensions that are effectively unmeasurable. Benchmarking techniques are also widely used to compare operations, compensation and financial performance with those of other similar operations, both internally and externally. Yet further models have emerged – such as the Strategic Measurement Analysis & Reporting Technique (SMART) pyramid and the Results and Determinants framework, for example – but these have not been widely adopted by organizations.

The point is not to criticize these different frameworks and methodologies, because they all add value in their own right. The problem with them, however, is that all are partial or point solutions. They offer insights into some of the dimensions of performance that should be measured and managed, but by no means all of them. The framework proposed in this book – the Performance Prism – seeks to rectify this shortcoming by building upon the strengths of the existing measurement frameworks and methodologies, integrating them and offering a more comprehensive and comprehensible measurement framework.

Delivering Stakeholder Value with the Performance Prism

Underpinning the Performance Prism framework is the notion of stakeholder, as opposed to shareholder, value. So what is stakeholder value and how can executives be sure that the organizations they control are delivering it? The truth is that there is no simple answer. There is no off-the-shelf solution. There are no well-established methodologies for assessing whether or not organizations are creating and delivering stakeholder – as opposed to shareholder – value. True, there are a number of sub-methodologies – such as techniques for measuring customer and employee satisfaction – and, as we have noted above, partial solutions, most notably the ubiquitous balanced scorecard. But how do these sub-methodologies and partial solutions integrate with one another? How do they enable executives in organizations to track whether the strategies they are pursuing, the processes they are operating and the capabilities they are developing are actually enabling the organization to deliver stakeholder value today and will continue to be able to do so in the future? The answer, of course, is that they don't. This does not mean that they are not valuable solutions. It just means that they are contributions to a larger scheme of things. What is lacking is an integrative framework that builds upon these partial solutions and presents a rounded picture of what executives have to manage and measure if they are to be sure that the organizations they control are to deliver sustainable stakeholder value. And put quite simply (and somewhat ambitiously) it is the aim of this book to present and explain such an integrative framework – namely, the Performance Prism.

Unlike the first generation of performance measurement and management frameworks – the Performance Prism is holistic in orientation. It does not assume that the only stakeholders which matter are the shareholders and customers. It does not assume that financial measures should be supplemented with a few non-financial ones. Instead, the Performance Prism encourages executives to focus on the critical questions. It begins by prompting the question – 'Who are our stakeholders and what do they want and need?' Then it prompts questions about what strategies are required to deliver value to these stakeholders. What processes need to be put in place to execute these strategies? What capabilities – bundles of people, technology, practices and infrastructure –

are required to underpin these processes? A subtle, but vitally important, twist in the Performance Prism is the distinction between what the stakeholders want of the organization and what the organization wants of its stakeholders. All organizations want certain things of their stakeholders, just as all stakeholders want certain things of organizations. The Performance Prism encourages management teams to think through this issue and ask explicitly – What is it that our stakeholders want and need from us? And what is it that we want and need from our stakeholders? In other words, what is the quid pro quo?

The Performance Prism is the key theme in this book, but it is not the only one. For the book also recognizes that, in today's rapidly evolving world, the way that organizations measure and manage performance will have to change. For years people have been criticizing measurement systems for providing the wrong data too late. So what is the answer? How should we be using performance measurement data in today's turbulent economy? Fundamentally, we have to move away from thinking about measurement in the traditional sense – the process of quantification – and start to think about measurement as the process of gathering management intelligence. We need to develop intelligence gathering systems that allow managers to answer quickly the critical questions they have to answer if they are to successfully manage a business in the 21st century. As an analogy, managers have to behave with data-feeds more like journalists do with news-feeds. They have to access and then use the data/facts to construct intelligent theories about what is happening in their businesses so that rapid, but well-informed, decisions can be made in the context of the business environment in which they are competing. The Performance Prism provides a framework for thinking about the structure of this intelligence-gathering process and practice. The more effective the application and evolution of the management intelligence gathering system in an organization, the better equipped its managers will be to manage in the 21st century.

Overall then, the message is that in order to survive and prosper in an increasingly complex and connected world, executives have to understand what their various stakeholders want and need from the organization and what the organization wants and needs from them. They have to align their strategies, processes and capabilities to satisfying those diverse sets of wants and needs so that they can deliver value to their stakeholders. And they have to construct flexible performance measurement and management systems that allow them to see continuously and adroitly whether their organizations really are delivering value to all of their stakeholders today, and whether they will be able to continue to do so tomorrow. Essentially, the Performance Prism is intended to provide a structure for thinking through these critical business issues in a rational way so that intelligent business decisions can be made based on the best available data.

The Measurement Mantra 2

We now had an accounting department full of people who only stopped cranking out numbers to pick up their paychecks. And we had so damn many numbers, inside so many damn folders, that no one was looking at them. But no one would admit it. Everyone just bluffed their way through meetings, pretending to be familiar with every detail.

Ricardo Semler • *CEO of Semco, in his book 'Maverick!'*

What unites diverse global businesses such as GE, Toyota, Nokia, Bayer and Shell? That they all have to compete for demanding and fickle customers in an increasingly fragmented and global marketplace? That they all have to work in partnership with the most powerful and influential members of their global supply base? That they all have to attract and retain talented people in a world where, if they have the right skills and competencies, it is easy for employees to hop from job to job and country to country? That they all have to meet the demands imposed upon them by local, national and international legislators and regulators? That they all have to operate under the ever watchful and prying eyes of the media and of pressure groups? The answer is that they all have to manage their relationships with each of these stakeholders – customers, suppliers, employees, regulators, legislators, media and communities – while simultaneously growing shareholder value.

Managing Business Performance in the Information Age

It is clear that the rules of the game for business have changed materially over the last decade. Or, at the very least, the rules of the game are in the process of radical change. Success for organizations today is measured very differently than it was yesterday. Of course financial performance is still essential. Delivering profit growth or enhancing shareholder value is still at the top of every executive's agenda, but it is now widely recognized that delivering financial performance alone is insufficient. Even more importantly, it is now generally accepted that the level of financial performance achieved today is a function of decisions made 6–18 months or even longer as, for example, in the pharmaceuticals industry. The reason Volkswagen established a manufacturing operation in Mexico was to access a lower cost base. The delay, however, between the time the decision was taken and the time the plant came on stream (and hence when the lower cost base was accessed) was in the order of several months or years, not days or weeks. Similarly, multi-million dollar investments in CRM (customer relationship management) technology, or in restructuring a global supply base that no longer meets future requirements, cannot typically be expected to pay off for at least 18 months to two years.

Clearly executives have to manage today's financial performance, but we have to recognize that they can only do so within the constraints imposed upon them that result from the decisions taken by yesterday's executives. Furthermore, we have to recognize that the choices made by today's executives will affect the financial performance that can be delivered by tomorrow's. Effectively our definition of success, especially for executives, has to change. To define success solely in terms of financial performance is tantamount to rewarding today's management on the basis of how well they execute the strategies imposed upon them by yesterday's management. Obviously, this is important for them. But, particularly for tomorrow's executives, it is just as important – in fact, it is probably even more important – to track whether or not today's management team are positioning the organization so that it will be able to deliver excellent financial performance tomorrow.

If you accept this line of argument then a whole host of sub-issues arise. Have today's executives made the right choices about products/services? Have they put in place the infrastructure that will allow the organization to develop, produce and deliver these products/services? Have they made the right choices about markets and customers? Are they building relationships with the right suppliers and alliance partners? Are the people in the business happy to work for them? Do they share their vision of the future? Do they have the right skill-sets? Do they see a future with the firm? Will the best people stay and help the firm create that future? These questions are about the long term. They are about where the organization is going, not where it has been. Senior executives have to get the balance right between short-term harvesting and long-term sowing. That, after all, is what they are paid for and, if they are directors of public companies, what they are elected to do by their shareholders.

Success Redefined: The New Corporate Agenda

Success for today's executives then should be defined in terms of both the short- and longer-term view. But what does this mean in practice? How are organizations coping with this changing mind-set and what new frameworks and methodologies are they using to help them? Ask these questions and it becomes obvious that management is undergoing a revolution. Businesses the world over are no longer defining success purely in terms of the traditional measures of financial performance – profit, margin, return on investment, return on capital employed (ROCE), and so on. Instead, they are adopting new frameworks and methodologies, some of which are purportedly better methods for measuring financial performance, for example, economic value added.[7] While others – such as balanced scorecard approaches – are designed to supplement financial measures with non-financial ones which, in turn, are assumed to be the drivers of future financial performance.

The evidence that points to a revolution is compelling. Survey data, gathered from a variety of sources, and covering both the US and Europe, suggest that some 40–60 per cent of firms have recently re-engineered their performance measurement systems and, by implication, their definitions of success. Mark Frigo and colleagues, for example, surveyed some 132 members of the Institute of Cost Management's Management Accounting Group in 1999. They found that some 55 per cent of respondents were in the process of changing their measurement systems, with 37 per cent of them willing to describe the changes that they were making as a 'major overhaul'.[8] Research conducted by the Balanced Scorecard Collaborative in 2001 confirms these figures.[9] The Collaborative found that 52 per cent of firms surveyed were now using a balanced scorecard, 21 per cent were planning to use one soon and 23 per cent were considering whether they should use one. Interestingly, despite the impressive adoption figures, another survey found that even those that were actively using a balanced scorecard still only rated their performance measurement systems as adequate.[10] And this may explain why yet another recent survey found that 92 per cent of companies questioned – and 100 per cent of those with turnovers of over $5 billion – believed that they still had to improve their performance management systems.[11] Our own Cranfield/Accenture survey, based on 50 companies' approaches to business performance measurement in 2000, ratifies these findings with 96 per cent of survey respondents claiming that they are seeking to improve their measurement systems.

An important question that these studies raise is why do managers in so many firms currently feel the need to re-engineer their organization's performance measurement systems? After all, the often cited homily 'you can't manage what you can't measure' suggests that measurement must have been an issue for the world's first managers. While the history books don't go into great detail on this subject, it seems reasonable to assume that managers must have been around for quite some time. How else could the Seven Wonders of the Ancient World have been completed on time and to budget! And assuming that managers have been around for some time, then it also seems reasonable to assume that measurement must have been an issue for some time. So why are we still worrying about it in the 21st century? Surely it can't be that difficult to identify and implement the right measures for a given set of activities.

The sad truth, of course, is that it is extremely difficult to establish the right performance measures for any given business or business unit. Survey data, for example, suggest that managers experience difficulty in establishing appropriate performance measures for key strategic drivers, such as:[12]

- Intellectual capital (67 per cent report difficulty).
- Value from research and development (59 per cent report difficulty).
- Customer lifetime value (59 per cent report difficulty).
- Brand effectiveness (56 per cent report difficulty).
- Innovation (52 per cent report difficulty).

And it is not just developing appropriate performance measures that is proving difficult. The same survey identifies other challenges, such as:

- Choosing correct leading and lagging indicators (56 per cent report difficulty).
- Benchmarking against competitors (49 per cent report difficulty).
- Balancing financial and non-financial indicators (44 per cent report difficulty).
- Applying measures consistently across business units (44 per cent report difficulty).
- Capturing different stakeholder interests (43 per cent report difficulty).
- Using appropriate numbers of measures (41 per cent report difficulty).
- Applying measures consistently across regions (39 per cent report difficulty).
- Identifying key value drivers (37 per cent report difficulty).

And all of these difficulties are just the logical and scientific ones. They ignore many of the illogical challenges. The dark side of measurement! The politics. The gaming. People's fear of measurement. The challenges associated with capturing robust and valid data. And perhaps most significantly of all, as we have already hinted in the previous chapter, the behavioural consequences of performance measures. People react to whatever measures are introduced. They modify their behaviours depending upon how they are measured. Hence the other frequently cited homilies – 'tell me how you'll measure me and I'll tell you how I'll behave' and 'you get what you inspect, not what you expect'.

The chaos that can result, especially when the wrong measures are chosen is often amazing to behold and potentially frightening to experience. Take, for example, one of the classic measures of police department performance – the percentage of crimes that are not solved. There is an easy way to make this measure look good. Simply 'encourage' a few criminals to own up to crimes, even if they did not commit them. In the UK, this strategy was used to great effect by the West Midlands Serious Crime Squad, which managed to achieve an impressive clean-up rate for crimes in the 1970s and 1980s. Unfortunately, it emerged in the mid-1980s that the Serious Crime Squad had a habit of fabricating evidence. Among the most celebrated cases was that of the so-called Birmingham Six, who spent 16 years in jail between them before their conviction was overturned on the grounds that the Serious Crime Squad had basically made up the evidence used to secure their conviction. For a few years at least, the Serious Crime Squad delivered great performance numbers. Unfortunately, some of the methods they were using to do so were questionable to say the very least!

Of course, it is not just in the public sector that measures result in dysfunctional behaviours. Similar examples abound in the private sector. In fact, a significant stimulus for the measurement revolution that gripped the world during the late 1980s and on through the 1990s was the widespread recognition that the measures traditionally used in firms were wholly inadequate. They often encouraged short-term behaviours, especially when they were linked to the stock and share options of senior executives. Some of the most damning criticism came from highly influential authors, such as Professors Bob Hayes and Bill Abernathy of the Harvard Business School, who blamed America's economic decline in the 1970s and early 1980s on American management's obsession with the short term.[13] Others, such as Professor Bob Kaplan, argued forcefully that the measurement systems used in many organizations actively undermined the business's competitiveness.[14] Fundamentally, the theme underlying these criticisms was that the performance measures used in many firms were too narrow in focus and concentrated solely on short-term financial gains for a subset of the organization's stakeholders.

Upping the Stakes

The pressure on executives to improve their organization's performance measurement systems appears to have increased inexorably throughout the 1980s and 1990s. A significant driving force appears to have been some extremely potent social and technological forces, as well as some very pragmatic challenges.

The pragmatist's approach stems from the fact that the performance measurement systems used in many organizations proved to be fundamentally incompatible with the strategies being pursued by those same organizations. The emergence of Japan as a significant economic power provides a case in point. Businesses, such as Toyota and Kawasaki, were able to radically improve their manufacturing performance through the adoption of manufacturing management techniques such as Just-In-Time and so-called Lean Manufacturing. The principle underlying these techniques was that we should eliminate the buffers – both time and inventory – that we have used to protect manufacturing from the turbulence of the marketplace. Instead of making large batches of product and selling them ex-stock, we should make only what the customer needs and only when the customer needs it. The natural extension of these concepts is to look constantly for ways of making supply chains more responsive and agile. If Toyota is only going to make what its customers want, when they want it, then Toyota is going to ask its suppliers to perform in the same way. It is going to expect them to develop the capability to manufacture and deliver in batches of 50, rather than 5,000.

The results achieved through this radical rethink of manufacturing were astounding. For example, Womack, Jones and Roos, in their book *The Machine that Changed the World*, reported that the performance differentials between the world's best and worst performing car plants were in the order of two to one.[15] That is the best plants in the world were twice as productive as the worst plants. But the performance differential did not stop there. For not only were the best plants twice as efficient, they were also more than twice as effective – reporting defect levels of 35.1 defects per 100 vehicles, as opposed to 190.5 defects per 100 vehicles. Managing quality, by focusing on prevention rather than inspection, is a vital component of the mix (see Figure 2.1).

The impact on manufacturing was profound. As more and more people began to realize that a manufacturing resurgence lay at the heart of Japan's economic growth and more and more companies saw themselves losing market to Japanese competitors – e.g. Xerox, General Motors and Harley-Davidson – ever greater numbers of executives and academics made the journey to Japan to try and understand what was happening. Time and time again they came back with the same messages – involve people, improve processes, drive out inventory, simplify work flows, reduce set-up time, develop closer relationships with suppliers. Manufacturers from around the world tried adopting these principles, but they consistently ran into problems when trying to drive through the associated behavioural and cultural changes. How do you involve people and encourage teamwork in an environment where people are assessed and paid on the basis of how well they work as individuals? How do you drive out inventory in an environment where inventory is counted as an asset and,

Figure 2.1 Lean Enterprise Data

Assembly plant productivity, volume producers, 1989 (hours per vehicle)

	Best	Weighted average	Worst
Japanese owned plants in Japan	13.2	16.8	25.9
Japanese owned plants in North America	18.8	20.9	25.5
American owned plants in North America	18.6	24.9	25.5
American & Japanese plants owned in Europe	22.8	35.3	57.6
European owned plants in Europe	22.8	35.5	55.7
Plants in newly industrialized countries (Mexico, Brazil, Taiwan & Korea)	25.7	41	78.7

Assembly plant quality, volume producers, 1989 (assembly defects/ 100 vehicles)

	Best	Weighted average	Worst
Japanese owned plants in Japan	37.6	52.1	88.4
Japanese owned plants in North America	59.8	54.7	59.8
American owned plants in North America	35.1	78.4	168.6
European owned plants in Europe	63.9	76.4	123.8
Plants in newly industrialised countries (Mexico, Brazil, Taiwan & Korea)	27.6	72.3	190.5

therefore, reducing inventory can have an adverse impact on the balance sheet? How do you encourage people to make only what the customer wants, when the customer wants it, in an environment where machine and labour utilization are key metrics? The way to make the numbers look good is to get everyone working as hard as possible. Keep them producing regardless of whether there is a market for what they are making. What executives the world over found was that the measurement systems they were using were incompatible with the new strategies/approaches they were adopting. Repeatedly, horror stories about the incompatibilities between lean thinking and traditional accounting unfolded. The net effect of these emerging paradoxes was that the accounting community began to question its own long-held beliefs and assumptions about how to measure organizational performance and the very role of measurement in managing culture change.

The Social Agenda

Accompanying the pragmatic need to ensure that measures matched strategies and operational priorities was the more subtle, but nevertheless powerful, need for organizations to exhibit a social conscience. A key theme underpinning this is the gradual shift in society from a 'trust me', to a 'show me', to an 'involve me' attitude.[16] A decade ago it was perfectly acceptable for those with social status – politicians, doctors, lawyers, academics – to say to those around them 'trust me, I know what I am doing'. But in the intervening years we have witnessed a catalogue of disasters. Politicians have demonstrated on numerous occasions that their whiter-than-white image is merely a thin veneer – Bill Clinton and Monica Lewinski, for example. Doctors have fundamentally abused the trust patients have placed in them – Professor Van Hewsen and the Alder Hey hospital scandal, for instance, which involved the systematic 'harvesting' of organs from children without parental consent. Increasingly, society is saying to those in power and with authority – we won't trust you. We want you to show us. We want evidence that what you say is true.

So how do we provide evidence? The answer is simple – through measurement data. Hence the rapid emergence and dissemination of league tables, performance standards, accreditation kitemarks, and so on. In the university sector, management schools across the globe are regularly ranked in terms of teaching and research performance by the *Financial Times*, as well as the Higher Education Funding Council and the government sponsored research councils. In health care, performance league tables, summarising operation success rates and recovery times, are widely available. In education, school league tables, identifying the percentage of pupils graduating and gaining other levels of achievement, are produced so that parents and policy-makers can be better informed about school performance.

And it is not just in the public sector that organizations have to demonstrate how well they are performing across a broad spectrum of measures. In November 2000, a Business in the Community taskforce reported to the Confederation of British Industry conference on the results of its two-year study into corporate social responsibility. It said: 'What a business produces, how it buys and sells, how it affects the environment, how it recruits, trains and develops its own people, how it invests in the community and respects the rights of people – all these add together to form the impact of that business on society.' The taskforce report advocates that appropriate measurement and management of social impact protects and enhances a company's reputation, improves business competitiveness and helps to reduce risk. It also proposes a Business Impact Self-Assessment Tool, enabling companies to assess their community activities against standard criteria.

Intangible Assets

In the private sector too, organizations have invested millions of dollars developing sophisticated internal and external reporting processes. A particularly important current development is in the area of intellectual capital and intangible assets. This has been stimulated by the realization that the traditional balance sheet fails abysmally to capture a company's true worth. Take, for example, Oracle.[17] The company's market capitalization in August 2000 was $254,509 million, 39.4 times the value of its assets. How can this be? How can a business with physical assets of only $6,460 million be valued at $254,509 million by the market? The answer of course lies in the firm's intangible assets – brands, market position, capabilities, organizational knowledge, etc. The point is that a firm is far more than simply the

The Hidden Value[18]

Industry	Knowledge Capital ($ millions)	Knowledge Capital/Book Value	Market Value/Book Value	Market Value at 31/8/00 ($ millions)
Aerospace and defence	23,447	3.58	1.8	11,407
Airlines	7,949	2.12	1.0	5,496
Biotech	4,393	5.18	16.3	13,940
Chemicals	9,948	3.08	2.2	7,746
Computer Hardware	49,857	6.69	17.5	202,719
Computer Software	38,908	5.68	15.2	48,465
Electrical	7,690	3.70	3.6	6,081
Electric Utilities	10,351	1.11	2.1	19,418
Food/Beverages	18,565	7.48	9.1	27,007
Forest Products	8,884	0.87	1.6	10,322
Home Products	19,296	8.10	6.6	29,257
Industrial	23,132	3.65	3.3	16,922
Media	16,759	0.94	2.7	82,396
Motor Vehicles	13,413	3.50	1.9	9,205
Newspapers	5,619	3.77	3.2	6,594
Oil	24,559	1.71	3.4	55,150
Pharmaceuticals	75,224	8.44	12.2	116,073
Retail	15,406	2.89	3.8	18,486
Semiconductors	42,029	6.23	12.6	89,911
Speciality Retail	10,320	2.62	8.0	17,154
Telecom	81,221	3.26	3.5	118,288
Telecom Equipment	26,947	3.25	7.7	96,184

sum of its physical assets. Indeed, in today's information oriented society, often the firm's intangible assets far outweigh its physical assets (see the box *The Hidden Value*). So the question becomes: how can executives and investors track whether a given firm is increasing or decreasing the value of its intangible assets? Hence the flurry of activity around intangible asset accounting.

There are reasons to be cautious. As Peter Drucker, the mangement thinker, has said: 'Unless you can show these values, management will pay no attention to them. It's an old rule that you only attend to what is reported. The investment you put into those people is incredible: and until it's reported all the top management talk about managing knowledge and the knowledge worker will remain rhetoric' (*Financial Times*, 27 April 1999).

The Power and Pitfalls of Information Technology

The social and economic factors associated with the move from a 'trust me' to an 'involve me' world and the radical re-engineering that has taken place in many businesses as a result, have undoubtedly had a massive impact on the measurement revolution. But there is also a third factor – information technology – that has also facilitated many of the most recent developments. Software vendors the world over now offer performance reporting and analysis packages that would have been unheard of ten years ago. OLAP (On-line Analytic Processing applications) coupled with data warehousing technologies mean that executives can now slice and dice data in any way they wish to. Vendors such as Oracle, Peoplesoft and SAP are building entire businesses around their software and its capabilities. Multinationals are now able to gather and compare information on multiple sites around the world.

In the world of procurement, for example, executives can use the technology available to them to consolidate their materials inventories across the globe. Not only does this allow executives to see what stock is where, but it also allows them to manage its movement and rationalize its volume. Furthermore, the technology offers the opportunity to glean new insights into how much is purchased, when it is purchased, from where it is purchased, and so on. It is now far easier for the central purchasing manager of a company like IBM, for example, to track how much the firm spends globally on stationery items, on packaging materials, on travel services, as well as on electronic components. With access to such data, it becomes far easier for the organization to exploit its purchasing power and negotiate bulk discounts. No longer is it necessary to conduct a lengthy exercise gathering data on how much is spent on hotel bills or airfares annually. Instead, these data can be accessed at the click of a button.

The same is true of sales data. With the technology available today, executives can sit in their office and drill down through reams of data to find out the sales achieved by individual salesmen on particular days of the week. In fact, it goes even further because now those same executives can access the same data over the internet, and then they can e-mail their views directly to the sales representative concerned. The more these arguments develop the more a 'nightmare scenario' emerges. Yes, the technology is incredibly powerful. But it can either be used very wisely or very foolishly.

Some years ago one of the authors was working with the production manager of a factory just outside Manchester in the UK. This production manager had 60 KPIs (key performance indicators). To most people this is unbelievable. How can anyone cope with 60 KPIs? But to the production manager it was clear that every one of them was essential. Despite repeated questioning and debate there was no way that he was going to accept that he should reduce the number of KPIs on his list. Why? Because every so often, about once a month, his boss's boss's boss – the main board director with responsibility for manufacturing worldwide – would phone up and ask 'How much did you produce on line two last week?' or 'How much did you scrap on line three last Monday?' Why the company's manufacturing director wanted answers to these questions nobody knows. But the behavioural ramifications were profound. The production manager concerned believed that he had to be able to answer the manufacturing director's questions immediately otherwise it would look like he was not in control of his part of the business. And the only way he knew of doing this was to keep hold of every performance report he could get his hands on. That way, when the call came and the question was asked, he could give a rapid response simply by leafing through the filing cabinet.

Now roll this scenario forward a few years. With today's technology the manufacturing director could log on and drill down to the same level of detail. He could then pick out a particular issue and e-mail it to the production manager concerned and – if he had the time and felt so inclined – repeat the process for every other production manager in the business around the world. Just imagine the chaos that would ensue. Every time a new e-mail arrived a whole new set of hares would be set running. Meetings would be held, discussions scheduled, improvement programmes initiated. The organization would lose all sense of strategy and the people within it would simply react to e-mailed comments on performance reports.

Of course, this is a crazy way to run a business. Of course, everyone knows the dangers of this approach. Of course, nobody would really behave like that. Or would they? In February 2001, one of the authors attended a software demonstration from Cognos, one of the world's leading IT vendors of business intelligence software. The demonstration revolved around a mythical company – Airwave

Technologies – and the problems that they were currently experiencing. The theme behind the demonstration was that the president of the business used the Cognos software to identify where the problem was in his organization, compile a performance report that illustrated it and then sent the report to the supplier concerned to action, with a copy to the Airwave's director of procurement. You could see the eyes of some of the executives in the room light up. You could see (and hear) them saying 'that's how we should run our business', 'that's the level of control we need'. The Cognos demonstration clearly had its desired effect. It sold to the assembled throng the notion of a mythical future – one in which understanding the root causes of performance shortfalls and communicating them to those who have to act on them is as easy as pressing a few buttons on a PC.

Management utopia? Perhaps, but it will only seem so for those naïve few who still believe in the much discredited management model of command and control. Software is clearly important for performance reporting. It has clearly helped to facilitate the measurement revolution. The opportunities it offers for eliminating tables and spreadsheets and moving towards graphical and pictorial representations are immense, but we should not get too seduced by the technology. It certainly enables significantly improved performance management when used appropriately, but it also opens up the opportunity for mindless micro-management when abused.

The New Measurement Crisis

Micro-management is not the only issue. The rapid developments in information technology have also opened the doors to a new measurement crisis. When organizations began to get interested in re-engineering their measurement systems in the mid- to late 1980s, the challenge that many executives faced was quite simply that their organizations were measuring the wrong things. Far too often they focused on financial figures, such as return on investment, profitability and cash flow. These narrow financial measures all too often resulted in short-term behaviour. Hence the tendency for managers to delay capital investment expenditures towards the year end, in an attempt to make the figures look better. Or the tendency for managers to delay the booking of sales to the following year, if their sales targets had already been met. Or the tendency for managers to negotiate with suppliers to delay payment to the following year to reduce their current year costs. These short-termist behaviours were made even more dramatic when pay was linked to performance, for then the incentives for executives and managers throughout the organization to deliver the numbers became significant. Short-term manipulation of the numbers could result in bonus payments being increased by several tens – even hundreds – of thousands of pounds/dollars for people at senior levels in these organizations. It is no wonder then that people played the numbers game and delivered the figures. Unfortunately, they often did so without improving – or even worse, actually damaging – the firm's underlying performance.

As this problem became increasingly evident and an ever greater number of people began commenting and reflecting upon it, then the nature of the measurement crisis became more and more obvious. The excessively short-term, narrowly focused measurement systems adopted by many organizations were quite simply leading to the wrong behaviours. In many ways these arguments have been won. There are few executives today who would argue that solely relying on financial measures is the right way to run a business, if you really want to run the business for the long term. There is no need then to dwell on the old measurement crisis, as most people now accept its root causes and consequential effects. The problem is that today the nature of the measurement crisis is changing. And this problem is compounded by the fact that not many people yet recognize the situation. The fundamental problem today is not that people are measuring the wrong things. Instead, it is that they are trying to measure too much.

The supermarkets are an excellent case in point. Most of them now operate some form of loyalty scheme, which is effectively an attempt to buy loyalty from customers. Tesco, the number one retailer in the UK, for example, operates a club card system. Each time you enter the store and purchase goods, you hand over your club card and earn points based on the value of the goods that you have purchased. Points can subsequently be redeemed for reward vouchers and discounts. However, the supermarket is able to use these data to analyze and understand customer buying patterns, so that they can then tailor in-store promotions and segment their customers for marketing purposes. The insights that Tesco is able to generate through these data are highly significant and this capability enables them to retain their edge as one of the world's leading retailers. The problem is that even they believe that they are only using about 2 per cent of the data to which they have access.

There are numerous reasons for this state of affairs. One of the most significant is just the volume of data that is being captured inside these organizations. Imagine a typical transaction. As a shopper you will buy 50 to 100 items. Many of these stores will have 10 to 20 different tills operating at any one point in time. They can process about one customer every five minutes, giving an average of 12 customers an hour for 10 hours a day. So, each and every day they are working, they are gathering between 60,000 and 240,000 data points per store. In a mid-sized country we are talking about 200 stores, working 7 days a week. The supermarkets, therefore, are gathering something like 65 million to 340 million different data points per working week. No wonder they are only looking at 2 per cent of the data. Of course the problem gets worse, because it is not only that they are gathering so much data, but also that some of that data is of questionable validity or robustness. A large US supermarket chain recently provided a wonderful example of this (see the box *All Eggs in One Basket*).

All Eggs in One Basket

One of the senior corporate managers was due to visit a particular branch of this supermarket in Texas. Prior to going he had a look at the sales figures for the branch and noticed that one of their best selling items was hard-boiled eggs! This appeared crazy. Most people have never bought a hard-boiled egg from a supermarket so why should so many be sold in Texas? So, when he visited the store, he asked a few people if they sold a lot of hard-boiled eggs. He received the same response from everyone: 'We don't sell any hard-boiled eggs.' Puzzled, he started to explore what was going on.

The root cause of the problem? Hard-boiled eggs were valued at 50 cents each. Whenever an item that had no bar code on it had to pass through the scanner, it was valued in terms of hard-boiled eggs. So oranges were valued as seven hard-boiled eggs. Packs of washing powder were valued as 40 hard-boiled eggs. Toilet rolls were valued as 16 hard-boiled eggs, and so on. No wonder it appeared the store was selling so many hard-boiled eggs! Imagine the implications for an automated inventory management system though …

Information Proliferation

You can't walk into a hotel these days without receiving at least one customer satisfaction questionnaire. If you stay and eat in a hotel, then you will often end up with a customer satisfaction questionnaire for every meal that you take, and another one for each room you stay in, and in extreme cases, for each night you stay! All the data that these measurement systems generate are displayed around the hotel. Often in the back office, but increasingly in the front office too. Displays of facts and figures showing customers how good the service is that is being delivered are becoming more and more commonplace. The underground railway in Singapore is littered with such information. The charts all show the same thing: that the railway works pretty well (unlike train services in some other countries). The point is that more and more people – customers, employees, shareholders and even governments – are demanding that organizations release information about what they are doing, why they are doing it and how well they are doing it. The net result is that organizations are trying to capture more and more data. To capture the data, they are putting in place more and more measurement systems. They need access to this data so they have to build the information technology infrastructure. This problem is not set to stop.

In fact, some serious issues face executives today. If, for example, you are running a relatively simple business with ten products, which are sold in five different regions, each of which consists of 20 countries, and you collect sales data for 52 weeks for your five customer categories and 50 sub-categories, then you would be able to generate any one of 13 million different performance reports for sales data alone! The Gartner Group estimates that by 2004 the average company will have collected 120 terabytes of customer data alone. Since a single terabyte equates to 38 miles of full filing cabinets, this is a mind-boggling amount of information. With this abundance of data, there is much that it is *possible to know* that would have been virtually impossible to know only a few years ago. However, the trick of course is not to know what it is possible to know (it's impossible anyway), but what it is that you *must* know. In other words, what will make a significant difference to the performance of the organization in satisfying its various stakeholders wants and needs better, and ultimately more profitably.

Recently, one of the software vendors illustrated this point to one of the authors when discussing their software. With great glee the software vendor pointed out how their software could generate 600 million different performance reports for sales. The author's response was quite simple – it was one of horror. As an executive in a business, I would not want to be faced with 600 million different performance reports. I want the one or two or five performance reports that really help me to understand what is going on. More data is not necessarily good. What we need to do in organizations is focus on measuring what matters. The role of the software and accompanying infrastructure is simply to enable us to do this. Merely developing systems that provide access to more and more data will only add fuel to the fire and leave yet more executives with a fundamental problem – namely, drowning in data.

Fuelling the Fire

The new measurement crisis – drowning in data – should not be blamed on IT alone. As we have noted in the previous chapter, the problem has been further compounded by the number of solutions that the academics and consultants have offered to the market. In the last few years, we have seen the emergence of Activity Based Costing, Activity Based Management, Economic Profit, Economic Value Added,[19] Market Value Added, Shareholder Value Analysis, Balanced Scorecard, Comparative Benchmarking, Baldrige Award criteria, Business Excellence Award model, and a host of regional and sub-regional awards derived from these. The academic and consulting community have had a field day, offering to managements new measurement frameworks and methodologies, each of which is designed to provide tangible value adding benefits in its own right, and each of which inevitably does add value when intelligently implemented (otherwise no one would ever adopt it). The problem is that there are just too many of these frameworks out there and many of them seem to offer partial, rather than comprehensive perspectives on performance (see Chapter 5 for a fuller discussion of this issue).

It is not only the measurement frameworks and methodologies that have grown in number in recent years, but also the desire to measure individual dimensions of performance. In organizations today, people frequently express a desire to measure customer satisfaction, customer complaints, customer loyalty, customer retention and customer profitability. Then they think about employees, and say we had better measure attrition, morale, absenteeism, health and safety, accidents, motivation, skill-sets, training, comparative compensation, length of service, employee advocacy, and so on. Then they think about suppliers, and say, for our suppliers we should be measuring how well they are performing, how much they are costing us, whether they are developing, whether they are taking cost out of the supply chain, whether they are sharing those cost savings with us, and so on. Then they think about the core processes in the business, and decide that they should be measuring both process efficiency and process effectiveness. They need to measure on-time delivery performance and how quickly they can deliver. They want to measure quality levels, so they introduce a measure of parts per million (ppm) or percentage of defects, or scrap produced, or quality costs, etc. Then they decide they had better have some measures of productivity too, so they can check whether they are actually using the resources they have access to efficiently. Then there is the problem of innovation. How do we measure innovation? Maybe we should be measuring the amount of sales turnover we get from products introduced in the last 18 months. But that will not allow us to track time-to-market or development costs, or progress against milestones, so we had better measure these as well!

The list is endless. Gather any group of executives in a room and ask them what they would like to measure and they'll fill ten flip charts full of suggestions in 30 minutes. Give them another 30 minutes and they'll likely fill ten more. Each performance measurement will be valuable. Each will be appealing. Each will be important. And each will cost the organization. But, realistically, no organization can afford to measure everything they would like to measure. And, even if it could, its executives would not be able to manage with them all. So it is time to prioritize and decide what really matters in organizations, and focus on measuring the critical few. Importantly too, decisions need to be taken as to which key measures the executive team should own and be accountable for, and which measures are still indispensable but need to be delegated to managers or supervisors further down the organizational hierarchy. Responsibility and accountability for managing the latter also needs to be addressed. This can represent a significant and challenging cultural change.

The Cost of Measurement

An alternative way to look at this argument is simply to think about the cost of measurement. And this is a fascinating question to ask executives. Generally, if you ask a senior executive in an organization: 'How much does your organization spend on capturing measurement data?' The answer will be, 'A lot, but I don't know exactly how much.' Think about the question for a minute. All we have asked is how much do you spend on capturing measurement data. We have made no mention of collating that data, of sorting it, of putting it into meaningful displays that actually allow it to be interpreted, analyzed and acted upon. The costs associated with capturing data and converting it into valuable information that can be acted upon are immense in most organizations. Ford, for example, estimate that they spend $1.2 billion a year on planning and budgeting alone. Research data gathered by the Hackett Group suggest that the average $1 billion company spends 25,000 person days a year on planning and measuring performance. Yet it is rare to find an organization where anyone has been given overall responsibility for managing the measurement system. It is even rarer to find an organization where anyone actively seeks to improve the measurement system. How often do people remove measures that are obsolete? Even in organizations that have re-engineered their measurement systems, the tendency is to add more measures, not take out the obsolete ones.

This chapter has been critical of performance measurement in organizations. And in many ways it is exactly right to be critical, because of where we are today. In most organizations measurement is a mess. There is too much wasted data. There is too much wasted effort. It costs too much. The measures are not clearly communicated. They are not aligned with each other. They are poorly linked to reward mechanisms. They are not clearly understood. They are distrusted. They get gamed. Organizations have too many performance measurement and management frameworks, all of which appear to be inconsistent with one another. What is needed is for us to take a step back from all this activity and think for a while about why we are measuring performance in organizations. What are we trying to achieve through our performance measurement systems? And how best can we achieve it? These are the issues that Chapter 3 will deal with, as meanwhile we take a fundamental look at the role of measurement in organizations and at the processes that allow good measurement systems to be designed, implemented and cascaded throughout the business.

3 Managing with Measures

In God we trust, but all others need data.

Creed and challenge adopted by the CEO of a food manufacturer to anyone presenting a recommendation not supported by facts.

Managing with measures makes such intuitive sense to most people that it is easy to assume that the majority of organizations must have got it cracked. After all, all that managing with measures involves is deciding which measures to track and then using these measures to drive performance improvement. A simple statement, but one with hidden complexity. What really makes a good measurement system? Should measures be linked to reward? Should measures be derived from strategy? How can measurement systems be structured so that they actually drive the behaviours you want in an organization? These are easy questions to ask, but they are invariably much harder to answer. So far, we have been highly critical and somewhat damning of performance measurement practice as it exists in many organizations today. The point, however, is not that it is impossible to establish good measurement systems and measures of performance. Instead, the point is that it is *difficult* to establish good measurement systems and measures of performance. So, how should it be done?

The Four Processes

There are four fundamental processes that underpin the development and deployment of a performance measurement system (see Figure 3.1). The first is to do with design of the measures – this is all about understanding what should be measured and defining how it should be measured. The second is to do with preparing for the implementation of the measurement system – this is about planning how to gain access to the required data, building the measurement system, configuring data manipulation and distribution, and, crucially, overcoming people's political and cultural concerns about performance measurement. The third is the act of managing with measures – that is actually operating with the measures, using the measurement data to understand what is going on in the organization and applying that insight to drive improvements in business performance. And, finally, there is the act of managing the measurement system itself – making sure that it is refreshed and refined continuously and ensuring that measures remain relevant to the needs of the organization.

Fig 3.1 The Four Fundamental Processes

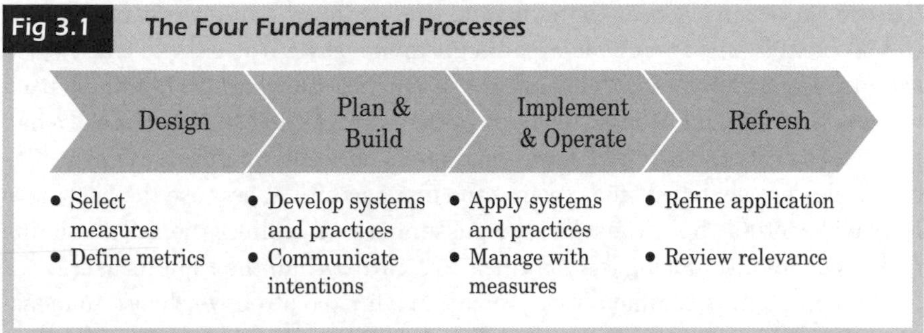

Design

Most of the rest of this book is about designing performance measurement systems using the Performance Prism framework as a guiding beacon for appropriate measures selection. There are, however, a number of general measures design principles and considerations that we need to consider here first.

Designing robust performance measures that encourage the right behaviour is just the starting point when it comes to the process of developing and deploying a good performance measurement system. The process of deciding what and how to measure is an intellectually challenging one though. It certainly requires careful thought. And it definitely requires some significant choices to be made about the behaviours to be encouraged in the organization and, therefore, the characteristics and structure of the appropriate measures. But, universally, those with experience agree that while intellectually stimulating, the process of designing the measurement system is the easiest stage of developing and deploying it. On the other hand, if this first process is not done well, then the game is lost from the outset.

Some organizations do it well and develop excellent measurement systems. Others mess it up completely. Executives the world over frequently get it wrong. Take for example, the airline that introduced a new measure: 'Time taken to unload bags'. One day, one of the senior executives in the airline observed a baggage handler sprinting across the runway with a small bag under his arm, press a button on the baggage carousel, throwing the bag onto the carousel and then sauntering back to his colleagues to have a chat. Puzzled, the executive began to explore what was going on. It emerged that the airline was measuring the time taken to unload bags by using the metric of tracking the elapsed time between a plane landing and the first bag being put on the baggage carousel. So the game the baggage handlers were playing was: get the first bag on the carousel quickly and don't worry about the rest!

Clearly, this is an inappropriate metric and a far better one would have been the time between the plane landing and the *last* bag hitting the carousel. But the problem is this is much more difficult to measure. It is easy to track when the first bag hits the carousel because this is when the operator hits the button to start the carousel. Hence the data capture process can be automated. When the last bag hits the carousel, however, there is no similar defining moment. The carousel is not switched off as soon as the last bag hits it, because the bags have to travel around the carousel so the passengers can collect them. The airline had ended up introducing the easy measure, rather than the right measure.

This problem is common in organizations, far too often we choose to measure what is easy to measure, rather than what is right to measure. And then employees play the numbers game. They deliberately game measures in order to evade blame, with the consequence that the real purpose of the measure (say, to help improve customer satisfaction) is lost without trace. If we don't pay enough attention to the design of the measures we use, then we simply end up creating measurement systems that drive behaviours which are completely inappropriate – albeit unintentionally. You certainly get what you measure, but you may not get what you want.

Measures Definition

During the process of designing measures we need to think about what it is that we are actually trying to measure. Often, when people set out to design a performance measure, they think about the title of the measure (what the measure should be called) and consider various options for the metric(s) that will define the measure, and then they worry about the formula – what data they are actually going to collect. These questions are clearly important and it is impossible to define a measure without addressing them, but they are not the only questions that should be asked when designing a measure. Just as important are questions like:

- What is the reason for this measure?
- Why do we want to measure it?
- Who is going to act on the measure once the data become available?
- What do they then do with the benefit of this knowledge?

These three questions: (i) what is the purpose of the measure? (ii) who is going to act on it? and (iii) what do they do? are often missed during the definition of measures. Yet this is essential if the loop is to be closed and action is to follow measurement.

Answering these questions, however, does not yet ensure that the measure is fully defined. There are also some pragmatic questions that have to be addressed, such as:

- Where are we going to get the data from?
- Who is going to collect the data?
- How often are they going to collect the data?
- How often will the data be reviewed?

Even after these questions have been addressed, there is still one further issue to consider – namely, the target. How will you know, without an appropriate target, whether you are achieving the level of performance you actually want to? How will you actually set the target to make sure it reflects the level of performance you should be striving for? Do you want targets set based on potential? Do you want targets using last year, or the competition, or industry best practices as the basis for comparison? Or do you want targets that enable progress versus budget/forecast to be tracked (even if those figures are often somewhat arbitrary at best)?

These questions come together to form the measures definition template (when completed, called a performance measure record sheet) shown in Figure 3.2.

Fig 3.2 Measures Definition Template

Measure:	
Purpose:	
Relates to:	
Metric/Formula:	
Target Level(s):	
Frequency:	
Source of data:	
Who measures:	
Who acts on the data (owner):	
What do they do:	
Notes/Comments:	

At one level, the questions contained in this template can appear superficial or, at least, simple to answer. Experience shows, however, that while the questions appear simple to answer, in practice they rarely are, especially when the process of designing new or improved sets of measures is taken seriously. Take, for example, a basic measure such as on-time delivery. The appropriate metric for this measure will be one that tracks the number or percentage of on-time deliveries within a given period. But what is an on-time delivery? Is it one that leaves the factory on-time or one that arrives at the customer's premises on-time? And what is on-time at the customer's premises – delivery in the right week, or the right day, during the correct pre-specified half-hour delivery window? How about deliveries that arrive when scheduled, but that are not complete – are these on-time? How about deliveries that arrive on-time, but are only on-time according to the negotiated delivery date, rather than the customer's original request date – are these deliveries still on-time, or is that a separate metric? As this simple example shows, the subtleties associated with the design of measures are legion.

The template should help in the measures definition stage as it identifies the awkward questions to address when confirming the specification of the measures design. This type of template has been used to great effect in numerous organizations, not least because they force measures designers to clarify the appropriate formula for each metric and to specify the data source. They may not be the most exciting part of measures design, but we are sure that they are nothing less than an essential discipline.

For example, take a simple metric such as gross profit (say, where the level of an operating unit's profitability is the measure). Should this be calculated on the basis of dollars or percentage? The advantage of using value is that the measure encourages sales people to think about the total profitability of the order. Conversely, measuring gross profit in terms of percentage encourages sales representatives not to give away margin – in fact, it may even encourage them to turn away business that is not profitable enough. Similarly, measuring the conversion ratio of quotations or proposals submitted in terms of volume, rather than value, can encourage people to focus on converting many small quotes rather than a few very large ones. However, if you wanted to diversify, it might well be that the number of quotes converted, rather than the value of quotes converted, is the right measure to implement. Alternatively, if you want to build a relationship with a particular client segment, then it might be that you decide only to measure quotes converted with that particular set of clients – or the proportion of all quotes converted within that segment. You need to be very clear what it is that you want to achieve from applying each measure.

The point is that individual measures require precise and careful design if they are to achieve the desired ends and encourage the appropriate behaviours. In terms of individual measure design then, 'good enough' is simply not an appropriate strategy. Instead, time, effort and thought has to be devoted to the process and the measures definition template shown in Figure 3.2 provides a framework for structuring this thought. The facilitator's checklist shown in Figure 3.3 will help to configure the content of the template.

Fig 3.3 Measures Definition Template: Facilitator's Checklist

Measure:
- What should the measure be called?
- Does the title explain what the measure is?
- Is it a title that everyone will understand?
- Is it clear why the measure is important?

Purpose:
- Why is the measure being introduced?
- What is the aim/intention of the measure?
- What behaviours should the measure encourage?

Relates to:
- Which other measures does this one closely relate to?
- What specific strategies or initiatives does it support?

Metric/Formula:
- How can this dimension of performance be measured?
- Can the formula be defined in mathematical terms?
- Is the metric/formula clear?
- Does the metric/formula explain exactly what data are required?
- What behaviour is the metric/formula intended to induce?
- Are there any other behaviours that the metric/formula should induce?
- Are there any dysfunctional behaviours that might be induced?
- Is the scale being used appropriate?
- How accurate will the data generated be?
- Are the data accurate enough?
- If an average is used how much data will be lost?
- Is the loss of 'granularity' acceptable?
- Would it be better to measure the spread of performance?

Target level(s):
- What level of performance is desirable?
- How long will it take to reach this level of performance?
- Are interim milestone targets required?
- How do these target levels of performance compare with competitors?
- How good is the competition currently?
- How fast is the competition improving?

Frequency:
- How often should this measure be made?
- How often should this measure be reported?
- Is this frequency sufficient to track the effect of actions taken to improve?

Source of data:
- Where will the data to track this measure come from?

Who measures:
- Who – by name, function or external agency – is actually responsible for collecting, collating and analyzing this data?

Who acts on the data (owner):
- Who – by name or function – is actually responsible for initiating actions and ensuring that performance along this dimension improves?

What do they do:
- How exactly will the measure owner use the data?
- What actions will they take to ensure that performance along this dimension improves?

Have You Designed a Good Measure? – The Ten Tests

Once you have completed the measures definition template, you have produced a specification for the measure. Frequently the specification will highlight specific issues within the organization that need to be addressed. It also often prompts a discussion about whether the measure itself will drive the behaviours that are actually required. So, for example, in the case of measuring the time to quote, a sales organization might become involved in extensive discussions about whether quotes should be considered complete (signed-off) at the time they are sent to the customer or the time that the customer actually confirms their receipt. The advantage of the latter is that it actually encourages sales teams to talk to customers more. If quotes are signed-off when they are put in the post, or in the fax machine, then that would be the end of the process. However, if they are signed-off when the customer has verbally confirmed that they have been received, then the behaviour encouraged is for sales people to fax or post quotes to customers and then phone them to check that they have been received. If an organization has a strategy of trying to build stronger relationships with customers, then this might well be an appropriate approach.

The point is that the act of defining the measure, and particularly defining the metric and the formula for calculating it, is crucial because the way you structure the measure affects the behaviour of individuals within the organization. Designing measures that stimulate the right behaviours is intellectually challenging. But simply having a measure that encourages the right behaviour is only part of the challenge, for there are several other questions that have to be addressed when assessing whether or not the designed measure is a good one – these are the Ten Tests.[20]

Test 1: The Truth Test

The first test to subject a measure to is the truth test. Here we are asking: are we really measuring what we set out to measure? Far too often poorly designed measures result in us tracking things we never wanted to track in the first place. Customer loyalty, for example, provides a case in point. Numerous commentators state that loyalty can be tracked by checking whether customers come back and buy again. But all that this measures is customer retention (and this is important in itself of course). But customer retention is just one face of customer loyalty; the other side is about satisfaction and advocacy. Customers who buy repeatedly are not necessarily particularly satisfied or advocates for the business. Many banks and telephone companies, for example, retain their customers not because of loyalty, but because their customers feel trapped – trapped because of the effort involved in rearranging numerous direct debits and payment agreements in the case of banks, or telling all of your friends, colleagues and business contacts about your new phone number in the case of the telephone companies. Some other measure will be needed to establish whether customers are happy with the products or services they get and, possibly, whether they are likely to recommend the product or service to colleagues, friends or family. This can be especially vital in industries where new competitors are entering the market. To establish whether or not you really are measuring what you set out to measure, you have to compare the items on the measures definition template entered under the headings – measure, purpose and formula. If these three line up then it is fair to assume that you are measuring what you set out to measure.

Test 2: The Focus Test

The second test to subject measures to is the focus test. Here we are asking not whether we are measuring what we set out to measure, but instead whether we are *only* measuring what we set out to measure. The reason this is important is that sometimes poorly defined measures end up measuring multiple dimensions of performance simultaneously. Take, for example, a measure like sales to existing clients. This measure can track both customer retention and cross-selling simultaneously. Sales to existing clients can increase because of cross-selling activities, but can be adversely affected by the loss of customers or business. So there is a need to differentiate between sales to existing customers in terms of cross-selling, and sales to existing customers in terms of customer retention. The way to do this is to identify two separate metrics. One that specifically focuses on customer retention – are we getting more or less of the same business than last year from particular customers? And a second metric that focuses on cross-selling – are our customers buying more multiple products and/or services from us this year than last year? Separating out the metrics in this way makes it much easier when it comes to analyzing and identifying real trends in performance.

Test 3: The Relevance Test

It is all very well measuring what you set out to measure and not confounding multiple performance issues in the same measure, but you also need to ask yourself if it is the right measure. This is the focus of the relevance test and here we are asking: are we definitely measuring the right thing? Take, for example, a measure such as the number of suggestions made by employees. Numerous organizations have adopted this performance measure as a proxy indicator of employee involvement in their improvement initiatives. But is it a valid indicator? Do organizations really want lots of suggestions? Surely what is wanted are valid – and implementable – suggestions. Hence a better measure might be the average number of implementable suggestions. But even this does not measure employee involvement. A single employee might offer 2,000 implementable suggestions and this would make the figure look good, but it would hardly be indicative of widespread involvement. If widespread involvement is the aim then 1,000 employees each offering two suggestions, should score more highly than one employee offering 2,000 suggestions. So, a more appropriate measure could be the percentage of employees offering two or more implementable suggestions.

Test 4: The Consistency Test

This test is concerned with whether the measure is consistent, whoever makes the measurement and whenever they make the measurement. If the measurement is not clearly specified – or at least the measurement process is not clearly specified – then different individuals will track different data and hence the results will vary depending upon who takes the measurement. In many ways the consistency test is effectively a scientific approach to measurement. In designing laboratory experiments, the scientist would be very precise about how the measurement was to be made so that others could replicate the study. The same is true of business performance measurement. Unless we are precise about how the measurement should be made and when it should be made, we will end up making invalid comparisons. This is particularly an issue in organizations that have wildly different numbers of customers at different points in time. Take, for example, measuring customer satisfaction at a tourist attraction. Early in the morning, on a school day, there will be relatively few visitors. Queues will not have built up. Attractions will be easy to see. But equally the atmosphere may be low. So, early in the morning, before numbers have built up at the visitor attraction, customer satisfaction scores are likely to be good in terms of accessibility and visibility, but poor in terms of atmosphere. Later in the day, or on a public holiday, the scores may be completely reversed. There will be lots of people around and the atmosphere may be great, but the queues unacceptable. The key point, in terms of designing measures, is that we have to understand the context within which the measurement data are being collected so we can know whether or not we are comparing like with like.

Test 5: The Access Test

This test asks whether the data can be easily accessed and understood. Is it easy to track and capture the data that are needed if we are to make the measurement? Far too often people design sophisticated measures that can – or should – never be used in practice because of the challenges associated with accessing the necessary data. The implications of this can be seen most clearly in terms of cost (also see Test 9). For example, a typical consideration might include whether a smaller data sample that is much easier to access will do just as well as a comprehensive data collection system.

Test 6: The Clarity Test

This test is concerned with whether there is any ambiguity possible in interpretation of the results. If the measure is not clearly specified, or if the source of the data is ambivalent or inconsistent, then different people can interpret the data in different ways and this can cause chaos – lots of debate and little action. This is a particularly important issue when one bears in mind some of the politics and gaming that can be associated with implementing new measurement systems – especially so when 'performance league tables' will be published either internally or externally. Furthermore, one of the first lines of defence used by those who want to avoid being measured is to question the validity of the measurement and claim that the basis of the calculation is bogus or inappropriate.

Test 7: The So-What Test

This is a fundamental test of a good measure. Underlying it is the notion of checking whether the data can and will be acted upon once they have been collected. As we have already discussed, for measures to deliver value to a business, the insights the data provide have to be acted upon. Unless it is clear that the data will be acted upon, then there is no point actually having the measure in the first place. Measures that are not acted upon are simply a waste of time and effort. The items on the measures definition template that address the questions: Who acts on the data? and What do they do? will help to resolve any 'actionability' dilemmas. If you cannot answer those questions, why are you measuring it?

Test 8: The Timeliness Test

This test is concerned with whether or not the data can be analyzed and accessed rapidly enough, so that timely action can be taken. Far too often measurement reports appear so long after the event that it is almost impossible for anyone within the organization to do anything useful with the data. Take the monthly sales report. Receiving these figures at the end of the month, or a few days after the end of the month, is almost useless – it's historical data. It is far too late to take any action to affect repairs at that stage, although it may help to establish if a trend is forming. Frequency of measurement is often an issue here too – for example, annual customer and employee perception surveys are simply too far apart to judge whether improvement initiatives resultant from the previous survey are having the desired effect. We need to ensure that necessary and sufficient data become available within the organization in a timely fashion, so that people can actually act on it in a meaningful way and see the results of their actions. Note the use here of the words 'in a timely fashion', rather than 'as rapidly as possible', as it denotes the *appropriateness* of the timing.

Test 9: The Cost Test

Before introducing a new measure it is essential that we think about the cost of actually tracking this particular dimension of performance with the frequency of measurement specified. Consideration needs to be given as to whether the particular performance measure is worth the cost that will be incurred in capturing the data? If not, then there is no point in introducing the measure. A cost/benefit deliberation may well be a relevant design consideration. The UK government's 'Best Value' programme, for example, is said to have added £29 million a year to the cost of running the police force because of all of the extra effort involved in reporting against specific, government-imposed, key performance indicators.

Test 10: The Gaming Test

The final test is to think – once again – about the behaviours that the performance measure will encourage. Is the measure, in its proposed form, likely to encourage any behaviours that are undesirable to the organization? If so, what can be done about this? How can the measure be changed so that it actually encourages appropriate behaviours, rather than potentially inappropriate ones? Or does some compensating metric also need to be addressed alongside? For example, if the level of output is introduced as a process measure, will quality be compromised by people taking short cuts? In this case, probably both sets of data need to be combined so that the level of good quality output is measured. It may seem obvious, but it is astonishing how often this type of consideration is overlooked. Gaming is most frequently found where allocation of responsibility for performance failures is sought through measures and, therefore, blame may be attributed. See the box *Measures Gaming and Dysfunctional Behaviours in the Airline Industry* for a further illustrative example.

Measures Gaming and Dysfunctional Behaviours in the Airline Industry

Standard practice for tracking the cause of departure delays in the airline industry is to assign each delay to the party that caused it. Delays that are caused by gate agents (e.g. failure to check all passengers on time) are assigned to customer service. Delays that are caused by the baggage handlers (e.g. failure to load all bags on time) are assigned to baggage. Delays that are caused by flight attendants (e.g. failure to get all passengers seated on time) are assigned to in-flight. Delays that are caused by cabin cleaners (e.g. failure to get the aircraft cleaned on time) are assigned to cabin cleaning. And so on.

The purpose of this system is to assign accountability for delays accurately, in order to evaluate the performance of individual employees and their managers, to motivate better performance, and to improve the departure process over time. However, there was some evidence of dysfunctional behaviours associated with the airline on-time departures system. Some indicators of this are listed below:

- Miscoding of delays was prevalent. At some stations, employees reported that delays were coded to weather and air traffic control whenever possible, to shift the onus to outside parties.
- There was often a failure to focus on the actual goals of the departure process. According to a supervisor, 'If you ask anyone here, what's the last thing you think of when there's a problem, I bet your bottom dollar it's the customer. And these are guys who bust their butts every day. But they're thinking "how do I keep my ass out of the sling".'
- One customer service employee observed, 'Here ... the ultimate goal is not the customers. It's the report card. You spend so much time filling out delay forms and fighting over a delay – just think what we could be doing.' A similar sentiment was expressed at another airline. 'There is so much internal debate and reports and meetings. This is time we could be focusing on the passengers.' Rather than focusing on the process itself, managers tended to focus on meeting their numbers to avoid punishment. One manager complained about being 'harassed on a daily basis ... Headquarters has a performance analysis department that is looking at my MAPS [minimum acceptable performance standards] every day, analyzing the station's performance. Failure to meet MAPS is perceived to result in punitive action.'

- Working relationships between groups suffered as well. 'There was always a lot of finger-pointing,' according to a ramp manager at one carrier. 'Barriers between groups – it all comes down to the delay coding system,' said a station manager at another airline.
- Managers were willing to do what was necessary to meet their performance goals, even if it meant doing things that were not in the company's best interests, in their judgement. 'The field manager is judged on the numbers and not on how he got them,' said the manager of human resources. The employee relations manager concurred, 'All that matters is the numbers – how you achieve them is secondary. This is part of the culture of fear.' According to a field manager, 'The penalties that go along with [such] accountability make people afraid to take risks.'
- Managers transmitted to the front-line workers the pressures they perceive from headquarters. As a result, employees were well aware of their managers' performance evaluation system, and how it affected them. 'Here you only care about delays,' said a customer service agent. 'Otherwise the little report card won't look good that week. The ultimate goal is not the customers, it's the report card.'

The airline with the industry's fewest delays, mishandled bags and customer complaints – the best performer on aggregate – had introduced a new delay code, called a 'team delay'. The team delay is used to point out problems between two or three different employee groups. The team delay became the single most-used delay category for station-controllable delays. Within this airline, the team delay was regarded as an innovation that partly explained its superior on-time performance.

This airline is also deliberately vague about the basis of managerial evaluation. When asked, field managers were vague about how their own performance was assessed. 'I'll hear about it if I'm not doing a good job,' was one typical response. 'It is watched but there is no fear factor,' said another. Field managers at this airline expressed a comfort with the relationship with headquarters that contrasted dramatically with the resentment expressed by field managers at other airlines. They described a dialogue with their superiors, and a flow of information that was focused on identifying problems and finding solutions.

So, the best performing airline both introduced an innovative measure and used its set of performance measures in a very different way from the industry norm.

Source: Adapted from a research paper 'Anomalies of High Performance' by Robert D. Austin and Jody Hoffer Gittell, Harvard Business School.

These ten tests are summarized in Figure 3.4.

Fig 3.4 The Ten Measures Design Tests

The Ten Tests

1. *The Truth Test* – Are we really measuring what we set out to measure?
2. *The Focus Test* – Are we only measuring what we set out to measure?
3. *The Relevancy Test* – Is it the right measure of the performance factor we want to track?
4. *The Consistency Test* – Will the data always be collected in the same way whoever measures it?
5. *The Access Test* – Is it easy to locate and capture the data needed to make the measurement?
6. *The Clarity Test* – Is any ambiguity possible in interpreting the results?
7. *The So-What Test* – Can and will the reported data be acted upon?
8. *The Timeliness Test* – Can the data be accessed rapidly and frequently enough for action?
9. *The Cost Test* – Is the measure worth the cost of measurement?
10. *The Gaming Test* – Is the measure likely to encourage undesirable or inappropriate behaviours?

Plan and Build

Once you have designed (or redesigned) your measures, clearly you have to implement the supporting measurement system. You have to introduce the new measures into your organization. You may have to overcome the fears and concerns that can be associated with the introduction of measurement. You have to persuade people, or cajole them, or otherwise reassure them that the new measurement system is not there as a big stick to beat them over the head with if and when they fail to deliver. You have to convince them that it will be there to help them to manage better and to deliver benefits to the organization they work for. And you will probably have to explain to people how to use the measurement data to actually understand what is happening inside the organization and how to improve performance. You will likely also have to acquire or develop the necessary technology aspects of the measurement system, which may well involve some information systems testing. You will have to introduce new measurement acquisition mechanisms and then access the data they provide. And you will have to tell people how the data will be presented to them, probably involving them in the development process. This is likely to involve a not insignificant communication, education and training requirement too that will normally demand some substantial planning effort.

Data Acquisition

For example, just in terms of establishing the measurement system itself, imagine introducing a new measure of customer satisfaction. If you want to measure on-time delivery of components, or customers' perception of service quality levels, and you have never done so before, then you will need to establish a new performance measurement system for that/those measure(s). You will have to acquire data that allows you to track how well you are doing. Much of the data will have to be captured at the individual transaction level – i.e. was that order on time, was that customer satisfied with the particular service they received at that time, and so on. But tracking at the transaction level often means tracking hundreds, thousands or even tens of thousands of interactions every day. So are you going to track every single interaction? Or are you going to track a sample of interactions? And if you track a sample of interactions, which sample are you going to track?

There are important issues at stake here. If you track people's perceptions of service quality first thing in the morning in the banking sector, when a bank is relatively quiet, you will get a very different set of results to when you track people's perceptions of service quality when the bank is busy, such as at lunchtime. Alternatively, if you track people's perception of service quality *in the bank*, what about all the people who never come to the bank? Those who use the phone or the mail or the internet to do their banking, for instance. Market research shows us also that people who are informed beforehand that they will be interviewed or surveyed after a service interaction tend to be more critical of their experience and more negative in their responses than those who are not pre-warned. The choice of how you access and acquire the data you require to make your measures is absolutely crucial, as it will fundamentally affect the results you see from your measurement system.

Collecting the data is of course not the end of the process, for then you have to collate it – you have to gather together the data from diverse sources and integrate these into a single data set. Many organizations fail to do this and as a result fail to extract much of the value from their measurement data. Too often, for example, different branches inside a banking network will run their own customer satisfaction survey or their own customer complaints process. Typically, each branch will gather data on how satisfied its customers are with its local service. But how consistently is it done? And then who collates this data? Who ensures that data which concerns the same customer, who visits different branches of the same organization, is actually pooled? Clearly, some organizations do this very well. But there are many where different databases exist in different parts of the organization, each of which contains complementary but independently managed data of variable consistency in the way it was gathered. Collating the data can be incredibly difficult, not least because it often exists in different forms and formats around the organization.

This problem is even more severe when you cross the traditional functional boundaries. Most organizations have customer satisfaction databases, many of which are owned by the marketing department. These tend to contain vast amounts of data on customers' perceptions of the organization, customers' experiences with the organization, and customers' views of the service that is delivered by the organization. Then, in a separate department – usually the human resources department – there is an employee satisfaction database. This contains all the latest information on employee opinions about the organization: whether people think that the organization is a good place to work; whether they think that the organization has a clear vision and strategy; whether they think that managers in the organization actually know where the business is going. Then, in a completely separate database, there is all the operational data. Nowadays, this is often contained in an ERP – Enterprise Resource Planning – system. The data inside these databases relate to all of the operational activities within the business. They describe how efficiently resources are being utilized within the organization. In a manufacturing company, for example, they would explain where stocks are held and where quality problems are being experienced. Then there is yet another set of data (either in the same ERP database or in yet another database) – often owned by the finance function – that contains all the information about sales revenues, operating costs and the profitability of particular products, accounts and orders.

The problem is that these three or four separate databases all contain data about how well the organization is performing, yet rarely are these data-sets collated into a single integrated set so that some broad-based performance analysis can be carried out. Consequently, a number of organizations have implemented data mining and warehousing software that enables the collation and analysis of data from multiple sources.

Data Visualization

Of particular importance in the planning process is the need to find visualizations that communicate information. Sadly, efforts in this regard have been rather limited to date. Even the more sophisticated software vendors that sell performance reporting solutions have only helped organizations move from spreadsheet-based displays to trend charts (albeit sometimes three-dimensional ones). What is really needed is some creative thought on how to present and display data in ways that communicate at multiple levels. Or perhaps our use of display media has become too standardized and we have just lost the art of creative visualization?

Take, for example, the 19th-century representation – or *carte figurative* – of Napoleon's march through Russia (see the lower element of Figure 3.5). This simple visualization is incredibly rich in information. The length and direction of the line shows the distance travelled and the direction of the troops at any point in time.

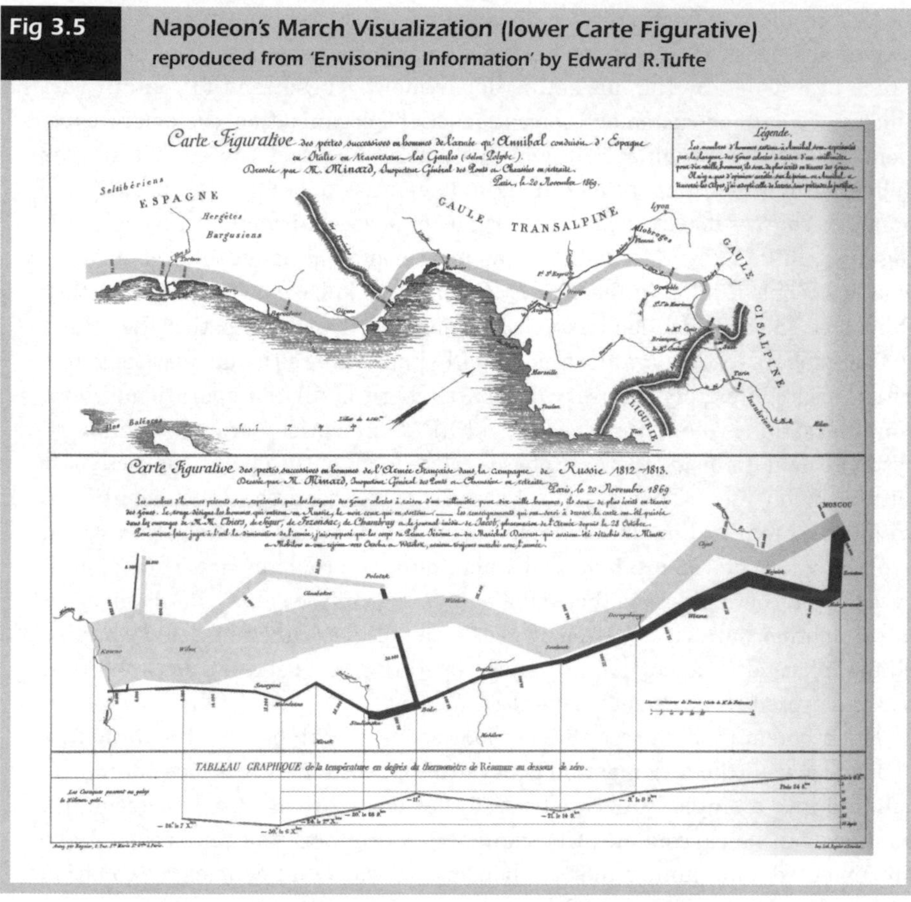

Fig 3.5 **Napoleon's March Visualization (lower Carte Figurative)**
reproduced from 'Envisoning Information' by Edward R.Tufte

The width shows the number of troops still alive. The scale, at the bottom, shows the changes in temperature as time goes by. The power in the visualization is obvious to all who see it. It is a very simple picture, yet extremely rich in information. The picture itself prompts you to ask questions. Why did the army split in two? Why did so many people die? Were adequate precautions against the cold taken? What were the characteristics of those who survived? What differentiated them from those who died? The point is that the way the information is displayed is conducive to analysis, interpretation and questioning. Why do we not seek equivalent visualisations for our performance measurement data? Why instead do we content, or constrain, ourselves with the limited capabilities of PowerPoint and Excel?

Forward-thinking organizations are beginning to understand the power of well-designed visualizations. Ford, for example, developed the Ford QOS (Quality Operating System) as a means of tracking performance improvements. At the heart of this system is a very simple visualization of the format shown in Figure 3.6: a single sheet of A4 split into four quadrants. The first quadrant

Fig 3.6 The Ford QOS Visualization – Defect Levels

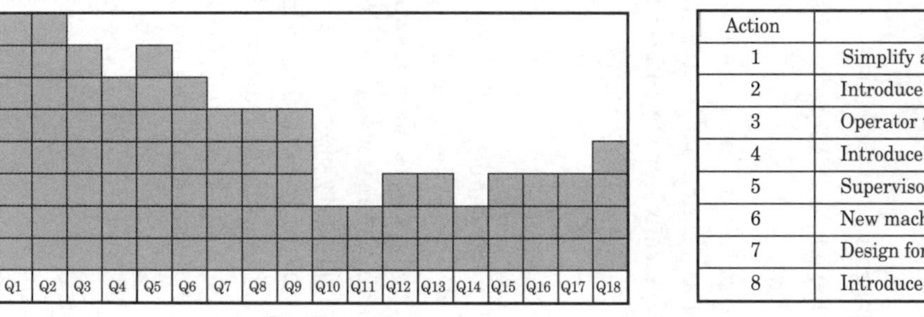

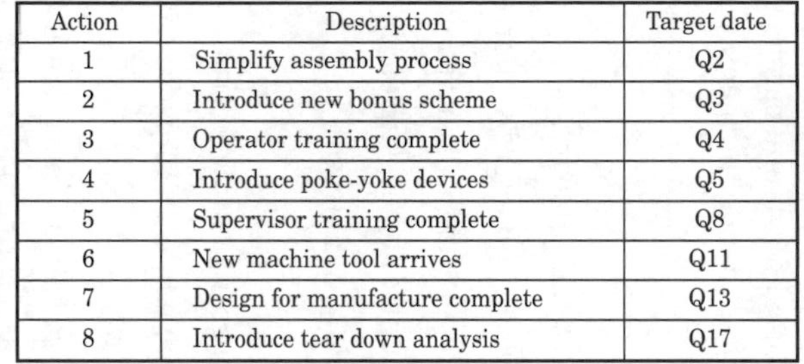

Action	Description	Target date
1	Simplify assembly process	Q2
2	Introduce new bonus scheme	Q3
3	Operator training complete	Q4
4	Introduce poke-yoke devices	Q5
5	Supervisor training complete	Q8
6	New machine tool arrives	Q11
7	Design for manufacture complete	Q13
8	Introduce tear down analysis	Q17

Frequency of occurrence

Q1	Q2	Q3	Q4	Q5	Q6	Q7	Q8	Q9	Q10	Q11	Q12	Q13	Q14	Q15	Q16	Q17	Q18
Y	Y																
Y	Y	Y		Y													
Y	Y	Y	Y	Y	Y												
R	Y	Y	Y	R	Y	R	Y	Y									
R	Y	Y	R	R	Y	R	R	Y									Y
R	R	R	R	R	R	R	R	R			R	R		Y	Y	Y	Y
B	B	B	B	B	B	B	B	B	B	B	B	B	B	B	B	B	B
B	B	B	B	B	B	B	B	B	B	B	B	B	B	B	B	B	B

Type of Defect: B = blue; R = red; Y = black

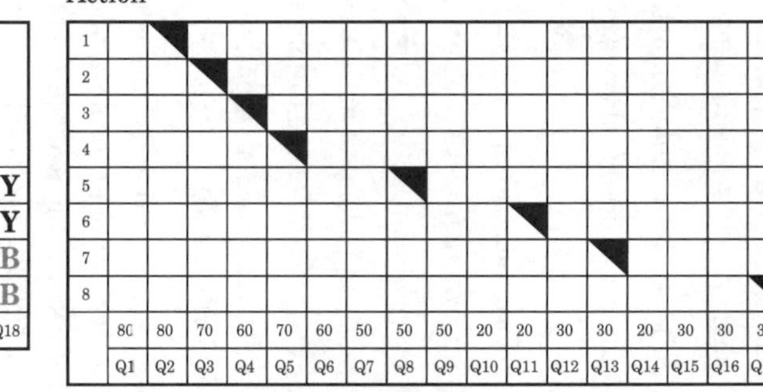

contains a straightforward trend chart. The second (bottom-left) contains an analysis of the trend chart, i.e. a detailed breakdown and categorization of the data. The third contains an action. And the fourth an implementation plan. From this simple chart it is possible to identify:

- The number of defects each quarter.
- The number of different classes of defect each quarter.
- The rate at which performance is improving quarter by quarter.
- Why performance is improving as it links to actions carried out.
- When improvement activities are scheduled to be completed.
- When improvement activities are actually completed.
- The rate of improvement activities.
- The relative pay-off of the different improvement activities.
- Whether the improvement activities have had an impact across all dimensions of performance.

Other typical visualization examples show graphical representations of overall performance achievement for a number of associated parameters versus target levels or historic moving averages. These typically have facilities to allow 'drill-down' to more detailed information, as illustrated in Figure 3.7.

The Bigger Picture

We have talked a lot about the practicality of designing individual measures of performance so far in this chapter. This is deliberate because this detail is completely missing from most texts on the subject. Books on frameworks, such as the balanced scorecard, for example, explain the framework but offer little in the way of insight when it comes to the practicality of measures design. Yet it is at this detailed level that many measurement initiatives come unstuck. True, you have to select an appropriate measurement framework. True, you have to align your measures to your strategy. But once you have done so, you have to make your measures practical and this is where the material covered so far in this chapter comes into its own.

We'll return to the bigger picture later, when we explore the Performance Prism framework in more detail in Chapter 5 and explain why we think it addresses some of the shortcomings in the measurement frameworks that exist today. But before we do that we want to continue with the practicalities and explore the issues associated with successful measures implementation.

Fig 3.7 Example of a Customer Experience Scorecard Visualization
with drill-down facilities illustrated by magnifying glass symbol[21]

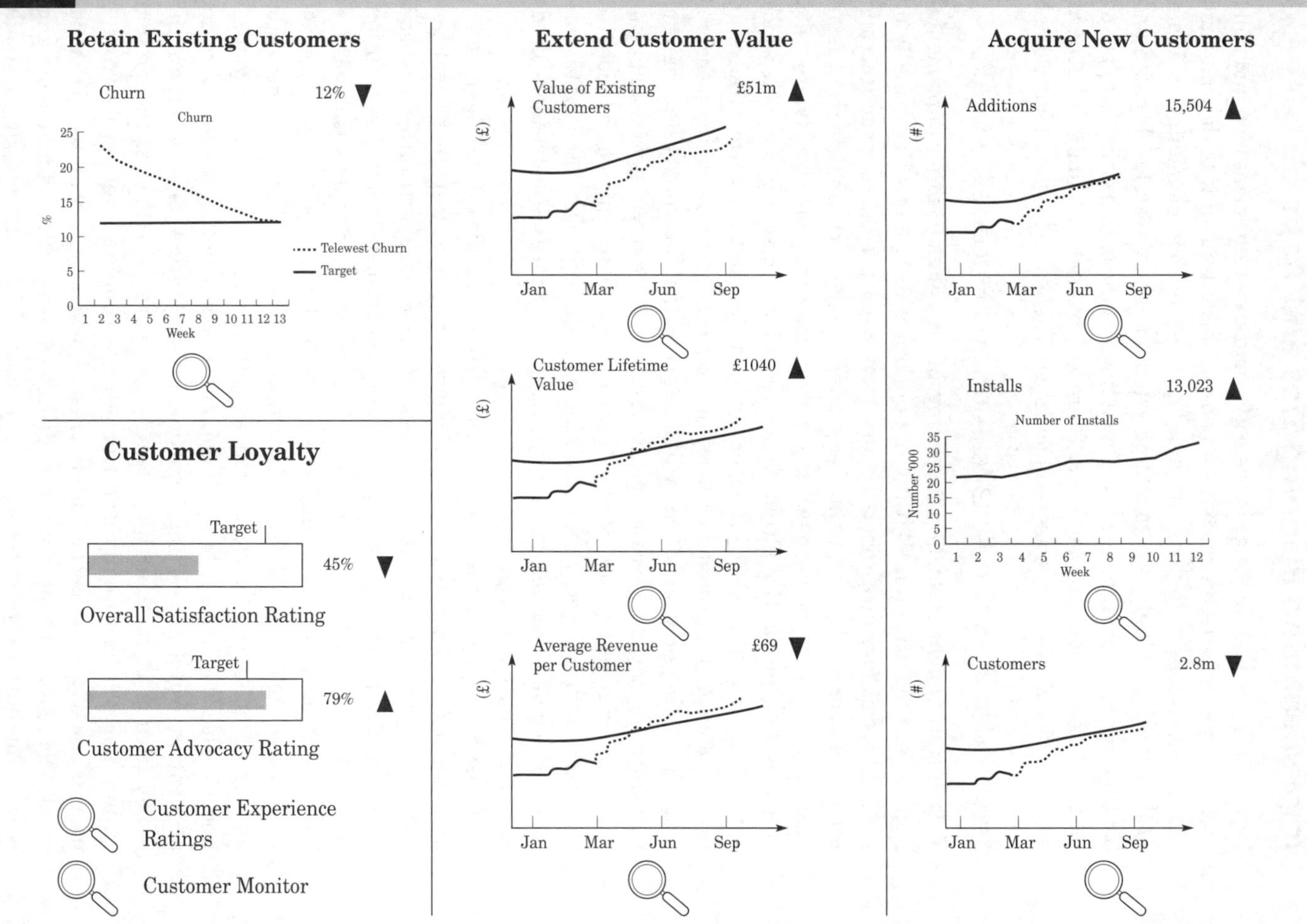

Implementation Planning Tips and Traps [22]

Perhaps the greatest challenge in the performance measurement plan and build process, however, is the implementation phase. This is fraught with difficulty and challenges. Of course, there is no single 'best way' to do implementation. What needs to be done will depend to a large extent on both the scale – breadth and depth – of the intended change and the maturity of the organization in applying measures to managing its business. There are, however, a number of generic activities that we would suggest be undertaken. These are shown in Figure 3.8.

Step 1: Identify Redundant Measures and Processes

This first step might be slightly surprising, but it is important for implementation's sake that it is done. Within any organization, there will normally be a whole set of measures, metrics and associated processes, practices and procedures currently used to measure and manage performance (that is, in addition to the ones you have just selected – some new, some already existent). Organizations miss a trick if they do not take this opportunity to review which of the existing measures are no longer required and can be discarded. However, there is often an unfortunate tendency towards retaining all existing measures and only adding new ones. This will seldom be the most effective means of implementing new performance measurements, since it will give the appearance of solely creating more administrative work, making implementation and acceptance within the organization all the more difficult. The potential to eliminate redundant measures and their associated processes – 'metricide' – needs to be evaluated quite aggressively.

To perform this step, first compare the current measures – and their associated management practices – with the new set of measurements developed during the prior measures design process. Then seek opportunities for measures rationalization, challenging the validity of obsolete measures retention. However, note that any measures required in order to comply with essential legal or obligation requirements, but not specifically for business management purposes, will clearly still have to be retained. Agree a list of those measures no longer required and assess the impact of their redundancy on the organization. Consider the impacts from the point of view of removing the need for data acquisition, collation, sorting, analysis, interpretation, dissemination and review (that is, if you think they were ever reviewed at all). Note though that elimination can be a highly iterative effort – 'comfort levels' with existing measures and reports may be hard to break. It will be important too to communicate the redundant measures and processes to the affected managers and, where appropriate, to external stakeholders. The communication should include a reason why the measures have become redundant within the context of the new/improved measurement system.

Fig 3.8 Implementation Planning Schematic

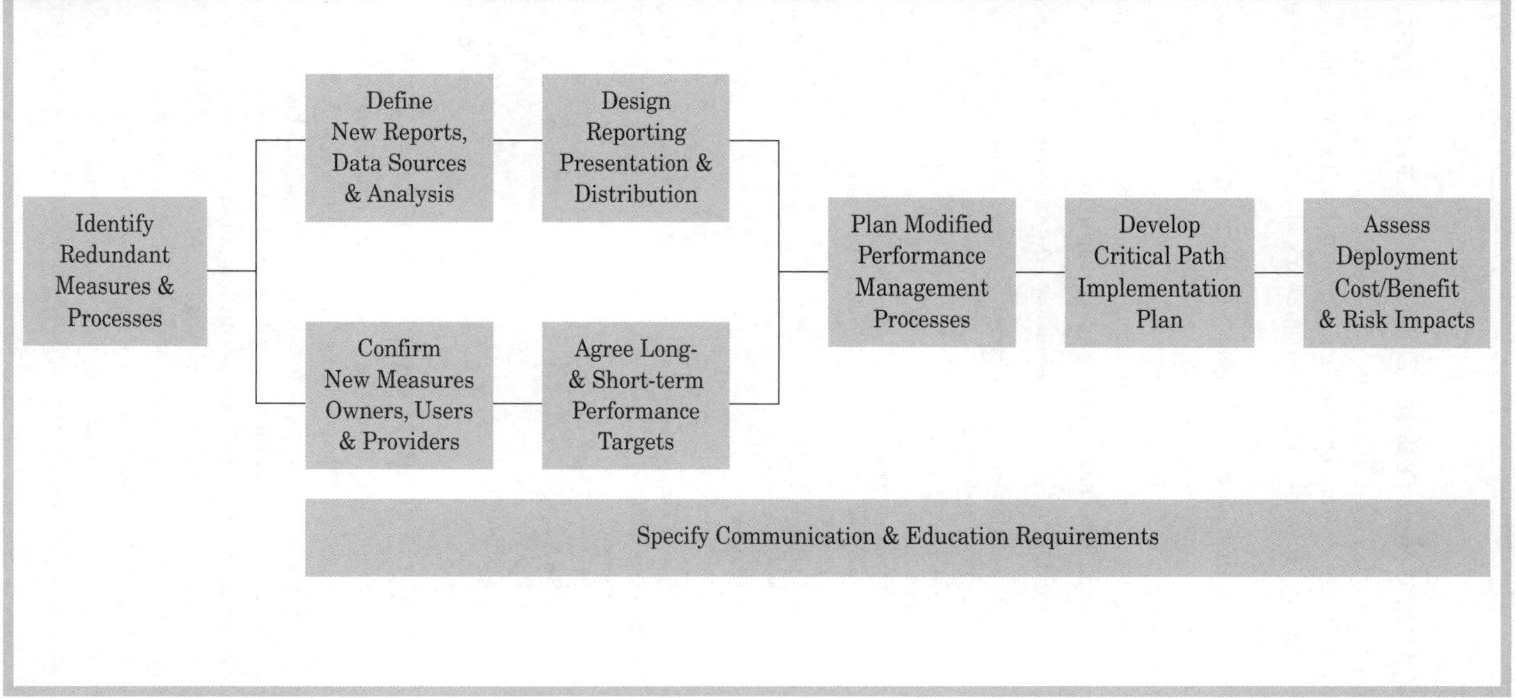

Identify Redundant Measures & Processes

Define New Reports, Data Sources & Analysis

Design Reporting Presentation & Distribution

Confirm New Measures Owners, Users & Providers

Agree Long- & Short-term Performance Targets

Plan Modified Performance Management Processes

Develop Critical Path Implementation Plan

Assess Deployment Cost/Benefit & Risk Impacts

Specify Communication & Education Requirements

Step 2: Define New Reports, Data Sources and Analysis

Once the rationalized set of measures has been defined, then it will be necessary to specify the content of specific reports that will be required for different review purposes, together with the frequency of each report and the specific sources of the data.

Furthermore, the raw data will generally be of little practical use on its own if there is no accompanying analysis and interpretation, followed of course by an improvement action based on the insight provided by the analysis. So, identify what data analysis is required for each report and define how the information needs to be 'sliced and diced' for reporting purposes. For example:

Report	Content	Frequency	Data sources	Data analysis
Period Management Report	All measures and metrics consolidated from the weekly report containing: – Financial Data – Sales Data – Production Data – Quality Data – Service Data – HR Data – Safety Data	Monthly	Transactional system consolidated with the weekly reporting and HR reports.	Data analysis carried out by business analyst. Historic performance and moving average trends extrapolated. Split by: Business unit and sales region. Business analysis software to be used.
Performance Update Report	Measures and metrics of performance including: – Financial Data – Sales Data – Production Data – Distribution Data	Weekly	Transactional system.	Data analysis carried out by team leaders supported by the business analysts. Analysis of performance vs. plan carried out.

Step 3: Design Reporting Presentation and Distribution

The next step towards developing the performance management system is to plan how particular reports will be structured and disseminated. As we have described earlier, if it is difficult to understand or visualize what the data implies, then people are less likely to relate to it and apply the information. Decisions as to whether performance data will be distributed in paper report format or whether they will be made available through electronic accessibility/distribution may need to be taken too. If the latter, then access and editing issues may need to be addressed. Also consider here the use of regularly updated measures displays (e.g. noticeboards) so that all team members or where appropriate, the whole site's personnel (and its visitors too) can see the progress that is being made in relation to the specific initiatives they are collectively pursuing. As we shall describe in more detail later in this chapter, the broader communication considerations are vital.

The example shown below illustrates the kind of planning documentation that will typically need to be prepared – in practice, however, it can probably be consolidated with the frequency, data sources and analysis table shown above:

Report	**Content**	**Frequency**	**Recipients & broadcast methods**
Period Management Report	All measures and metrics consolidated from the weekly report containing: – Financial Data – Sales Data – Production Data – Quality Data – Service Data – HR Data – Safety Data	Monthly	– Issued to key stakeholders via e-mail. – Paper copies issued to departmental managers >24hrs prior to monthly review meeting. – Summary posted on communication noticeboards.
Performance Update Report	Measures and metrics of performance including: – Financial Data – Sales Data – Production Data – Distribution data	Weekly	– Paper copies to departmental managers. – Key measures displayed on canteen communication boards. – Intranet availability.

The structure of all reports should allow users to view the data easily and preferably pictorially. It should also enable them to identify the performance trend, and whether it is a good or bad performance outcome for that reporting period. Users will normally want to be able to make quick reference to what the primary causes of changes in performance were and what the proposals or action plans are to improve performance too. The structure in which reports can be presented is highly variable but some frequently applied types include for example:

- 'Traffic lights' highlighting positive performance in green and negative in red (orange for within tolerances).
- Smiling or unhappy faces (known as 'smilies').

In general, the more graphical the representation the easier it will be to identify what is performing well and what not so well – and, therefore, where management action needs to be taken to improve, sustain, or 'raise the game' in relation to target performance. Consideration also needs to be given to the level of detail to be represented in reporting charts. Too much detail can create an unintelligible mess; not enough will often leave key cause-and-effect questions unanswered.

The latest developments in information technology mean that executives and managers need no longer be so reliant on receiving periodic reports in order to receive the data they need to manage. Increasingly, data can be distributed (and shared) automatically, for example, via company intranets. Where appropriate too, they can receive and review data, such as the customer response to special promotions for instance, in 'real time'. The ability to make *ad hoc* enquiries in order to obtain specific 'cuts' of the available data without having to engage the services of IT programmers is also becoming increasingly possible. So, one of the most significant considerations here may be that of making decisions about data *availability* – what information can be readily viewed directly from information systems rather than specific distributed reports?

Where a major upgrade of performance measurement systems is being planned, consideration may also need to be given to appropriate reporting software selection at this point. Today, many of these tools are web-based, making for easy access and distribution at multiple sites. Whether the data is to be reported using existing or newly acquired software, it is likely that the interfaces required to legacy systems, such as data mining/warehousing applications, will need to be addressed as part of the implementation planning effort.

Step 4: Confirm New Measures Owners, Users and Providers

In parallel with the definition of performance reports and the design of reporting solutions, the human interfaces with the data should now be formalized for each new measure to be introduced. That is to say:

- Who will use the data?
- Who will own the measure?
- Who will provide the data?

Much of this information will have been defined as part of measures selection and completing the associated performance measure record sheets. Nevertheless, it will normally be useful to consolidate and sort this information so that each user, owner and provider can see and confirm the totality of the measures for which they have a use, responsibility or accountability. For example:

Measure	Users	Owner	Providers
Number of new customers	Telesales manager Accounts manager Sales managers Marketing managers	Marketing director	IT analysts (ERP system)
Retention level of existing customers	Telesales manager Accounts manager Sales managers Marketing managers	Marketing director	IT analysts (ERP system)

Measure	Users	Owner	Providers
Call-out response time	Field operations manager Sales representatives	Operations director	Customer Services (logging records)
Proportion of bills paid on time	Accounts manager Finance manager Team leaders	Finance director	IT analysts (ERP system)

Don't assume that the measure owner is simply implicit from the type of measure – for example, the financial director will not necessarily own all financial measures and, in the above example, for instance, there could be some debate about who should own customer retention measures (marketing or operations?). Also ensure that the responsible (and accountable) executive is committed to owning the measure and try to involve him/her in the development process. In particular, we recommend that implementation planning team leaders spend time with measures owners to consider what realistic target levels of performance are achievable within which periods of time, what the critical dependencies are, and whether there are relevant sub-sets of measures that capture those dependencies.

Step 5: Agree Long-term and Short-term Performance Targets

Target setting can be tough. Set target levels too low and little effort is likely to be put into achieving them; set targets too high and no one will believe they are achievable or, more likely, they'll apply their creative energies to find ways of cheating the numbers rather than improving the process. Targets need to be set at an achievable, but challenging, level. Indeed, sometimes it will be necessary to set two or more targets – first, an ultimate goal to be achieved but that may take some years to accomplish and, second, a short-term milestone target that represents where the organization wishes to get to within a few months or a year.

The organization's *ambition* also needs to be reflected in the target levels set. Does the firm want to be the best, within the upper quartile of comparable companies, or just on a par for its industry? Will the performance factor create a distinctive competitive advantage? Is a given level of performance a qualifier for doing business in the markets the business wishes to operate? Or does performance merely need to be contained within upper and/or lower thresholds? These are important considerations that will also help to determine whether the target level of performance needs to be a moving one so that continuous improvement is encouraged.

A further consideration is whether the target level to be set (for both the long and short term) should be the same throughout the organization, or whether there need to be different target levels for different component parts of the firm – in different business units, market sectors, regions, countries or districts for instance. It will often need to be different, especially for achieving short-term targets.

The greatest difficulty with target setting comes when there is a new measure to be introduced and, therefore, there is no historical performance data on which to base the target level. Without actual data, target setting is largely a guessing game of wishful thinking. However, there are some ways to 'educate that guess' by, for example:

- Asking relevant stakeholders to suggest what the target level should be (if it is not far too embarrassing to do so).
- Finding out what performance levels competitors achieve.
- Gaining an understanding of what best practice (or even good practice) levels are achieved by other companies in comparable businesses with similar capability requirements.
- Checking what standards (such as 'minimum service floors') are applied by regulators for the industry or comparable industries.
- Applying a statistically proven mathematical formula (such as the normal distribution curve).

The other alternative is to withhold target setting until actual data is available and a trend emerges. However, in such cases we would generally recommend setting an objective, a longer-term achievement goal, but perhaps postponing short-term milestones until the pertinent data is available.

Where data is already available, then targets can be more easily dictated or, preferably for buy-in, negotiated. However, we would also recommend conducting a gap analysis that compares current or recent performance with both stakeholder expectations and external benchmarks in order to help set the appropriate target level by drawing attention to the existing performance differentials.

Step 6: Plan Modified Performance Management Processes

After identifying the data, reporting, ownership and targets, next consider the processes needed to manage with the selected measures. If the data is not analyzed, reviewed and – where needed – acted upon, then it is all a wasted effort. What needs to be captured is:

- Who is involved in the end-to-end process.
- Who is responsible for doing what actions.
- What the sequence of actions are.
- How this activity sequence fits together to create a desired outcome.

Ideally, each of the processes defined should be documented in a simple procedural format, preferably containing a process flow chart. Documenting the measurement processes in a simple format enables quick and easy reference for users, owners and providers. Process flow charts are also important for deployment communication and education purposes (see Step 9). These processes will normally continue to be refined and modified over time: if they are created in a simple standard format, then the subsequent updates can be easily maintained.

All this may seem somewhat bureaucratic, but our experience is that it is worthwhile where major changes to current practices are required. In practice too, it is unlikely that it will be necessary to define the process for each and every measure to be introduced or modified. Usually a common process can be defined around 'families of measures', around measures owners, or around particular types of review mechanism. Consider which groupings follow the same or very similar paths. A typical output might look something like the example shown in Figure 3.9 (p. 60).

Step 7: Develop Critical Path Implementation Plan

In this step, an outline for the implementation plan should be developed. Develop a critical path plan of when each stage will be commenced and is to be completed and what outputs are required at each deployment stage. Each of these stages should also be signed off, wherever possible, by the relevant management representatives to ensure their commitment to deployment.

At this step also, some key deployment decisions will need to be made. Typical questions to address are:

- What other deployment initiatives will be implemented in parallel?
- How will these parallel initiatives be integrated with the measures?
- Will the new measurement systems and practices be piloted?
- If yes, where will it be piloted (geographically/functionally/etc.)?
- What are the criteria for pilot selection?
- What is the pilot feedback process?
- How will the feedback be fed into the main roll-out?
- What criteria must be met to allow full roll-out to commence?

Be sure too to develop performance measures for monitoring the progress and the success of the implementation project plan. Establish realistic deployment targets and milestones, plus the essential accompanying reporting procedures and performance review processes for these.

Fig 3.9 Managing with Measures Process Flow Chart

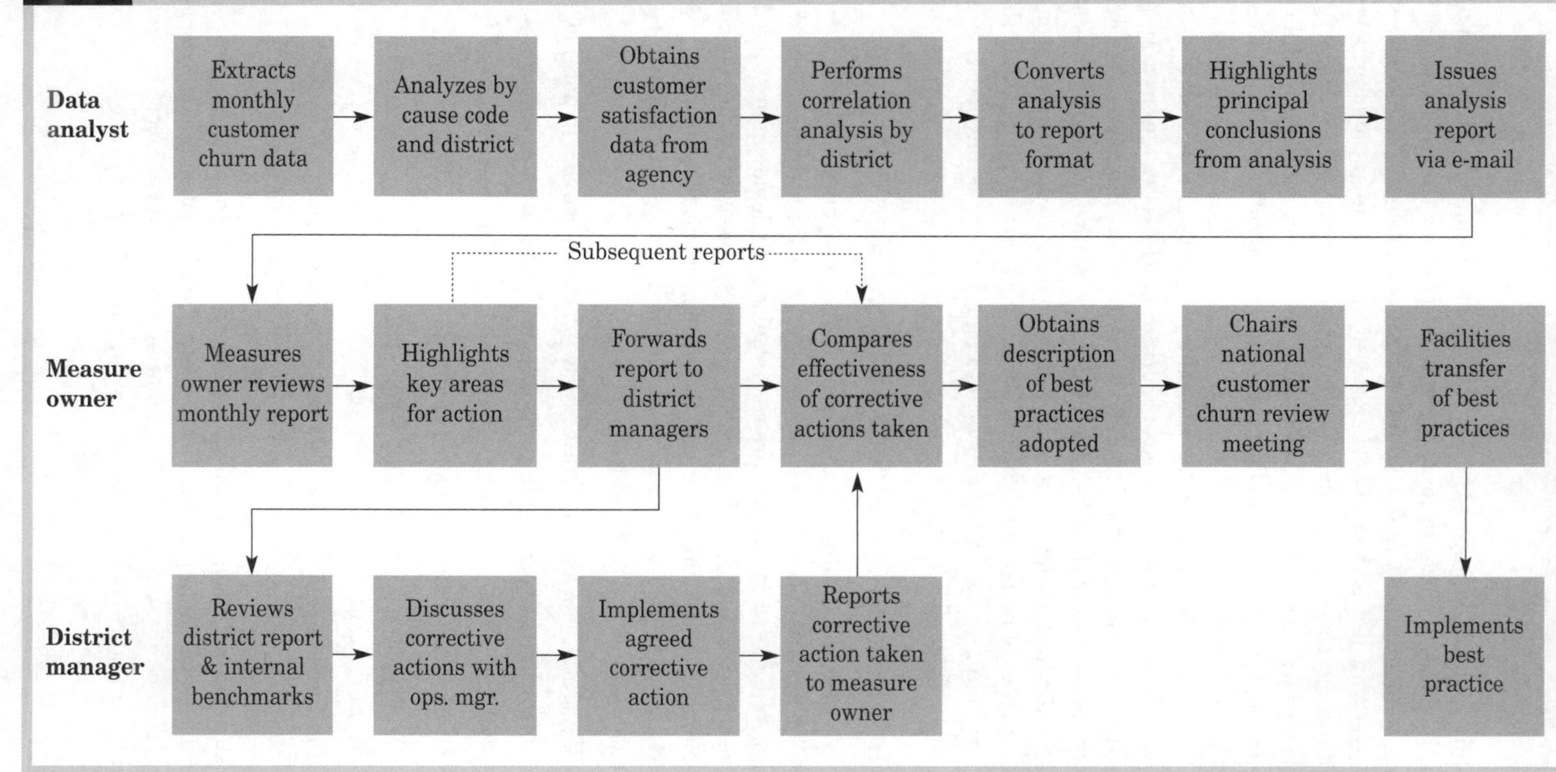

Step 8: Assess Deployment Cost/Benefit and Risk Impacts

In this step, a review is required of the necessary resources to implement the system, and also what resources will be required on an ongoing basis to manage the performance measurement system. To do this, consider for example:

- *Implementation costs*: software installation/integration, temporary staff, education and training, etc.
- *Maintenance costs*: business analysts, software, IT staffing, management time (*less* the time saved), etc.
- *Tangible and intangible benefits*: revenue generation, cost reduction, stakeholder satisfaction, access to capital, improved visibility, greater predictive capabilities, better decision-making, etc.

During the early stages of implementation especially, there may well be a need for some additional specialist resources to carry out statistical data analysis. Consider whether these resources will be required on a permanent basis, or whether – after the initial set-up of collation and analysis programmes – the data analysis task can then be passed on to the measures owner, for instance.

Management impacts must not be underestimated either, with action planning meetings and increased workloads to complete the actions needed to solve the problems shown up through the data analysis. Conversely, it should be remembered that, by eliminating a number of redundant measures and reports, some spare capacity and time may have been generated too. There will also be a potential impact on the organization as the performance measurement system is introduced. Developing action plans and making individuals accountable for feeding back the results to the firm's executives is likely to impact a number of individuals and teams.

As with many implementation programmes, there is a risk that there could be some resistance to this type of change. The likelihood is that there will be areas of the organization that have not been measured in the past, or managers who have not previously been fully accountable for their actions. The proposed system could appear threatening to a number of individuals, particularly if – in some cases – their performance is to be reported for all to see. A clear communication plan (see Step 9) and a series of review sessions between, say, managers and team leaders, or team leaders and individuals affected by the changes, can help to counteract this. This review should highlight to the individuals the benefits of introducing the system and provide reassurance that it is not designed to create a 'stick to beat them with'.

Note too that some organizations immediately try to align their personnel recognition and reward systems to the implementation of the new performance measures. Whereas this might be a practical option where the organization has a successful track record of implementing such practices in the past, for others it can spell disaster. Many well-intentioned measurement systems have failed due to this cause. Normally, to avoid this risk, it will be advisable to postpone this alignment until such time as the new measures are firmly established and reliable data is available. Indeed, for less experienced organizations, the best time to implement such practices is very often when a new 'push' is required to take performance to a higher level of target performance (see 'Link to Human Performance Programmes' later in this chapter). Nevertheless, it may still be appropriate to include an assessment of the adoption of the new measurement systems and practices within personnel appraisal systems in order to help 'make it happen'. We recommend that implementation teams work closely with the firm's Human Resources/Personnel department to include these parameters within their frameworks.

It is at this stage that the time, effort and cost of the implementation – if it is a substantial change programme that is being planned – will sometimes 'come home to roost'. The firm's executives may look at the resources required in terms of hardware, software and people, both on a short-term basis to get the system running and on a longer-term basis to keep the system operational, and decide that it is too costly to implement. This is a potential risk to be acutely aware of and, in these circumstances, the benefits of the introduction of the system may need to be actively 'sold' to the executive management team to justify the implementation budget. Alternatively, some scaling back or rephasing of deployment plans may be required.

Step 9: Specify Education and Communication Requirements

Note that this step is not chronological – it runs *throughout* the implementation planning process. Clearly, the magnitude of the changes planned will influence the amount of resource planning needed. Assess and specify the particular resources required to prepare and deliver this entire education and communication effort and when it will be required. Ensure that they are included in the overall implementation plan and budget too.

The education and communication programme required for the implementation of the performance measurement and management system can be developed in two phases, or components:

- *Initial briefing sessions* – for all managers and employees – describing the fundamentals of the proposed changes and the reasons for them.
- *Formal training sessions* – for those individuals who are most affected by the changes.

The initial briefing session should build on:

- Why performance measurement is important.
- What needs to be done differently in future.
- Which business performance model is being adopted.
- How it fits with the overall business goals.
- When and where the new practices will be implemented.

Communication of the performance system itself should answer questions such as:

- What is it?
- Who will use it?
- What are the impacts likely to be?
- Why is it different from what was used in the past?
- How does it link with the strategic intents of the organization?
- How will it be used to improve the performance of the organization?

This communication could be supported by a briefing document that each team leader or manager communicates to their people. This might be supplemented by a question and answer sheet to facilitate any anticipated questions that should come from the briefing session. It is important to consider how these messages will be received. Expect resistance. As management guru Peter Senge says,[23] 'Resistance to change is neither capricious nor mysterious. It almost always arises from threats to traditional norms and ways of doing things.' A format that encourages two-way communication about the topic should be adopted.

The second component of the education and communication plan should cover more detailed information, such as:

- Communication of the actual output of the performance system.
- What reports will be published.
- How they will be distributed.
- Where and how the outputs will be displayed.
- How to interpret the data produced.
- How to use it to create action plans.
- How action planning will be managed (e.g. review meetings).
- How feedback will be received.

A vehicle for delivering this communication could be a similar briefing document to the first component above, supported by a concise user training and frequently asked questions manual/booklet providing specific details about the performance system. If new computer software is being introduced, then separate user training will need to be scheduled and budgeted too. For each component, consider also what additional communications may be required in relation to external stakeholders.

Implement and Operate

This is the third fundamental process that underpins performance measurement. Implementation first involves executing the plans and deploying the systems developed as part of the previous planning and building process. Second, it means operating with the selected measures and the defined measurement system in practice on a day-to-day basis. The first will likely require first-rate project management, but the skills demanded are not performance measurement and management specific. The second, however, should be of great interest to practitioners.

Beyond Measurement to Management

Once the performance measurement infrastructure has been built, once the data are available, once you are actually accessing them, analyzing them and interpreting them, then you get into the most difficult part of performance measurement – actually managing with the data. If you want to get real value from your measurement system, someone, somewhere has got to act on the data that the measurement system is generating. Why do we find this so difficult? Why do we find it so challenging in organizations to actually take account of measurement data and take appropriate action on the basis of it?

There are numerous reasons for this, but among the most pressing is simply the confusion that exists in many organizations. People do react to measurement data. But in many organizations there are so many different inputs that it is not clear which set of data individuals are supposed to react to. People need clarity. They need to understand which are the key priorities in the organization. They need consistency. If an organization's scorecard says that customer service, increasing sales revenue and improving productivity are the top priorities, then no wonder people get confused when the managing director asks about relationships with suppliers, or employee retention. The point is that we have to consistently reinforce the measures that matter and consistently encourage people to take action to improve performance against them. To do this we need to think about how we incentivize people. We need to think about how we encourage people to act on the data. We need to think about how we can make it meaningful to them. We need to communicate how measures in different parts of the business link together to deliver stakeholder value.

It is important to recognize too that it is not until this third stage that we start to get real value from the measurement system. Until and unless the data is acted upon, there is no value in measuring (apart from perhaps a degree of 'comfort', if the measures happen to be showing a serendipitously positive trend). Far too often, however, there is a complete failure to act on data. This was recently brought home to one of the authors while he was working with a firm that manufactured pens and markers. During a review of the measurement reports that existed in this particular organization, the author came across two different reports, each of which had different values on them for current work-in-progress. One report said that current work-in-progress was running at £275,000. The second said that current work-in-progress was £350,000. Both of these reports carried the same date. Both of these reports purported to be dealing with the same issue – current work-in-progress. And yet they were out of kilter by a factor of 25 per cent. When the author asked why, the management team was perplexed – the immediate response was, 'Oh, we never noticed that before.'

This is symptomatic of an organization where the data that exist within it are not being used. If you have two different reports in the same organization for the same time period with different values for supposedly the same measure and nobody has ever noticed the discrepancy before, then it is a clear sign that nobody is using the performance reports. And the only way this particular organization could find out why the difference existed? By going back to the original computer code and looking up the basis of calculation for inventory in these two different reports. When that activity was completed, it emerged that the value in both reports was correct, because the organization had more than one way of defining work-in-progress.

Sadly, this is not uncommon. In fact, it is not even extreme. Another organization that one of the authors recently worked with has six different definitions for revenue! How do you manage in a business where you have got six different definitions for sales revenue? How do you know whether you are comparing apples with apples? How do you know whether sales are improving year-on-year? You can keep changing the basis of calculation (in the same way that many governments do) simply to make the figures look better!

Apply the Data to Gain Understanding and Learning

But even when the data has been properly standardized and collated, it is not the end of the process of course. You then need to analyze the data. Analysts have to actually mine the data and understand what messages it contains for the organization – seeking to identify trends, patterns and correlations across the separate data sets. And once that analysis is complete, then someone has to interpret the analysis. They have to explore what the insights are and what they mean for the organization. They have to identify what is going well and what is not going well. They have to make judgements about what has to be changed in the business and how it can be changed. And only then can we start to worry about acting on the data – actually ensuring that the data are used to drive decisions, which in turn drive business performance.

The Data to Decisions Cycle (see Figure 3.10) illustrates the whole process of creating and applying this vital knowledge capital. The cycle starts with the performance measurement process of gleaning data and information, which then needs to be analyzed and interpreted. As a result of this process, 'cause-and-effect' understanding is acquired since the analysis allows the drivers of better or worse performance to be identified. This then enables the performance management process to come into play, whereby insights and judgements derived from the analyzed data are converted into decision and actions. The cycle then repeats itself in 'double-loop' learning mode to monitor the effects of the decisions and actions taken. In this way, firms can build an immense amount of empirical knowledge capital, which is hard for competitors to replicate easily.

Fig 3.10 The Data to Decisions Cycle

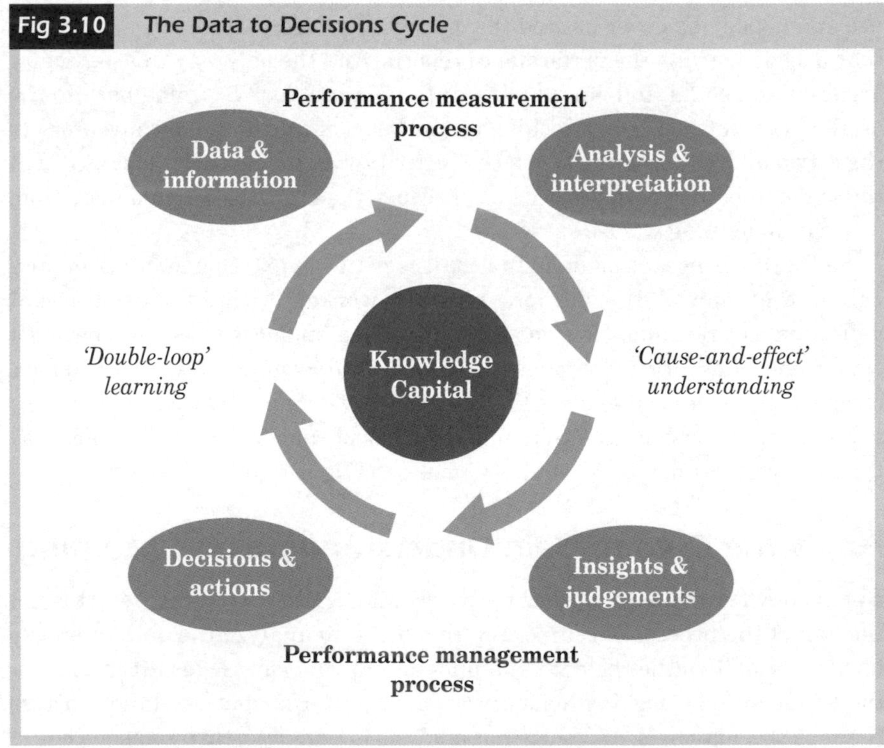

Of course, to gain that benefit, there needs to be room for making mistakes and learning from them. A culture of blame or punishment for failures will not be conducive to experiment or to taking risks. The late W. Edwards Deming, the quality management expert and teacher, warned that in such environments the value of the information contained in a measure must be counterbalanced against the fear of reprisal. Because of that fear, people will systematically subvert the measurement system, causing a decline in the accuracy of the measures and hence undermining their usefulness.

Check Data Veracity

'Garbage in, garbage out' has long been the credo of information systems users, and so it is with performance measurement systems. Checks on the validity of the data being used for analysis and, therefore, decision-making purposes need to be made as part of the implementation process. There will typically be four types of data input abuses to look out for:

- Data that is dubious because it is new and people have not yet got used to reporting it in the way required.
- Data that is being collected or collated in a different way to how it was done previously – thus comparing the 'new data' with the 'old data' is likely to throw up anomalies.
- Data that is being collected in a sloppy (but not malevolent) fashion – for example, large proportion of coding to 'miscellaneous' categories.
- Data that is deliberately being manipulated or 'gamed'.

Clearly, great care needs to be exercised when data is suspected of being tainted by any of these attributes. While the first three may usually be resolved by follow-up education and fine-tuning, the last is far more serious.

Where it seems that data is being deliberately falsified, then management needs to think carefully about the organizational culture that is being encouraged. Clearly, those that are manipulating the data perceive a significant threat and that it will be used against them. More worrying still, this normally indicates that co-operation has broken down and that, therefore, the measurement system is actually causing sub-optimal performance. In such cases, if there isn't a simple reassurance solution, it may be that the measurement system needs to be substantially modified. There are a number of instances where reducing the granularity of the measures applied (especially where they attempt to attribute responsibility, i.e. blame) can in fact improve performance achievement through improved co-operation.

Monitor and Analyze Performance Trends/Correlations

Following the planned launch of the performance measurement system, the data produced will need to be analyzed and the performance trends identified. The main purpose of this effort is to enhance the organization's knowledge and understanding of 'the problem'. The primary focus then will be on performance improvement and the development of action plans to improve performance. See the box *Managing with Measures* for an example.

Managing with Measures

A telecommunications company had been running a performance measurement system for three months following the introduction of its new call centre in the North Eastern business region. One of the key metrics of service performance measurement is the time taken to repair customers' telephone lines. The target is to achieve this within 24 hours of the fault being recorded. The information is consolidated weekly and is reported by district (the North Eastern region has been split into four districts North, South, East and West).

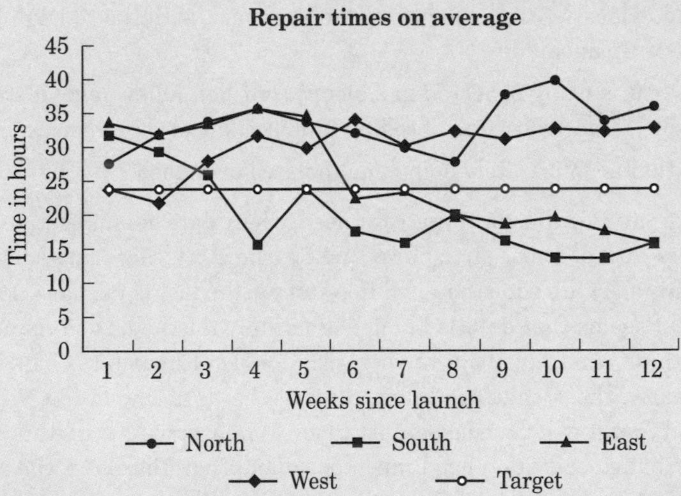

As can be seen from this example, a couple of districts have improved over the three months – in particular the South and East – while the others have declined, most notably the Western district (which started within target performance levels before deteriorating). From this data an action plan can be drawn up.

By carrying out some internal benchmarking and applying best practices within its own organization the company should be able to apply the lessons learned in the South and East to the other districts.

Source: Accenture's *Managing With Measures Implementation Guide*, written by Chris Adams and Neil McTiffin.

Beware though that it would not be unusual to see an improvement in performance just because a factor is being measured for the first time. When it is measured, then it is getting focus and therefore some level of improvement often takes place as a result (which is sometimes called a 'Hawthorne effect'). Over time the level of improvements will tend to stabilize and a trend will often be identified quite rapidly. However, the challenge is to identify those areas where the trends are less obvious and where a deeper understanding of the data is required. It is important to try to identify the root cause of any adverse trends so that better insights can be gained and focused action planning carried out to address the cause.

Link to Human Performance Programmes

A common 'trap' is to try to link the new performance measurement systems to attendant human performance programmes too early – although this does depend to a large extent on the prior sophistication of the organization's employee motivation practices. In our view, in most cases it is advisable *not* to attempt the link at least until the system has been running for some time, the processes are established and the data are – and are perceived to be – 'clean'.

Even then, think twice before implementing performance-related incentives. The principal concern is that dysfunctional behaviours are more likely to be encouraged when particular measures are linked to financial rewards. These measures then automatically gain greater importance than the others. And so unintentional dysfunctions can arise, such as, for example, sales may become more important than margins; business growth more essential than business ethics; output comes above quality; delivery cost takes priority over customer service; individual performance is perceived as of greater merit than teamwork; and so on. In the wrong hands, it can be a dangerous weapon and we shall explore some of the fatal consequences in later chapters. Now compound that with newly-available data that is less than assured, set some arbitrary performance improvement target, don't audit the way the measure is recorded, and there we have all the ingredients for a lethal cocktail – a disaster waiting to happen.

However, once the measurement system has had a chance to 'bed in', the data are being captured consistently and the performance reporting mechanisms are maturing, the system outputs may then be considered for linking to the human performance systems – but *with great care* in their selection. Often indeed, it may be tactically astute for management to hold motivational incentives back until 'the low-hanging fruit has been picked' and then brought into play when a more concerted effort for further improvements in performance is needed in order to reach yet more demanding targets – 'the push to the summit', in a mountain climbing analogy. We would also recommend that such incentives are predominantly team-based, given the 'concerted effort' requirement and the likely need for high levels of co-operation to reach the summit of performance and a distinctive competitive advantage.

Assigning specific accountability for a particular reward-laden measure or group of measures is not as easy as it might seem either. There will inevitably be the usual dependencies on other individuals, functions, departments or external suppliers doing their part that is outside their direct span of control. Sharing such responsibilities between functions and even within individual's performance appraisals can usually be negotiated relatively easily when the onus is focused on achieving improved levels of performance for the benefit of the company or organizational entity. However, change that to achieving the benefit of someone's wage packet or promotion prospects, then civil war between them can be anticipated. Some organizations still perceive these types of tensions and conflicts to be healthy, our experience suggests that more often than not they are misguided.

Seldom then, despite the vaguely logical appeal of making the connection from the outset (and perhaps the easy management answer to the ubiquitous question from the workforce at the announcement briefing: '*What's in it for me?*'), does there need to be a great rush to implement parallel HR incentive schemes. A good measurement system design may achieve much of what needs to be accomplished in the name of the greater good of the company, rather than the greater salary, bonus or prospects of the employee.

Refresh

What an organization chooses to measure should be dynamic. While many measures may be indispensable, others – perhaps 20 per cent or more – should be temporary. Some measures may be introduced in order to learn more about a specific factor or aspect of performance; others may be introduced as the result of a specific problem or failure. However, it is easy for them to remain embedded in the measurement system, even after the threat or opportunity that they represented at the time has been resolved. Conversely, there are likely to be emerging areas of interest or concern that require management attention but which have not been properly addressed due to a deficit of information. Furthermore, even existing, indispensable measures can need fine-tuning – especially in respect of their target performance levels.

To paraphrase the popular slogan that 'a dog is for life, not just for Christmas', a performance measurement system is for life too – it is a living entity, not a passing whim that will eventually evaporate. It must evolve and be nurtured over time.

Managing the System

The fourth and final process is the notion of managing and refreshing the measurement system so that it remains relevant and useful. This stems from the fact that many organizations have measurement systems that are in a mess. They have tended to grow like a fungus over the years. All too often we are great at introducing new measures of performance, but awful at deleting the obsolete ones. Whenever a new executive arrives, or a new problem is encountered, or a new conference is attended, someone says, 'Ah, we should be measuring customer satisfaction', or 'customer loyalty', or 'customer complaints', or 'customer profitability', or any one of a whole host of other dimensions of performance. The measure is introduced to the organization. The measurement system is established. The data are gathered and – hopefully – collated, analyzed and even acted upon. And then we attend another conference, or another new executive arrives, and they bring with them another new measure that they would like to add. And so the cycle repeats itself. And we end up constantly adding more and more measures, and hence more and more complexity to our measurement systems. Today's business world is complex enough already without exacerbating the problem.

What we need to do is delete – as well as introduce performance measures – on an on-going basis. We need constantly to evaluate whether or not the measures we have are the right ones for the organization. And if they are not the right ones, we need to find a way of getting rid of them so that we don't waste time and effort capturing data that no one is going to use. A good rule of thumb is to say that for every new measure introduced, an obsolete one should be deleted. An alternative is to simply stop issuing performance reports and see who complains! It is disturbing to see in organizations the effort that is wasted on producing stuff that is just baggage – performance reports sent to people that nobody wants or uses.

We have come across organizations where people religiously produce and circulate meaningless data, such as the average price of a litre of petrol during the previous week. In this particular business, 150 people received an e-mail on a weekly basis telling them the average cost of a litre of fuel in the previous week. None of the 150 could do anything at all about the cost of fuel – as the price was negotiated centrally – and so the data was completely meaningless to them. Yet someone, somewhere, in the business sat down religiously every week to write the e-mail.

Another example was provided by the manufacturing director of a small manufacturing firm. Halfway through a conversation between one of the authors and the manufacturing director, someone walked into the room with a thick performance report and put it on the manufacturing director's desk. The manufacturing director waited until the person delivering the report had walked out of the room, then picked it up, threw it straight over his left shoulder into the bin, without even looking at the report, or where the bin was! When asked why, the manufacturing director commented, 'Oh, that was last week's absenteeism figures. They are completely useless. We had a big problem with absenteeism about five years ago and it was really important to track it then, but we have cracked that problem now. We don't have many issues with absenteeism. And anyway I can't do anything about absenteeism; it is the responsibility of the cell supervisors. So I really don't need the information. They just deliver it to me every week and then I just chuck it in the bin.' Many measures are, like this one, the scar tissue of previous mistakes or problems. But once the root cause has been understood through data analysis, acted upon, and then the action confirmed as eliminating the problem or error, is the measure still needed? Keep asking these two questions: Do we need it? Why do we need it?

Similar conversations in other organizations have taken place. Take, for example, sales as a measure. How do you use information provided in a sales report? One particular sales report that one of the authors came across recently – the so-called Flash Report – contained 156 different performance measures in it. Sales were compared with this year, with last year, with forecast, with budget, across lines, across products, across regions, across customers, and so on. If this is just the flash report, one wonders what the final report looks like. But how do you use all this information? How does it actually help you manage the business? Most of the time all you can look at is whether we are doing better or worse than last year and this year's plan – and, therefore, do we need to panic or can we feel comfortable? Maybe it reinforces a culture of achieving 'results'. Nevertheless, it is history – what happened last month and before. To manage the future, however, we really need some predictive measure of sales. We need to know what are likely to be the sales figures in a month's time. And for many businesses the best way of doing this is to track the forward order book, or the number of tenders submitted, or the number of quotes requested, or the number of prospects requesting sales visits compared with some previous period. All of these are indicators which give some insight into the level of activity being experienced in the business and hence the likely demand for products or services in the future.

The key message is that we need to question constantly what is measured in an organization. We need to question regularly whether we are measuring the right things, and if we are not, we need to get rid of the obsolete measures. We don't just need to add new measures on top of the old ones. Unfortunately, this is very rarely well-managed in organizations. Perhaps one in ten organizations actually go through the process of deleting obsolete measures on a regular basis. Ask any executive audience and you will find that the vast majority of people in the room have never asked for a performance report that their organization produces to be deleted. They have never asked someone to stop providing data to them, even when they never use and never need the data!

Establish Continuous Improvement Policies

By this stage, the implemented performance measurement system *should* be running effectively and efficiently, with key reports being produced, with appropriate data analysis in place, with – where appropriate – widespread IT system availability of insightful analyzes and trends, and with action plans being developed for the areas that need attention. In order to avoid complacency and misalignments, the next step is to establish continuous improvement policies for the performance measurement systems and management practices.

In recent years, many organizations have introduced programmes aimed at company-wide continuous improvement, such as quality circles, suggestion schemes, total quality management, 'six sigma' and balanced scorecard initiatives. Some have achieved spectacular successes, while others have failed to achieve their aims – mainly due to a variety of poor implementation practices. Nevertheless, there are enough success stories to demonstrate that an internal culture of continuous improvement, if appropriately nurtured, can have dramatic cumulative impacts on the performance of the organization. However, with all of these initiatives, one of the critical success factors is in implementing contiguous performance measurement and management systems. Indeed, whatever the organizational strategies and initiatives are, performance measures must be adapted and implemented to match the drive for improved performance. Unfortunately, it is another process that is often neglected. It is vitally important that organizations' performance measurement systems and practices evolve over time in parallel with their changing objectives. Many of the factors that can present barriers to and help enable the evolution of measures are summarized in Figure 3.11.[24]

Fig 3.11 Barriers to and Enablers of Measures Evolution

Critical factors	Barriers to measures evolution	Enablers of measures evolution
Culture	• Management inertia towards measures due to other priorities • Ad hoc approach to measurement • Measures not aligned to strategy • Actions not aligned to measures • Lack of management concern for non-investor stakeholders	• Senior management sponsorship • Consistent communication of multi-dimensional performance to staff • Open and honest application of measures • No blame/No game environment • Integration and alignment of reward systems
Process	• Lack of proactive multi-dimensional performance review process • Poor measures selection approach • Lack of data analysis and insights • Insufficient measure ownership delegation • Ownership of cross-functional measures not addressed	• Integration of measures with strategy development • Integration of measures with process redesign • Inclusion of non-financial measures in business performance reviews • Formal measures review process conducted at regular intervals
People	• Lack of manager/supervisor training in managing with measures • Shortage of data analysis skills and specialist resources • Shortage of expert IT data extraction programming staff • High staff turnover	• Provision of appropriate performance measurement resource • Investment in measures usage and analysis skills-building • Inclusion of appliance of measures in employee performance reviews • Community of measures users who make improvement suggestions
Technology	• Inflexible legacy systems • Poorly or partially implemented ERP systems • Difficult to tailor 'off-the-shelf' performance reporting software • Poor use of graphical representation • Excess of raw data	• Investment in IT hardware and software • Data mining/warehousing capability • Readily customizable information systems • Internal systems development and adaptation capability
External/Internal Triggers	• Changes in regulatory/legislative requirements • Changes in competitive environment • Changes in company ownership • Changes in management • Changes in technology	

Once again, one of the keys to embedding a continuous improvement philosophy is that of education and communication. At its most mature level, self-directed teams within the organization will set their own continuous improvement targets, apply diagnostic techniques they have been taught and develop action plans to achieve these goals. They may also hold regular peer reviews and display or broadcast their results with limited input from their management groups. More typically though, management will need to initiate the introduction of new improvement programmes and performance measures – for example, in the light of changes in stakeholder demands or in strategic direction – or reset the target levels of performance once milestones have been achieved (or nearly achieved). However, do remember that some things are more important to improve than others – 'rearranging the deckchairs on the Titanic' isn't going to make a substantive difference. Select the ones that will make a real difference to the company's business performance and/or reputation.

Conduct Regular Measures and Management Practice Audits

Once the system has been running for some time and the data output is reliable, the initial measures and reporting mechanisms should be reviewed to ensure their continued validity: that the key stakeholders' wants and needs have not changed, that the organization still wants and needs the same things *from* its stakeholders, that these sets of wants and needs are being satisfied, and that the organization's strategies are working effectively to satisfy them. While the audit's principal function is to seek imperfections with the status quo, it is prudent as well to balance this with a review to see what has been achieved since the revised measurement and management practices were implemented.

As part of the audit process, it is necessary to identify any measurement gaps and redundancies within the system. The management practices should also be reviewed to ensure that nothing has slipped. In some cases, the management team may have changed and the new team or individuals may see their role differently from the previous management, focusing on different areas. It is important that these individuals are identified and interviewed in order to establish the reasons for the change of focus or practice.

An audit of the key dependencies and assumptions used as a basis for the development of the measurement system should be carried out too. The audit should review the dependencies and challenge the assumptions, identifying whether they still hold true for the strategic direction of the business. If they are still valid, they can continue to be built into the next stage of the system's development; but if they no longer fit, then they should be removed and replaced with new assumptions based on analysis of the available data and with dependencies that are relevant to today's market environment.

Furthermore, some of the measures introduced as part of the initial implementation are likely to have been put in place in order to gain a better understanding of the drivers of some aspects of performance. If the collection of data and its statistical analysis has now fulfilled that purpose, and assumptions have been confirmed or disproved, then are these measures still required on an ongoing basis?

The ten tests outlined earlier in this chapter (see Figure 3.4) are, we believe, an excellent way of assessing the quality of the individual performance measures used in an organization. They enable two fundamental questions to be addressed:

1 Are the right things being measured?
2 Are they being measured in the right way?

However, that analysis is essentially concerned with the individual performance measures. To have a truly effective performance measurement system we also need to consider the performance *management* process and address two further questions:

1 Are the necessary data captured, collated and sorted?
2 Are the necessary data analyzed, interpreted and acted upon?

Bringing these four questions together allows us to develop an audit framework shown in Figure 3.12. It is the questions contained in this framework that we need to address when assessing the effectiveness of the organization's performance measurement system.

The output from the audit should of course be recommendations for improvements – new measures, better measures, measures deletions, measurement frequency changes, ownership changes, improved data analysis, adherence to existing review procedures, streamlined performance management processes, and so on.

It can also make a lot of sense for the audit team to record 'benefit of hindsight' perceptions about implementation of the system and obtain views from a cross-section of the organization as to what worked well, what didn't work so well, whether resource allocations were about right, and what they would do differently if they had to do it again. Asking open questions about the key achievement 'enablers and blockers' will normally elicit this information. The views should be documented for reuse in future improvements and, where applicable, passed on to other business units implementing best practices in performance measurement and management.

Fig 3.12 The Diagnostic Audit Framework

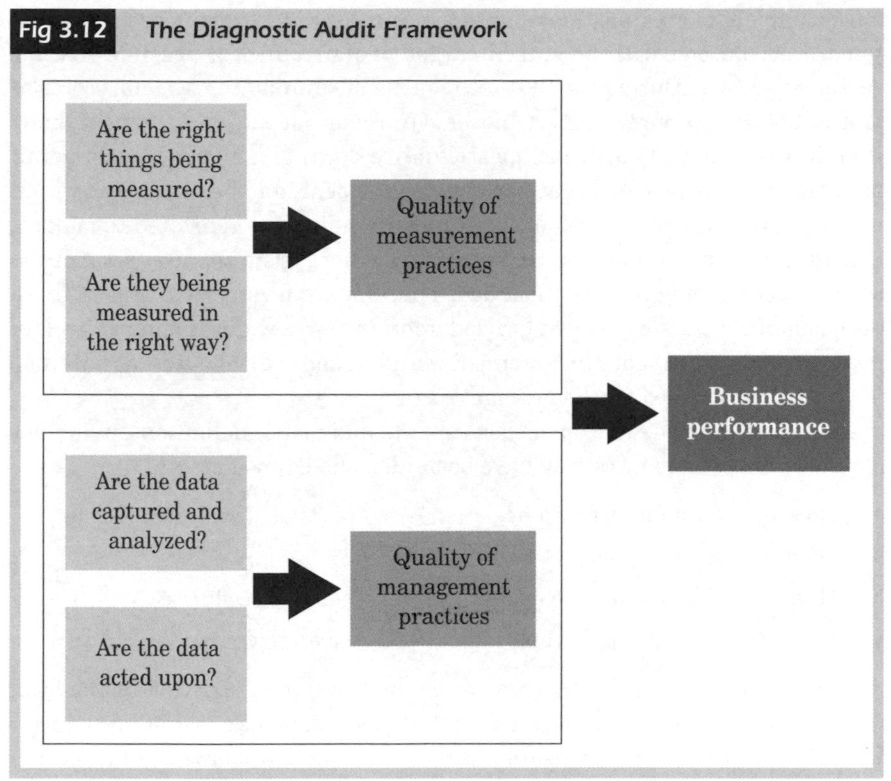

Refine Targets, Metrics and Management Processes

Once the system has been operational for a few months and the data collected is reasonably 'clean', the targets that have been set for the performance system should also be reviewed. It could be that the targets set have been easily achieved and exceeded and so new targets are required to improve performance even further. In this instance, new 'stretch targets' should be set that are achievable but which still offer a challenge to the organization. Other targets may have been more difficult to achieve (or it may even be that the business strategy on which the performance measurement system was built has been modified) and the performance metrics need to be focused in other areas or against new targets.

A similar process should be carried out for metrics and management processes in light of the information gleaned since the initial implementation.

For example, the organization might have introduced a broad measure of customer satisfaction with an initial target of four out of a possible five for customer service. During the first six months of running the system, scores of four out of five were regularly achieved. On review of the measurement, however, it was decided to drill the questionnaire down to a higher level of detail because analysis revealed that performance appeared to be consistently high in some areas but poor in others. The questionnaire was redrafted to make it more specific on a number of service factors where, from the first six months data, a score of only two was recorded. Therefore, relevant measures of these performance factors have been focused upon in the new questionnaire and an initial target set at 3.5. The amended management review process will also have been established for the new measures.

As part of the review of the measurements and metric definitions, a number of new or modified metrics may have been identified, consider:

- Do they have a full definition?
- Do they have an owner?
- How will they be linked to existing processes and procedures?
- Have they been properly communicated to the organization?

Any measures confirmed as needing to be made redundant should be removed from the system as well as their associated metrics, processes and procedures. Ensure that performance measure record sheets and other process flow records are updated to reflect all the changes implemented.

Looking Forward: The Role of Measurement

Most executives would accept the premise that performance measurement is a vital component of integrating and managing their business. But if you look at any business and ask what the business's performance measurement system is, it is almost invariably impossible to find one answer. Defining the single performance measurement system is almost impossible in many businesses today. This does not mean that it *should* be impossible, however. Indeed, one of the reasons for the widespread interest in performance measurement, especially strategic performance measurement, is the fact that isolated, essentially function-based, measurement systems are an absolute curse in a world where organizations are seeking integration around their business strategies and processes. So what are we to do about this? In a world where organizations operate multiple independent, or at best loosely connected, measurement sub-systems, how are we to answer this question: Do we have a good measurement system?

The Characteristics of Excellent Measurement Systems

There are numerous comments in the academic and practitioner literature about the characteristics of good measurement systems – measures should be derived from strategy, measures should be internally consistent, measures should be linked to reward, measures should drive action and behaviours, and so on. Other commentators often suggest that a good measurement system has certain characteristics, such as the right balance of 'leading and lagging indicators'. This is a popular concept. But just how helpful is it?

The idea is that certain measures indicate future performance, while others provide insights into past activities. These commentators use this concept to argue, for example, that customer satisfaction is a leading indicator of financial performance. If customers are happy today then they are likely to come back and buy again tomorrow, so future financial performance should be assured. This rationale can be further developed in so far as not only are happy customers more likely to buy again, but they are also more likely to recommend your business to others and they are more likely to be willing to accept premium pricing too. Therefore, you can generate future sales by satisfying today's customers.

Yet customer satisfaction is also said to be a lagging indicator of employee satisfaction. If you have unhappy employees, who are not enjoying their work and see no value in the organization, then they will deliver poor service and this will be recognized by the customers. Hence dissatisfied employees result in dissatisfied customers (on which more later). Taking this argument to its logical conclusion, customer satisfaction is both a leading indicator of financial performance and a lagging indicator of employee satisfaction. So does that make customer satisfaction a leading or a lagging indicator? In reality, the answer of course is that it is both. And the only way that you can use the concept of leading and lagging indicators is to explain the context about which you are talking. The truth, however, is that many commentators in the field don't recognize this and simply bandy around words like leading and lagging indicators. Proponents of the balanced scorecard, for example, sometimes say 'the scorecard is balanced because it contains a balance of leading and lagging indicators'. Well, any set of measures will contain a balance of leading and lagging indicators because any measure can be defined as either a leading or lagging indicator depending upon the context. So, in many ways, the terminology associated with leading and lagging indicators is not helpful.

No, the answer to the good measurement system question lies in the question itself. Executives typically want to know whether they have a good performance measurement system in place. And clearly, given the complexity of the measurement systems operated by most organizations and the level of confusion that reigns over leading and lagging measures, the answer will be an emphatic 'no' in the majority of cases. But it is necessary to go further than this. It is necessary to go back to the fundamental question – why do we measure? At one level, this is purely a philosophical question; at another, it is a highly pragmatic question and one with a multitude of answers.

We measure in organizations because we want to be able to manage. We measure because we want to know where we are. We measure because we want to know if we are getting better. We measure because we want to be able to reward people on the basis of their collective or individual performance. We measure because we want to focus attention. We measure to protect ourselves. We measure because we are told by other parties that we have to do so. These, and a host of others, are all valid reasons why we want to measure (see Figure 3.13). But what seems to happen in most organizations is that once we have established the need to measure, then we immediately move to the questions of: what should we measure and how should we measure it? The problem is that these are the wrong questions. Look back at the list of reasons why we measure and ask yourself what underpins all of them. The answer: the need to be able to answer specific questions. Essentially, the role of measurement is to provide us with the data we need to be able to answer questions about the organization's performance.

Fig 3.13 Why Measure?

Why Measure?

Traditional:

- To track recent/current actual performance against targets/predictions/history
- To track recent/current performance against external regulations/internal policies
- To track perceptions of performance deficiencies and monitor their improvement
- To motivate managers and employees to achieve specific performance objectives

Emerging:

- To help predict future trends
- To validate or challenge existing assumptions
- To discover new insights (through data analysis)
- To stimulate the creation of new initiatives, objectives and targets

Ultimately:

- To aid decisions and substantiate improvement/investment recommendations
- To show the achievement/realization of anticipated benefits resultant from actions

Asking and Answering the Right Questions

However, that simple statement involves a fundamental shift in mind set. To be able to answer questions about the organization's performance, we have to have access to the right data. We have to be convinced that these data are valid and reliable. And we have to be able to manipulate and analyze these data. True, measures influence behaviour. True, measures can translate strategy into action. True, measures can be used as the basis of reward. But these are all secondary attributes of measurement. It does not mean they are not important or valuable. But it does mean that we have to recognize that the primary role of measurement data is to enable us to answer specific questions about how the organization is performing. The implication of this line of reasoning, of course, is that the starting point for assessing whether or not you have a good measurement system is not: are the measures well-designed, or are they used? Instead, it is: do the measures furnish you with the data you need to answer the questions you need to answer in order to manage?

As a way of thinking about this, take customers as an example. What are the questions that executives in organizations actually need to be able to ask themselves about their customers? Well, one of them will be: are our customers happy with what we are giving them? Another might be: are we retaining our customers? Yet another might be: are we attracting the sort of customers that we want? This list of questions will differ from organization to organization, although of course there will be some generic themes. But, once the list of key questions has been defined, it then becomes possible to establish what measures should be put in place in the organization so that the data needed to answer the questions can be made available.

So, let us assume for a minute that we have done an analysis of an organization, we have looked at the individual measures and understood that they are good individual measures. We have looked at the measurement system as a whole and said, 'Yes, it allows us to answer the questions that we really want to answer.' Then we are in a position to answer the question we set out to, namely: Do we have a good performance measurement system? It is the authors' contention that the answer is 'yes'. Forget balance. Forget deriving measures from strategy. Forget leading and lagging indicators. If you have a set of measures in place in your organization that meet the ten tests in Figure 3.4 (p. 45) and satisfy the four questions in Figure 3.12 (p. 77), then you have a robust performance measurement system. If this system allows you to address the questions you need to address in order to establish how your business is performing, then you have a good performance measurement system.

Of course, in the Yossarian tradition, the Catch-22 that this then raises is: what are the questions you need to address in order to establish how well your business is performing? It is this critical question that the rest of the book seeks to explore. If we don't get that right, we shall be managing with the wrong measures.

Managing Stakeholder Relationships – The Business Issues

4

The starting point is understanding a company's value drivers, the factors that create stakeholder value. Once known, these factors determine which measures contribute to long-term success and so how to translate corporate objectives into measures that guide managers' actions.

Chris Ittner and David Larcker • *Wharton School of the University of Pennsylvania.*[25]

So far, in the first three chapters, we have identified a number of problems and challenges with performance measurement as it is typically applied in organizations today. In particular, we identified that measurement systems and their related frameworks tend to take a too two-dimensional view of the business issues that need to be managed in today's more complex business environment. But, perhaps above all, we have advocated the abandonment of the linear and misguided principle that underpins much of the work on shareholder value. It is the naïve and simplistic, but still prevalent, tenet that the investors are the only constituency that counts. Oh, if only it were that simple!

The shareholder value premise, while focused and occasionally useful, ignores a whole host of fundamental challenges that 21st-century executives now have to face up to. The point is, if it is not already clear, that no longer can the company's owners, or even their proxy – the senior executives – determine alone what should matter and, therefore, what the business should measure. Instead, businesses have to look to *all* of their organization's stakeholders and take account of what they care about. It may not be the message that executives want to hear, but they ignore it at their peril.

The inclusion of a broader spectrum of stakeholders within the measurement system that provides some illumination as to how the organization manages its relationship with each of these stakeholders is a critical facet of that emerging environment. We have identified earlier too the fact that the relationship is a two-way one – while stakeholders have wants and needs of the organization, the organization has wants and needs of its stakeholders as well. In that case, it would perhaps be more appropriate to talk of an *inter-relationship* between the organization's managers and these several constituencies. Nevertheless, for clarity's sake, we'll generally stick to the term 'relationship' from hereon, but on the understanding that it is a reciprocal one.

If the primary role of performance measurement is to provide data to managers that enables them to answer the questions which matter about the business's performance, as we have suggested at the end of the last chapter, then some of these questions should address this new complexity and a broader view of performance management. This chapter will expand on this thinking and examine the pertinent business issues.

The Stakeholder Mix

Some commentators talk about this challenge as the 'New Bottom Line' or the 'Next Bottom Line'. By this they usually mean the mix of financial and non-financial performance measures that make up the so-called 'triple bottom line'– economic performance, environmental performance and social performance.[27]

These are important emerging issues that businesses need to address, but at the same time we do not wish to overstate their importance to managing stakeholder relationships. There is still much to be put right with the 'old bottom line' too. And those traditional stakeholders – such as investors, customers, employees and suppliers – seem to be becoming more demanding and the nature of the company's relationship with them has changed or is in the process of changing quite radically. So, before we address the relationships with emerging stakeholders, we should first consider the traditional ones. After all, it is the mix of having to manage multiple stakeholders – traditional *and* emerging – that has made management life so much more complex. This complexity that is inherent in stakeholder relationship management is significant and fundamentally different to the business environment that existed even ten years ago.

Today, it is clear that executives have to manage within the web of stakeholder relationships encapsulated in Figure 4.1. The Stakeholder Relationship Web illustrates the complexity of the relationships that have to be managed in today's business environment. It also highlights the typical strengths of the relationship that need to be built (through the width of the arrows), although these will vary considerably from industry to industry – for example, food manufacturers will typically need to build very close and deep relationships with the retailers who are their intermediary and conduit to the consumer market. Generically speaking though, the strongest links are normally between the organization and its investors, customers, employees, suppliers and regulators. Chapters 6 to 10 will address each one of these primary relationships, examining the key components of the relationship and how to derive relevant measures that are appropriate to each. Chapter 9 also deals with alliance partners as well as suppliers. Chapter 10 looks at communities and other socially conscious stakeholders, such as pressure groups, as well as the emergence of regulators as significant business stakeholders.

Fig 4.1 The Stakeholder Relationship Web

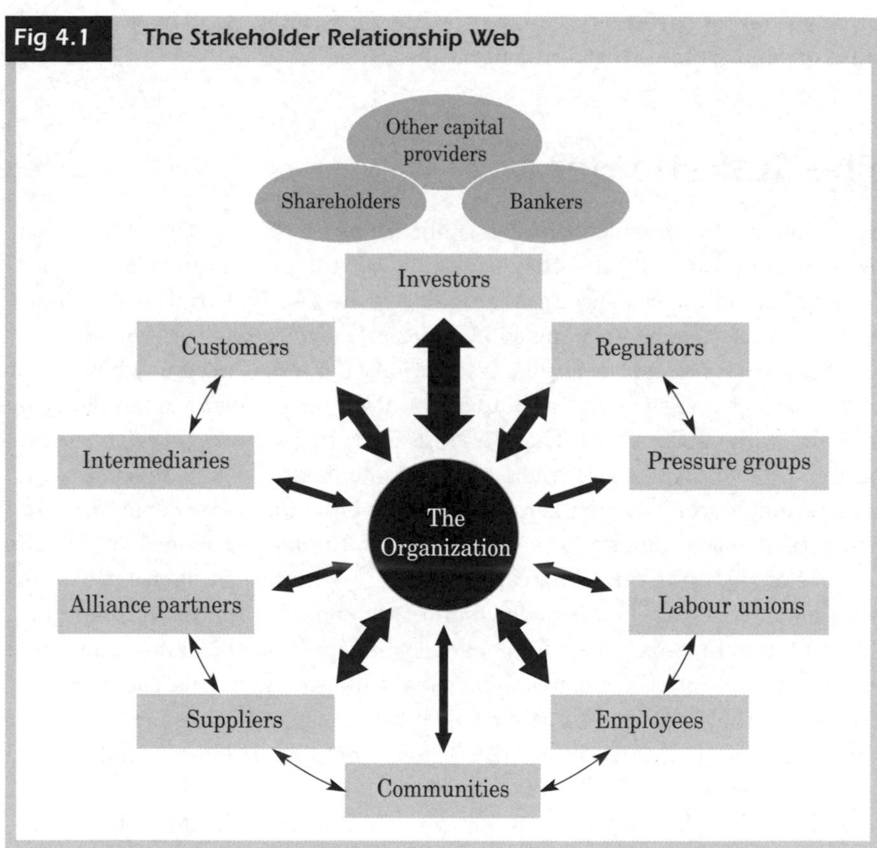

However, before we get into the realms of designing measures and more specifically how the Performance Prism framework helps to develop them, let us first explore some of the essential business issues surrounding the management of stakeholder relationships. The relationships that exist today between organizations and each of their primary stakeholders need to be seen in the context of how the nature of these has changed substantially in recent years. We should be aware too of how our knowledge about them has expanded through both practitioner and academic research initiatives. Where appropriate, we shall also provide examples of these contexts where they help to illustrate the particular management challenges they present.

Investor Relationship Management Issues

Not many years ago the term IR used to be shorthand for industrial relations and the relationship of the organization with trade unions and shop-floor workers in particular, but today IR most commonly stands for investor relations. While investors have always been important stakeholders, the vogue for creating shareholder value that spread from the US during the 1990s has ensured that they are on the radar screen of every senior executive of a publicly quoted company. Today, managing the investor relationship with the right measures is critical.

The shareholder value mantra has been pervasive. Originating in the US, it has infiltrated the formerly resistant bastions of German and Japanese business culture, and even many former communist bloc countries. The economic benefits have been felt in terms of prosperity, but there has been a price to pay for this upheaval. As we have suggested in earlier chapters and will return to again later, there have been a number of warning signals which seem to indicate that the 'unacceptable face of capitalism' has become too tunnel-visioned and that the first decade of the 21st century will be marked by some revisionism. This is likely to accept the principle of shareholder value as being first and foremost to create economic health, but it will surely be one which is also tempered by and inclusive of a broader stakeholder viewpoint that is more sustainable.

Should this mood change be welcomed? Do investors simply view it as just another distraction? The professional investment community is certainly not oblivious to this development. Many equities analysts and fund managers now expect companies to report certain information which goes considerably beyond legal and accounting norms. In fact, it is companies who have been slow to respond to these new investor expectations that are most likely to be at risk. In an economic climate that is now becoming far more closely geared to 'bear market' realities than 'bull market' fashions, the right level of information provision to investors is likely to count more than ever.

Who is Running the Show?

In business, a company's shareholders are normally considered to be its owners and, therefore, entitled to reasonable jurisdiction over its management. The more shares (or stock, in US parlance) each shareholder owns, the more power and influence they can theoretically wield. For most large companies, this effectively means that they are owned by a cluster of institutional fund managers. In smaller companies and a few large ones, however, it is not unusual for its founders and their families to maintain a substantial shareholding in the company. This enables them to retain control of the firm's destiny and directorships. That's the theory of corporate ownership.

In practice, if the company were to go into liquidation, it is (in the laws of England and Wales at least) the firm's bankers who get paid out first by the liquidators using the proceeds from the sale of the remaining assets, or of the whole business as a 'going concern', usually at a knock-down price. Indeed, the banks may actually precipitate a bankruptcy against shareholders' wishes by calling in an overdue loan that cannot be paid. The shareholders then have to wait to see if there is anything left for them after the receivers responsible for liquidating the firm have done their work and have been paid for it. Now who owns the company?

An even more astonishing phenomenon exists in the US. Incredibly, there seems to be no law which determines who is really in charge of a company. Is it the CEO? The board? Or the shareholders? Fairly fundamental principles you would imagine. But, for example, at Chubb – the New Jersey incorporated insurer – management turned over a large majority shareholder vote to change one of its bylaws, arguing that the law of New Jersey prohibited the company from changing a bylaw solely on the basis of a shareholder vote. Apparently even Delaware's Court of Chancery (Delaware is where most US companies are incorporated) has yet to rule on the subject.[28] This revelation might come as something of a surprise to those who think that 'owners' should have some control over what they own.

Return on Investment

Nevertheless, most Western companies do claim that their raison d'être is to create shareholder value. Whether that is, or should be, their *sole* purpose is a separate question of course. Yet few firms proclaim their desire to create value for their bankers (although of course they often do). But both sets of investors provide the company with vital sources of capital. Banks loan money to organizations and charge them interest for the privilege. They essentially establish how they will obtain value at the time that the loan is agreed; they then collect it over the lifetime of the loan. Shareholders are quite different, however. They too provide the company with money – by buying the shares or stock that it issues – but have no guarantee that it will deliver value to them. Of course shareholders *hope* that the investment they are making – their stake – will gain in value over some period of time. They may also wish that meanwhile, if the company is mature enough and the investors are not 'day traders', the firm will generate sufficient cash to enable the payment of periodic dividends. The total shareholder return (the value of share price movements plus dividends) on their investment needs to be greater than, say, putting the money in a 'safe' deposit account at the bank or other fixed interest investments, such as gilts or low risk corporate bonds. Otherwise, why bother? And indeed, historically, investment in a broad spectrum of shareholdings has outstripped that of fixed interest investments over time. But therein lies the rub – some share investments perform considerably better than others.

The risk that shareholders are taking, therefore, would seem to be substantially greater than that of bankers (although the latter of course do have the risk of 'bad loans'). In exchange for this increased level of risk, shareholders – not unreasonably – feel that the opportunities for reward should be substantially greater. There is, therefore, a significant amount of pressure on the management of most quoted companies to deliver that value to shareholders. If they fail to do so, the shareholders are likely to simply transfer their investment funds elsewhere or in extreme cases – if they are powerful enough – to remove the existing incumbents (by voting them off the board) and finding someone else that will.

Charities and not-for-profit organizations do not have shareholders of course. But they do still have people to whom they are answerable for what they do. Again, it is essentially the people who provide them with money. Donors and sponsors of charitable organizations, who can decide at any time whether or not to continue funding the charity's good works, also seek a tangible return on their investment. For governmental organizations, taxpayers – who, in democratic societies at least, have the opportunity to vote for whomever they wish to manage the public purse – also want to see tangible benefits in return for parting with their money. But, in the latter case of course, the 'investors' are also the *customers* of the public services and infrastructure provided, while government funding is mostly mandated rather than attracted. Nevertheless, there is an increasing trend for government departments to impose market-focused measures of efficiency and effectiveness on the public sector, for example, in essential public services, infrastructure development, and especially education and healthcare provision.

It is possible that the importance of shareholders may be overstated or overhyped in today's working environment. We should remember that a large share of economic activity is carried out by organizations other than profit-seeking corporations with quoted shares. These range from professional partnerships to employee-owned companies, include mutual funds (although these are in decline), and small and medium-sized enterprises. These account for 66 per cent of all European Union non-agricultural market sector employment. But, whereas these enterprises exhibit significant differences in the way they are governed and capitalized, many of the same performance management principles hold true. In this book, however, we focus our attention principally on business and how organizations can use measures to help manage their relationships with shareholders and the broader investment community.

Investor Relationship Communications

Much controversy has been raised recently by the 'special relationship' that exists between financial analysts and companies. The concern has centred on analysts receiving price-sensitive information not available to other investors. In the UK, following several profit forecast downgrades after private briefings, the Financial Services Authority (FSA) said that cosy relationships between companies and selected analysts were 'corrosive to market confidence' and would be tolerated no longer. See the box *Cobbler's Children* for an allegedly excessive example of this behaviour. When the FSA took on new powers in 2001, it was able to impose fines and take action against directors.

Cobbler's Children

In 1999 Reuters, the UK-domiciled international media group, was accused of flying analysts to New York to tell them some bad news. Its share price dropped sharply immediately afterwards.

It is a cruel irony that Reuters should disastrously mismanage its own communications with shareholders, given that it is one of the world's leading purveyors of financial information ...

Meanwhile, in the US, selective disclosure – whereby chosen analysts or journalists are given details of sensitive company plans ahead of the rest of the market – has already been banned by the Securities and Exchange Commission (SEC). Arthur Levitt, then chairman of the SEC, campaigned vigorously on behalf of the retail investor, railing against market 'gamesmanship': companies that feed information to analysts, or quietly guide them to reasonably accurate estimates of earnings; and analysts who put their relationships with companies before the production of unbiased research (see the box *Buy, Hold, Sell*).

Buy, Hold, Sell

According to research company First Call, of 28,000 analysts' recommendations on 6,700 companies, less than 0.7 per cent were ' sells', while 75 per cent were ' buys' or ' strong buys'. We should conclude then that a ' hold' recommendation is tantamount to a polite or politically correct way of saying 'sell'. No wonder then that some regard equities analysts as the prostitutes and investment banks as the pimps of the financial services industry.

Further circumstantial evidence of the complicity of investment banks is provided by the fact that J.P. Morgan, the US investment bank, wrote to its equity research analysts in March 2001 instructing them that they must notify the bank's corporate financiers and clients about any forthcoming changes in stock recommendations. While the firm insists that this is a communication process rather than an approval one, many see this as a further infringement of analysts' independence.

A study published in 2001 by Reuters, echoes the warnings by regulators that the quality of analysts' research is falling. It suggests that equity analysts are increasingly mistrusted by fund managers because they are letting themselves be bamboozled by spin put out by the companies they cover. Some individual analysts are rated significantly more highly by the companies they cover than by the fund managers who actually buy and sell shares. A subsequent *Global Investor* magazine survey found also that fund managers rated the importance of analysts' independence at an average score of 4.13 (on a scale of 0 to 5). When asked to score their *actual* independence on the same scale, they awarded the analysts a score of just 2.36.

Several investment banks are now in the process of trying to 'clean up their act' – partially motivated by a wave of litigation from investors, especially in the US, and criticism from regulators and politicians. HSBC, for example, is encouraging its analysts to recommend roughly equal numbers of 'buys' and 'sells' and cut back on the use of the weasel word 'hold', which should now only be used for a company expected to perform in line with the average for its sector (not the market as a whole). But the very fact that HSBC perceives this common sense approach as a radical move is another indicator of just how corrupt the system has become.

The regulators, on both sides of the Atlantic, have taken the view that selective disclosure is hardly distinguishable from insider trading in its effect on the market. In the US, Regulation FD (Fair Disclosure) mandates that any news with the potential to move stockmarket prices must be released to everyone at the same time. Other large stockmarkets worldwide are expected to follow suit. Needless to say, this trend is not appreciated by the analysts and fund managers. One commented: 'It has gone from one extreme to the other … it is hard to even have a sensible conversation with a lot of companies because they start clamming up.' While a fund manager retorted that 'There is a risk that they might clam up. But it is in their interest that professional investors get a feel for how the management is performing and the company is doing.' More surprising perhaps is that Henry Paulson, chairman of Goldman Sachs, went on record at its annual general meeting in April 2001 as saying, 'I think Regulation FD in general is a big negative. What was well intentioned, I think, has added to the volatility of the market … There is no free flow of information, so you get profit warnings.'

Portfolio managers that invest millions of pounds or dollars or euros in a company understandably want to hear the story direct from the key executives driving a company's strategy and responsible for delivering the results. They have much they would like to talk about on a regular basis, but the mechanisms by which they are allowed to do this are changing rapidly. Given the new regulations on disclosure, analysts and investors are likely to be going to have to do more footwork in order to obtain insights into company performance. From a company perspective too, managing investor expectations – within the law – have never been so essential to an organization's credibility, reputation and, potentially, survival as an independent entity.

Just how close should the relationship between investors and companies be? Some commentators consider that companies should spell out their investment plans, consult investors on them and report back in detail what they have achieved. They say that this approach would give shareholders an opportunity to engage in a much more creative dialogue than presently exists. They also believe that discipline would be improved with poor performers held to account before too much value is destroyed. Company directors, on the other hand, may regard this as investors with limited detail knowledge meddling with their jobs and yet another layer of 'red tape' to contend with. Investors naturally think they are better at 'seeing the wood for the trees'.

The likely solution to these dilemmas is that companies will make more information available – simultaneously to all interested parties – on their websites, providing selected corporate presentations, financial and non-financial data, plus special 'webcasts'. In the US, where a generally more enlightened attitude prevails than elsewhere to the public provision of corporate data, a number of service providers have created content-rich investor relations pages on the website, making imaginative use of the opportunities to offer interesting analytical tools and information. However, some analysts worry that announcements and their accompanying webcast will become increasingly bland and less informative events than face-to-face meetings. This remains to be seen. But, whereas one can understand that it may not be quite as attractive as flying across the Atlantic to get the news (c.f. Reuters), at least everyone has the opportunity to receive it at the same time.

Indeed, the UK's recently introduced Electronic Communications Act now allows companies to conduct any or all of their business – including that pertaining to investor relations – by electronic means. If its shareholders agree, the Act permits annual reports, accounts, press releases, electronic voting and virtual AGMs to be transferred online. This has the potential to save considerable sums of money for companies' Investor Relations departments. BP, for example, has 800,000 global investors and under half are in the UK. But even some of the smallest stock exchange quoted companies boast 25,000 shareholders, amounting to about £375,000 per year in administration costs. Even these smaller companies are now beginning to create websites for investors with facilities such as almost real-time share prices, analysts' forecasts, slide presentations, news and announcements, the ability to register for e-mail alerts, and the opportunity to correspond directly with company directors by e-mail. For an example, see the screenshot in Figure 4.2 of the investor research resource website of chemicals company European Colour (capitalized at around £20m). This site won a Best Investor Communications award in a *Financial Times* competition in March 2001.

Fig 4.2 **Example of Investor Research Resource Website**

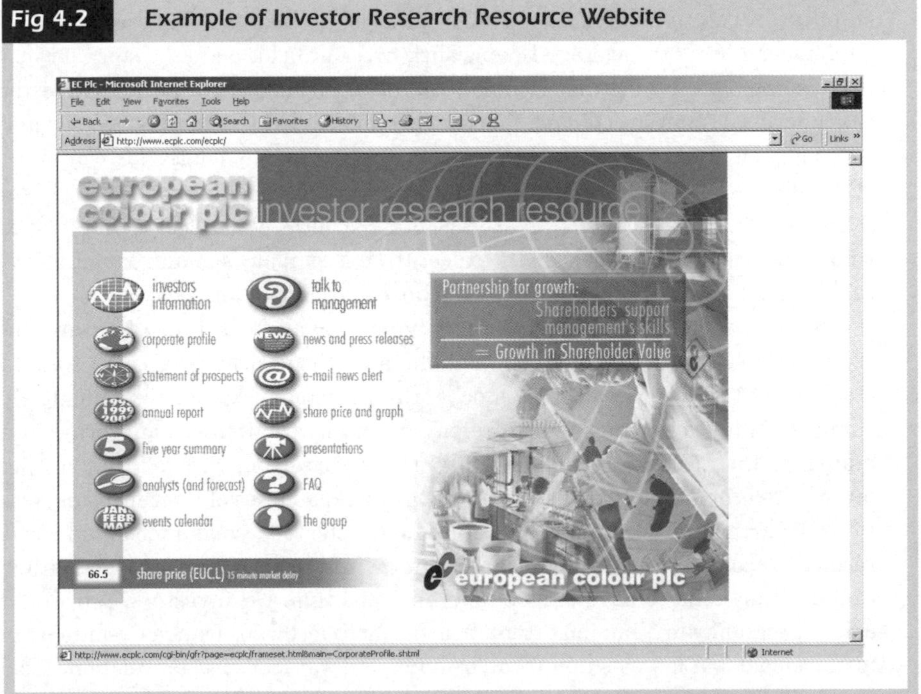

Investor Loyalty in the Information Age

The pace of corporate information gathering and dissemination to investors has moved on by a quantum leap in recent years. While not all investors (nor executives) have fully come to terms with instant information yet, there is no way the tide can be turned back. Information technology has forever changed the quantity of information that it is practical to collect and the pace at which it can be analyzed and shared across the globe. As Louise Kehoe, the *Financial Times* journalist based in San Francisco, points out: 'In theory, more information, gathered and shared with all investors more efficiently, should result in greater clarity and transparency – and perhaps less market volatility.'[29] Yet, so far, the biggest users of this technology, the IT companies themselves, have experienced tremendous volatility in the stockmarkets of the world as the slowdown in their industry during late 2000 and early 2001 is reflected in real-time sales information. Knowing more, faster may mean that there will be greater volatility.

However, the increased application of the world wide web has its downside for companies too. DoubleClick illustrates another e-business phenomenon. Chairman and CEO, Kevin O'Connor, said during the height of the dot-com and day-trading boom, 'It's very easy to sit here and measure your success by the stock price, but we want to make long-term strategic decisions, even at the expense of the short-term.' Admirable sentiment, but that attitude infers some reasonable level of stability in capital availability. The trouble is, as *Business Week* reported in September 1999,[30] the average DoubleClick investor holds on to the stock for just five trading days. It's not that DoubleClick has been singled out for high investor churn levels – Amazon.com and Yahoo! shareholders held on to the stock for just seven and eight days respectively. That compares with 18.5 months for Wal-Mart, 29.6 months for Exxon and over 33 months for General Electric – even Cisco Systems' investors hold on for an average of 8.5 months. What does a shareholder who holds a stock for a week really expect from a company's management team? Probably not a strategy that positions the business for long-term success.

Although some of these excesses may have gone away as a result of the subsequent bursting of the dot-com bubble and the consequent correction in stockmarket valuations of these stocks, the principles are not fundamentally changed. Many companies today are paying more attention to monitoring and managing their core shareholders, while others are setting targets for recruiting more long-term investors and strengthening the capabilities of their investor relations departments. For example, Philip Morris, the tobacco and food giant, was recently reported to be trying to sign up more institutional investors in Europe because they tend to have longer time horizons than US investors. You would expect geography to be an important measurement factor in customer relationship management, but it seems that it can be highly relevant for investor relations too.

The Sources of Shareholder Value

Many commentators have attempted to make correlations between share price, corporate financial performance and the drivers of corporate performance (e.g. customer satisfaction, employee productivity, and so on). Tying the key drivers to actual financial performance is a well-worn path and we describe much of the research done in these areas later on. Even some of the evidence provided for this can be somewhat shaky in terms of proving that genuinely valid correlations consistently exist. However, it is the step beyond that which presents the greatest difficulty – the translation of corporate financial performance to share price movements and hence shareholder value. You might imagine that this would be one of the most obvious and intuitive links, but it is not that simple. Far from it.

Share prices and consequently the market value of quoted companies can change every day. Price movements can be driven by the occasional announcements made by the company about its results or its expectations, but much more often they are driven by what is known as 'market sentiment'. Sentiment consists of an amalgam of constantly changing perceptions, rumours, fashions and trends. And this sentiment itself is driven by a number of factors, which boil down to just two: fear and greed – fear of losing lots of money and greed for exceptional investment opportunities. Investors take their cue from, for example, the announcements of other companies in a particular industry sector; analysts' reports on specific companies and sectors; other investors' perceptions and actions relating to the future of that sector; press reports; the cost of basic raw materials (such as, oil or metals); the economic prospects of various countries and regions in which a company trades; and so on (see Figure 4.3, p. 94).

Special factors can come into play too, such as the hiatus caused by the anticipated 'Y2K' bug that never quite seemed to materialize, but certainly polarized the investment community. Sentiment is a highly complex and unstable compound. Consequently, in the relatively short term at least, share prices often seem to live in a kind of 'parallel universe' to actual company performance. Don't just take our word for it though, apparently there is a scientific basis for the assertion (see the box *Herd Instincts*).

Fig 4.3 Market Sentiment

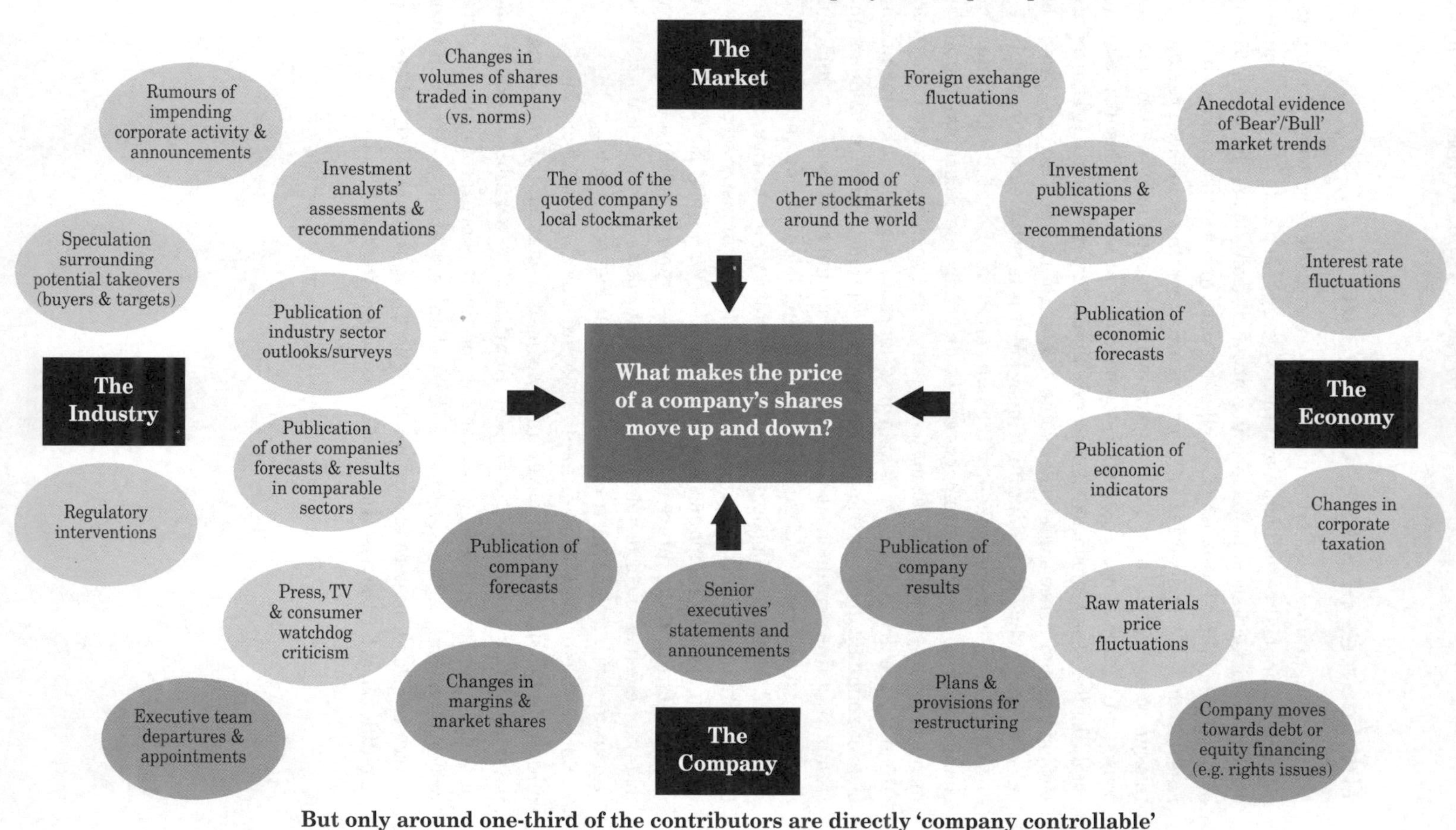

Herd Instincts

Research carried out by scientists Thomas Lux of the University of Bonn and Michele Marchese of the University of Cagliari dismantles the 'efficient market hypothesis' of economics, which claims that securities prices reflect an unbiased view of all incoming news. They say, instead, that prices are largely the result of herd behaviour.

Using a sophisticated computer simulation model, the scientists were able to come to the conclusion that the real force behind market movements are 'noise traders', who base their buying and selling decisions not on fundamentals but on what other traders are doing. Changes in sentiment by just a few players can shift the entire market mood and cause a stampede. Slight optimism can quickly turn into a raging bull market, while a touch of pessimism is likely to induce a plunging bear market. Bear and bull markets, they found, are predominantly caused by mood changes among noise traders and, during periods of high volatility, there were more noise traders in the market.

On the other hand, the fundamentalists – traders who based their decisions on corporate earnings, interest rates, market news, and so on – did have a stabilizing influence on securities prices over the longer term. From their point of view, large deviations from underlying asset value represented buying or selling opportunities. However, according to Lux and Marchese, their calming influence was apparently also undermined over time. Impressed by the superior short-term returns achieved by the noise traders, the fundamentalists tended to desert their principles and join the herd.

Managing Investor Relations

This 'noise' factor makes it very difficult for those companies and executives that profess a commitment to creating shareholder value, since a substantial component of it *cannot* be within their span of control. While company performance and its share price are heading in the same direction, it is tempting to claim the correlation and to broadcast it both internally and externally. The problem comes when the trends diverge. While few executives overtly suggest that their company is overvalued, many proclaim that their shares are undervalued by the market and that the prospects of their company are misunderstood. And so Investor Relations departments have flourished in many companies in recent years and are likely to continue to do so – they are the new 'spin doctors' and image-mongers of this corporate era. When budget for such activities is so directly related to the chief executive's income (through share options), funding can be remarkably forthcoming.

Customer Relationship Management Issues

'The Customer is King.' Throughout the 1990s and late 1980s a host of popular management initiatives, such as Just-In-Time, Total Quality Management, Customer Care, Business Process Re-engineering and – most recently – Customer Relationship Management have put customers centre stage in their business philosophies. And of course, as we have noted earlier, wherever management initiatives go performance measures will tend to follow closely. Indeed, in the early 1990s, the Balanced Scorecard placed customer-focused measures alongside financial ones.

Much has already been written on the subject of the importance of customer relationships over the last decade and we have no intention whatsoever to conduct a comprehensive review that documents each of the sources of all this knowledge. That is not the primary subject of this book. Conversely, however, it would leave a hole in this passage of the book if we were not to point to some of the essential substance within this literature and the extensive research that has been undertaken. In order to set the context for customer relationship measures development and to understand the business issues that affect measures selection, therefore, we have striven to identify the relevant major themes.

Customer Benefits Delivery

Have all these customer-focused programmes delivered on their promises? The obvious answer is that some did and some didn't. It largely depends on how well they were implemented. While it is easy to pick on those that didn't – and we shall not shirk from this task! – let us first just reflect on how products and services *did* get better for customers over the last decade or so. We tend to take it for granted once it becomes part of our day-to-day lives. It seems as though we have become almost immunized to good news. While that may give us even more energy to whinge and moan about what is still wrong with the products and services we use daily, a better balance is called for (see the box *A Dozen Product and Service Improvements*):

A Dozen Product and Service Improvements

From a purely consumer point of view, life got better in the following ways:

- We can obtain cash 24 hours a day/365 days a year from ATMs.
- The choice of products offered by supermarkets is immensely greater.
- A vast array of information is available from our homes via the internet.
- Compact disks provide superior audio and video quality of reproduction.
- New pharmaceuticals can repair or prevent many of our bodily ailments.
- Low-cost airline services have opened up affordable new markets for travel.
- Cars and electrical equipment are generally more reliable and longer-lasting than ever before.
- Mobile phones allow instant communication wherever we are.
- Twenty-four hour helplines and longer store opening hours make it easier to cope with our busy lifestyles.
- The variety of restaurant cuisine available in most cities and towns has exploded.
- The number of TV channels and programmes available to subscribers has grown significantly.
- Telephone banking and insurance services are available from our homes (rather than via branch offices).

And this is just the most obvious stuff. There have been a 1,001 other incremental improvements that we might welcome but seldom acknowledge. Some of these are product innovation led, while others are due to process innovations. And in almost all cases – unseen by consumers – process improvements have had to quickly follow product innovations in order to bring them to market. We should be grateful for these too.

Product and Service Offerings

The internet enables companies to provide enhanced services to its customers and can help them to build unique relationships with those customers. Only a few do it well. Land's End, the US-based mail order clothing retailer, has built a website that allows you to create a virtual model of yourself. As you spot an item of interest, you can call up the virtual model and see what you look like dressed in these clothes. Benetton's online shop theex.it has versions in three languages, provides excellent pre-sales support, offers online discounts and 'takes the navigator on a trip that will define their own style through an innovative browser experience'. Home Depot, the leading US DIY retailer and builders' merchant, gives small contractors – its most valuable customers – a log-in and password for a website that is full of helpful applications. The builder provides details of the job and the website tells him what materials he needs, how to schedule the work and what snags he might encounter. The site can then provide availability information and schedule deliveries on a just-in-time basis. If the builder needs an electrician or a plumber, Home Depot will post the details on its site and operate as a virtual labour exchange. The point is that these features have been designed to increase what these days is commonly called 'stickiness' – increased customer loyalty.

Michael Hammer, the process re-engineering guru and teacher, coined the phase 'Fast, Right, Cheap and Easy (to do business with)' as the snappy maxim to describe what customers want and need. They want rapid availability to very good products and services at reasonable prices without any hassle both before and after getting them. Jeff Bezos, founder of Amazon.com, one of the internet's strongest brands and favourite e-commerce destinations, says much the same thing: 'There are four things that customers care about: selection, ease of use, prices and service. You have to be excellent in all four of those areas, you can't pick one out to leave another. If you do, you will not be successful.' An organization then should be set up with the operating strategies, business processes and attendant capabilities to deliver these apparently simple wants and needs. Most of us would instinctively go along with that objective. It may not be so easy to achieve, but these are the fundamental principles for customer fulfilment.

Today, many companies actively seek to continuously improve the products and services they provide to customers. To achieve this aim, they introduce customer-participating focus groups, they conduct surveys and they track not only their own performance but also that of their competitors. In other words, they measure. And measurement has a big role to play in helping to quantify the scale and nature of product and service problems, to prioritize executive attention and to monitor progress in this area of managing customer relationships. One of the secrets is to identify each of the interfaces that the organization has with its customers and gain an understanding of the processes and capabilities involved in satisfying customers' wants and needs at each interface point – or 'moment of truth', as it is sometimes known. Once the 'customer experience' has been identified, appropriate qualitative and quantitative measures can be selected which address both the essential process outcomes and the execution of the process itself.

Customer Care – Who Cares?

Branding is also closely associated with building customer relationships. Brands, in fact, reside in the perceptions of customers and of course non-customers too. Advertising and promotions can help raise the awareness of brands, reinforce brand values, and help to influence the positioning of brands in certain target markets. However, as several dot-coms discovered, you can throw as much money at it as you can afford but you don't build brands by advertising alone. The perception of customers (and, to a certain extent, prospect customers) revolves around their whole experience of the brand, including the experience of acquiring and using the products and services advertised, plus – and by no means least – the experience of friends, family, work colleagues and other users too.

The most common way to find out what customers think is to ask them. And so customer surveys are commonplace today. In fact, some would argue that they are so commonplace that they have become just as annoying as telesales calls, junk mail and internet spam. But customer survey data provides much information that is invaluable to organizations in gaining an understanding of existing customer and prospect customer perceptions. While this is still most common in consumer product industries, it is becoming increasingly common in the service industries too (see the box *Customer Satisfaction In An 'Oily Rag' Business*).

Customer Satisfaction in an 'Oily Rag' Business

Kwik-fit, the leading UK fast-fit car repairs group, has long taken customer care very seriously. Its forecourt promise is to deliver '100 per cent customer delight', leaving employees little room for a bad day at the air hammer. The company strives to make its strategy a success by providing 'the best training and self-development programmes in the business' and by 'listening to customers'. Customer satisfaction is monitored via reply-paid questionnaires distributed after work is completed and through a 24 hours a day free-phone helpline. Standard fare? Maybe, but its customer survey unit makes contact with 5,000 customers each day, within 72 hours of their visit to a Kwik-fit centre, to check whether they were satisfied with all aspects of the supply of products – vehicle exhausts (mufflers), tyres, brakes, batteries, etc. – and, particularly, the fitting services they received.

Fast, Right, Cheap and Easy. Alas, it is simply astonishing how many companies foul-up the execution of this simple premise. Research organizations, such as J D Power in the automotive industry, publish league tables of consumer satisfaction with particular products and services. Many TV and radio programmes and regular sections of popular newspapers are these days dedicated to consumer complaints. The ritual naming and shaming of errant vendors would be entertaining if it were not for the sad fact that every one of us has been stitched-up at some time or other. Every reader will have their own collection of 'war stories' to relate on the subject. What is also surprising – or perhaps it isn't really – is that certain types of complaint are common and repetitive. The UK's *Sunday Times*[31] newspaper recently published the following list of problems their consumer champion receives that crop up time and again:

- Bank errors and general banking inflexibility.
- Computer warranties that offer no consumer protection.
- Motor insurance claims that take forever to resolve.
- Incomprehensible mobile phone contracts.
- Interest-free loans that don't work out that way.
- Travel insurance claims that are rejected on dubious grounds.
- Paltry compensation paid to unhappy holidaymakers.

Special doses of vitriol are reserved for banks and complaints are up 20 per cent.

Another *Sunday Times*[32] investigation found that staff at NatWest, one of the UK's biggest banks, had been ordered not to recommend its highest interest paying accounts and that they lose earnings if they break the rule. The policy also means that the lower the rate of interest on the accounts they sell to customers, the more they earn. The report claims that up to 40 per cent of the salary of branch staff is made up of commission earned by selling certain products. Typically, the lower the rate of interest on the product sold, the higher the commission that staff get paid. Each branch has to produce a certain level of 'income' for the bank each month for branch staff to be entitled to bonuses, but they do not earn any such income for selling high interest savings accounts. Furthermore, they also receive higher levels of income if they are able to persuade customers to keep their cash in a current account, rather than switching it to a savings account. No prizes for guessing how staff behave. The deliberate encouragement of such behaviour is simply scandalous and shows a cynical contempt for customers' [pun intended] interests.

The problem is not confined to the UK. One US bank wrote to a section of its customer base telling them that it no longer wanted their business – the terminated customers had seemingly not used the bank's credit card sufficiently to make them worthwhile customers. In Germany, it was recently reported that complaints from customers about the service provided by its largest telephone service provider had become so frequent that all Deutsche Telekom's shops had gone ex-directory and operators were refusing to give out the addresses. Indeed, some companies seem to have turned antagonizing their customers into something of an art. Our favourite though is that of the UK's Anglian Water. Its research department wrote to its customers saying: 'We are developing new products and services, which aim to make your life easier. We are very excited and we think you'll be excited too.' The only problem was that one of its customers receiving this letter had already been dead for six months – something that was presumably known to Anglian, since the letter quite astonishingly began: 'Dear Mrs Deceased'.[33]

One of the most famous cases of creating customer aggravation and simultaneous brand busting occurred over an incompetently managed promotion (see the box *Hoover Sucks*).

Hoover Sucks

In November and December 1992, Hoover Europe – a subsidiary of Maytag Corp. of the US – offered its UK and Irish customers a very special deal. In an attempt to pursue its market strategy to increase its share of the local domestic appliance market, it offered two free flights to Orlando or New York for every purchase over £100.

However, it grossly misjudged the success of the promotion. Following a £1 million TV advertising campaign, shops sold out and its factory was switched to seven-day working. More than 100,000 people bought products – many purely to qualify for the free flights, creating a flourishing second-hand market in new domestic appliances still in their boxes.

This demand created a huge bottleneck of applications and many customers were told they could not fly when they wanted. The fiasco created much adverse press and TV comment at the time. Instead of supplying the demand through cheap charter flights, the company was forced to purchase large numbers of scheduled flight tickets.

Its focus on market share also seems to have blinded it to another detail: customers purchasing the cheapest qualifying product, a £119 vacuum cleaner, on which it might expect to make a profit of about £10–£15, received flight tickets costing Hoover £200–£500. Simple cost/benefit analysis seems to have been overlooked.

Maytag, Hoover's parent, sent a task force to the UK, fired three top executives and set up a fund of £20 million to save face. It later admitted that this reserve was insufficient and it took a *further* charge of $30 million against its first quarter results to cover the extra costs. The company subsequently imposed draconian and controversial cost cuts on its European operations (involving factory closures) in order to restore profitability.

From Customer Satisfaction to Customer Contribution

Organizations do not help themselves in their quest for customer loyalty – and profitability – when they make such fundamental errors. In the main, they don't *deliberately* set out to antagonize customers; it is usually the result of some dysfunctional business process or reward mechanism that is not attached to the organization's overall business strategy. We should note also that some companies can be very good at certain aspects of customer relationship management, but be equally appalling at others (see the example shown in the box *Kwik-fit – The Sequel*).

Kwik-fit – The Sequel

It's ironic that Kwik-fit, the car repairs group now owned by Ford that we praised earlier in this chapter for its exemplary attention to customer satisfaction surveillance, was recently criticized by the UK's Consumers' Association. The consumer watchdog found it to be one of the worst offenders for recommending work on its customers' vehicles that simply did not need to be done. In its investigation, five out of eleven Kwik-fit outlets visited recommended unnecessary work (such as brake replacement, fitting new shock absorbers and new tyres) at an average cost of £150. While customers might be very satisfied with the work and the way it was done, they will be less than delighted by the resultant hole in their bank accounts.

When malpractices such as this are publicly exposed, it leads other existing and potential customers to be suspicious and to take their business elsewhere. This would seem to be a case of short-term profitability – customer contribution – overtaking customer satisfaction in a way that is ultimately counterproductive. It may of course also be a reflection of how *employees* are measured and rewarded.

The principal point here is that some companies have lost the plot in terms of customer interrelationship measures. We are no longer looking at customer measures from the point of view of the customer, but from the point of view of the organization's wants and needs *from* its customers. Customers have no latent desire to be especially profitable or even loyal – indeed, if they were aware of it, they might well feel uncomfortable with the notion that they are being segmented and profiled, except for the few (that is the wealthy) who can see some tangible benefit to it. On the other hand *everyone* does want excellent products and services at reasonable prices (unless perhaps if they are buying luxury goods, where exclusivity matters).

Some businesses necessarily rely purely on one-off sales (domestic housing real estate agents might fall into this category, for example – and this might help to explain their almost universal disregard as pariahs), but most need repeat business in order to cover the cost of attracting new customers. If the incoming customers aren't enamoured enough of their experience to keep coming back for more, then the sales and marketing cost invested in winning them is a sunk investment that has been wasted. In the main, customer loyalty is a major business issue for companies. Nowhere is this more true than in the industrial context, where winning customers can often involve a long tendering and negotiation process that involves corporate entertainment and other sorts of pampering in order to win business. A small one-off job simply will not cover the costs of winning the business. It may well be necessary, however, in order to gain entry and establish credibility but it will not be enough on its own account. Such businesses almost certainly need to identify and analyze the value of the 'entry level' investments they promote versus the longer term benefits they enjoy as a result.

But not all loyal customers are necessarily profitable ones. In an industrial context again, the customer who places small orders very frequently for delivery to a remote address may not be as profitable as one who buys a large quantity of the same product at infrequent intervals for delivery to a relatively adjacent conurbation to the point of supply, for example. The distribution costs are significantly different. This is something that most of the national postal systems of the world have always known, given their variable delivery costs per item matched to fixed-price pricing policies based on weight and speed rather than on domestic destination. Consequently, some items of mail are inherently less (or not at all) profitable than others. But few measurement systems capture this crucial level of detail.

In general, industry has not been much smarter though – until now, that is. The emphasis has recently moved much more decisively towards measurement and analysis of customer profitability. Often this has produced results which have been truly shocking to the providers of those products and services. The bad news: several firms have found that they have an alarming proportion of customers who are not profitable. One bank, for example, found that 130 per cent of its profit came from just 20 per cent of its customers. (Old friend Vilfredo Pareto missed a neat trick there.) The good news: companies can now know who their most profitable customers are and can give them the 'red carpet' treatment in order to retain their loyalty. Of course, if you are a customer, that is only good news if you happen to be on the receiving end of this preferential treatment. *Business Week* has dubbed this 'The New Apartheid'[34] (see the box *Some Customers are More Equal than Others*).

Some Customers are More Equal than Others

Maxims and corporate mission statements from the 1990s, such as 'the customer comes first', gave consumers across the world the impression that nothing was more important than their patronage. It also conferred an essence of egalitarianism. All customers deserved equally high levels of service. Now though, in the age of data, it turns out that only some customers come first – and many of those not in their number are starting to feel unwanted.

For example, calls from the most profitable customers can now be quickly answered by the most senior operators, while those from less profitable ones are put on hold. At one US electric utility, the top 350 business clients are served by six people. The next tier of 700 is handled by six more. The remaining 30,000 other business customers are serviced by two further customer service representatives. You don't need us to tell you what the impact of that is if you happen to own or run a small business.

This isn't a tale of a woolly-minded utility being oblivious to customers' wants and needs. It is CRM – Customer Relationship Management. Improvements in information systems have allowed the mass of customer data that organizations have available to them to be analyzed so that insights can be gained and better business decisions made. So-called 'data mining and warehousing' software is used to sift through the enormous quantities of data that a business generates, using a number of different algorithms, in order to find the hidden patterns that will help a company to maximize its profits.

In its first phase, for example, supermarkets have introduced a form of two-tier pricing through the use of loyalty cards, which reward frequent customers with discounts and special offers not available to other shoppers. Airlines, hotels and car rental companies also give preferential treatment to frequent users.

All very discrete selectivism, in fact. However, the battle lines are now being drawn up for the next phase – ' Big Brother allows fat cats to get fatter'. In the UK, supermarket stores are planning to give gold loyalty cards to about 5% of their customers who spend the most (primarily upper- and middle-class families). Gold card holders will be served personally and promptly. The lower spenders will have to wait in queues. Cardholders will enjoy express checkouts, discounts and a free, prompt delivery service. Others will have to pay £5 for next-day deliveries. One supermarket has even developed a 'smart chip' so that gold card holders can be identified as soon as they enter a store and immediately offered a superior service.

It is not specifically a retailer-led phenomenon. First Union bank in the US codes its credit card customers with coloured symbols that flash when service representatives call up an account on their computer screens. Green means the person is a profitable customer and should be granted waivers or otherwise given kid-glove treatment. Reds are the money losers who have virtually zero negotiating power. And yellows are a more discretionary category between the two extremes – for now, but it'll surely get even more selective soon.

Continental Airlines recently started rolling out a Customer Information System, whereby all of its 43,000 reservation, service and gate agents will immediately know the history and value of each customer. An 'intelligent engine' not only mines data on status but also suggests remedies and perks, from automatic coupons for service delays to priority for upgrades. The technology will even allow Continental staff to note details of customer preferences so that the airline can offer them 'extra services'. How far that goes remains to be seen, but there is a downside. Continental staff can also add their comments about customers – so it's probably not a good idea to have that bust-up argument with the 'gate agent from the Gestapo' over how much hand-luggage you are carrying any more. It may be recorded and used as evidence against you.

What is perhaps even more discomforting to some consumers is that data about you and your transaction history can be sold to other companies. So you can be 'pigeon-holed' before you even walk in their door, since your buying potential has already been measured. This is a social revolution which has the potential for a significant backlash. The 'new apartheid' created by these systems, based on pure spending power with more overt benefits discrimination, is an emerging issue that will have to be addressed in the 'Age of Data'.

Sharpen that guillotine blade, Monsieur Robespierre!

Customer Lifetime Value

Don Peppers, co-author with Martha Rogers of *The One to One Manager*, dismisses the egalitarian one-size-fits-all approach because it means treating your best customers the same as your worst. 'It is patently absurd,' he says. 'The truth is that customers are different in two very significant ways. They are different in their value to the enterprise, so the more valuable and growable customers should get higher priority in marketing time, effort and resources. They also differ in the value the enterprise has to give to them, so understanding customers' different needs allows you to treat different customers differently according to what they want and create loyalty from a learning relationship.'

However, customer segmentation according to their historic profitability is not only a simplistic view in terms of its potential consequences but also in terms of its execution and – as usual, where overly simplistic views prevail – there are predictable dangers lurking here. For example, new customers are inherently unlikely to be immediately profitable and, if they are *treated* as second-class customers because of that, are they likely to stick around long enough to become profitable ones? Similarly, some products or services are only required by customers on an infrequent basis, but may be required for a very long period thereafter – mortgages or life assurance, for example. In the industrial sector, shunning a customer who pays his invoices rather slowly may mean foregoing involvement in a major new project. Conversely, for an insurance company, individual customers can be highly profitable for many years – until the day they make a substantial claim. How to treat them now?

Eroding the customer base by actively or passively angering (so far) unprofitable customers enough to send them elsewhere can be a fatal mistake though. An organization with relatively high fixed costs will then have to allocate these overheads across a lesser number of customers and so is likely to make some previously profitable customers now seem unprofitable. This of course is the beginning of a downward spiral. The data relating to customer profitability has to be applied with great care in terms of how it is used. In some cases, it may be possible to apply variable pricing to address the problem, but if competitors fail to invoke the same criteria then the spiral effect is likely to be much the same. Far better then to think of customers' future potential lifetime value than their past history. For example, by some estimates, an 18–25-year-old viewer is worth 18 times more than a middle-aged housewife to a commercial television channel. 'Your goal,' says Don Peppers, 'is to come up with some mechanism that allows you to rank your customers from top to bottom in terms of their long-term value to you so that you can prioritize your decision-making.' This may not come as particularly good news to elderly consumers, however.

Having the right measurement data for making decisions is just one aspect, it is how that information is *used* that really matters. It is easy to make mistakes by taking some of the available data and looking at it from too narrow and superficial a focus. Inadvertently sifting out profitable customers in the interests of seeming to create better product profitability would be an example (see the box *Caveat Vendor*).

Caveat Vendor

A British supermarket recently carried out an examination of its sales data in a certain store. Looking for unprofitable product lines, it discovered a certain type of fancy cheese that was only bought by a few people every week. The answer seemed to be simple: axe the cheese, replace it with something more popular, increase profits.

But then the company looked more closely at the data. It discovered that the few people who bought this particular cheese were people who had much higher shopping bills than the average. These same customers were also buying fine wine, expensive delicacies such as caviar, and other gourmet foodstuffs. The decision was reversed. Rather than risk losing these high-value 'foodies' to a rival outlet, the supermarket continued to stock the cheese, taking a small loss but retaining the customers.

This is an example that illustrates the ease with which data can be (or, in this case, could have been) used to make the wrong business decisions if too simplistic or superficial approaches are taken.

Source: *Financial Times*, 23 August 2000.

Furthermore, even though sales people generally tend to think it a more important element of buying decisions than customers do, a key element in winning sales and retaining business in most industries is price. Price too high and customers will tend to move elsewhere (if they have a choice); price too low and you will attract large quantities of unprofitable business. In order to manage customer profitability, pricing has to be matched to costs. If 20 per cent of your customers equate to 130 per cent of your profits, you probably aren't doing this very well. While price is a factor of generating demand for products and services, many of the determinants of cost (and, therefore, many of the discretionary parameters for pricing flexibility) are determined within the prior process of developing those products and services. When costs rise faster than prices, then clearly margins will be eroded. If it isn't measured and regularly reviewed, it's likely that the process is totally out of control.

Managing with Customer Perceptions

It is often taken as a 'given' that improving levels of customer satisfaction will also improve company financial performance. It seems intuitive, but what is the factual evidence? Not all the evidence is conclusive.

The National Quality Research Center at the University of Michigan Business School, headed by Claes Fornell, established what it calls the American Customer Satisfaction Index in 1994. Starting with limited sample beginnings about perceptions of companies and government agencies, it now surveys more than 50,000 organizations. Results issued in early 2000 indicated an overall customer satisfaction score of 72.8 out of a possible 100. Not a meaningful statistic in itself, but when it is compared with the original 1994 score it represents a *decline* of 1.4 points. The usual suspects are responsible for the decline: for instance, airlines are down 12.5 per cent, telephone companies down 11.1 per cent, banks down 8.1 per cent and retail stores down 6.5 per cent. Other service providers, such as broadcasters and life insurers can be included in this dismal litany too. The better news is that although there has been this longer-term decline, there appears to be an improvement – albeit a fairly small one – in the index average since 1997.[35] However, this evidence would seem to indicate that improved levels of customer satisfaction are not driving corporate profits, which shattered all previous records in the intervening years while the Dow Jones index tripled in value. What has happened? Has product and service quality in the US really declined? Have US companies become complacent while the economy has been on a roll? Or have customers just become more demanding?

The pundits claim that customer perception of what is possible has moved on considerably over the last five to ten years. Customer expectations of product and service quality have increased significantly. Consumers do, in general, show a greater readiness to complain. This is evidenced by, for example, a 1997 UK National Consumer Council survey which found that in 1992 just 25 per cent of people surveyed had made at least one complaint about service levels in the previous year. Four years later this had risen to 43 per cent (and remember that Brits may be famous in some parts of the world as whingers, but they are not well known as formal complainers).

What is more, the trend to provide the facility to complain helps. A study conducted by the Chapman University of California shows that by simply encouraging customers to complain helps to increase the level of satisfaction (even if the complaint never gets resolved). In an experiment, published in the *Journal of Consumer Marketing*, consumers were given a free trial at a gym. Those who were actively encouraged to complain on joining the gym were 59 per cent more likely to enrol for regular membership than those who were not encouraged to do so. There can be other types of 'halo effect' too. For example, when trains run to published timetables it turns out that passengers also believe that trains are cleaner and queues to buy tickets are shorter, and so on. Finding the principal drivers of customer satisfaction is a key factor in measuring and managing customer relationships. But if you never collect and analyze the data in the first place, it is unlikely that you will ever find out what the drivers are.

While customer expectations may represent a moving target that distorts comparative analysis at an industry level, fortunately some organizations have enjoyed better fortune in proving the tangible links between customer satisfaction and customer behaviours and, hence, customer profitability. The box *Customer Satisfaction to Customer Profitability Link is Proven* illustrates an important pioneering example of best practice in this field.

Customer Satisfaction to Customer Profitability Link is Proven

Research carried out at PNC Bank in Pennsylvania in 1996 and 1997 by a joint client, consultant and academic team produced some fascinating results (published in a relatively obscure briefing within the March/April 1999 edition of the *Harvard Business Review*). They found clear evidence that companies harvest far greater economic rewards from highly satisfied customers than they do from the merely satisfied. They also confirmed that increasing a customer's level of satisfaction can substantially increase the economic attractiveness of that customer.

Using data from a 1996 survey of 1,500 PNC customers, the researchers were able to tie customers' satisfaction ratings to their actual behaviour in terms of their actual bank balances and transaction histories. They found that the account balances of those customers who ranked themselves as highly satisfied were nearly 20 per cent greater than those of customers who ranked themselves as just satisfied. Indeed, the balances maintained by just satisfied customers were no higher than those maintained by customers who classified themselves as less than satisfied.

When the research team turned their attention to around 400 of PNC's bank branches, thay found that branch profitability was 23 per cent higher than average for those branches with the highest proportion of highly satisfied customers. The other branches, with a higher average of less satisfied customers, fell below average in their profitability levels. So, wealthy people *are* happy people after all! No, this would be a deeply cynical view. The link seems to be indisputable and the researchers did deliver one further *coup de grâce*.

Finally, and perhaps most interestingly, the joint research team considered what happens when customers' level of satisfaction changes. They compared the satisfaction levels and account balances of the 1996 survey respondents with their satisfaction levels and bank balances following a second survey conducted 15 months later. They found, first, that customers who were highly satisfied in the first survey and remained so in the second one increased their bank balances by an average of $4,800. Furthermore, customers who moved from being satisfied to highly satisfied increased their balances by an average of $4,500. However, highly satisfied customers whose level of satisfaction dropped between less than satisfied reduced their balances by about $1,000, while satisfied customers who became less than satisfied reduced their balances by an average $1,400.

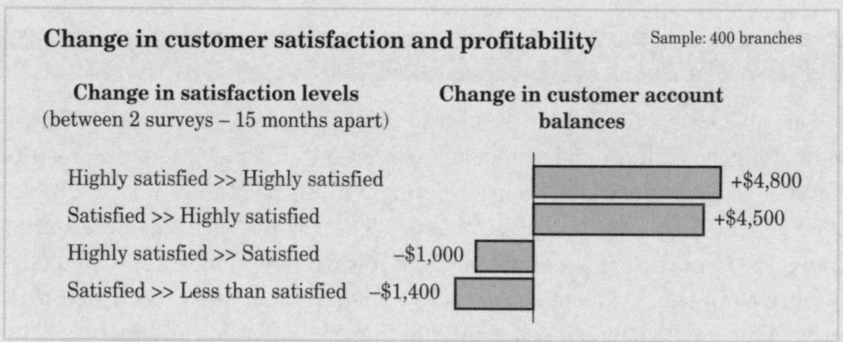

Clearly then, highly satisfied customers are economically much more attractive than those who are only moderately satisfied. Customers who stay highly satisfied become increasingly more attractive over time. You might argue that this is intuitive, but as far as we are aware this was the first documented instance of its proof. Previous research had addressed very satisfied customers' *intentions*, but this study captures their actual behaviours. It also shows that the majority of bank customers do act quite rapidly on their perceptions about their level of satisfaction. And it must be reasonable to assume that these important conclusions are not exclusive to the banking industry.

To reiterate then, there are two separate agendas at work here: what the customer wants and needs is the first, what the organization wants and needs of its customers is another. This is where we believe the Performance Prism framework is uniquely positioned to help differentiate between these contrasting, but interlinked, agendas. It forces us to segregate Customer Satisfaction from Customer Contribution and to identify appropriate measures for each.

Employee Relationship Management Issues

Employees form the third leg of a triumvirate that most practitioners seem to pretty much agree includes the most critical stakeholders for the vast majority of organizations – investors, customers and employees (although, as we have noted elsewhere, other stakeholders are becoming increasingly important too). Even balanced scorecard users frequently turn the innovation and learning quadrant into an employee measures one.

Our own research, carried out in 2000, shows that 72 per cent of our sample of companies measure employee satisfaction (which was second only to customer satisfaction at 80 per cent and well ahead of investor satisfaction at just 42 per cent). Of those that don't already measure employee satisfaction, 86 per cent believe that they should. On the other hand, a very similar proportion of companies – 68 per cent – claim to monitor employee contribution (for comparison, only half as many organizations say they measure customer contribution), while 88 per cent of those firms who don't measure it think that they should. So it would seem that there is a relatively substantial and uniform degree of usage of both employee satisfaction and contribution measures. There is also a high level of intention, agreement that these are key management issues that should be measured in the future.

The relationship between employees and business performance has been the subject of a vast amount of academic and practitioner research. This has been ongoing for nearly 100 years, but still we do not have all the answers. Just a fragment of this body of knowledge is acknowledged within this chapter.

Employee Behaviour Studies

There has almost certainly been more research done on employees and their behaviour than any other facet of business. Factory workers, for example, have been subject to the measurement of their contribution for decades. Frederick Taylor, who published his *Principles of Scientific Management* in 1911, advocated that managers should gather together all the traditional knowledge possessed by workers and then classify it and distil it down to laws, rules and formulae. He went on to prescribe a system whereby they should develop a 'science' for each element of a man's work to replace old rule-of-thumb methods and 'scientifically' select and train workmen in the new methods. Taylor's work has had a profound and far-reaching influence on factory works management and many other working environments today still reflect his ideas.

Not long after Taylor's work, in 1917, Frank and Lilian Gilbreth gave us the almost eponymous *therblig* – a set of symbols to enable the detailed analysis of an individual's work. Indeed method study, work study, and 'time and motion' study went on to dominate industrial management productivity thinking and employee measurement practices through to the 1960s and 1970s. Many now discredited methods, such as 'piece-work', were implemented on the back of it. But other predominant measures of the period were the number of days workers were on strike and the level of absenteeism. Meanwhile, the relationship between management and workers (and their trade unions) became a battleground between what management could get its workers to do and what its workers could get away with not doing.

Other researchers pursued different lines of enquiry. For example, in the late 1920s and early 1930s, Elton Mayo helped conduct the famous studies at the Hawthorne Works of the Western Electric Company, which examined the human social, motivational and emotional factors affecting industrial employees' performance. A whole series of management gurus – from the pioneering works of Maslow, Herzberg and McGregor to the more recent deliberations of Drucker, Deming and Senge (to name but a few) – have contributed to our body of knowledge about the human side of the enterprise. It is the products of their thinking that tend to predominate in today's more enlightened, but still far from perfect, business world.

From Employee Contribution to Employee Satisfaction

Throughout most of the 20th century, management's focus was on maximizing the contribution of a plentiful supply of employees to ensure that they worked as efficiently (but not necessarily as effectively) as possible. While wages and living standards in most industrial nations have generally increased beyond recognition in the meantime, it is the number of employees that has become the principal denominator in measures of productivity.

Today, with considerable competition for the best people and, in many countries, relatively full employment, employers complain about skills shortages. Recruiting and retaining enough people with the right skill-sets is one of today's key employment issues. For a while at least, employees have the whip-hand as the so-called 'war for talent' is pursued between leading companies with the consequent impact on the remuneration packages offered. Employee satisfaction has become increasingly important and now ranks on a par with employee contribution. Whether that trend will continue with the advent of a downtown remains to be seen. We suspect that it will, but it is likely to be more concentrated on specific job functions.

While it might seem obvious that increased levels of employee contribution that lead to greater efficiency and effectiveness will help to improve the performance of the business, it may be less transparent that employee satisfaction achieves the same end. Skills shortages can cause operational constraints and a high employee attrition rate infers a not insignificant replacement cost (see the box *Sorry You're Leaving*).

Sorry You're Leaving

Traditional measures of the cost of employee turnover focus on the cost of recruiting and training replacements, but ignore the costs of lower productivity and customer satisfaction. A study of a US automobile dealer's sales staff by Abt Associates found that the average monthly cost of replacing a sales representative who had five to eight years' experience with one who had less than one year of experience was as high as £36,000 in sales. While the costs of losing a broker at a securities firm can be even higher. The research estimates that it takes around five years for a broker to rebuild relationships with key institutional clients that can create as much as $1 million per year in commissions to the firm. It is not hard to see that losing such an individual might then have a punitive impact on the firm's financial returns.

A quick check on *Fortune* magazine's annual 'The 100 Best Companies To Work For' league table gives an indication of the lengths that highly-rated US employers will go to in order to keep their staff. Apart from often ample wages, employees can expect significant additional financial benefits. These include cash bonuses, free equity shares or stock options, generous retirement plans, 100 per cent health insurance premiums (even extending to the employee's entire household, including nannies), clothing allowances, free laptops with internet connections, grants towards external training courses (up to $4,500 a year), and so on. But it isn't all about indirect money benefits, other firms offer paternity leave (up to six weeks on full pay), on-site health care, state-of-the-art fitness centres, subsidized on-site child care (Cisco's even has web cameras to give parents a real-time window on their child's play). And then there are recreational benefits to be enjoyed too, such as access to company condominiums, lake cabins and mountain retreats, while one firm allows veterans with 20 years' service to take an all-expenses-paid trip anywhere in the world. At the other end of the generosity scale, there are those simple things like free bagels, muffins and candies. Being an employee of a major corporation has certainly not always been this good!

Employee Retention and Motivation

Despite these attempts, according to the California-based Saratoga Institute, employee attrition rates at US companies have increased by nearly 20 per cent during the past five years to an average of 16.5 per cent (but as high as 34 per cent in services businesses). In Europe, employee turnover was up by 10 per cent in 1999 to an average of 14 per cent, according to Saratoga Europe. While this is alarming in itself, there is worse news in that attrition rates for new hires is nearly 30 per cent in the first year of employment. Employee retention has become a significant business issue for executives in many industries (see the box *Retaining Talent – Stemming the Tide*).

Retaining Talent – Stemming the Tide

In an attempt to keep people, companies in several industries have resorted to the bluntest of instruments: money, and lots of it. Bonuses are the financial incentive of choice, but companies also offer higher salaries and stock ownership or options. The attitude of management seems to be that money is the universal motivator, and that the highest bidder takes all. Not surprisingly, these organizations eventually discover that money doesn't necessarily buy loyalty. Indeed, such thinking runs counter to most studies on job satisfaction and the attitudes of new recruits – which routinely identify such things as learning opportunities, professional growth, type of work, autonomy at work and intellectual stimulation as more important factors than compensation.

Nevertheless, it is difficult for executives to understand what factors influence people's decisions to stay with or leave a particular company – and, subsequently to craft the ideal mix of pay, perks, and personal and professional development that will motivate each employee. Most companies also have an inability to measure specific employee contributions and correlate them with overall financial performance.

Research conducted by Accenture, including in-depth interviews with nearly 500 senior executives from ten different industries around the world, reveals that to win the war for talent, companies must adopt a new approach to retention: one that focuses on communication as well as compensation; on opportunities as well as options; on performance as well as perks. This research has uncovered several common traits among companies that have been able to actually buck the turnover trend and not only keep their talented employees but also motivate them and improve their performance. These companies:

- learn what employees really want most by communicating with them, including receiving continual feedback
- provide a wide range of growth and development opportunities for all levels of employees
- adopt measurement and reward systems that clearly articulate what is expected from employees and reward them accordingly.

Accenture's research also shows that the most motivated and loyal employees are those whose companies help them become star performers by providing a comprehensive set of personal and career development opportunities across the whole enterprise, without functional or divisional restrictions. In effect, companies must make their employees more attractive to the external market so that they satisfy the employees' real desires for growth and development.

One of the more surprising findings from the research was that a majority of survey participants claim they gave employees the chance to be involved in creating the company's overall business strategy. Swedish financial services leader Skandia, for example, has created a 'Future Centre' in which teams of employees representing a broad mix of age groups, functional roles and cultures are encouraged to create a vision of the company's future. By getting involved in this way, Skandia's employees get a level of insight into the business and exposure to issues that they don't encounter in their day-to-day responsibilities.

A common situation that can lead to employee dissatisfaction, or even departure, is the lack of a well-articulated and consistent performance measurement and reward system. Accenture's work in this area indicates that employees who leave organizations often complain that they never knew what their previous employers or supervisors expected of them, and that there seemed to be no identifiable relationship between performance and rewards. To address such situations, many companies are becoming more rigorous in how they measure and reward their employees. They are not only making it clearer to employees what their roles are in the greater organization; they are also infusing a much higher level of accountability into every position in the company.

Source: Adapted from 'Stemming the Tide' by Tony Clancy and Arnaud Andre. Accenture's journal *Outlook* – 2001, Number 1.

However, in our view, there is a real danger lurking in over-zealousness too. For example, one company claims that it is creating a 'causal map' that spells out the relationships between individual employee behaviour and business strategy. This document clearly identifies the financial and customer objectives that are critical to attaining the company's goals; the specific behaviours that are needed from each employee to achieve the financial and customer objectives; the metrics that would measure each behaviour; and a set of key performance indicators for each employee's job. It has a sort of plausible ring to it, but also a sense of déjà vu

– Managing By Objectives (MBO) was a similar initiative widely implemented back in the early 1980s. It frequently failed because of the emphasis placed on individual performance at the expense of team performance.

Most people want to work in a meritocracy, but it needs to be a co-operative one if the synergistic benefits are to be realized by the employer. Dysfunctional or not, people's behaviour will be driven by how they are measured and, especially, how they are rewarded. Where the individual is the focus of reward mechanisms, there is significantly less incentive to co-operate with work colleagues to achieve what is best for the organization. There is almost certainly a higher likelihood that related measures will be 'gamed' by individuals too. A classic example of this phenomenon is illustrated in the box *Playing a Drinking Game*.

Playing a Drinking Game

A Scotch whisky distiller, Glenmorangie, measured its sales and provided *performance related bonus incentives* to its sales manager, based on his ability to push their products into the market. The metric applied was the level of shipments to its local distributor, Westbay.

The distiller's senior management were surprised to discover – shortly after terminating the manager's employment – that 16,000 12-bottle cases of whisky, which it thought was being enjoyed by consumers, were languishing undrunk in the distributor's warehouse. The value of this stock was approximately £4 million at retail prices and the company was forced to issue a profit warning, which sent its share price tumbling some 15 per cent on the day of the announcement. Faith in the management's ability to ensure proper controls through appropriate measures was severely dented, as witnessed by some of its major shareholders' comments to the press: for example, 'If companies are going to offer these kinds of incentives, it's imperative that they have proper controls in place to check up on their employees. Someone senior must take responsibility for this disaster.'

Management had wrongly assumed, of course, that as fast as the cases were going to the warehouse, they were leaving it again for the retail market. A new measurement system was subsequently put in place, by which the metric of sales is logged based on depletions – or sales to retailers – rather than shipments to the distributor.

Maintaining Employee Morale

There come times too when firms need to shed substantial numbers of staff. It is important then to do everything possible to maintain productivity levels, especially when attitudes towards the company and its executives may be quite negative.

Nowhere is this more evident than in the case of mergers and acquisitions. In Chapter 6, we say that the goal of mergers and acquisitions is to enhance shareholder value and that all other stakeholder considerations are essentially about 'damage limitation'. Clearly, a critical part of that damage limitation is that key employees should not leave and that major customers should not defect. Typically, there will be some selective 'culling' of executives and employees resultant from major mergers and acquisitions in order to deliver the cost savings expected by investors as a result of the deal. Duplicated roles and functions (sometimes known as 'Noah's Ark Syndrome' because there are two of every position) are usually the first to go. Nevertheless, after this initial upheaval, those executives and employees selected for retention are the ones that the combined business wishes to retain. It is vital that they do not become disaffected by the 'radiation' and decline in morale that frequently occurs in anticipation of and as a result of the organizational changes. It is not unusual for 'head-hunter' activity to increase substantially just after a merger or takeover. They will be seeking talented, but disaffected executives. All the post-merger integration manuals say that these decisions need to be executed rapidly. The loyalty of the experienced senior executives selected for retention will often be 'mission critical'. It is essential, therefore, to make sure that there is a means of tracking that all these key people are comfortable with the messages they are receiving and that they understand that they have a valuable role in the creation of the future of the combined organization.

If employee morale is allowed to deteriorate to too great an extent, then this can easily have a knock-on effect in the way customers are treated. These days, it is relatively unusual for the business combination related redundancies to result in labour strikes (although they can still happen). However, customer services tend to deteriorate in other, more subtle, ways: orders get lost, telephones don't get answered, stock levels don't get replenished, queries aren't responded to, complaints remain unanswered, and so on. Employees spend their time speculating about – and talking about – what will happen to them, or how long it will be before it happens to them, and not going about some of their individual responsibilities. If this comes at a time that any major customer was considering an alternative supplier, more than likely it is now that they will vote with their feet and walk away. The loss of a major customer – or, in a retail environment, a significant number of valued customers – has the potential to wipe out most or all of the benefits of the business combination.

That linkage between employee satisfaction, attitudes and behaviours with that of customer satisfaction and retention is vital to success and is one we shall return to later.

Although increasingly common in today's business environment, mergers and acquisitions are by no means the only type of major corporate change programme. Indeed, employees frequently complain that their workplace is constantly in a process of upheaval and crave a period of stability from the constant restructuring going on around them. Executives, on the other hand, have to execute. Shareholders expect the performance of the company to go onward and upward, and few will be too concerned about the employees' worries. As Sir John Harvey-Jones, former chairman of ICI, says in his book *Making It Happen*: 'Management is about maintaining the highest rate of change that an organization and the people within it can stand.' In 1999, nearly half of the 500 largest companies in Europe had restructured and/or been involved in a merger or acquisition during the past three years. It would not be surprising if the other half have been affected since then, such has been the pace of corporate activity (although the most recent evidence shows that it is now slowing).

Often, in order to generate enthusiasm and legitimacy for its proposed initiatives, senior executives try to identify so-called 'burning platforms' as a rationale for why the business has to change direction yet again or for why it needs to modify aspects of its ingrained corporate culture. These, it has to be said, are often 'sheep in wolves' clothing', but executives have reputations to make, brokers' analysts to impress and the annual general meeting next week. It may seem somewhat devious to employ such tactics, but otherwise inertia is likely to rule. And inertia is not allowed. We may think we live in an age of 'spin', but as Niccolo Machiavelli noted back in the early 16th century: 'Although it is detestable in everything to employ fraud, nevertheless in the conduct of war it is praiseworthy and admirable, and he is commended who overcomes the foe by stratagem.'

As an alternative form of creating change (with less pain), many chief executives have tried to modify their corporate cultures through what are known as 'values programmes'. However, despite one or two success stories where executives have really 'walked the talk', numerous research papers have cast doubt on the effectiveness of these top-down employee re-education initiatives. After a spectacular and expensive launch with much propaganda, they invariably come to nought when it is realized that senior managers behave in ways that contradict the very values they so recently proclaimed. Increasingly, we have found, such programmes are greeted – perhaps more so on the European side of the Atlantic than in North America – with rampant scepticism. As John Hunt, Professor of Organizational Behaviour at London Business School, suggests: 'What may sell in California or Hong Kong will not sell in London or Paris. Europeans have seen it all before. If people think they are being emotionally manipulated by value statements, they raise their defences.'

When companies try to impose synthetic 'just add water' cultures on their organizations or are over-zealous in policing cultural consistency, they should not be surprised if there is some backlash from a core of employees struggling to maintain their individuality. The story that follows may be aprocryphal, but it illustrates the point. At Disney, which is earnest about maintaining its values, many employees had taken to referring to the company as Mauschwitz in internal e-mails. When its management discovered this, a directive was sent to all employees threatening that anyone found using this 'irreverent' term would be instantly dismissed. Within a few minutes, employees were circulating e-mails referring to the company as Duchau!

However, while the right choice of change programme must be of paramount importance to senior executives, it will be the middle management band within the organization that will be primarily responsible for implementing it (necessarily with visible senior executive commitment to the programme). And whatever internally focused strategies and initiatives executives decide should be deployed, employees are inevitably at the forefront of the implementation programmes that must follow. Small or large, where there are change programmes, performance measures must follow to monitor their implementation and evaluate their impacts. Without appropriate measures, executives and managers won't be in a position to track progress, to manage the transition, or to assess the outcomes. What precisely needs to be measured will be largely dependent on the outcomes the organization's executives wish to achieve and how they propose to go about implementing it. There are, however, some generic patterns and we shall address these in Chapter 8.

But what do employees themselves think about their contribution to these initiatives and their firm's success? And how does their point of view differ from that of their bosses? For some insight into this, see the box *Sources of Success*.

Sources of Success

The 1999 European Workplace Index survey conducted by Towers Perrin found that 84 per cent of employee respondents across Europe agreed that they understood their company's goals and direction. However, while as many as 90 per cent of managers agreed they made a direct impact on achieving their company's success, only 69 per cent of non-management employees felt this was true for them – although little separated these groups when it came to personal satisfaction at work.

The study also found that employees in European-based companies had a much more positive attitude towards business goals than their counterparts in the US. European workers are apparently more optimistic about the future of the companies that employ them, generally believe they are treated fairly and that company success will translate into personal success for themselves.

Perhaps more surprising, business leaders and employees in Europe share the same views about corporate strategy. There was a similarity of outlook about the need for customer focus, employee business understanding and management effectiveness.

The report says: 'If the past decade has taught us anything, it is that sustained success – financially and operationally – is highly dependent on the dedication, skills and commitment of employees at all levels in the organization.'

Labour Unions

The power of labour unions has been considerably eroded in a number of countries during the 1980s and 1990s. Many perceive that their threat to productivity improvement and implementing change had become too strong and that their power was abused, and so good riddance to their influence. However, in other countries, the unions have remained strong and are even perceived to be beneficial, if somewhat bureaucratic (for example, where works councils have to endorse a wide variety of decisions). But even labour unions will accept that, in some circumstances, there is a certain amount of compromising that has to be done in business in order to retain jobs over the longer term.

Maintaining a close relationship with labour union representatives is important and they need to see much of the data that the company collects in order to understand its competitive position, the challenges and threats that it faces, and how well it complies with labour-related regulations and internal policies.

Listening to Front-line Employees

A further key issue we should identify here is that executives generally have little understanding of the circumstances in which their middle managers and employees operate on a day-to-day basis. With few (sometimes legendary) exceptions, the executives of large companies work at a level of abstraction where they cannot relate to the operational problems that employees face every day when they deal with the firm's customers. They assume that operational managers below them will resolve these issues. But it is a risky assumption. Middle managers are driven by the initiatives that senior executives promulgate. The demands of 'head office' will readily divert their attention from mundane operational decisions and the responsibility for these is then further delegated to powerless and budgetless supervisors.

A series of documentaries on UK television's BBC2 network called 'Back To The Floor' illustrates this syndrome vividly. In these programmes, senior executives from diverse industries voluntarily spend a week performing a variety of menial tasks normally carried out by their lowly workers. These consistently illustrate the vast gap that exists between executive perceptions about the way things work in their organization and the stark (and often ludicrous) reality of what actually happens where the rubber meets the road. Employees naturally use the opportunity to bring various long-standing grievances and idiocies to the executive's attention. In virtually every programme, stunned executives go back to their offices at the end of the week with a long list of operational glitches where policies, processes and practices can easily be improved with a little investment. Miraculously of course the budget is then found to implement these initiatives.

The point, however, is that the voice of the employee invariably does not reach the boardroom. Incumbent operational managers work principally to the priorities handed down to them from above. They are also likely to be preoccupied by the need to 'put out fires' that are breaking out all around them. So, bottom-up suggestions from employees about what should be done and how money should be invested to make practical operational improvements fall on deaf ears, and then rapidly dry up. As Harvey-Jones again correctly points out: 'Every annual report by every chairman all over the world ends up by paying a tribute to "our people – our greatest resource". Yet boards of directors hardly ever take time out to look at the totality of the environment in which "our greatest resource" works.'

While going back to the floor is probably a healthy thing for most executives to do anyway, there are ways to save their blushes when they get there. One size won't fit all, but an appropriately designed and implemented performance measurement system that relates to the key elements of employee relationship management, and in which senior executives take a genuine interest, will normally have highly beneficial effects. Obtaining regular anonymous feedback from employees may be a feature of such a system, but that is just a way of measuring the outcomes and should, therefore, be just one aspect of the solution. By also ensuring that the right management measures are put in place, and that managers are made individually and collectively accountable for achieving target levels of performance, the desired change in behaviour patterns can be achieved. There is also a significant body of evidence now to demonstrate that taking good care of the 'interrelationship' that employees have with the organization will result in the positive impacts on the bottom line that senior executives crave. We shall explore this 'value chain' further in Chapter 8.

Supplier and Alliance Partner Relationship Management Issues

In many respects this section is the obverse of the Customer Relationships one. In principle, an organization wants much the same of its suppliers as its customers want of it. And suppliers want much the same of the organization as it wants from its customers. But of course entirely different people and disciplines are involved. Suppliers tend to have a greater overall importance in industrial and consumer goods companies than they do in pure services industries, and we reflect those differences here.

Managing Outsourced Manufacturing

Nike, the US sportswear company, is illustrative of a phenomenon that has grown massively over the past decade, during which there has been a strong trend towards outsourcing 'non-core' activities. However, it is also illustrative of the dangers that such strategic policies can bring upon companies if their execution of these policies is perceived to be exploitive of its suppliers or, more importantly, its suppliers' workers.

Nike manufactures virtually none of the trainers and garments that you and/or your children wear. It designs and develops its products and it ably markets and distributes them. It considers that those processes and capabilities are among its core competencies and that production is not. And so the task of physically making its products is outsourced under license to a host of external suppliers. In order to offer its customers (within its very particular market segment) competitively priced goods, while at the same time optimizing the value it provides to its shareholders, it arranges to have the vast majority of its products made thousands of miles away from its headquarters in Oregon, and its biggest markets in North America and Europe, in countries that have some of the world's lowest labour costs. About 500,000 workers in over 350 factories across the globe make Nike footwear and apparel. Does it have a core competence in managing its suppliers? This is open to debate. And it has been a very public and controversial one at that.

Since 1992, Nike has been the focus of international scrutiny of how huge Western companies treat their suppliers in some of the poorest parts of the world. It has frequently been accused of promoting the use of 'sweatshops' in Indonesia, Vietnam, China and South America, where labour abuses, forced overtime and unsanitary conditions abound. Activist groups, such as Global Exchange, bombarded the media alleging, for example, that seven-year-old Pakistani children sewed Nike soccer balls for 6 cents a day. By 1997–98, an anti-Nike campaign led by human rights activists culminated in several 'Protest

Nike' days in the US. Nike's initial response was sluggish, but quickly gathered momentum when it realized the damage that could be done to its brand and also to its college campus sales. It, therefore, introduced a code of conduct for its suppliers, created a remediation plan and implemented independent monitoring of its suppliers' factories. It even published the location of many of these factories, which it had previously refused to do on competitive grounds.

Nike now claims it is a market leader not only in shoe design but also in labour standards. However, each time it thinks it has won the publicity war, another damaging revelation surfaces. During the Sydney 2000 Olympics, the Australian arm of Nikewatch called for athletes to boycott Nike products and implored them to visit factories in south-east Asia. Recent findings by aid agencies claim that workers are still forced to work overtime and are still abused by their Taiwanese and Korean supervisors. A further report, by the Global Alliance for Workers and Communities in February 2001, uncovered allegations of sexual harassment and physical and verbal abuse in nine of Nike's Indonesian contract factories. Interviewees claimed two employees in different plants had died at work having been denied medical attention. Workers in one factory alleged that female recruits were encouraged to 'date' managers to ensure promotion. While 2.4 per cent of the 4,000 workers interviewed complained of 'sexual touching' by supervisors and managers. Nike, although it has born the brunt of the negative publicity campaigns, is not alone of course. Companies such as Gap, Reebok, Adidas, Levi Strauss, Liz Claiborne, Mattel and even Ikea have been actively addressing their global supplier management policies, many requiring factories to meet hundreds of detailed standards. Today, effective supplier management is a vital issue for many companies.

The Growth of Outsourcing

The march of supplier relationship trends through the last century is well illustrated by the automotive industry. Henry Ford's vertically integrated system of owning mines, blast furnaces, component manufacturing, product assembly and sales offices of the early part of the last century is legendary. It was also expensive and inefficient during a downturn in demand. In the 1920s, General Motors' Alfred Sloan decided that he could preserve the prevalent coordination advantages of a unified company, but impose the cost efficiency disciplines of the market, if the internal supply organizations were treated as independent businesses by giving then divisional status. Even 60 years later, about 70 per cent of the parts in each GM car and truck was made by its in-house parts divisions. By the 1950s, however, Ford – now under Henry Ford II – put out to bid, to completely independent supplier firms, many categories of components formerly supplied from within the company. These suppliers were given detailed drawings of the required parts and asked for their price per part. The lowest bidder then generally won a one-year contract to supply the part. The cost savings obtained through this approach led both companies to drastically reduce the level of internally produced components and, eventually, to allow their erstwhile component divisions to become independent companies, free to sell to competitors as well as to their former parents.

The relationship between vehicle manufacturers and their suppliers has undergone a seismic shift in recent years. Today, automotive suppliers no longer merely deliver batches of parts to order, but instead provide entire and often very complex modules, from complete suspension systems to ready-to-install driver cockpits. In Brazil, and in other fast-growing regions where car production is currently the subject of significant investment, entire greenfield assembly plants have been designed from scratch with adjoining 'supplier parks' populated by component manufacturers. At VW's truck and bus factory in Rio de Janeiro, suppliers have even been brought inside the factory to assemble modular units around a central production line.

The trend towards outsourcing is by no means exclusive to the automotive industry or to manufacturing businesses, many other industries and companies have followed suit. Outsourcing an organization's non-core activities has become one of the mantras of contemporary management thinking. The theory is that companies cannot be excellent at doing everything. They should, therefore, focus their attention and resources on doing those things that they do best, and those that help to give them a sustainable competitive advantage, so that they can better differentiate themselves from their competitors' offerings. The mundane tasks of, for example, processing invoices, collecting and collating accounting data, or administering human resource management needs can be carried out by organizations that specialize in these fields of expertise. Why pour your company's capital into buying warehouses and a fleet of trucks, when there are many specialist companies who make their living out of doing nothing else? Of course, these outsourcers do need to make a profit, but – given their focus, expertise and scale – they are likely to be significantly more efficient too. A whole new outsourcing industry has sprung up over just the last few years. Market research firm Input estimates that the market for IT, business process, and processing services outsourcing will grow by 19 per cent a year until 2005, at which point it will be worth $260 billion.

Managing Supplier Relationships

Supplier management, or purchasing, is one of the least recognized activities in most organizations. Even after a decade of supply chain management and outsourcing hubris, the lot of the purchasing executive seems to have little more kudos than it did in 1991 when a report found:[36]

> A recent survey of 250 purchasing managers in over two dozen countries – in such industries as pharmaceuticals, consumer products, and laboratory supplies – showed that less than half agreed with the statement, 'Purchasing is highly respected and valued'. Often the activity is not closely monitored or measured.

A relatively small band of purchasing specialists – a tiny proportion of most company's headcount – often have control over a vast proportion of its operating costs. Typically, this amounts to 65 to 85 per cent in the majority of manufacturing companies and one-third to two-thirds of operating costs in more service-oriented companies. Not all companies, however, have a central purchasing function or shared service. Many divest the task to individual business units and local operating units in particular geographic regions, countries and districts. In purchasing, the procurement of goods and services is not the same as ordering them. So, many companies negotiate standard contracts with major suppliers centrally, based on rolled-up volumes across the group, and then issue a preferred supplier price schedule for local 'purchasing officers' to call off the specific quantities of goods or services that they need. Central purchasing groups need to target the high value, high overlap commodities purchased across the organization, which are typically not fully leveraged by localized purchasing agreements – for example, computer hardware and software, pallets, international transportation services, and so on. This requires data and analysis in order to gain an understanding of where the real opportunities lie.

Supplier management, therefore, has become a vital – if under-appreciated – skill-set in most companies. For example, Ford found when it started using external suppliers more extensively that it then had to develop the processes and capabilities to manage these suppliers. Ford's QOS (Quality Operating System) procedures for managing its suppliers and the quality of the components they produce in a very formal and structured way – known originally as Q101, and latterly as Q1 – became another Ford legend that was widely copied in other highly supplier-reliant industries, such as electronics. This system demands that measures are used to track the quality of components not only throughout the supplier's production process but also to trace it back into the supplier's supplier processes so that, in theory at least, the whole supply chain is kept under strict quality control. While suppliers may get irritated by the burden of implementing different quality control and measurement systems for each of their major customers, it is nevertheless true to say that such systems are generally far more effective than the standard accreditation systems (such as ISO 9000) to which buyers sometimes insist that their suppliers adhere, but which have highly variable results. While perhaps imposed on them, the advantages of practices such as SPC (Statistical Process Control) have not gone completely unnoticed by the suppliers themselves.

The Differing Nature of Supplier Relationships

A predominantly dictatorial approach is typical of the autocratic (no pun intended) style of supplier management developed by the US automotive industry, but which is prevalent in several European assemblers' supply chains too. Here the customer–supplier relationship is essentially an adversarial and bullying one. For instance, if new model sales do not reach forecast levels, the unit costs of components rise at the very time that pressure grows to cut prices and, therefore, to pare costs. The assembler will then typically respond by seeking alternative bids for parts at lower cost. These are huge companies and, therefore, have the 'whip-hand' in terms of the procurement power they wield and the purchasing practices they adopt. Incumbent suppliers, who have just tooled up and are likely to be already selling at below cost, may then be unceremoniously dumped in favour of a lower bidder. As Womack, Jones and Roos observed in their book *The Machine That Changed The World*: 'This step no doubt cuts costs in the short term but reconfirms all suppliers, including the new winners, in the belief that information must be guarded from the assembler and that trust placed in a long-term relationship is trust misplaced.'

There is, however, an alternative way. Japanese automotive assemblers, and especially Toyota, embrace an altogether different approach to managing relationships with their first-tier suppliers, who provide complete sub-assemblies of components. The first-tier suppliers then tend to largely replicate the relationship with their second-tier suppliers. The essential features of this approach can be summed up as follows:

- Long-term relationships with a few key suppliers that are seldom changed.
- Key suppliers are involved in new model development at an early design stage.
- They have a mutually co-operative and trusting interrelationship with the assembler.
- They do not bid for work on a price basis, but instead are given target costs to achieve.
- They take on responsibility for designing, developing and integrating major sub-components to given performance specifications.
- There is a recognition that production costs can be reduced over time through continuous improvement programmes, but this can only be gained through experience of manufacturing the sub-assemblies.
- The company and its suppliers build cross-functional teams to smooth process flows and eliminate waste.
- The supplier's costs are freely interchanged with the assembler and the benefits of productivity improvements are shared.

- Suppliers also share information with each other, especially benchmark data, through 'supplier clubs' and work co-operatively to improve performance through the application of best practices (in the knowledge that if the assembly line goes down because one of them has a quality problem or fails to deliver, it will affect them all).

Because so-called 'lean producers', like Toyota, have long devolved much of the responsibility for engineering and making parts to their suppliers, by the late 1980s their internal cost of making a vehicle represented just 27 per cent of the whole. General Motors, by contrast, added 70 per cent to the value of a vehicle. Benchmarks show that Toyota needed just 37,000 employees to produce 4 million vehicles, while GM needed 850,000 employees to produce 8 million vehicles. A large part of that difference was due to the more sophisticated relationship Toyota had – and continues to have – with its suppliers. And yet, in 1987, GM had 6,000 employees in its parts purchasing operations while Toyota required only 337.[37] Toyota has spent Y3 billion–Y4 billion ($28 million–$37 million) in recent years on developing network computer links with its suppliers. It can now bring a car from the drawing board to production in 12 months, while US carmakers take as long as three years. These are remarkable differences in operating efficiency, created through advanced supplier relationship management practices, from which many other industries (and nations) could also learn and benefit.

Nick Oliver and Barry Wilkinson, in their book *The Japanization of British Industry*, describe the attempts of automotive suppliers to implement Japanese management practices in the early 1990s. This was not an entirely smooth process and, not unexpectedly, there were some rigorous reactions to the changes being enforced ('encouraged') upon them, dubbed by one Managing Director as 'Japanese Induced Terror'. Yet they also describe instances where first-tier suppliers were in the process of implementing 'strategic sourcing' initiatives with their own suppliers that emphasize the term 'co-makership', with the aim of reducing the incidence of non-conformances by integrating the supplier into the design process. By combining the product performance knowledge of the customer engineer with the process performance knowledge of the supplier, the objective was to achieve a more manufacturable design and increased levels of parts standardization. Naturally, some suppliers preferred the traditional 'arm's length' relationship, but most welcomed the 'leopard's new spots' one.

Which Way Works Best?

Of course not all Japanese manufacturers are 'world class' and, as Nissan so harshly discovered, highly efficient supply chains do not necessarily guarantee commercial success. The right product range, distinctive marketing flare and sound financial controls are needed too. In general, however, the Japanese have worked fastidiously at improving quality and productivity for decades, while their US and European counterparts were late starters (but have since tried to play catch-up), especially in terms of quality management. During this time many have come to realize that intimate long-term relationships with their suppliers is a crucial component of the struggle to optimize the supply chain and hence the cost of making vehicles. For more observations on the relative efficiency of automotive component manufacturers (see the box *Benchmarking Supplier Performance*).

Benchmarking Supplier Performance

In 1992, Accenture (then known as Andersen Consulting) teamed up with the University of Cambridge and Cardiff Business School to carry out a comparison of manufacturing performance in the Japanese and UK automotive components industries. The *Lean Enterprise Benchmarking Project* found that Japanese component factories outperformed the UK by a 2-to-1 margin in productivity and had a 100-to-1 quality differential.

One of the key reasons cited for the difference was the Japanese world-class plants' attention to supply chain management. The world-class and non-world-class plants had about the same number of suppliers, but the volume of business per supplier was twice as high in the world-class plants. There was also less 'buffering' in the world-class plants, such as fewer hours of inventory and more frequent deliveries between suppliers, plants and customers. More schedule stability in the world-class plants resulted in a much lower variation between what customers forecast one month before delivery and what they actually required. And, crucially, the difference in the incoming parts defect rate was 50-to-1 between world-class and non-world-class plants.

In a follow-up study in 1994 Accenture (Andersen Consulting), Cambridge and Cardiff examined the characteristics of high-performing automotive components manufacturers in nine countries around the world in their *Worldwide Manufacturing Competitiveness Study – The Second Lean Enterprise Report*. Of 71 plants included in the study, 13 showed both high productivity and high quality. Only five of the nine plants located in Japan were world class. Others were located in North America (3), France (3) and Spain (2).

In the area of supply chain quality, for example, it found that Japanese factories had incoming defect levels far below those in Spain, France, Italy, Germany, UK, US and Mexico. Inventories of incoming parts, levels of schedule variance and incoming late deliveries were all significantly better in the Japanese plants (and, remember, not all of these were rated as world class). The report also highlights the poor on-time delivery performance of 'second-tier' suppliers in the US. It says: 'This coupled with the high level of defective parts produced by the second-tier suppliers implies that these suppliers are not as advanced as their first-tier customers in terms of process control and discipline.'

One of the reasons often cited for such national differences is the level of sophistication in the buying organization's relationship with its suppliers. The latter benchmarking report addresses this in terms of benefits sharing and information exchange. It says: 'We measured the percentage of plants who have agreed rules with their customers and suppliers as to how the benefits of any joint cost reduction activities are shared. Such arrangements have gone furthest in Japan, although the UK leads the rest of the world, probably owing to the influence of the Japanese transplants.'

On the subject of information exchange the report notes: 'There are clear national differences in the use of suppliers' associations and again Japan stands out. Seventy-five per cent of the Japanese plants have customers who run suppliers' associations and they in turn run associations for their suppliers. In Japan, these associations take various forms, but typically serve as places for information exchange and learning within the supply base of a carmaker. Opinions about these associations vary, and there were conflicting views about their function and utility. Honda, for example, does not have a supplier association at all ... There is some supplier association activity at first-tier suppliers in the West, mainly in France and the UK, but this has not generally penetrated to the second tier of the industry. France provides an interesting alternative model to Japanese style supplier associations. Given the domination of the French industry by Renault and PSA, tacit co-ordination is easier than in countries with many customers. The French automotive components industry has a strong industry association, FIEV, which appears to perform many of the functions of the Japanese supplier associations, but at a national level. Knowledge about best practice was high in France, and the nature of the French industry facilitates the spread of learning.'

One final reflection on the 'Which way works best?' debate within the automotive industry – in 2001, JD Power, the market research agency, ranked Ford, one of the manufacturers that has a reputation in the trade for its less than fully collaborative relationships with its suppliers, as the worst among the world's top-seven carmakers in defects per vehicle.

What about other industries besides automotive? The grocery industry launched an initiative in the early 1990s, known as Efficient Consumer Response (or ECR). Leading members of the industry believed that as consumers became increasingly sophisticated and demanding, it needed to respond by being more efficient and by giving consumers 'More-for-Less'. The underlying concept that this initiative set out to achieve was to introduce a philosophy and practice of 'working together to fulfil consumer wishes better, faster and at less costs'. The essential idea was, first, that groceries manufacturers and the retailers who distribute their products to consumers needed to work together more closely to achieve mutual efficiencies and, second, that internal operational efficiencies within each type of organization also needed to be achieved if consumer value was to be fully realized.

Undoubtedly, some progress was made, especially through the implementation of retail EPOS (electronic point of sale) systems linked directly to major suppliers, who were then able to react more rapidly to supermarkets' replenishment needs. Others have implemented so-called collaborative planning systems (see the box *Collaborate or Die*).

Collaborate or Die

J Sainsbury, one of Britain's largest retailers, joined with several of its big suppliers to implement a collaborative planning system. The system allows suppliers to warn the supermarket of impending delays or shortages and lets Sainsbury warn suppliers of forthcoming promotions and potential surges in demand.

It claims that this application has led to a 25 per cent reduction in out-of-stock items. 'Quantities can be predicted and managed in a much more accurate way, whereas previously there was a difficulty in matching the correct stock to demand ratios,' says John Rowe, Sainsbury's director of logistics. 'With the new system we have clear ownership and control of the supply chain process and we can effectively keep products moving, allowing the supply chain to be far more responsive to the needs of our customers than it has ever been before. Companies really need to think about how they can work more closely with other companies around the world, be they suppliers or even competitors. The best way to use technology in this area is to collaborate on common functions, whereby everyone wins.'

This kind of technological solution to co-operation seems to be acceptable. However, the ECR movement as a whole largely petered out in the late 1990s because, some say, the largest – and apparently impenetrable – barrier to be overcome was that of trust. The long-standing enmity between food manufacturers and retailers over sharing cost information and the distribution of realized benefits was too ingrained for much more progress to be made. The impasse may have been exacerbated too by the parallel initiatives of the major retail grocers to rapidly expand their range of private label products, which often look remarkably similar to the branded equivalent, but are sold at significantly lower prices. Branded foods manufacturers, on the other hand, need to support their products with sizeable marketing promotions and, therefore, were unable to compete on pricing with unadvertised but carefully placed (on supermarket shelves) private label goods. Retailers are always shy about sharing profit margin information on individual product line items (and, in any case, these depend to a large degree on how they allocate certain costs); while manufacturers hold deep suspicions that cost benefits passed through to the retailer will not be passed on to customers, but simply added to profits. So-called 'open book accounting' approaches, where everyone involved can see what is going on, are unsurprisingly rare in the grocery industry.

Single or Multiple Sources of Supply?

Chemicals are just molecules. Outside of specialized pharmaceutical and fine chemical formulations, there is not much of a design element. Neither is branding so important. Polyethylene is polyethylene. Why, for example, would any business want to have a partnership with a bulk chemicals supplier, when they can buy from several suppliers and trade them off against each other on price? Several reasons. Using a single source of supply means that the whole annual off-take can be used to negotiate a volume discount. Greater raw material consistency is likely to be experienced in production. The organization has to process far fewer supplier invoices. More efficient communication mechanisms, such as Electronic Data Interchange (EDI), can be set up between buyer and supplier, or it may even be that the supplier can be persuaded to manage the purchaser's inventory of the product it supplies by monitoring stock levels (for example, some liquids and gases suppliers use remote telemetry techniques) and by arranging appropriate replenishment shipments, further relieving the purchaser of a not insignificant administrative task.

Not likely to convince the accountants and not a specific industry characteristic, but significant nonetheless, suppliers keep in touch with the industry they supply. It's their job to know what is going on. They are far more likely to volunteer competitor information to their best clients if they believe that co-operation is the 'name of the game'. Much strategic information can be gained through such informal connections.

Finally, the one thing that businesses which use large quantities of organic chemicals fear most is volatility in the price of oil. Products derived from oil are subject to rapid price fluctuations too. If these supply-side price increases come through before selling prices can be renegotiated with customers, then margins will inevitably suffer (unless other cost savings can be achieved). This, and its cyclical nature, has always been the bane of the chemicals industry. A long-term supply partnership on a predominantly single source basis, however, is far more likely to be able to agree a mechanism to achieve greater levels of price stability than can be negotiated by market opportunist buyers.

However, one sector of the chemicals industry needn't worry about that. Manufacturers of industrial and medical gases oxygen, nitrogen and argon (such as BOC, Praxair, Air Products, Air Liquide and Linde) don't need raw materials suppliers – they simply suck what they need out of the air! But, instead, they do have to buy relatively sophisticated equipment in order to make pressurized gases and deliver them to their customers all over the world. The principles relating to supplier partnerships will still apply in almost all sectors of purchasing.

Leapfrog Relationships Within the Supply Chain

Collaborations between customers and suppliers need not necessarily be confined to raw materials and operational capital expenditure items. Back in the late 1960s and early 1970s, DuPont's textile fibre division was early in collaborating with and actively supporting its UK customers' marketing initiatives. It shared a substantial part of its marketing budget with those of major carpet retailers and tufted carpet manufacturers in order to help promote its 'Antron' brand of stain-resistant nylon carpet fibres. It also formed marketing partnerships with ladieswear retailers and the manufacturers of so-called 'intimate apparel', promoting its 'Lycra' brand of elastomeric fibres for lingerie and 'Cantrece' fine-denier nylon fibres for hosiery. Apart from providing in-store promotions and advertising, it hosted a number of major trade fashion shows and also sponsored a national 'lovely legs' competition, made fashionable by the then recent arrival of the mini-skirt and the necessity of tights. The point is though that rather than just marketing to its direct customers, the manufacturers, it looked forward in the supply chain and sought to pool its considerable marketing and branding clout, co-operating with its customer's customers in order to influence its customer's customer's customers [sic]. The 'pull-through effect' on its fibres sales could then be measured.

More recently, for example, Intel has achieved a similar feat through its 'Intel Inside' campaign with computer manufacturers. Nevertheless, such success stories in the use of branding and co-marketing efforts are still relatively rare in the world of manufacturing. Where they do exist, however, their effectiveness and efficiency clearly need to be tracked.

The Trend Towards Joint Ventures

Although not new, business alliances and joint ventures have become ever more popular instruments of collaboration over the last decade. These vary from relatively small and specific initiatives, such as major drugs companies' co-operations with tiny biotechnology development companies to huge deals such as the $4 billion turnover joint venture announced by Coca-Cola and Procter & Gamble in 2001 to sell fruit juices and salty snacks [although, at the time of writing, this venture seems to be in some jeopardy; but there are many other such arrangements, such as those between pharmaceuticals companies to market each other's products in different geographical regions]. The odd thing, given their popularity, is that few of them actually work. For example, Accenture's Alliance Survey in 1999 found that just 39 per cent of alliances were considered unequivocal successes by the executives surveyed, while nearly one in three were considered outright failures. Of the rest, 17 per cent wind down as priorities and people change, 9 per cent are bought out by one of the partners and 5 per cent are spun off as independent entities.

On the other hand, alliances do have the advantage of generally being less messy and traumatic than full mergers. In fact, many of the larger alliances frequently consist of a series of joint ventures. For example, the General Motors alliance with Fiat of Italy (involving a 20 per cent minority shareholding), announced in 2000, plans to benefit from pooling their purchasing, sharing technologies and exploring possible common platforms for volume cars. The companies expect to cut the mounting development costs for new models, while eradicating overlaps in research, component development and supply chain management. However, unlike a full merger, the individual partners apparently intend to retain their own separate manufacturing facilities (perpetrating the endemic over-capacity which exists within the industry), continue their own end-product distribution channels and actively compete against each other in certain markets.

This is an increasingly common phenomenon in today's business world, sometimes known as 'co-opetition'. In this scenario, there exists a spirit of co-operation to reduce costs but an ongoing competitive approach to winning and supplying customers. It is not difficult to imagine, therefore, how these kinds of relationships do generate difficult-to-manage tensions – especially in terms of how much information and performance measurement data is transferred between the two organizations – and how easy it can be for trust to evaporate and the joint venture to become dysfunctional.

Determining the Nature of Supplier Relationships

Should all supplier relationships become partnerships? Accenture's research in a number of industries shows that indiscriminate collaboration is as unhealthy a practice in business as it is in other facets of life. Some relationships are dangerous, others waste time and money, and only a few justify taking the risks demanded by fully integrated collaboration (see the box *Dangerous Liaisons*).

Dangerous Liaisons

Accenture has developed a framework for analyzing customer–supplier relationships. This is based on the key criteria of market sophistication and operational complexity that interact to shape four basic types of supply chain relationships. These four categories are: Transactional, Unique, Operational and Integrated. The features of each of these are summarized in the diagram below:

The right fit

Determining what kind of relationships you should have with each of your suppliers should be a function of the operational complexity and the sophistication of the suppliers' marketplace

Operational complexity	Low market sophistication	High market sophistication
High	**Operational** Collaboration is driven by operational requirements	**Integrated** Collaboration is driven by both operational requirements and supply market forces
Low	**Transactional** Supply market is fragmented and operational requirements are low	**Unique** Collaboration is driven by strategic importance of the commodity but requires little operational integration

Operational complexity influencing factors

- Length of component cycle
- Order lead time
- Distribution network infrastructure
- Custom design
- On allocation/not on allocation
- Volume units

Market sophistication influencing factors

- Market structure (e.g. monopoly oligopoly, open market)
- Brand impact
- Unit cost
- Barriers to entry

Clearly, there are certain circumstances under which collaboration with a supplier has the potential to cut costs, increase revenues or lower risk. Under some market and operating conditions, suppliers deserve a great deal of attention and consideration. Under other circumstances, suppliers will provide their goods and services without any expectation of commitment or co-operation beyond timely payment of the invoice. There is no point in investing more than is necessary in any supplier relationship – or, conversely less than enough.

Relationships with suppliers ought to be dictated by operating and market conditions; this framework can help define the appropriate relationship – the bounds of intimacy, as it were – for each component organization in any supply chain.

Source: Adapted from 'Dangerous Liaisons' by Timothy L. Mould and C. Edwin Starr, *Outlook*, 2000, Number 2.

Information sharing is fundamental to achieving the business objectives of supply chain relationships. In operational relationships, it may be necessary and sufficient to share planning and forecasting data. Integrated collaborative relationships, though, typically involve even more information sharing – for example, about capacity, production schedules, inventories, marketing plans and costs. This degree of sharing will inevitably deepen the collaboration and build such a high degree of trust that competitors will find it very hard to threaten the relationship by simply undercutting on price.

Internet Exchanges

Much has been made – in the press, at least – of the potential of internet exchanges and the purchasing benefits that will be derived through Business-to-Business (B2B) transactions. Buyers will get better prices through rapid auctions, while sellers will get access to a wider market for their products. Essentially, B2B e-commerce cuts companies' costs in three ways. First, it reduces procurement costs, making it easier and faster to find the cheapest supplier. Second, it cuts the cost of processing transactions. And third, it allows better supply chain management and makes possible tighter inventory control, so that firms can reduce their stocks or even eliminate them. Through these three channels B2B e-commerce reduces firms' production costs, by increasing efficiency or by squeezing suppliers' profit margins. In economics jargon, the economy's aggregate supply curve shifts to the right.

The biggest savings are likely to come in procurement. A report by Martin Brookes and Zaki Wahhaj, at Goldman Sachs, estimates that firms' possible savings from purchasing over the internet vary from 2 per cent in the coal industry to up to 40 per cent in electronic components. Brookes and Wahhaj reckon that doing business with suppliers online could reduce the cost of making a car, for instance, by as much as 14 per cent. Their report looks at industries that account for about one-quarter of America's GDP, and uses input–output accounts to include second-round effects of cost savings – i.e. that lower costs in one industry will reduce the price of inputs for other industries. They conclude that, in the five big rich economies, B2B e-commerce could reduce average prices across the economy by almost 4 per cent. And this probably understates likely cost savings because it is based on lower procurement costs alone. While this prediction was given – just a few months ago – at the height of the B2B internet hype, we wonder whether Goldman Sachs is sticking to their analysis today.

B2B certainly promises big benefits. In 2000, British Telecom announced that it intended to make 95 per cent of routine purchases online. It claims that procuring goods and services online will reduce the average cost of processing a transaction by 90 per cent and reduce the direct costs of goods and services it purchases by 11 per cent. Guilbert, one of the Niceday stationery brands, reports that an order placed through their e-procurement system costs $80, where it used to cost $135. In 2000, GE alone bought $6 billion worth of goods online. It claims to have cut transaction times from two weeks to 24 hours and reduced the average contract cost by 70 per cent. United Technologies, the maker of Otis elevators, Sikorsky helicopters, Pratt & Whitney aircraft engines and Carrier heating and air conditioning equipment, expects the number of supplier invoices it handles to fall from 300,000 a year to 12,000 by automating its indirect purchases. In March 2000, BASF sold several tonnes of methanol over an internet auction site for the first time. The deal was done by one or two people in just three hours. Under normal procedures, it claims, a similar transaction would have taken six people a week to complete. However, white-collar employees at BASF are concerned about resultant job losses as the company ramps up the volume of its online sales.

Nestlé is a partner in CPGmarket.com, a pan-European B2B exchange for the consumer packaged goods industry. It reckons the biggest benefit has been to give it a view of the entire supply chain. 'Previously that data was all over the place, but getting a clear view of the entire chain has been amazing, and gives us a big edge,' says Chris Tyas, its supply chain director. 'We can improve efficiency radically and make sure our customers and suppliers always know what is going on.'

In theory, B2B exchanges offer big companies big savings: Ford, GM and DaimlerChrysler have set up a joint exchange called Covisint to buy components from suppliers over the internet. It is expected to have a potential $300bn in worldwide parts purchasing. The companies first established joint ventures with IT businesses – Ford with Oracle, a leader in the database market, and General Motors with Commerce One, a fast-growing supplier of web-based procurement software. The new ventures were set not only to handle Ford and GM's own purchasing requirements, but also those of their suppliers and partners, thereby vastly enhancing purchasing power and economies of scale. However, after some dissension among their suppliers over multiple exchanges, Ford and General Motors subsequently agreed to merge their online purchasing operations. Then DaimlerChrysler, and subsequently Renault and Nissan – and possibly Toyota – announced that they were seeking to join the consortium. Morgan Stanley, the investment bank, estimated that B2B procurement could save the automobile manufacturers $2,700 per vehicle. However, a separate study – by Deutsche Bank Alex Brown and the Roland Berger consultancy – suggested that savings would work out at only about $1,188 per vehicle. Nevertheless, when carmakers are making $700 net profit per car on average, that is still a considerable prize.

The sage Toyota though is wary about the exchange and may not attach itself to it. If it does, it has said that it is likely only to use it to trade in basic commodity items, such as fasteners and office supplies, with a focus on its US operations. Quality assurance and security are critical issues for them. The company's executive vice-president in charge of procurement, Tadaaki Jagawa, explains: 'Our parts are not purchased through a bidding process. We buy them by building a relationship with our suppliers over time ... We meet face-to-face with every one of our suppliers. We are continually traipsing all over the world to see the factories and the managers that make our products, to see if they really make high-quality goods. You just can't do that on the web.' He adds to this judgement his concerns about exchange security: 'The other companies are our rivals, and we are competing on parts ... we do not share information about our components.' Nevertheless, he admits: 'We have to keep up with the changing times. So we cannot deny that we will have to use the internet.' However, rather than participating in industry-wide consortia, several companies have overcome the security issue by electing to run their own 'private exchanges'. Already Volkswagen claims to have conducted auctions on its private exchange worth over $1 billion.

Building a huge shared exchange turns out to be more complicated and expensive than anyone imagined. Fourteen months after Covisint's creation, Forbes Global reported:[38] 'The B2B exchange is floundering and has no hope of living up to its hype ... Covisint's owners have spent a combined $170 million on their fat company, including $50 million on a pack of consulting firms. The site now burns through $12 million a month. The partners expect to spend up to $350 million before Covisint breaks even, which they hope will be before the end of 2002. And for all that cash Covisint last year handled less than 1 per cent of the carmakers' purchases. This year it aims for 30 per cent, $75 billion, a nearly impossible goal.'

Meanwhile, in Europe, it turns out according to a 2001[39] study that only 27 per cent of almost 60 first-tier automotive component suppliers have even heard of Covisint and nearly two-thirds have no strategy for using online trade exchanges. This would suggest that there is still much to be done to win suppliers over to this new mode of trading.

In an economy taking a break from exponential growth at the time of writing, the stampede is over and many companies are reining back their investments in such schemes. Nevertheless, the quest for purchasing efficiencies is unlikely to deter them for long. The automotive experience does suggest though that the capital needed to build such exchanges (and probably to maintain them too) is going to be far higher than previously estimated. Their efficiency and effectiveness will need to be monitored carefully.

By no means everyone is convinced that more and more investment in IT solutions is the answer to supply chain improvement either. Quite apart from how good the software itself may be (and there have been some very public criticisms of certain vendors' implementations), few companies can demonstrate tangible benefits (see the box *Supply Chain Efficiency? – Drop IT*).

Supply Chain Efficiency? – Drop IT

Companies are on the wrong track if they think that information technology is the solution to streamlining their supply chains. They have been putting 10 per cent of their IT investment into supply chain management software and spending has been growing at 20 per cent per annum. Even in the downturn, a recent supply chain study by Bain & Co. shows that supply chain management is still a priority with 68 per cent of executives. Yet the average company's supply chain is half as efficient as the industry's best and inventory turns have barely changed in a decade. Why then are so many companies making so little headway?

The secret is not in IT – everybody can buy the same software and do a bit of customizing to make it fit the business. The top performers in this field – exemplars include Wal-Mart, Dell, Nokia and Toyota – understand that supply chain processes and disciplines are vital to containing costs. They spend just 4.2 per cent of their revenues on their supply chains, compared with over 9 per cent for the average company.

The Bain study found that almost 80 per cent of companies' efforts were focused inside the organization. Of those running supply chain improvement initiatives, less than 10 per cent reach out to their network of key suppliers. Furthermore, fewer than 25 per cent of companies polled have full information on their supply chain. Not tracking performance means not knowing how much their supply chain inefficiencies cost and that impacts the bottom line.

Dell, for example, claims that its few days of inventory – compared with more than a month for most competitors – adds five percentage points to its margin. Wal-Mart makes direct deliveries for products with rapid obsolescence and time-to-market pressure, putting other products through traditional distribution centres when velocity matters less than cost. Nokia's advantage comes from product designs that share parts and make its vendors' work easier, while its competitors struggle with complexity.

While better IT systems can help, the big benefits come from first examining the end-to-end process, then re-engineering the supply chain for efficiency and effectiveness, and tracking performance for continuous improvement.

Source: 'Weakest Links in the Supply Chain', *Financial Times*, 11 December 2001

Within more and more industries, it is becoming apparent that the competitive game is no longer played by the contestants Company A versus Company B. The game has become a team sport played by supply chain network versus supply chain network, with an increasing reliance on collaborative relationships to create value. It is a high-stakes game that has considerable potential risks when there is a significant investment in time, human resources, information technology, proprietary information and, not least, performance measurement systems to monitor progress.

Regulator and Community Relationship Management Issues

This section completes our examination of the key stakeholders that are vitally important to the measurement and management systems that corporations need to develop in today's business environment. If you thought some aspects of other stakeholder relationships and their attendant measurement systems were underdeveloped in many companies, you are more than likely to enjoy reading what follows. Or – health warning – you may become even more deeply concerned about the adequacy of your own company's existing performance measurement and management systems.

The Regulatory Phenomenon

Even Jack Welch, CEO of General Electric and one of recent history's most popularly celebrated corporate executives for sound judgement, misjudged the impact that regulators can have on his business. A whole host of other executives have made the same underestimate.

When, in October 2000, GE announced its $35 billion takeover bid for Honeywell in a press conference. Jack Welch repelled an investor question about antitrust problems with the deal. The investor asked whether the deal would take four months to complete. 'No, I think faster than that,' replied Welch. 'Oh, I believe this deal will be done by the end of February.' The European Commission's decision to open an in-depth inquiry into the merger at the end of February 2001 added a significant and embarrassing delay to the ambitious timetable anticipated by Welch. Furthermore, if GE were obliged to offer substantial concessions to the Commission in Brussels, the rationale for the deal would be severely dented. Jeffrey Immelt, GE's chairman-elect and Jack Welch's successor, implied that it was prepared to abort the deal if the regulators imposed overly stringent conditions. Regulators then questioned GE's rivals and customers about issues raised by the deal as part of a four-month inquiry. However, even after GE offered some conciliatory concessions, the deal to merge two US companies was blocked by a European regulator.

This is just one example of the kind of powers that regulators exert today. In many countries all over the world, regulatory powers have increased substantially over the past decade. Several factors have helped to create this phenomenon:

1 increased privatization of formerly government-owned institutions
2 greater public protection legislation (e.g. product liability and environmental concerns)
3 increased employee protection legislation, particularly in a regulation harmonizing Europe
4 an extraordinary escalation in merger and acquisition activities on both sides of the Atlantic
5 revelations about the scale of companies' anticompetitive abuses.

FDA regulators have long held the power to close food and pharmaceutical plants that do not match up to stringent health and safety regulations, but other regulatory bodies have only recently been in a position to, for example, fine companies for taking part in price fixing cartels. It is not so much that large quantities of legislation have been enacted to make this happen – although, in many countries, the law has certainly been strengthened – but more that regulators have discovered that they do actually have the 'teeth' to take action, such as by raiding the offices of suspected companies in order to establish evidence of their anticompetitive practices. Consequently, having achieved some successes, they have turned their attention to more controversial abuses and to major corporations that they would never have dreamed of tackling head-on just a few years ago. It is likely that a 'snitch factor' has come into play too. Competitors of major companies are now far more likely to report perceived abuses to the respective regulatory authorities and this has further fuelled the volume of cases requiring investigation.

Many former publicly-owned monopolies have been privatized within the past decade. Gas, electricity, water and telecommunications utilities, coal, oil, steel, transportation and mail monopolies have been taken out of direct government control in many countries and shares sold wholly or partially to financial institutions and the general public – sometimes at knock-down prices, sometimes not. However, although they have been removed from government ownership they have certainly not been relieved of government control. Most are subject to close regulatory control by influential and powerful government agencies. This is essential where a monopoly (or virtual monopoly) exists. It is inevitable that a significant amount of time must elapse before a real competitive market for their formerly monopolistic products and services can emerge; and indeed, in some, a true market may never do so because of the sheer cost of entering the market and establishing the required infrastructure.

Ofwat, the UK regulatory body with responsibility for overseeing the operations of the UK's water companies recently completed a substantial price review. The outcome of which was that water companies across the UK were forced to reduce their prices on average by 12.3 per cent. This equates to a reduction in annual operating profits across the sector of between £800 and £850 million.[26] Different water companies were forced to reduce their prices by different amounts, partly as a result of their performance against performance measures defined not by the business concerned, or by the consumers, but by the regulator and his team.

We find, however, that there is a tendency to imagine that regulators are only a significant factor for these recently privatized, formerly government-owned, industries. Understandably, these industries tend to draw media attention because of their often very public and consumer-oriented face. The inevitable tensions that frequently exist between regulators, acting on behalf of consumers, and the directors of former monopolies that are in the process of adjusting to shareholder pressures are the stuff about which journalists dream. However, to suppose that these are the only industries where regulators matter is a massive misconception. The fact is that all businesses and not-for-profit organizations are subject to regulatory pressures to a greater or lesser extent. And the trend is definitely towards greater.

The purpose of regulatory bodies of course is to obtain and put in place legal powers; to make judgements; to set performance targets; and to intervene where abuses exist and can be proven. Regulations are intended to protect customers, employees, suppliers, investors and communities from malpractices. They seek to control what organizations are and are not allowed to do and to moderate corporate (mis)behaviours within the given standards they define. The penalties for non-compliance range from the veto or qualification of a strategic plan (such as a merger or acquisition) to substantial fines and jail sentences for senior executives.

Other Critical – *Highly Critical* – Stakeholders

Complying with regulatory requirements is just one aspect of this phenomenon. Communities, pressure groups and the media – press, web and TV reports – are becoming increasingly important facets of maintaining, and often defending, corporate performance in the realm of public opinion. Opinion can quickly translate into reputation and that really does matter. It affects whether customers want to buy from you, whether employees want to work for you and whether suppliers want to deal with you. Yet many companies seem to be virtually oblivious to getting a handle on the measurement and, therefore, the management of this fundamental issue.

Where regulatory powers are absent, but certain perceived abuses exist, there is a tendency for pressure groups to evolve. These aim either to create the demand for more stringent regulation or, in the absence of provisional standards that are likely to be legally established in the near future, to create sufficient public outrage that their efforts lead to changes in corporate behaviours. Organizations such as Greenpeace, Friends of the Earth and other vigilante organizations have been prepared to take a stand against arrogant multinational companies who put their own self-interest – and those of its shareholders – ahead of the broader interests of society. Their several successes in helping to institute new regulatory powers and in embarrassing companies into modifying their attitudes through co-ordinated media campaigns has been a significant feature of business during the past decade or so. (See the box *Genetically Modified Market* for a classic example of this phenomenon.)

Genetically Modified Market

A recent history has emerged of 'blue chip' companies who have fundamentally underestimated the importance of communicating with all key stakeholders in their business; such has been the contemporary corporate emphasis on investors' interests. Their neglect of the 'radar systems' to track the wants and needs of other stakeholders has caused tangible damage to their respective reputations as public companies.

In February 1999, the *Financial Times* reported that: 'When the next book about great public relations disasters is written, it is safe to bet that it will be dominated by the story of Monsanto's woes over genetically modified (GM) foods in Europe. It is the biggest fiasco since Shell became the target of public outrage over plans to sink the Brent Spar oil platform in the North Atlantic.'

Monsanto's mistake was in failing to foresee public reaction to their plans, allowing themselves to be wrong-footed by the subsequent outcry. The report indicated that:

- As a US company, it badly misunderstood the differences in attitudes towards nutrition in Europe and the US (following controversies over 'mad cow' disease and 'artificial ingredients').
- It failed to recognize that consumers would resent being asked to shoulder the risks of a technology – dubbed 'Frankenstein foods' by the press – that brought them few obvious rewards.
- It thought international trade agreements would force Europe to open its doors to GM products whether it liked them or not, but reckoned without public concerns about the competence of regulators.

Monsanto's chief executive admitted at the time that in the public relations area: 'Greenpeace is doing a better job than we are.' Its failure to effectively monitor a broad enough range of stakeholders' wants and needs and take appropriate actions to address their concerns led to a consortium of leading European supermarket chains to drop all private-label goods containing GM products. One retailer who pioneered the boycott commented: 'The GM issue has done more for our image than anything we have ever said on the value of frozen foods.' The issue subsequently escalated further and seriously impacted the company's European ambitions. Monsanto was taken over by Pharmacia in 2000.

Success has done little to pacify organized pressure groups' level of activity. They take the view that there is much that needs reform. Highly media-centred disruptive actions are the easiest and usually most effective way to get attention. For example, an internet campaign co-ordinated by Greenpeace against Coca-Cola persuaded the drinks company to change its mind about the use of hydrofluorocarbons (HFCs) in its refrigerators at the Sydney Olympic Games. In the majority of cases, the experience has been that pressure group activitists are prepared to go to extensive – even excessive – ends to achieve their public and governmental recognition aims. Few corporations can afford not to take notice. Those that bury their heads in the sand will only make it more certain that they will be the subject of significant amounts of adverse publicity, boycotts, attacks on employees and their possessions, plus intimidating threats to their major customers, shareholders, investment bankers, and so on.

Newspaper editors were particularly titillated when bra manufacturers Triumph International became embroiled in a protest over its manufacturing plant in Burma (Myanmar). The protesters objected to the Swiss company's support of a regime run by a military junta that openly abuses human rights and they wished to make sure their views were well publicized. Not difficult – the campaign was backed up by a dramatic image of a woman wearing a barbed wire bra and posters urging women everywhere to: 'Support breasts, not dictators'.

Most organizations are ill-prepared for this attention. Companies need to have these organizations well and truly on their radar screens and have their media relations machines ready to address the challenges they can activate. Being aware does not necessarily mean a need to capitulate to demands, but it does mean being fully informed as to where the missiles are coming from and how much destructive power they are carrying. To be informed should be to be prepared. Provided that this vital intelligence is used appropriately, then relevant responses can be crafted. But they may also need to be supported by the law (see the box *Fighting for Life*).

Fighting for Life

Huntingdon Life Sciences is a UK drugs-testing company that has been targeted by animal rights activists, who have taken the law into their own hands and very nearly brought about its bankruptcy. Stephens, a US investment bank, saved the company from the brink of receivership in January 2001.

The anti-vivisection group, Stop Huntingdon Animal Cruelty, has waged a long, bitter and violent battle against HLS, targeting its shareholders, customers and employees. Barclays, Philips & Drew, HSBC, Credit Suisse First Boston, Citibank, Bank of New York and Merrill Lynch have all been targeted by SHAC and, concerned for their employees' safety, have cut their investment links with HLS. Not surprisingly, Stephens is the latest bank to receive attention from the activists. Market-makers Winterflood and Dresdner Kleinwort Wasserstein threw in the towel too. Customers such as GlaxoSmithKline, British Biotech and DuPont Pharma – who, after all, are legally bound to have their drugs tested before they can be marketed in the country of use – have also been bullied. Bill Barry, a director of DuPont Pharma's UK operations, received threatening letters at his home address, had protesters sitting on his roof, and both his and his wife's car were damaged with paint stripper. Brian Cass, HLS's managing director, was attacked outside his home and beaten by three hooded assailants wielding baseball bats. Another senior manager at the firm was also attacked as he returned home at night.

The government is considering changes to its criminal justice legislation to crack down on animal rights extremists and directors of companies at risk may be allowed to keep their home address private.

In spite of their sometimes aggressive tactics, organizations like Greenpeace claim that they are developing an increasingly constructive relationship with companies. Indeed, a surprisingly large number of prominent industrial executives – for example, from BP, Unilever and, more recently, Monsanto – have appeared at conferences organized by Greenpeace. Thilo Bode, a political economist and former banker, who is Greenpeace International's executive director says: 'Corporations are very susceptible to public opinion and vulnerable to consumer pressure.' Companies, therefore, face a trade-off between the cost of addressing an environmental issue and the cost of the damage to their image if they do not. 'The really interesting thing is we have the best talks with companies we are having campaigns against,' he says. Greenpeace talks, for example, to BP's chief executive Sir John Browne despite campaigning against its exploration work in the Arctic. 'I say: "You are an adversary at the moment but we think that you can change things",' Bode explains.

Social Responsibility

The emergence of the 'green movement' has also had a significant impact on regulatory activity – particularly, in Europe. For example, new laws relating to the recycling of packaging materials have been enacted in Germany, and other countries expect to introduce them in the near future too. The automotive manufacturing industry also faces pressures to take responsibility for the full lifecycle of the vehicles they produce. The European Commission is pursuing an initiative to make manufacturers responsible for recycling their own products.

The 'end-of-life vehicle directive' is expected to be implemented fully by 2007. Under its terms, vehicle makers will have to bear the expense of recycling their cars, buses and trucks. The directive requires that 85 per cent of the weight of all new vehicles sold in the European Union after 2007 be made of reclaimed materials. A further directive, expected to be implemented a year earlier, bears the unlikely acronym 'WEEED' – the waste of electrical and electronic equipment directive. Under this legislation, manufacturers – and, potentially, even retailers of own label products – must collect and recycle their electrical products, such as freezers, washing machines, personal computers, television sets and electrical toys. The directive sets targets for the amounts of production that must be recycled, from 50 per cent for toys to 75 per cent for big household appliances. The principle adopted by the Commission is that it is the polluter who should pay.

The US, the world's largest industrial polluter, has so far remained largely oblivious to this movement but it too faces many environmental issues – especially in California, where local authorities seem unable to manage electricity supplies but have long taken a far more relevant and urgent position on pollution than Washington typically does. At the time of writing, the US government also faces much global criticism over its attitude towards the Kyoto accord on global pollution reduction targets. But could the US be missing an economic trick here? What is the impact of 'greening' on companies' profitability? Surely there is a divide between shareholder interests and behaving as a responsible company (whether legislated or voluntary)? Arguably, not. A study by seven leading companies suggests that environmental policies bring real benefits to shareholder value, but some financial analysts predictably remain sceptical (see the box *Greenbacks for Green Companies*).

Greenbacks for Green Companies

Following a two-year study, a consortium (consisting of ICI, Volvo, Unilever, Monsanto, Deutsche Bank, Electrolux and Gerling, the German insurer) sought to show that improving environmental compliance and developing eco-friendly products can enhance earnings per share and profitability. Furthermore, the report warns that institutional investors are becoming increasingly wary of companies that ignore or play down the importance of the environment.

'Investors are beginning to look at the downside risk of investing in companies that are either only just complying with environmental law or those companies that make empty mission statements about it,' argues Leif Johansson, chief executive of Volvo and chairman of the consortium. His message is that shareholders will soon expect companies to use environmental strategies to maximize shareholder value by exploiting opportunities for cost-cutting or achieving premium prices.

The report claims that environmentally aware companies derive savings from improved management of raw materials and energy resources. More efficiency means less waste. It also argues that consumers are prepared to pay a bit more for more energy efficient products. Electrolux has enjoyed rising demand for its green range of household appliances even though these are sold at a higher margin than standard models. The report also suggests that environmental focus helps to stimulate innovation. Research that develops more sustainable manufacturing processes should feed through to earnings per share.

The consortium, which also consulted companies such as DaimlerChrysler, BP Amoco, The Body Shop and 3M, says sustainable strategies are also beginning to feature more prominently as a 'pre-qualifier' for winning contracts or investment approval in emerging markets. For example, Volvo claims it has been forced to satisfy increasingly stringent environmental demands in India and China, two countries where it hopes to build a strong presence in trucks and buses. Closer to home, the company found that 80 per cent of buyers in the German and Swedish fleet market put environmental performance as a crucial factor in deciding which models to buy.

However, some investment banks consulted by the consortium question the direct link between sustainability and shareholder value, whether in raw material management or product compliance. Banks such as J P Morgan, Morgan Stanley Dean Witter and Lehman Brothers agreed that improving environmental compliance could help profitability, but only because it was a natural by-product of other 'value drivers', such as restructuring and more innovative marketing.

The consortium concludes that improved earnings can also be enhanced through responsible governmental interventions that encourage companies to exceed environmental requirements. For example, in Sweden consumers receive tax exemption for five years when they buy a car that meets best environmental standards. In other European countries, there are subsidies for energy-efficient household appliances.

Source: *Sustainable Strategies for Value Creation*, Consortium Report, 1999. Reported in *Financial Times* 28 April 1999.

Local Communities

Big companies have a tendency to take an arrogant attitude towards community affairs. They take what they want and often don't give much back, other than what they give passively in terms of creating wealth for the local sandwich bar owners, restauranteurs, taxi drivers, and so on. Other than the inevitable urge to sponsor the local football team (hardly an altruistic initiative anyway), they often seem to think that communities should just be grateful for their presence. Until, that is, they decide that it is in the best interests of shareholder value that they should close all or part of it down. Perhaps it's because head offices tend to be in large towns, where there is usually little sense of community, whereas operating units are frequently located in provincial cities and rural towns where community relationships with major employers are vital elements of the local social and economic climate. The trouble of course too is that by the time investors, customers, employees, suppliers and regulators have had their wants and needs satisfied, how much time do executives have to spend on managing community relations?

It has not always been that way though. In previous industrial ages, employers went out of their way to attract workers and take an interest in their welfare as part of a community. Cadbury, Rowntree and Lever, for example, all went to the trouble of investing substantial sums to provide for the communities in which they built their businesses and were comfortable with the fact that this policy would pay dividends in the longer term. If companies today were to think of their relationship with local communities as more of a two-way interrelationship, they would serve themselves and the community in which they reside far better.

Next time an industrialist whinges to you about the skills shortages they face, just ask him/her how many apprentice/trainee workers their company took on last year, and how much they have donated to specific faculties of local colleges and universities over the last three years. When they go on about the paucity of local suppliers and the quality of the goods they produce, ask them how much time and money they have invested in helping local companies acquire the skill-sets, practices, technologies and infrastructure that will enable them to reach the standards of production they require. You only get out what you put in, as they say. If you measure those inputs and outputs, then a better understanding of that process will be gained. Companies should consider being more charitable too. The return on that investment, if there has to be one, is that of the company's image within the community. Scott Bader, the employee-owned resins and polymers manufacturer, is certainly exceptional in that its statutes dictate that it donates 5 per cent of its profits to the charities voted by its employees.

Health and Safety

The chemicals industry though is not best known for its beneficial impacts on the community. Common abuses that have attracted regulatory intervention include failures to warn and protect users, customers and employees about hazardous materials and processes. Chemical manufacturing companies and the user customers of their products have become a particular target of regulatory attention. Many have had to make substantial investments in 'cleaning up their act' in order to avoid punitive fines by newly empowered regulatory authorities, created as the result of major catastrophes. The fatal disasters in nuclear plants at Three Mile Island and Chernobyl, the explosive destruction of a caprolactam chemical plant at Flixborough in the UK plus the shameful toxic pollution of the river Rhine have all helped to create the precedents for increased regulatory powers. As a result of these and many other less dramatic but serious incidents, the nuclear and chemicals industries have gained a poor reputation for safety and consequently now have the regulatory regimes they deserve.

To be fair to the chemicals industry as a whole, it has tried to face up to this challenge and significant effort has been expended on promoting self-regulating policies through 'responsible care' programmes and codes of practice. However, this involves a not insignificant cost. Yet many of these companies have to compete against companies who can make exactly the same formulations of chemicals in China and other parts of the world that experience few such pressures to adopt best practices. This naturally puts them at an immediate competitive disadvantage where their customers' buying focus is on price as the principal factor of purchasing decisions. It is clearly not then a 'level playing field'. On the other hand, a part of the same industry in the West has not helped its prospects by choosing to build manufacturing facilities in emerging market countries and, disgracefully, not applying the standards of their parent companies (see the box *Pesticide Homicide*).

Pesticide Homicide

Union Carbide, the US chemical company, achieved notoriety in 1984. An explosion at its plant at Bhopal, in India, killed 2,500 people, injured another 300,000 and destroyed 20,000 cattle (sacred cows). The immediate cause of the tragedy involved tanks of methyl isocyanate, a chemical used in pesticides, which were not sufficiently refrigerated. The refrigeration problem was not detected because the temperature alarm was shut down. The accident was compounded by the fact that the gas scrubber (which should neutralize escaped gas) was shut off and the flare tower (which burns escaped gas) was out of service. The subsequent investigation revealed a dismal litany of safety compliance negligence:

- Five other major accidents had occurred at the plant between 1981 and 1984.
- Operators had been given little or no training about safety and health hazards.

- All signs regarding operating and safety procedures were written in English, even though many operators only spoke Hindi.
- Gauges at the plant were consistently either broken, malfunctioning, off the scale, giving wrong data or considered 'totally unreliable'.
- Many of the control room's operators, not having oxygen masks, could neither see nor breathe when the leak began and had to run from their workstations at a critical time.

Union Carbide was forced to pay half a billion dollars to victims (a surprisingly low amount, as the legal trials were held in India), but its reputation was ruined and never fully recovered.

Corporate Abuses and Antitrust

A long series of major companies in a wide variety of industries have been caught rigging prices, employing other forms of anticompetitive practices and flouting regulatory standards. They do not do themselves a service by applying these tactics or by neglecting fundamental aspects of doing business. They discredit management teams and can do irreparable harm to hard-won corporate reputations.

The financial services industry in the UK, for example, has been accused of both mis-selling pension schemes to public sector workers and, more recently, the mis-selling of endowment mortgages. The industry faces not only significant fines but also massive compensation claims. The Financial Services Authority, which regulates the industry in the UK, has suggested that the total bill for pensions mis-selling alone is likely to hit £11 billion. Other estimates suggest that it might reach an astronomical £20 billion.

The retail industry is notoriously nationalistic, but a few majors have ventured beyond their national boundaries with varying degrees of success. Many struggle to manage their far-flung empires. Carrefour, the French hypermarket retailer, boasted that it had become the most successful foreign retailer in China. However, the Chinese government recently accused it of breaking central government regulations and Carrefour is being forced to negotiate a 'restructuring', which could include anything from punitive fines to store closures or forced store sales. Wal-Mart of the US fell foul of German authorities when it started pricing some of its commodities at below cost price, a 'loss-leader' practice it adopts elsewhere to attract custom – but one which is strictly forbidden in Germany, where legislation was put in place to protect the interests of small family-owned businesses. Marks & Spencer has been publicly accused of flouting French employment law over store closures.

The formation of pricing cartels is an obvious abuse and we detail some recent examples of these below, but other business malpractices are much more subtle. Executives might think that tying customers to their products within critical distribution channels through exclusivity deals makes good business sense in their quest to gain a dominant position in a given market. It gives them a competitive advantage and raises the cost of entry for any newcomers. However, such strategies reckon without fundamental regulatory principles centred upon consumer freedom of choice and that one company should not achieve domination by excluding fair competition. Major companies such as Coca-Cola and Unilever's ice cream brand Walls have been involved in such disputes with regulators. The 'dominate or die' philosophy of the early 1990s may need to be modified to one of 'dominate and spend a lot of money on lawyers' fees'.

Companies all over the globe are currently being investigated for accounting frauds. Let us just take some examples reported in the business press during February 2001. First, South Korean prosecutors indicted 34 Daewoo executives and accountants over one of the world's biggest accounting frauds. Acting under the orders of Daewoo's founder, Kim Woo-choong, it is alleged that they conspired to inflate the now bankrupt group's assets by Won41,000 billion (£23 billion) in order to hide losses and persuade banks to make new loans of nearly Won10,000 billion. In the same month, but in the US, the Securities and Exchange Commission announced that it is investigating fraudulent accounting practices at Lucent Technologies, the world's largest telecommunications equipment maker. The regulator's concerns centre on the booking of $679 million in revenues in the third quarter of its financial year 2000. It appears that sales figures were inflated by sales staff using one-off discounts on future orders as an inducement to customers to close an early sale, the booking of revenues before equipment had been fully shipped and, the biggest single item, $452 million worth of products had been shipped to distributors, but not sold to customers – a method known as 'stuffing the channels' – which the company was subsequently required to take back in order to preserve relationships. Still in February 2001, but this time in Germany, the Bonn public prosecutor opened a criminal investigation into Ron Sommer, Deutsche Telekom's chief executive, and other board members that relates to the alleged overvaluation of the group's property assets.

Ninety-nine per cent of this book was written before the dramatic implosion of America's seventh largest corporation, Enron. This scandal has at its root the use of highly dubious accounting practices. Whether they were illegally applied in Enron's case remains to be determined in the courts. However, if additional evidence were needed of the potential impact of accounting shenanigans; of the need for financial reporting reform; of the necessity for more stringent regulatory powers; of the uselessness of self-regulatory vehicles (in this case on the part of the auditors); and the 'profit is opinion, cash is fact' maxim, then this has to be it.

There are many other forms of regulatory deception. For instance, Mitsubishi Motors was recently embroiled in a scandal when Japan's fourth largest carmaker admitted that it had concealed the level of customer complaints from industry regulators for more than 30 years. An internal investigation found that the cover-up, aimed at avoiding product recalls, had been going on since 1969. It then proceeded to recall 620,000 vehicles at a cost of Yen7.5 billion ($69 million). These kinds of deception imply a cavalier attitude towards 'gaming' regulatory requirements that can, when exposed, severely damage corporate reputations. It must be reasonable to assume too that such revelations are merely the tip of an iceberg. The probability is that few get caught in flagrante delicto.

The UK Department of Trade and Industry inspectors, who spent nine years and £8 million preparing their report on the flotation of Robert Maxwell's infamous Mirror Group Newspapers, conclude that no regulations can eliminate fraud, malpractice and manipulation of markets. 'The most important lesson from all the events is that high ethical and professional standards must always be put before commercial advantage,' they write. Few would argue with such sentiments (apart from the late Robert Maxwell himself perhaps), but the fact remains that if the rewards for those individuals who take risks with such standards are significantly greater than the punishments for getting caught, then we should not be surprised by their repeated occurrence.

We have observed in an earlier section of this chapter how Regulation FD, and its equivalents in other countries, constrains how financially sensitive information that in the recent past was selectively leaked to financial analysts now has to be made available to all types of investors simultaneously. Yet, only a few months after its implementation, at least half a dozen firms are under investigation for flouting the new regulation. If they are found wanting and not made an example of, the practice will undoubtedly continue to flourish. Malpractice is hard to prove though and many regulators find it hard to prosecute offenders other than in the most flagrant of cases. In the UK, where similar selective disclosure legislation exists, the regulator – the Financial Services Authority – currently only has the power to reprimand (and shame) companies. One company, Baltimore Technologies, an internet encryption software company, is at the time of writing under investigation for releasing information to a select audience of analysts that wiped almost one-third off its market value. The contention is that the information it provided to the analysts was market sensitive and should have been made more widely available. The company, on the other hand, protests that it merely released information about the market in which it operates, not about its specific forecasts of its own financial prospects, which it released later the same day causing a further slump in its share price. It is a fine point as to what constitutes unfair disclosure, especially in such a specialized market. Analysts aren't stupid and read the runes about what is being said that may in fact be a thinly veiled profits warning. However, the FSA may be beginning to tighten its grip and new legislation came into effect in November 2001 that aims to give them greater powers to prosecute directors.

Corporate Reputation

In a more general sense, it seems as though the profit motive and the 'institutional shareholder is god' mantra has got out of control. Too many companies are now incapable of acting responsibly (especially if it costs money to make it happen) until they are either forced or shamed into doing something different. When corporate reputation is at stake, all the lights come on. We have seen earlier how automotive companies have had to address the activities of their component suppliers and how clothing manufacturers have been forced by the persistent action of pressure groups to improve the standards of their suppliers' employment practices in the Far East and other low-wage economies where regulations are poorly developed. Companies today have to be more alert, be more vigilant in monitoring activities in remote outposts of their empires, and take more care of practices conducted throughout their extended supply chains if they are to maintain their hard-won reputations.

To a certain extent regulators do act on behalf of communities too, protecting them from the worst excesses of corporate irresponsibility and, to be fair, ignorance. For instance, health, safety and environmental legislation has not only helped to protect employees and communities but also raised management awareness of the risks involved. Nevertheless, regulations are mostly just the scar tissue of abuses that managers should have identified and either weren't smart enough to find them or were irresponsible enough not to act on them.

In order to ward off the inevitable 'red-tape' that regulation brings, a number of industries have tried to implement self-regulation policies and practices. With just a few exceptions, these have not achieved much traction even where they are supported by the majority of participants. It only takes one rogue to bring a whole industry into disrepute. It is a further area Vilfredo Pareto overlooked when he developed the 80/20 rule. This is closer to a 99/1 rule, which of course is the rule of today's media (but one which was less obtrusive in the early part of the last century). Building corporate credibility is vital in today's marketplace and is a significant management challenge. Reputations take a long time to develop, but they can be shattered much more easily – sometimes by a single act of neglect or callousness, which subsequently gets publicized far more widely than could have been imagined. It means building relationships of trust: to a large extent with regulators but also with communities.

If any readers are still not convinced by the argument that this whole area of regulation and responsibility is a significant management issue – and that, therefore, some sort of measurement system needs to be put in place in order to manage it more effectively – they might care to consider the further examples contained within the box *Regulatory Interventions*.

Regulatory Interventions

Anyone outside the heavily-regulated privatized utilities, transportation and telecommunications industries, who regards Regulators as a relatively inconsequential or benign stakeholder, should consider the facts. Press reports – collected during 1999 alone – publicly exposed, for example, that:

In the United States:

- The vitamins division of **Roche**, the Swiss healthcare company, has been fined $500 million by the US Justice Department for indulging in antitrust cartel arrangements with its competitors. A former marketing executive was jailed for four months and personally fined $100,000 for his role in the cartel. The division's former president also received a fine of $150,000 and a custodial sentence of five months. Co-conspirator **BASF** of Germany was fined $225 million. A third conspirator, **Rhône-Poulenc** of France, escaped criminal punishment under an amnesty deal by supplying US prosecutors with the evidence that cracked the cartel. However, all three companies may face subsequent civil suits in the US and, almost certainly, actions in other geographical zones.
- **Hoechst**, the German pharmaceuticals and chemicals company, was also fined by the US Justice Department. It had to pay $36 million after it pleaded guilty to a 17-year conspiracy within its food ingredients business to fix the prices of sorbates, a type of food preservative. Its former marketing manager was forced to pay a $250,000 personal fine for his role in the conspiracy. **Eastman Chemicals** of the US was fined $11 million for its involvement in the same cartel.
- Food company, **Archer Daniels Midland**, was fined $100 million for its role in a global price-fixing cartel controlling lysine and citric acid. It's vice chairman, a well-known donor to political parties, was also prosecuted and jailed.
- **SGL Carbon** of Germany, **UCAR International** of the US and **Showa Denko Carbon** of Japan were fined a total of $277 million by the US Justice Department for price-fixing conspiracies involving graphite electrodes.
- **Microsoft** faced a hugely significant and highly public antitrust case brought by the Justice Department relating to its business practices and

dominant position. If it loses the case, which might drag on – expensively, in terms of its legal costs – for years in appeals court, the government is likely to seek stiff penalties. Legal experts also assert that Microsoft may face limits on its use of exclusive contracts and may be forced to make Windows more accessible to rivals. It may even be forced to restructure its business.

In Europe:

- **Coca-Cola**, doyen of shareholder value in the US, was under investigation in Germany, Austria, Denmark and Italy for abusing its dominant position. Following complaints from competitors, European Commission officials raided several of Coca-Cola's offices in a probe into whether the company was offering retailers and wholesalers incentives to increase sales volumes, carry Coca-Cola's full range (such as its Sprite and Fanta brands), or stop selling competitors' drinks through exclusivity deals.
- Separately, Karel Van Miert, the European Union competition watchdog at the time, warned **Coca-Cola** that it faced heavy fines for not seeking clearance from the European Commission for its proposed $1.85 billion acquisition of the Cadbury-Schweppes soft drinks business. The deal was subsequently restructured to exclude most of western Europe, and some other countries that objected, reducing the price by $1.1 billion.
- French government competition authorities also blocked **Coca-Cola's** plans to buy Orangina, France's second most popular soft drink, from Pernod Ricard.
- **Volkswagen** of Germany was contesting a record £69 million ($110 million) fine by the European Commission for preventing Italian VW dealers from selling cars to German customers at lower prices than in their homeland.
- **British Airways**, reeling from the collapse of its planned alliance with American Airlines due to regulatory issues, was fined £4.4 million by the European Commission for abusing its dominant position in the UK market by providing incentives to travel agents. BA subsequently announced that it was to issue writs against its European competitors, such as KLM, Lufthansa, Air France and Alitalia in an attempt to prove that other national airlines are using similar banned schemes.
- **Interbrew**, the world's fifth largest brewer, was on the receiving end of dawn raids at its offices by European Commission officials as part of an investigation into whether the Stella Artois producer was abusing its dominant position in Belgium.
- **Unilever** ice cream subsidiary Walls was being forced by the UK's Competition Commission to change its marketing and distribution practices – including supplying retailers with freezer cabinets for their products

only, paying volume bonuses that encourage retailers not to stock rival products, and recommending prices – because of its dominant position in the local market. The Commission is also seeking to prevent in-house or exclusive distribution networks where there is a 'scale monopoly'.

- Several well-known insurance and financial services companies in the UK have been fined substantial sums by the Personal Investment Authority (part of the Financial Services Authority) for their failures in relation to the mis-selling of personal pensions. **Brittania Life** and **Friends' Provident**, for example, have received fines totalling £950,000.
- **SAS**, the Nordic region's largest airline, whose entire board resigned in September 2001 following a cartel-building scandal, was fined €39.4 million by the European Commission for its involvement in the cartel. It had entered into an agreement with rival Maersk Air of Denmark to divide key routes between them.

In Asia-Pacific:

- **Coca-Cola Amatil**, 37 per cent owned by Coca-Cola, was under investigation by the Australian Competition and Consumer Commission for alleged breaches of the country's Trade Practices Act. These relate to CCA, which controls 65 per cent of the Australian soft drinks market, providing Coke at discounted prices to certain retail outlets, on condition that they did not stock rival beverages.
- **Novartis**, the Swiss pharmaceuticals group, was fined Yen3.3 billion ($28 million) by the Japanese tax authorities for under-reporting its income between 1990 and 1994 through the use of excessive transfer pricing. **Roche**, another Swiss drugs group, has also been in dispute with the Japanese tax authorities for diverting profits.
- The biggest case, however, involved the Japanese drugs group **Yamanouchi**, which allegedly failed to declare Yen54.1 billion in income over six years. The group had to pay Yen24.2 billion ($200 million) in additional taxes, including a fine. Its operations in Ireland, which has an extremely low tax rate for drugs manufacturers, were found to have overcharged the Japanese parent for raw materials used to make its top-selling ulcer drug.

These global examples are deliberately detailed in order to illustrate the variety, significance and extent of the regulatory compliance issues that major corporations face in today's business environment. However, it is reasonable to suppose that – in the majority of cases – the chief executives of the corporations investigated or prosecuted were not personally involved in making the decisions to exploit the company's position. They just didn't have the measurement and management systems to discover the malpractices. Indeed, their measurement and incentive practices may well have *encouraged* their employees – often in subsidiaries and business units far removed from corporate head offices – to behave in ways that actively invited abuses.

Source: Chris Adams, 'Regulatory Interventions' for Accenture's Managing With Measures Implementation Guide (1999).

Almost no industry is immune from increased regulatory pressures and potential prosecutions. Indeed, some people believe that regulatory authority has already gone much too far and is creating the levels of bureaucratic nonsense that 19th-century sociologist Max Weber and 20th-century novelist Franz Kafka would instantly recognize. One UK estimate found that companies faced an overall financial burden of £15 billion as a result of regulatory directives introduced between 1997 and 2002.[40] Governments may pledge themselves to eliminating unnecessary red tape, but few industrialists believe that significant progress will be made in reducing the workloads that regulations create. We'll have to learn to live with it.

This chapter has demonstrated the vital importance of a broad range of stakeholders to organizations in today's business environment. The success of companies and their executives needs to be measured in multi-dimensional terms, with both long and short time horizons. As we have seen, effectively and efficiently managing the relationship with these stakeholders presents many diverse business issues and management challenges. Just in the last few years the nature of these relationships has shifted considerably and will continue to do so. Executives need to have them on their radar screens if they are not to be caught short. The other take-away from this chapter, although we shall return to it again later, should be the reciprocal nature of the relationship between the organization and its stakeholders: each relationship has a quid pro quo. Everybody wants and needs something from the other. Perhaps the oddest thing though is that we do not have – until now – any management models that help us to find our way through this mire and to manage within this new complexity. The resolution to that problem is the subject of the next six chapters.

The Performance Prism Framework

5

Measuring more is easy, measuring better is hard.

Charles Handy • *business writer and professor at London School of Management.*

The main thrust of the previous chapter was that organizations in the 21st century have to take account of the wants and needs of all of their stakeholders – for several reasons. First because there is a danger that the stakeholders will rebel and refuse to co-operate with the organization if it does not satisfy their particular wants and needs. And that usually means less capital, fewer customers, lousy morale, higher costs and greater scrutiny. Second because organizations have legal, moral and ethical responsibilities towards their stakeholders. Third in this age of ever-present media and special interest groups, they also have hard-won reputations to protect. But what does this mean in practice and, in particular, in terms of measurement? How then should organizations structure their measurement systems? What dimensions of performance should they be reporting against? And how will these dimensions interact with one another? The aim of this chapter is to explore these issues and in so doing expand on the application of the novel performance measurement framework that we introduced earlier – The Performance Prism.

We think of the Performance Prism as a second-generation performance management framework. It builds on and strengthens existing (first-generation) measurement frameworks and methodologies, such as the balanced scorecard, the work on shareholder value, and the various self-assessment frameworks, like the Malcolm Baldrige Award criteria and the European Foundation for Quality Management's business excellence model, for example (although we acknowledge that the latter were not specifically designed with performance measurement in mind).

The Business Performance Revolution

Interest in performance measurement and management has rocketed during the last few years. Frameworks and methodologies – such as shareholder value added, activity-based costing, cost of quality, competitive benchmarking and the balanced scorecard – have each generated vast interest, activity and consulting revenues, but not always success. Yet therein lies a paradox. It might reasonably be asked, how can multiple, and seemingly inconsistent, business performance frameworks and measurement methodologies exist? Each framework purports to be unique. And each appears to claim comprehensiveness. Yet each offers a different perspective on performance.

The balanced scorecard, with its four perspectives, focuses on financials (shareholders), customers, internal processes, plus innovation and learning. In doing so it downplays the importance of other stakeholders, such as employees, suppliers, regulators and communities. The business excellence model combines results, which are readily measurable, with enablers, some of which are not. Shareholder value frameworks incorporate the cost of capital into the equation, but ignore everything (and everyone) else. Both activity-based costing and the cost of quality, on the other hand, focus on the identification and control of cost drivers (non-value-adding activities and failures/non-conformances respectively), which are themselves often embedded in the business processes. But this highly process-focused view ignores any other perspectives on performance – such as the opinion of shareholders, customers and employees. Conversely, benchmarking tends to involve taking a largely external perspective, often comparing performance with that of competitors or sometimes other 'best practitioners' of business processes or capabilities. However, this kind of activity is frequently pursued as a one-off exercise towards generating ideas for – or gaining commitment to – short-term improvement initiatives, rather than the design of a formalized ongoing performance measurement system.

How can this be? How can multiple, seemingly conflicting, measurement frameworks and methodologies exist? In fact the answer is simple. They can exist because they all add value. They all provide unique perspectives on performance. They all furnish managers with a different set of lenses through which they can assess the performance of their organizations. In some circumstances, an explicit focus on shareholder value – at the expense of almost everything else – could be exactly the right thing for an organization. In other circumstances, or even in the same organization but at a different point in time, it would be suicide. Then, perhaps, the balanced scorecard or the business excellence model (or some combination of them) might be the answer. The new CEO of a company, with too overt a current focus on short-term shareholder value, may find these frameworks a useful vehicle to help switch attention more towards the interests of customers, investments in process improvement and the development of innovative products and services. It is like sowing the seeds and harvesting the crop in different seasons of the year. To be sustainable though, *both* must be done – it's just that the cycle can be longer in business than it is in agriculture.

The key is to recognize that, despite the claims of some of the proponents of these various frameworks and methodologies, there is no one 'holy grail' or best way to approach the measurement and management of business performance. And the reason for this is that business performance is itself a multi-faceted concept, the complexity of which the existing frameworks only partially address. Essentially, they provide valuable point solutions.

The Performance Prism

Our solution to this problem is a three-dimensional framework that we call the Performance Prism. This framework has been deliberately designed to be highly flexible so that it can provide both a broad and narrow focus as required. If only a partial aspect of performance management is required, such as a single stakeholder focus or a particular business process agenda, then the Performance Prism can be applied to designing a measurement system and appropriate measures (and their attendant metrics) that address that context. Conversely, if a broad corporate or business unit performance management improvement initiative is required, then the Performance Prism is equally capable of supporting that too. How does it help to achieve these aims?

The Performance Prism consists of five interrelated perspectives on performance that pose specific vital questions:

- **Stakeholder Satisfaction** – who are our key stakeholders and what do they want and need?
- **Stakeholder Contribution** – what do we want and need from our stakeholders on a reciprocal basis?
- **Strategies** – what strategies do we need to put in place to satisfy the wants and needs of our stakeholders while satisfying our own requirements too?
- **Processes** – what processes do we need to put in place to enable us to execute our strategies?
- **Capabilities** – what capabilities do we need to put in place to allow us to operate our processes?

Together these five perspectives provide a comprehensive and integrated framework for thinking about organizational performance. Figure 5.1 illustrates these five basic perspectives of performance management and measurement.

Why does the framework look like this and why does it consist of these constituent components? Let us explain.

As the earlier chapters have demonstrated, it is clear that those organizations aspiring to be successful in the long term within today's business environment have to have an exceptionally clear picture of who their key stakeholders are and what they want or need. But having a clear picture is not enough. In order to satisfy their own work and needs, organizations have to access contributions from their stakeholders – usually capital and credit from investors, loyalty and profit from customers, ideas and skills from employees, materials and services from suppliers, and so on. They also need to have defined what strategies they will pursue to ensure that value is delivered to their stakeholders. In order to implement these strategies they have to understand what processes the enterprise requires and must operate both effectively and efficiently. Processes, in themselves, can only be executed if the organization has the right capabilities in place – the right combination of people skill-sets, best practices, leading technologies and physical infrastructure.

Fig 5.1 The Performance Prism

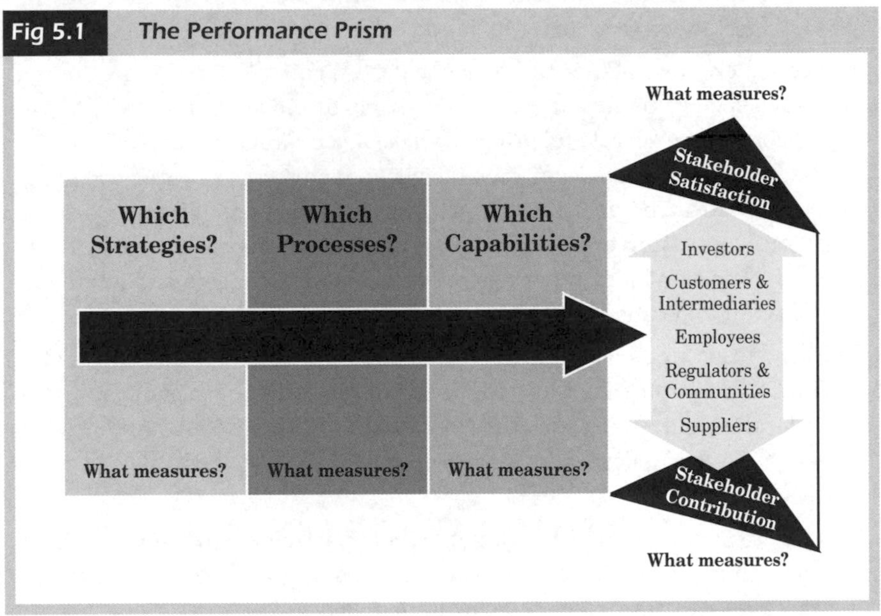

In essence then, the Performance Prism provides a comprehensive, yet easily comprehensible, framework that can be used to articulate a given business's operating model. An example should help to clarify the concept (see the box *The Performance Prism as a Management Framework*).

The Performance Prism as a Management Framework

Writing Inc. (an assumed name for a real company) is the wholly owned UK subsidiary of a large US conglomerate and manufactures pens and markers, primarily for the education sector. When the US parent aquired Writing Inc. in the late 1990s it set the business an explicit target of doubling its market share in Europe. Writing Inc.'s product range is already massive, with some 230,000 different SKUs (stock keeping units), so further product diversification was deemed inappropriate. Instead the business began to think about the wants and needs of its different stakeholders.

Clearly, a significant stakeholder was the US parent company. The wants and needs of this stakeholder were explicit. They wanted to increase their presence in the European market and felt the best way to do so was for Writing Inc. to seek to increase its market share.

The customers were also critical stakeholders. Writing Inc. specializes in the education sector and has an extremely strong brand, especially with those buying for the pre-school and primary school age groups. In terms of product, Writing Inc.'s customers want robust pens and markers that are good value for money. Robust, because this age group of customers are extremely good at destructively testing products on a frequent basis. Good value for money, because schools and play groups do not have massive budgets and are therefore constantly looking for ways to reduce unnecessary cost.

But in addition to their product requirements, Writing Inc.'s customers also have other requirements. First, they are interested in educational opportunities for the children in their care. Second, they are keen to identify ways of raising funds to support their work – hence the plethora of raffles, parties, school fetes, and so on.

So, is there some way that Writing Inc. could partner with their customers to enable them to achieve their broader wants and needs, while still satisfying Writing Inc.'s desire to double its market share?

Before exploring the solutions, let us just continue the analysis and consider some of Writing Inc.'s other stakeholders. The business's employees, for example, are keen to see the business continue and succeed. They are happy for the organization to seek to double its market share, but are not a particularly mobile workforce, so the prospect of moving to another location would not be appealing to them.

The local community would have a similar view. Writing Inc. is a significant employer in the locality. If the business were to expand and require additional staff, the local community would not only provide a source of appropriately skilled staff, but also be very supportive of any expansion plans.

It appears then that there are no barriers to Writing Inc. expanding, although there is a constraint. Namely that sales growth should come through existing products, rather than diversification. So, let us return to the issue of the customers and how Writing Inc. might help them satisfy their non-product wants and needs. If schools want to raise revenue then perhaps Writing Inc. could convince them to become a retail outlet for its products, in return for a percentage of sales. But this only addresses one of the school's requirements – namely they need to generate revenue. How might the second need be addressed?

Well, why not allow school children to design their own pens and markers? They could produce specifications for school specific pens and markers that the school could then sell to parents and grandparents. What would this mean in practice? Each school would develop its own unique design for a pen and/or marker, place an order for a batch and then sell them on Writing Inc.'s behalf. But to execute this strategy, Writing Inc. will have to modify its design and manufacturing processes. At the moment, Writing Inc. has processes designed to cope with large batches, but if it were to adopt this strategy then it would have to be able to cope with low volume and high variety.

How could it do this? One issue would be to reduce set-up times on machines, so the business could cope with small batch manufacture without the loss of significant time through repeated set-ups. The other issue would be to develop a process for capturing the designs produced by children. Perhaps this could be done over the internet? Maybe the business could establish a website that children could log onto where they could design their pens and markers online. The teachers could then sign them off and place the order. The order could be submitted electronically and the appropriate pens and markers produced and delivered.

The one thing we have not yet considered is what Writing Inc. wants and needs from its stakeholders to enable the above to happen. Writing Inc. has no web capabilities in house, so it will need to buy these in from a supplier. To do so it will need capital from its parent company. To secure this it will need commitment from schools that they will support the strategy. Finally, to manufacture in small batches the business will meed to reduce set-up times. To reduce set-up times, it will require the expertise of its production engineering people to develop the capability to analyze set-ups and eliminate non-value added from them. Hence, from its employers, Writing Inc. will require participation and ideas from its workforce to help make this a productive and profitable strategic initiative.

Let us think about the Writing Inc. example from the perspective of the Performance Prism framework for a moment. In terms of the five facets, the key themes are:

- ***Stakeholder wants and needs*** – double market share (financial results to parent company); robust pens and markers that are good value for money and provide educational opportunities (for customers); business growth and employment opportunities (for employees).
- ***Organization wants and needs*** – capital (from parent company); support, commitment and revenue generation (from customers); participation and ideas (from employees).
- ***Strategies*** – seek to use schools as expansive and profitable retail outlets.
- ***Processes*** – small batch design and manufacturing.
- ***Capabilities*** – web-based design capability; set-up reduction capability.

We can re-draw these themes in the form of a success or strategy map (see Figure 5.2).

Bob Kaplan and David Norton talk extensively about strategy maps in their latest book on the balanced scorecard.[41] But one of the advantages of the Performance Prism framework is that it makes explicit what elements should be covered in a strategy map. In traditional – balanced scorecard – terms a strategy map simply covers the four perspectives on the balanced scorecard – shareholders, customers, internal processes and innovation and learning. But, in our view, this is too narrow. Success maps, as we prefer to call them, should cover all five facets of the Performance Prism if they are not to fall prey to one of the greatest myths of measurement – derive measures from strategies.

Where to Start? – Stakeholder Satisfaction

One of the greatest myths (and fallacies) of measurement design is that performance measures should be derived from strategy. Listen to any conference speaker on the subject. Read any management text written about it. Nine times out of ten the statement will be made – 'derive your measures from your strategy'. This is such a conceptually appealing notion, that nobody stops to question it. Yet to derive measures from strategy is to misunderstand fundamentally the purpose of measurement and the role of strategy. Performance measures are designed to help people track whether they are moving in the direction they want to. They help managers establish whether they are going to reach the destination they set out to reach. Strategy, however, is not about destination. Instead, it is about the route you choose to take – *how* to reach the desired destination.

Fig 5.2 Writing Inc.'s Success Map

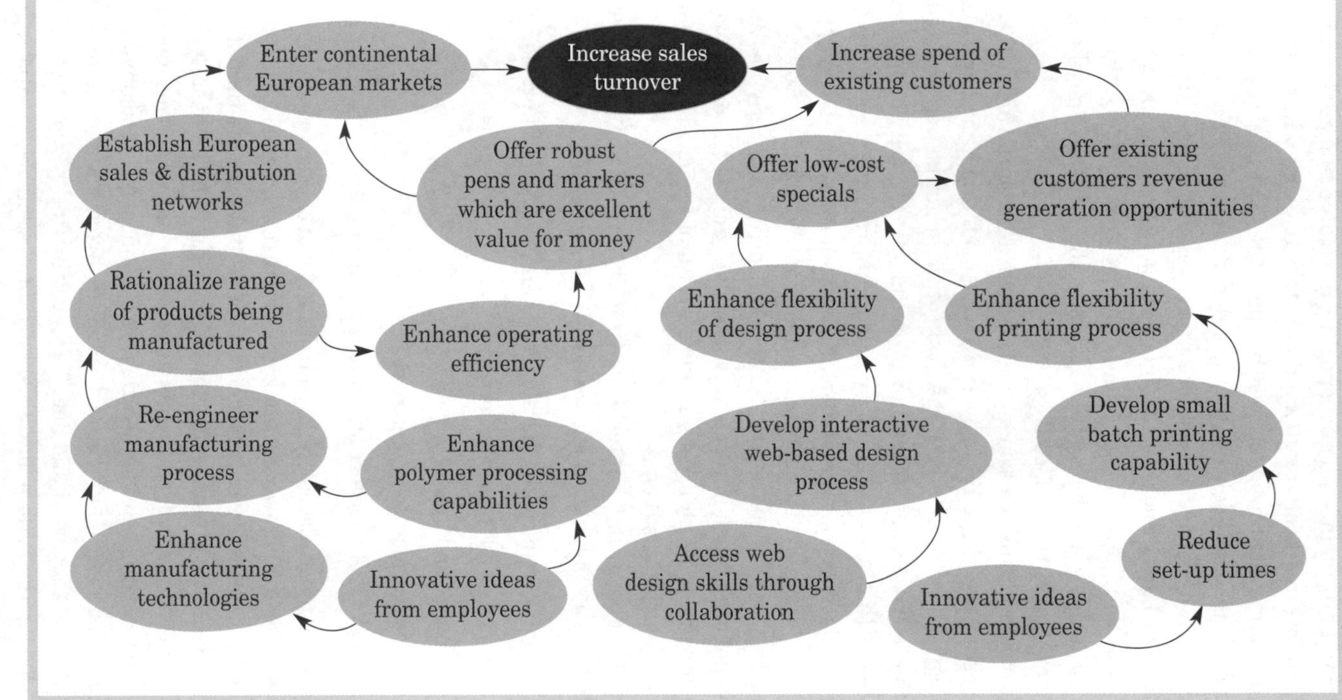

Organizations adopt particular strategies because they believe those strategies will help them achieve a specific, desirable end goal. Amazon.com, the original internet book retailer, did not start to expand into CD sales, toys and home improvement products just because they felt like expanding their product portfolio. They deliberately decided to leverage their e-commerce and operational expertise – their core processes and capabilities – to extend the range of products they sell beyond books *because* they want to increase sales revenues and, in the longer term, enhance shareholder returns. Expanding into CD sales and other product lines is the strategy they hope will enable them to achieve these objectives.

At one level this is a semantic argument. Indeed the original work on strategy, carried out in the 1970s by Andrews, Ansoff and Mintzberg, asserted that a strategy should explain both the goals of the organization and a plan of action to achieve these goals. Today, however, the vast majority of organizations have strategies that are dominated by lists of improvement activities and management initiatives – e.g. grow market share in Asia, extend the product range, seek new distribution channels, and so on. While these are undoubtedly of value, they are not the end goal. These initiatives and activities are pursued in the belief that, when implemented, they will enable the organization to better deliver value to its multiple stakeholders, all of whom will have varying importance to the organization.

We have seen in Chapter 4 that an organization's key stakeholders are likely to be a combination of a number of the following:

- investors (principally shareholders, but other capital providers too)
- customers and intermediaries
- employees and labour unions
- suppliers and alliance partners
- regulators, pressure groups and communities.

As we have noted elsewhere, organizations can choose to give more focus to one stakeholder group over another not because that particular stakeholder is implicitly more important than the others, but because that stakeholder has not received the attention it should have done in the past. Executives must decide which stakeholders' wants and needs their strategies must satisfy.

So, the starting point for deciding what to measure should not be 'What is the organization's strategy?' but instead: 'Who are the organization's stakeholders and what do they want and need?' Hence the first perspective on performance embedded in the Performance Prism is that of stakeholder satisfaction.

The Second Perspective on Performance – Stakeholder Contribution

The second perspective on performance is a subtle but critical twist on the first. For it is the 'stakeholder contribution', as opposed to 'stakeholder satisfaction', perspective. Take, for example, customers as stakeholders. In the early 1980s, organizations began to measure customer satisfaction by tracking the number of customer complaints they received. When research evidence started to show that only about 10 per cent of dissatisfied customers complained, organizations moved to more sophisticated measures, such as customer satisfaction. In the late 1980s and early 1990s, people began to question whether customer satisfaction was enough. Research data gathered by Xerox showed that customers who were very satisfied were five times more likely to repeat their purchase in the next 18 months than those who were merely satisfied. This, and similar observations, resulted in the development of the concept known as customer loyalty. The aim of this concept was to track whether customers: (i) came back to buy more from the same organization, and (ii) recommended the organization to others.

Even more recently, research data from a variety of industries, has demonstrated that many customers are not profitable for organizations. As we have noted in Chapter 4, it has been suggested that in retail banking, for example, 20 per cent of customers generate 130 per cent of profits! Other data illustrate that increased levels of customer satisfaction can result in reduced levels of organizational profitability because of the high costs of squeezing out the final few percentage points of customer satisfaction. Maybe – but most of the evidence would suggest that very few substantial companies have got anywhere near to running into that dilemma. Nevertheless, the reaction has been increasing interest in the notion of customer profitability. Sometimes the customer profitability data produces surprises for the organization, indicating that a group of customers thought to be quite profitable are in fact loss-makers and that other customer groups are far more profitable than generally believed by the organization's executives. Performance data allow assumptions to be challenged.

The important point, and where the subtle twist comes into play, is that customers do not necessarily want to be loyal or profitable. Customers want great products and services at a reasonable cost. They want satisfaction from the organizations they chose to use. It is the organizations themselves that want loyal and profitable customers. So it is with employee satisfaction or supplier performance too. In the main, organizations want loyal employees as well as loyal customers and they want their workforce to do their jobs with high productivity levels. Many organizations grade their employees based on their contribution and this grading may often have a very direct bearing on their remuneration also (an employee want and need of course).

For years, managers have struggled to measure supplier performance. Do they deliver on time? Do they send the right quantity and quality of goods? Do they deliver them to the right place? But these are all dimensions of performance that the organization requires of its supplier. They encapsulate the supplier's contribution to the organization. Supplier satisfaction is a completely different concept. If a manager wanted to assess supplier satisfaction then (s)he would have to ask – Do we pay on time? Do we provide adequate notice when our requirements change? Do we offer suppliers forward schedule visibility? Do our pricing structures allow our suppliers sufficient cashflows for future investment and, therefore, ongoing productivity improvement? Could we be making better use of our vendors' core capabilities and outsource more to them? Again, supplier satisfaction is different to supplier contribution.

The key message here is that for every stakeholder there is a quid pro quo: what the organization wants and needs from them, as well as what the stakeholder wants and needs from the organization (see Figure 5.3). We have found from experience that gaining a clear understanding of the 'dynamic tension' that exists between what stakeholders want and need from the organization, and what the organization wants and needs from its stakeholders, can be an extremely valuable learning exercise for the vast majority of corporations and, especially, their respective business units.

Fig 5.3 **Customer Satisfaction and Customer Contribution**

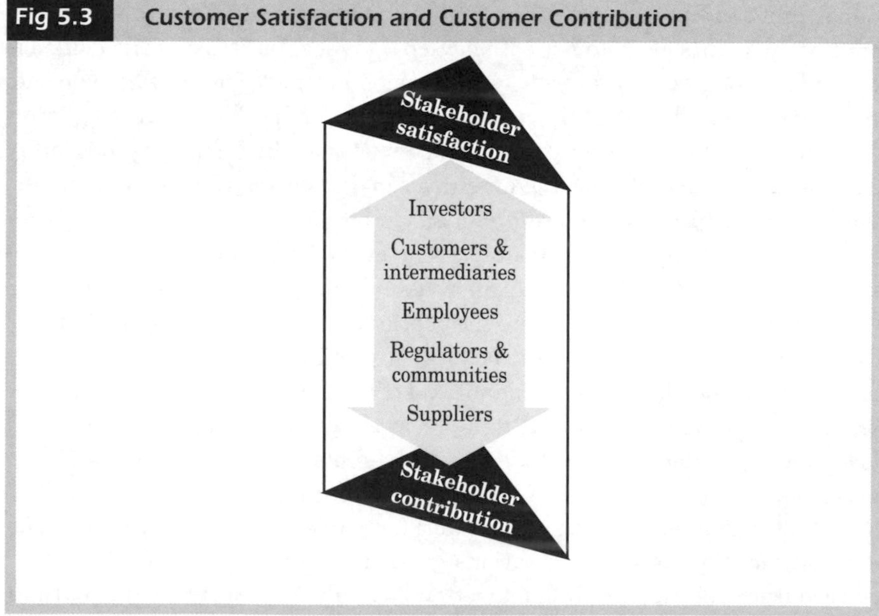

The Third Perspective on Performance – Strategies

As we have seen, the first perspectives on performance are the stakeholder satisfaction and stakeholder contribution ones. What managers have to ascertain here is: who are the most influential stakeholders and what do they want and need? And what do we (the managers) want and need from them (the stakeholders)? Once these questions have been addressed then it is possible to turn to the third perspective on performance: strategies. Most performance measurement design initiatives – wrongly – start at this point. They miss the essential context when they take that approach.

The key question underlying this perspective is what strategies should the organization be adopting to ensure that the wants and needs of its stakeholders are satisfied (while ensuring that its own requirements are satisfied too)? In this context, the role of measurement is four-fold. First, measures are required so that managers can track whether or not the strategies they have chosen are actually being implemented. Second, measures can be used to communicate these strategies within the organization. Third, measures can be applied to encourage and incentivize implementation of strategy. Fourth, once available, the measurement data can be analyzed and used to challenge whether the strategies are working as planned (and, if not, why not).

Strategies can be applied at different levels within an organization. Typically, corporate strategies will deal with the questions such as: What businesses do we want to be in? And how shall we be successful building them? Business Unit strategies will usually consider: What markets do we want to be in? And how shall we be successful serving them? Brands, Products and Services strategies address the problems of: What brands, products and services shall we offer to these markets? And how shall we be successful at offering them? Finally, operating strategies tend to look at: What processes and capabilities must we develop in order to serve these markets and provide these products and services effectively and efficiently? And how shall we successfully implement and achieve them?

The old adages 'you get what you measure' and 'you get what you inspect, not what you expect' contain an important message. People in organizations respond to measures. Horror stories abound of how individuals and teams appear to be performing well, yet are actually damaging the business. When call centre staff are monitored on the length of time it takes for them to deal with customer calls, it is not uncommon to find them cutting people off mid-call – just so the data suggest that they have dealt with the call within 60 seconds. Malevolently or not, employees will tend towards adopting 'gaming tactics' in order to achieve the target performance levels they have been set. Measures send people messages about what matters and how they should behave. When the measures are consistent with the organization's strategies, they encourage behaviours that are consistent with strategy. The right measures then not only offer a means of tracking whether strategy is being implemented, but also a means of communicating strategy and encouraging implementation.

Many of the existing measurement frameworks and methodologies appear to stop at this point. Once the strategies have been identified and the right measures established it is assumed that everything will be fine. Yet studies suggest that some 90 per cent of managers fail to implement and deliver their organization's strategies. Why? There are multiple reasons, but a key one is that strategies also contain inherent assumptions about the drivers of improved business performance. Clearly, if the assumptions are false, then the expected benefits will not be achieved. Without the critical data to enable these assumptions to be challenged, strategy formulation (and revision) is largely predicated on 'gut feel' and management theory. Furthermore, strategies can be blown off course by external dependencies that are beyond the control of the organization. Measurement data and its analysis will never replace executive intuition, but it can be used to greatly enhance the making of judgements and decisions. A key judgement is of course whether an organization's strategy and business model remains valid (see Figure 5.4).

Fig 5.4 **The Role of Measurement in Strategy Creation and Execution**

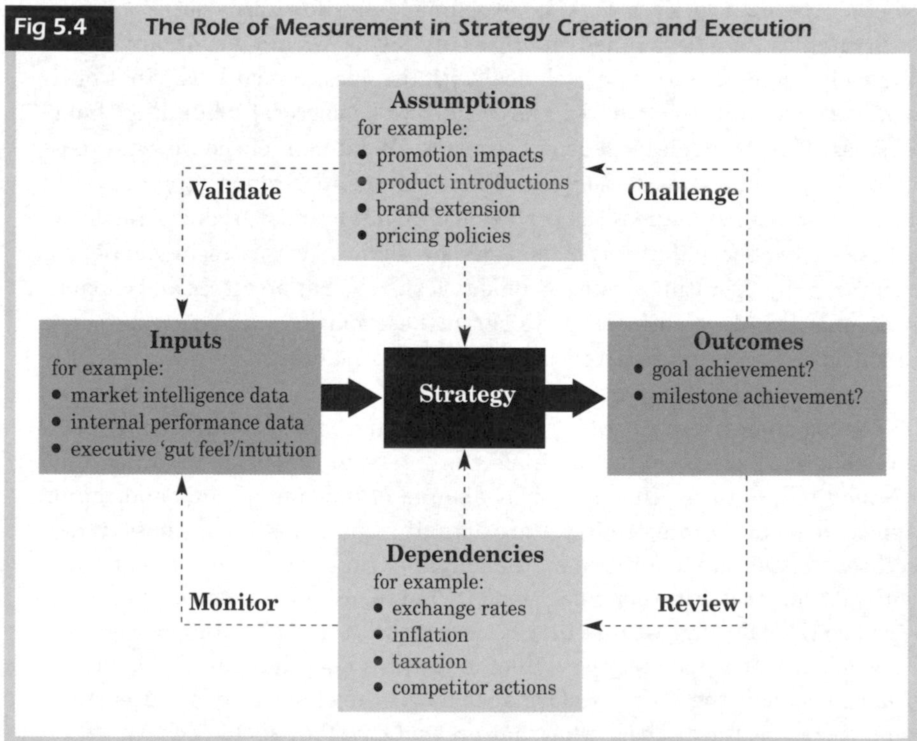

A further key reason for strategic failure is that the organization's processes are not aligned with its strategies. And even if its processes are aligned, then the capabilities required to operate these processes are not. Hence the next two perspectives on performance are the processes and capabilities perspectives. In turn, these require the following questions to be addressed – 'What processes do we need to put in place to allow the strategies to be executed?' and 'What capabilities do/shall we require to operate these processes – both now and in the future?'

Again, measurement plays a crucial role by allowing managers to track whether or not the right processes and capabilities are in place, to communicate which processes and capabilities matter, and to encourage people within the organization to maintain or proactively nurture these processes and capabilities as appropriate. This may involve gaining an understanding of which particular business processes and capabilities must be competitively distinctive ('winners'), and which merely need to be improved or maintained at industry standard levels ('qualifiers') – clearly, these are vital strategic considerations.

The Fourth Perspective on Performance – Processes

Business Processes received a good deal of attention during the 1990s with the advent of Business Process Re-engineering. Business Processes run horizontally across an enterprise's functional organization until they reach the ultimate recipient of the product or service offered – the customer. Michael Hammer, the re-engineering guru, advocates measuring processes from the customer's point of view – the customer wants it fast, right, cheap and easy (to do business with). But is it really as simple as that? There are often many stages in a process. If the final output is slow, wrong, expensive and unfriendly, how will we know which component(s) of the process are letting it down? What needs to be improved? In the quest for data (and accountability), it is easy to end up measuring everything that moves, but learning little about what is important. That is one reason why processes need owners – to decide what measures are important, which metrics will apply and how frequently they shall be measured by whom – so that judgements can be made upon analysis of the data and actions taken.

Many organizations consider their business processes in four separate categories. Generally, these are:

- Develop products and services.
- Generate demand.
- Fulfil demand.
- Plan and manage the enterprise.

Within these categories, there are various sub-processes, which tend to be more functional in nature (see Figure 5.5).

Fig 5.5 Industry Process Model Example: Aerospace

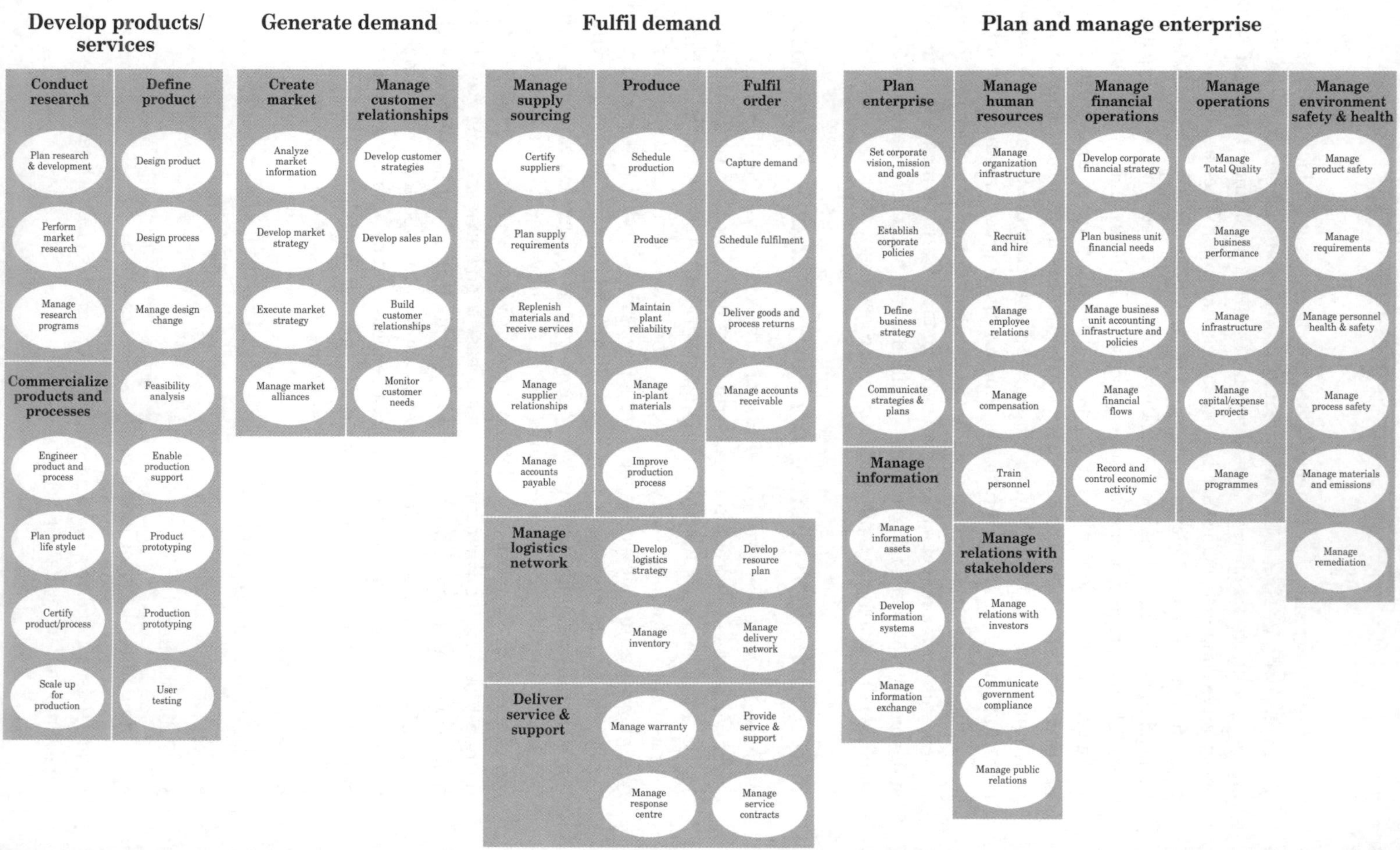

Processes are what make the organization work (or not, as the case may be). They are the blueprints for what work is done where and when, and how it will be executed. From a measurement point of view, we need to consider the aspects or features which it will be critical to measure. These can normally be categorized as follows:

- **Quality** (consistency, reliability, conformance, durability, accuracy, dependability).
- **Quantity** (volume, throughput, completeness).
- **Time** (speed, delivery, availability, promptness, timeliness, schedule).
- **Ease of use** (flexibility, convenience, accessibility, clarity, support).
- **Money** (cost, price, value).

These five categories will help to quantify the measurement criteria for the process issues that we identify as critical to success, i.e. *How good? How many? How quickly? How easily? How expensive?*

We should note though that not all critical processes are performed continuously or even regularly. Contingency processes such as disaster recovery, product recall or various types of system failure (e.g. power outage, labour strike, etc.) will be executed rarely – if ever – but nevertheless need to be prepared for rapid deployment at any point of time with formal procedures established. The key measurement issue here will normally be their level of readiness for action.

For an example of a product recall that was part well executed and part badly fouled up due to poor process measurement and management, see the box *À La Recherche Du Réputation Perdu*.

À La Recherche Du Réputation Perdu

In February 1990, Perrier, the French sparkling mineral water company, was forced to withdraw its products from supermarket shelves and other outlets. Worldwide, more than 160 million bottles of Perrier were removed and destroyed (over 72 million in the US alone). The water had been discovered in tests to be contaminated with minute – but unacceptably high – traces of benzene, a toxic solvent that can cause cancer, at its bottling plant in Vergeze.

When asked why the product was being recalled, Perrier's chairman laughed and said, 'Perrier is crazy! That's our advertising slogan in France.' Then, in its first press release, Perrier stated that an employee who incorrectly used a benzene cleaning fluid on the bottling machinery had caused the problem. In its second press release, however, Perrier recanted that statement, saying that employees failing to clean filters properly caused the problem.

Despite the speedy product recall and *nouvelle production* relaunch a few weeks later, the second press release had created doubts about the firm's famous 'naturally pure' water supply and the whole affair had raised questions about the integrity of its senior management.

In Washington, Senator Al Gore said, 'Personally, I am not going to be satisfied until thousands of rats have consumed millions of bottles of Perrier and survived.'

Six months later, Perrier was only being restocked by 70 per cent of old outlets. Competitors of course took advantage of Perrier's misfortune – well, actually, bad process performance measurement and management.

In May 1990, Perrier made a provision in its accounts of FF430 million ($79 million) to cover the cost. The following year, however, it admitted that the episode had cost FF1.01 billion ($171 million).

Lessons? Perrier's handling of the physical process of withdrawing potentially contaminated product was well done. On the other hand – Lesson 1 – its (seldom need to activate) crisis management process in relation to media handling was a shambles and, consequently, sullied its brand image. Clearly too, its management of regular maintenance processes – obviously vital because it would not have installed the filters if it had not realized that there was a potential problem with the water source – was not in control: Lesson 2.

Having the right process measures in place could have saved executive credibility, corporate reputation, market share, and a hugh amount of money.

Additionally, when measuring processes, we need to consider the component parts of the individual process itself. All processes have four common characteristics, which can be represented as shown in Figure 5.6.

Fig 5.6 The Four Common Characteristics of Processes

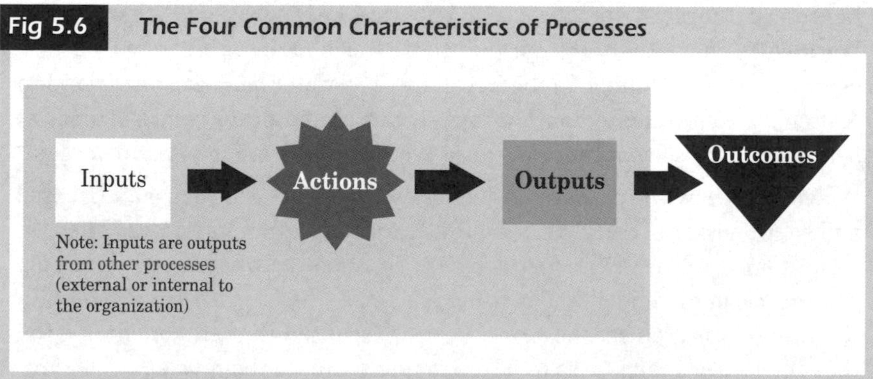

Starting with the process outcomes and outputs first, here we will normally need to identify measures of the **effectiveness** of the process:

- Does the process deliver or produce what it is supposed to do? [Output]
- How well does the process output perform for the recipient? [Outcome].

Process outcomes and outputs can be measured in terms of quality, quantity, time, ease of use and money (price). Outcomes can usually be measured in one of three ways – first, through surveying the recipients of the process outputs; second, through complaints or claims; and, third, through rigorous testing and/or simulation. It is often beneficial to implement *all three* types of measure. Next, we need to consider the actions and inputs of the process. Here we would typically be seeking measures of the **efficiency** of the process, for example:

- How long does it take to execute the process?
- How frequently does the process have to be executed?
- How much volume is processed (versus capacity)?
- What does it cost to perform the process?
- What are the levels of variability in – and into – the process?
- What is the level of wastage in the process?
- How flexible [e.g. multi-purpose] is the process?
- How simple/complex [e.g. transactional/knowledge-based] is the process?
- How ready for deployment is a [e.g. rarely required but essential] process?

Clearly, these factors can also be measured in terms of Quality, Quantity, Time, Ease of Use and Money (Cost).

Wastage and variability can be two particularly fruitful areas of process measurement. The classic categories of waste (described by Toyota's former chief engineer, Taiichi Ohno, but also applicable to many different non-engineering environments) are:

- Defects.
- Waiting.
- Transporting.
- Overproduction (regardless of demand).
- Inappropriate Processing ('hammer to crack a nut' syndrome).
- Unnecessary Motions (ergonomics).
- Unnecessary Inventory.

Today, we might also add the wastes of:

- Space.
- Pollution.
- Excess energy or power used.
- Unnecessary complexity.
- Human potential or talent.

One further feature of process measurement to mention is its ability to be measured at either a macro- or micro-level. As we mentioned above, process owners may indeed want to see the big picture, but they will also need to be able to pinpoint where quality, cycle time and bottleneck problems are occurring at the detail level. Figure 5.7 shows how some core processes can be measured on an end-to-end basis and then broken down into component elements.

Fig 5.7 Key 'Core Processes' Management Measures

Process focus	End-to-end measure	Sub-set measures
1. Product/Service fulfilment (selling & buying)	Order to cash	Sales/Purchase order to provision Provision to payment/Settlement
2. Product/Service demand generation	Prospect to customer	Potential prospect to 'Hot prospect' Hot prospect to sales closure (sign-up) Sales closure to repeat business
3. New product/Service development	Concept to market	Concept to prototype Prototype to launch/Roll-out
4. After-sales service (when applicable)	Notification to resolution	Notification to attendance Attendance to resolution (Assumes nil payment service contract – if chargeable, then to Payment)
5. Recruitment	Request to contribution	Request to start-date Start-date to competence level
6. Capex/Infrastructure/IT system projects	Definition to payback	Opportunity definition to RFQ RFQ to selection Selection to installation Installation to payback
7. Practices improvement/ Change programmes	Identification to results	Identification to implementation Implementation to predicted results
8. Mergers & acquisitions/ Alliances	Target to benefits	Target to deal Deal to benefits

The Fifth Perspective on Performance – Capabilities

Processes cannot function on their own, however. Even the most brilliantly designed process needs people with certain skills, some policies and procedures about the way things are done, some physical infrastructure for it to happen and, more than likely, some technology to enable or enhance it. Capabilities are bundles of people, practices, technologies and infrastructure (see Figure 5.8).

Fig 5.8 **The Components of Capabilities**

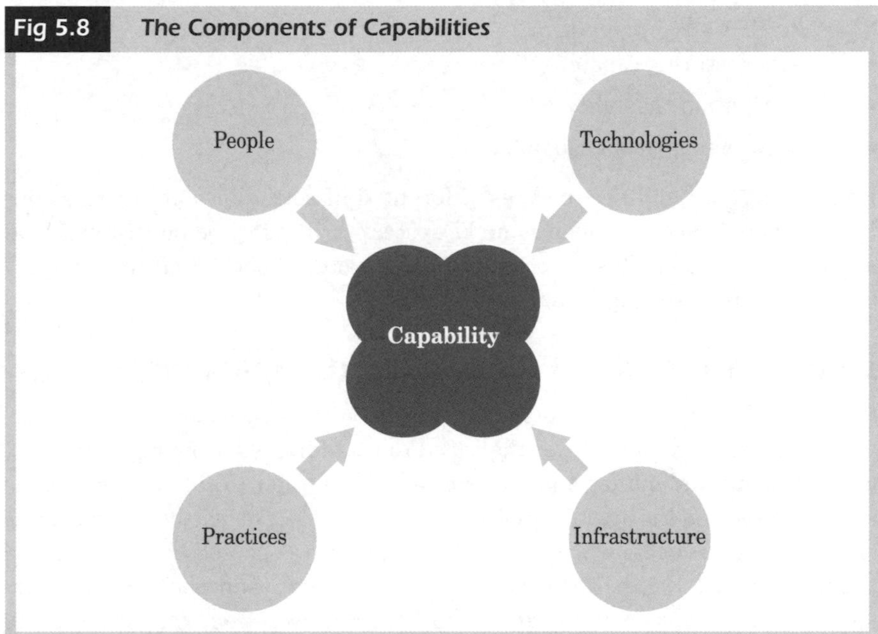

In fact, capabilities can be defined as the *combination* of an organization's people, practices, technology and infrastructure that collectively represents that organization's ability to create value for its stakeholders through a distinct part of its operations. Very often that distinct part will be a business process, but it could also be a brand, a product/service or an organizational element. Measurement will normally need to focus on those critical component elements that make it distinctive and also allow it to remain distinctive in the future. But that does not necessarily mean that those capabilities that only need to be as good as any other competitors do not need to be measured. How will you know that you are not beginning to lag behind in these areas if you do not measure them? Either way, competitive benchmarks will likely be needed in order to understand the size of the gap. Competitors will be seeking ways to create value for probably not exactly the same, but a very similar set of stakeholders too. The goalposts seldom remain static for very long.

So that there is no confusion about what we mean here by capabilities; consider a common business process, such as the order-to-cash fulfilment process in an electronic products business for example. The customer places an order, the company makes and delivers it, and then gets paid for it. It is a single process with multiple components and implies the presence of at least six different capabilities. These are:

- a customer order handling capability
- a planning and scheduling capability
- a procurement capability
- a manufacturing capability
- a distribution capability
- a credit management capability.

Each of these capabilities requires different skill-sets, different practices, different technologies (although some IT systems will likely be multi-functional and integrated) and different physical infrastructures, such as offices, a factory and warehouses (see Figure 5.9).

Linking Strategies, Processes and Capabilities

So, the Performance Prism helps to identify the critical components of strategies, processes and capabilities that need to be addressed, from a performance measurement and management point of view, in order to satisfy the various stakeholders' and the organization's wants and needs. Obviously, organizations can and need to choose which elements of these three perspectives or facets of the Performance Prism framework they need to focus their performance management attentions on at any given time in their evolution. The Performance Prism is a flexible enough tool to allow that selection process to be adapted in the initiatives and focus that organizations elect to pursue. Figure 5.10 summarizes the application of these three perspectives.

As we have seen from the Writing Inc. example described earlier in this chapter, an essential element is that these three facets or perspectives of the Performance Prism need to be linked to each other in order to understand how they fit together towards satisfying the stakeholders' and the organization's wants and needs. We illustrated how the creation of a success map is a useful technique that helps to facilitate this alignment. An alternative method, or perhaps most appropriately as a means of validating the outputs from the success mapping process, is to apply what we call a 'failure mode map'.

Failure mapping helps to check whether all the critical aspects of performance measurement have been properly addressed. We shall provide examples of these within each of the five chapters that follow. In essence, this technique takes the reverse approach to a success map by identifying particular scenarios that describe the opposite of success – failure. By examining each key potential failure

Fig 5.9 How Capabilities Enable Processes to Work

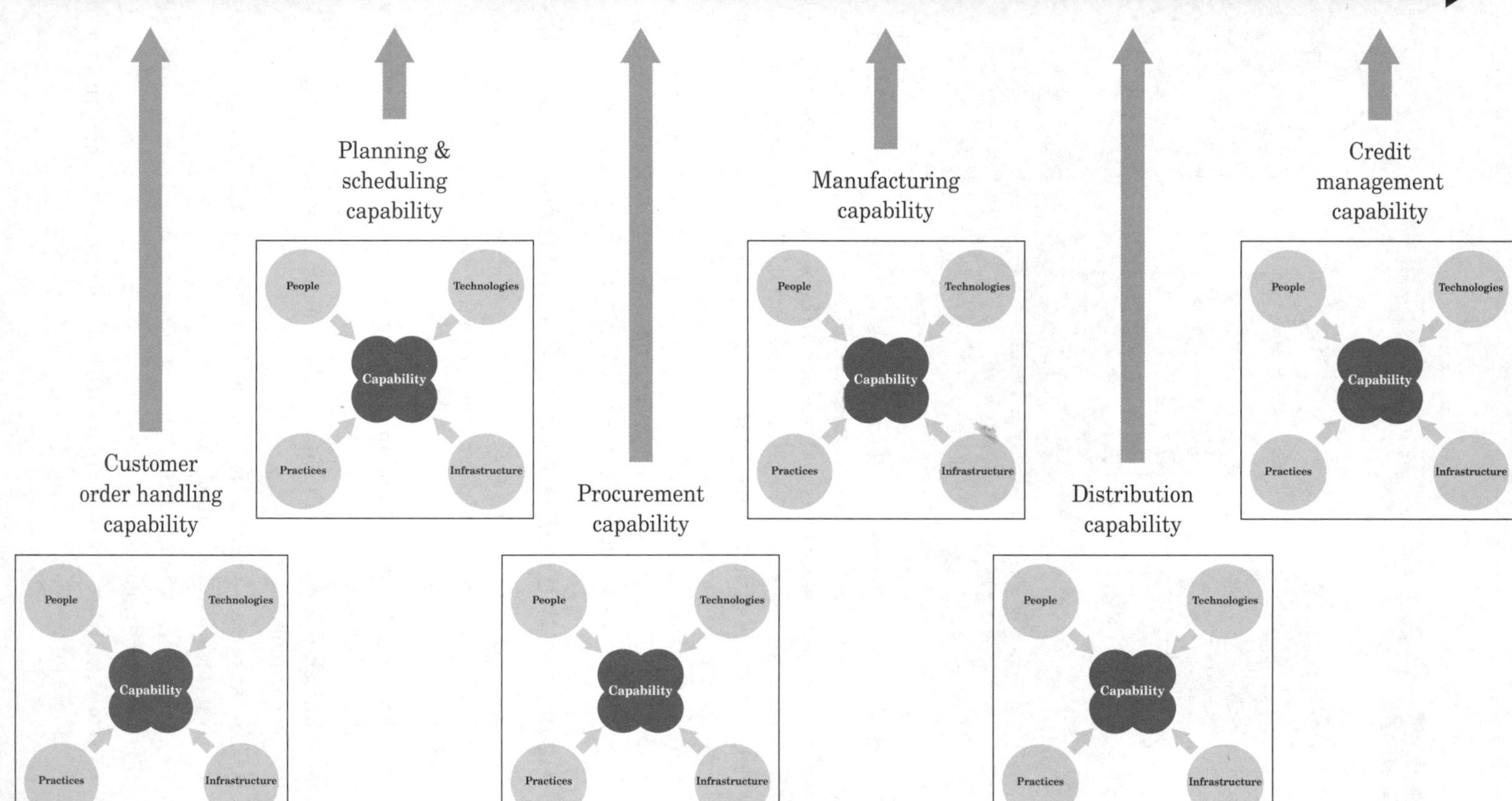

Fig 5.10 The Final Three Facets of the Performance Prism

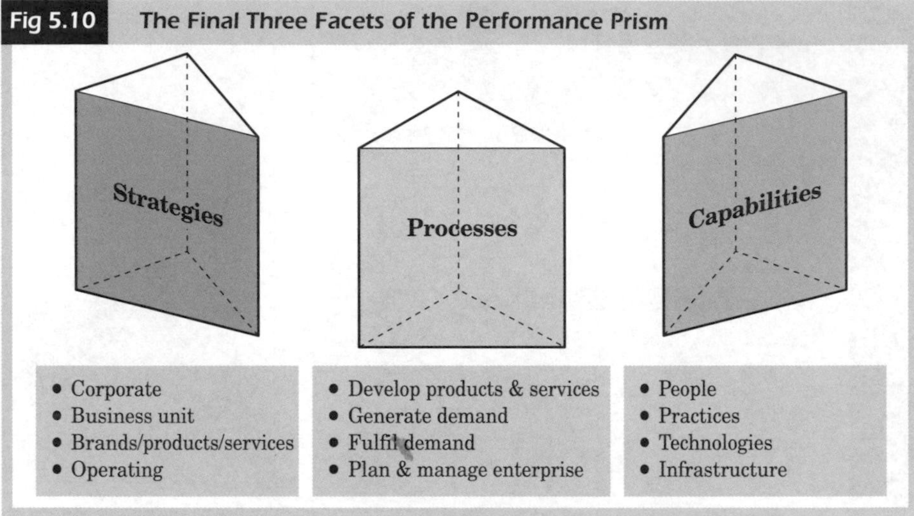

mode, a check can be made on the strategies, processes and capabilities that relate to this risk and whether the measures identified are sufficient to enable mitigation of the risk's occurrence or its malevolence. To be warned should be to be prepared.

Kaplan and Norton promote the application of strategy maps (as we have noted above), but they do not go far enough since they fail to break them down into their vital components – the potential for success and the potential for failure. Organizations have many opportunities but they also face several threats – their measurement systems need to be able to capture both so that executives can manage the business with a clear view of both scenarios.

Applying the Performance Prism to Measures Design

To summarize then, we have identified five distinct, but logically interlinked, perspectives on performance together with five key questions to apply that will aid measurement design:

- **Stakeholder Satisfaction** – who are the key stakeholders and what do they want and need?
- **Stakeholder Contribution** – what contributions do we require from our key stakeholders?
- **Strategies** – what strategies do we have to put in place to satisfy these two sets of wants and needs?
- **Processes** – what critical processes do we require if we are to execute these strategies?
- **Capabilities** – what capabilities do we need to operate and enhance these processes?

As we have seen, these five perspectives on performance can be represented in the form of a prism. A prism refracts light. It illustrates the hidden complexity of something as apparently simple as white light. So it is with the Performance Prism. It illustrates the true complexity of performance measurement and management. Single dimensional, traditional frameworks pick up elements of this complexity. While each of them offers a unique perspective on performance, it is essential to recognize that this is all that they offer – a single uni-dimensional perspective on performance. Performance, however, is not uni-dimensional. To understand it in its entirety, it is essential to view from the multiple and interlinked perspectives offered by the Performance Prism (see Figure 5.11).

Fig 5.11 **Delivering Stakeholder Value**

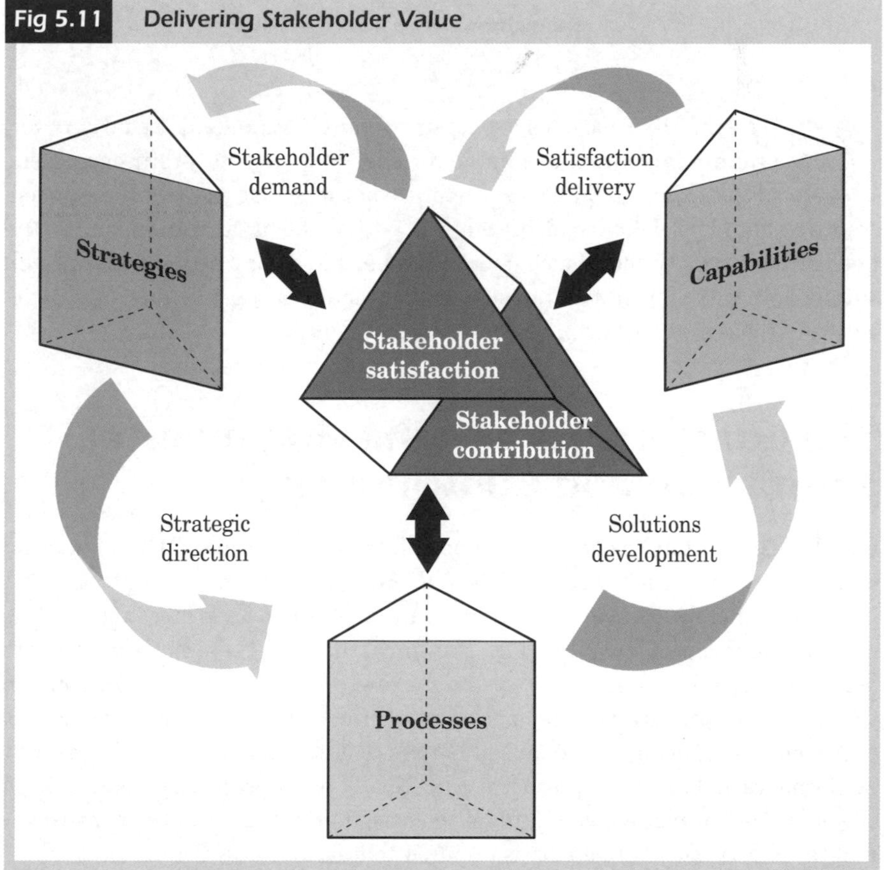

Let's explore this further through the next five chapters, each of which illustrates how the Performance Prism framework can be applied to specific stakeholders.

Managing Investor Relationships with Measures

6

Nobody who has been on a falling elevator and survived ever again approaches such a conveyance without a fundamentally reduced degree of confidence.

Robert Reno • *on the 1987 stockmarket crash.*

Given that its investors are as important a stakeholder that any for-profit organization can name (or even most not-for-profit ones, come to that), we should be clear about what it is that they want and need. And we should be clear too about what it is that the organization wants and needs from them. Without such clarity, it's hard to design strategies that will satisfy both sets of wants and needs. And without appropriate measures, execution of those strategies will be even more difficult.

The Components of Achieving Investor Satisfaction and Contribution

So, what do investors really want and need from an organization? Our shorthand terminology for this is *Return*, *Reward*, *Figures* and *Faith*. That is to say, investors – shareholders, in particular – want a return on their investment in the company in terms of a capital gain. But, until they sell their shares, investors only see a paper gain and so they also want reward for their loyalty meantime in the form of periodic dividend payments. Furthermore, they want the organization to present financial and non-financial figures that accurately reflect both its past performance and its future prospects. And, finally, investors want to have faith in the organization's management team to consistently deliver on the promises it makes – management credibility is an important factor for investors.

What does the organization want and need from its investors in return? Again in shorthand, we believe it is *Capital*, *Credit*, *Risk* and *Support*. That is the organization needs capital in order to grow, funding its capital expenditure and company acquisition requirements. Unless it is cash-rich, it will need credit – principally in the form of loans and bonds – in order to manage its working capital needs. It wants its investors to take an element of risk in lending it money or subscribing for its shares. And, lastly, it wants support from its major investors in terms of long-term loyalty and it may sometimes need patience from its bankers. In some circumstances, it may also need support in the form of practical advice from its investors – for example, whether to carry out an acquisition or not and, for fledgling companies, perhaps advice about how to run the company in unfavourable market conditions. The Investor Relationship model is presented in Figure 6.1.

Fig 6.1 The Investor Relationship

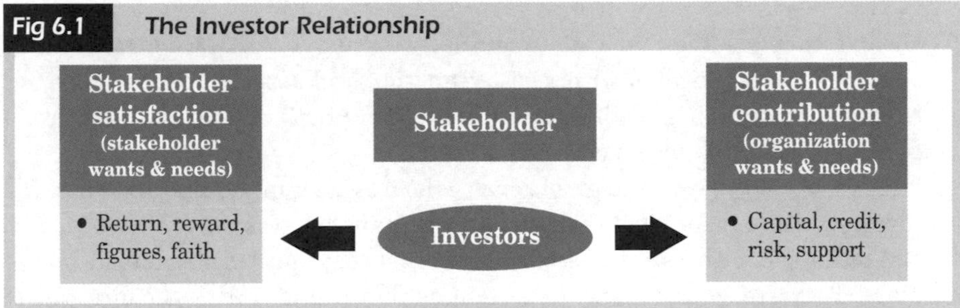

Investor Value Realization

What is it that actually creates the value that shareholders seek? We have seen in Chapter 4 that a company's financial performance will not always be positively correlated to its share price performance due to the many company-uncontrollable factors that go to make up stockmarket sentiment. In the longer term, however, the correlation is much stronger. So, what 'does the business'? Without doubt, over the longer term, it is principally the specific strategies (or, more fashionably, 'business model') the corporation both develops and executes that relate to satisfying its various stakeholders' wants and needs in the markets within which it operates. As Mark Goyder, director of the UK's Centre for Tomorrow's Company points out:[42] 'Investors urgently need better yardsticks by which they can interpret future financial returns from current value creation. This – and not the charting of [share] price fluctuations – is the proper territory for the study and enhancement of shareholder value.' However, it is the development and communication of strategy that tends to excite investors, but the execution of them that frequently disappoints. Those companies that consistently deliver on their declared strategies earn investors' respect and, normally, their long-term loyalty.

Corporate and even business unit strategies are often categorized as pursuing one of three disciplines: operational excellence, product leadership or customer intimacy.[43] Each of these approaches demand different core business processes, organizational structures, management systems and cultures. But, in whatever way they are dressed up, these strategies tend to revolve around six principal categories of management focus:

- Organic growth.
- Mergers and acquisitions.
- Cost optimization.
- Asset divestment.
- Capital investment.
- Optimal cost of capital.

Clearly, each strategy type is not mutually exclusive. An M&A strategy may very well run in parallel with a cost reduction and asset divestment one, for example. An organic growth strategy is likely, but not necessarily, to be accompanied by a capital investment requirement.

Organizations need strategies to enable them to steer in the right direction and investors like to hear what the company's captain believes those directions are. But the problem with strategies of course is that they only exist as intents and as plans. They are 'paper tigers'. Important as they are in setting the direction of where an enterprise is heading, strategies do not intrinsically deliver anything at all – other than speculation about the future perhaps. What does deliver tangible value though are the programmes and projects that firms start and complete in order to execute their strategic intents and plans. Managing these successfully is also an essential, but less glamorous and sometimes overlooked, executive function. (Note the words 'start and complete' – it is remarkable how many initiatives get started by executive edict but just how few reach a stage that could be considered complete, up-and-running, or even reach some sort of 'half-life'.)

Strategy development and implementation are part of a critical business process, which is commonly called Plan and Manage Enterprise. However, aside from the attraction and allocation of the capital it needs in order to execute its strategy, the 'real work' of a corporation is done through three other critical business processes. The first of these is developing new products and services. The business world does not stand still and the company that neglects an ability to renew itself will inevitably wither gradually (or occasionally flame-out spectacularly). Clearly, the level of R&D effort and expenditure is highly industry dependent. But how much a company spends on R&D is no *guarantee* of success, since it may not be spending it wisely on the programmes and projects that will benefit shareholders' interests most. However, as a general rule of thumb, it is commonly taken that the greater the R&D spend, the greater the investment in new products and services. For example, much of the rationale for mergers and acquisitions in the pharmaceuticals industry is driven by leveraging massive research and development resources to create new drugs.

The second core business process is generating demand for its products and services. Marketing and sales departments are charged with creating demand for these new products and services and for expanding sales into new or existing geographical regions and market segments. This may be achieved through an organic growth programme; as the result of a merger/major acquisition; or from a series of bolt-on acquisitions, which typically add either market penetration or geographical spread. Third, having created that demand, there is a requirement to fulfil it efficiently and effectively. This is an area that many dot-com start-ups found most difficult to deliver. Long before many of them 'threw in the towel', several surveys had highlighted major weaknesses in their ability to effectively deliver on the expectations of their customers, so newly won through expensive advertising campaigns. In their rush to achieve 'first mover advantage', poor execution gave many business-to-consumer dot-coms a bad name and contributed to their inability to secure sufficient repeat business to become profitable. Not surprisingly, investors currently have a negative attitude towards the sector. However, these weaknesses are by no means exclusive to the so-called 'new economy' companies and we explore this theme further in Chapter 7.

For companies to deliver on their strategies through their business processes, they must also develop particular capabilities which allow them to be better than – or, at least, the equal of – their competitors in the markets for their products and services. Anything less is probably unsustainable and likely to lead to the destruction of shareholder value. Typically, the capabilities that are likely to attract investors' interest are the ones that are either distinctive to the company in question or are essential components of a rational investment opportunity. The assessment of management's credibility will, to a significant extent, revolve around its ability to invest in – and sustain competitive advantage through – its distinctive capabilities. For example, at the operating level, a company's new/product service pipeline, its particular market focus and positioning, its business unit performance management, its management of its brands, and its investments in core competencies should all be of interest to investors who are not just intent on following the herd. Equally, the attitude of serious investors may be influenced by perceptions of, for example, a company's capabilities in managing investor relations, its executive leadership, its financial controls, its ability to manage risk, its track record for integrating mergers and acquisitions, and so on.

Furthermore, individual institutional investment funds today increasingly have a particular focus or speciality that is not necessarily driven by the most common segmentation criteria of geographical region, company size and industry. One of these emerging segments is in the area of 'socially responsible investments'. The ethical fund industry is growing rapidly and more than 200 such funds already exist in Europe alone. In April 2001, FTSE (jointly owned by the *Financial Times* and the London Stock Exchange) launched a series of four international tradeable indices, called FTSE4Good. These indices provide benchmarks against which institutions can measure and market the performance of their ethical funds. When similar 'sustainability indices' were introduced in the US by Dow Jones in 1999, companies started promoting their inclusion as a badge of honour in their annual reports. So, a significant factor for companies wishing to qualify and be retained in the portfolio of such investment funds will be to provide evidence of their social strategies, processes and capabilities. We shall address this requirement in more detail in Chapter 10, but it should be noted here that not only does this trend exist but that it may be an important topic in terms of managing investor relations. It also means executing particular internal programmes as well as providing evidential data to investors.

These are illustrations of – not recipes for – the components of delivering investor satisfaction in different operating environments. There is no single 'to do' list. Every public company (and private ones too) must determine how it relates to its investors if it is to survive and prosper. It is such a simple concept, but it is an area that many companies overlook and do not allocate the appropriate level of human and financial resources. Figure 6.2 summarizes the illustration we have described above.

For organizations that are subsidiaries or business units of parent companies, incidentally, the parent company's wants and needs can usually be substituted as a surrogate for the external investor. They essentially demand much the same things. We should note though that corporations may very well need to pursue significantly different business strategies within their various divisions and geographical regions in the pursuit of their overall performance objectives.

Measures for Investor Relationship Management

Typically, this stakeholder environment has been dominated by financial measures and it continues to be an extremely important factor today. However, there is a distinct movement to include more non-financial measures that provide indications of future performance and confidence in the management team to deliver on expectations.

Fig 6.2 Mapping Investor Relationships through the Performance Prism facets

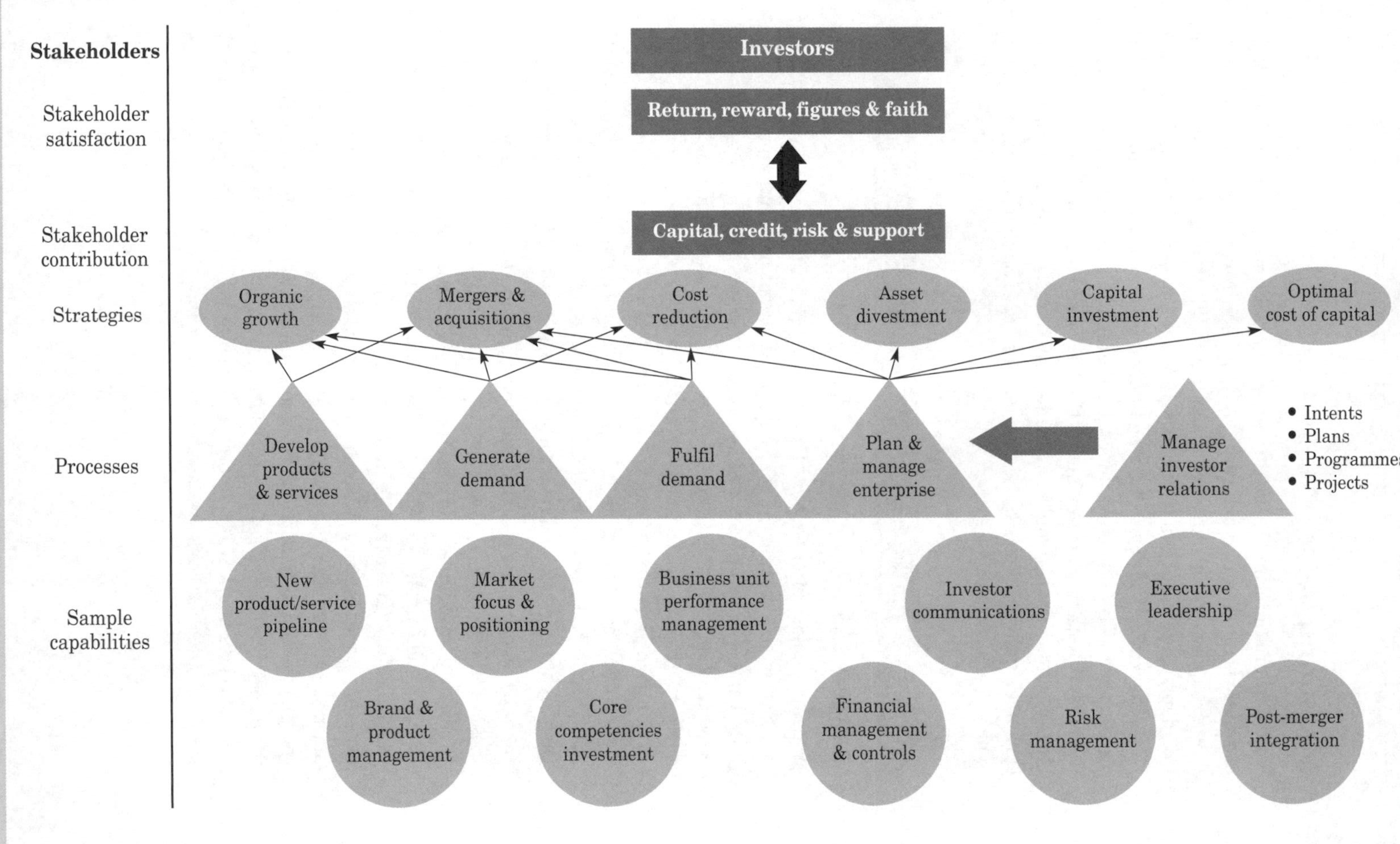

Measuring Value

The plethora of formulae used to assess – or often compare – the value of a company is an area of much confusion and controversy. Several methods are now used, the most common of which are EBITDA (earnings before interest, tax, depreciation and amortization), EVA™ (Economic Value Added) and Free Cash Flow (FCF). Many quacks peddle variants of these fashionable instruments, such as SVA (Shareholder Value Added), Cash Value Added (CVA) and Cash Flow Return on Investment (CFROI) – so much so that Stern Stewart has even gone to the trouble of trademarking the term EVA – and promote each one's individual merits. See the box *Alphabet Soup* for some more detailed explanations of these measures.

Alphabet Soup

EBITDA

Earnings before interest, tax, depreciation and amortization. Arguably, this is a reasonable measure if the company does not happen to have considerable capital expenditure needs and/or a substantial amount of debt to service. The trouble is that today most companies do not fall into one of these categories. The fact is that this measure is widely used by companies as a 'smoke and mirrors' mechanism to report rosier projections of its earnings growth potential than is really the case. The most worrying aspect of this is that it is a totally misleading measure of a company's access to further capital injection and its ability to pay interest on its existing debt.

Invented to overcome national differences in taxation and accounting standards, EBITDA also says nothing about the quality of a company's earnings. It can be manipulated through aggressive accounting policies relating to revenue and expense recognition plus other such accountancy shenanigans. Particularly, it does not take into account a company that depreciates costs over an extended period, when it would have been more realistic – and prudent – to charge them off against revenue. For example, media and cable companies tend to be particular proponents of EBITDA since it makes their income statements look more reassuring than they might otherwise be, yet they have to spend vast amounts of money upgrading their technology assets. So, in effect, this is a 'suspension of reality'.

EVA™ (and its derivatives)

Economic Value Added. Stern Stewart's method is based not on cash flow, as some people seem to believe, but profit restated (indeed others prefer to call it Economic Profit). It demands a whole set of complex adjustments [non-trained personnel need not apply for the job] – for its sole real virtue, which is making a charge against the restated profits for the weighted average cost of capital. The latter normally turns out at around 10 per cent in today's economic environment.

This adjustment is intended to take some account of the inherent risk of investing money in the firm versus putting the cash into other more risk-averse high interest bearing investments, such as gilts or bonds, called the cost of equity. The purpose of including this hurdle is to ensure that when executives make investment decisions, they make them on the basis that they are not squandering shareholders funds and a value adding return on investment is obtained. But how this is calculated can be fairly discretionary.

EVA is often also associated with MVA (Market Value Added). MVA is a longer-term measure and its calculation is complex too. Evaluating a company's MVA essentially involves calculating all the money that shareholders could theoretically take out of the business (the current value of its shares and its debts, sometimes called Enterprise Value) and deducting the sum of money that has been put into the company over its lifetime (money raised through share issues, borrowings and retained earnings). If a company has a positive MVA, it has created value; if it has a negative number, value has been destroyed. How useful that figure might be is debatable.

FCF

Free Cash Flow. Its principal advantage is that it does not require complex and intricate adjustments in order to calculate the appropriate figure. The calculation can be made by picking up any corporation's published statement of accounts and can be done by anyone with the wherewithall of a basic calculator.

It takes operating profit (before taxes and interest), removes the accounting depreciation and amortization charges plus working capital adjustments to profits [these are not cash sums, and are conveniently identified in most companies' cash flow statements] and then subtracts, first, the amount of tax paid. Next, interest payments and dividends distributed to shareholders – the principal *tangible* components of the cost of capital – are deducted.

Finally, the amounts of operating capital expenditure expended less the proceeds from any unexceptional asset sales should also be deducted. This is a 'fair and true' way to determine how a company is really performing. However, it does *not* include the cost of acquiring (or the proceeds of selling) companies, since these are considered as non-recurring transactions.

Arguably it would be better if companies were forced to declare this figure as part of their reporting requirements, but alas it still needs to be calculated in most instances. Companies make much of extolling the virtues of their P&L accounts, which are of course subject to manipulation. From an investor standpoint, the cash flow statement is usually much more interesting and can also be highly revealing.

While these methods all have their specific uses in particular circumstances, the authors are advocates of applying Free Cash Flow as the primary method of valuation, simply because it is unadulterated – it is what is left in the till after you account for all the cash coming in and all the cash going out during a given period. It can be applied from General Electric to the corner shop in the village. And it won't tell half-truths, in the way that EBITDA in particular flatters to deceive. Companies don't go belly-up just because their EBITDA fails to meet expectations, they simply run out of cash to continue doing business – as several banks, who loaned money on the basis of EBITDA projections, will be aware. As Peter Drucker once noted, 'You can only fake cash flow if you are willing to go to jail.' FCF is also simple to calculate and does not require a double-first degree in advanced mathematics and economics in order to understand the accounting adjustments that need to be made to come up with a figure. Cash is fact; accounting is opinion.

For start-up and fledgling companies, where initial 'cash burn' is high and profits often elusive for many years, other predictors of future success gain particular prominence. Today, for nascent organizations, the path towards profitability needs to be convincing and so credible evidence of progress must be provided to investors. A process of giving a monetary value to the customer acquisition projections to get to a future cash flow number is often applied for these purposes. Some other briefly fashionable instruments for evaluating non-profit-making companies, such as Real Option Pricing, are now scorned by most investment analysts. The UK's *Investors Chronicle* reports[44] that: 'Although this method proved popular with some analysts at the height of the tech boom, the mathematics involved is complex and the results are not always conclusive. Unsurprisingly, most analysts have abandoned the model.'

Projections of future cash flows are necessary for emerging companies to attract investor attention, but it is worth noting the words of Benjamin Graham, which still ring true nearly 70 years after he wrote them. In his seminal work *Security Analysis* (1934), he claimed: 'Analysts serve their discipline best by identifying such [new and unproven] companies as highly speculative and not attempting to value them ... The buyer of such securities is not making an investment, but a bet on a new technology, a new market, a new service ... Winning bets on such situations can produce very rich rewards but they are in an odds-setting rather than a valuation process.'

What Do Investors Really Want to Know?

Enough of the alchemy, a report entitled *Full Disclosure 2000: An International Study of Disclosure Practices* published by Shelley Taylor & Associates – the London and Palo Alto-based research consultants – analyzed the annual reports of 100 traditional and so-called new economy companies.[45] Their report listed the following criteria as those regarded as most important by the greatest number of investors:

- Strategy.
- Earnings per share growth.
- Free cash flow.
- Management experience.
- R&D expenditure.
- Short and long-term debt.
- Products.
- Bad news.
- Market leadership.
- Challenges and risks.

Only five companies were rated as addressing all of the issues investors cared about, and all of them had essentially old economy credentials: BP Amoco (UK/US), Ericsson (Swedish), Volvo (Swedish), Barclays (UK) and SCA (Swedish). Conversely, the five worst performers were all US internet and software companies. However, the report found that both new economy and traditional businesses of all descriptions were generally backward in coming forward with key information about their activities, beyond those financial metrics that they were obliged to disclose by law. The Shelley Taylor report is one of a stream of recent reports, papers and books calling for more detailed disclosure from public companies.

Earlier research carried out by Dr Richard Barker of The Judge Institute of Management at the University of Cambridge addressed the ratios and valuation models that both analysts and fund managers actually apply.[46] He found that they prefer the robust nature of the simple ones and the speed with which they can be applied. Top of this list comes:

- price/earnings ratio
- dividend yield
- return on capital employed
- price/cash flow ratio.

Other techniques appeared to be of little importance to them and both the analysts and the fund managers ranked the various technical tools in the same way.

Dr Barker found too that both analysts and fund managers rely on accounting data to judge value creation in the immediate future – using short-term extrapolation techniques – but when it comes to longer-term performance predictions they rank their assessment of management higher than anything else. He concludes that they see this judgement as a proxy for the capacity of the business to outperform the competition in the future. Interestingly, he also observed that again both analysts and fund managers rarely quantify risk, relying on subjective judgement rather than on quantitative analysis.

This UK evidence is largely born out by research carried out in the US as part of the *Measures that Matter* study.[47] This concluded that investors take non-financial measures into account when valuing companies. The research found that institutional investors not only pay attention to non-financial factors, they also apply that knowledge when making investment decisions. The researchers claim that, on average, 35 per cent of an investment decision is driven by consideration of non-financial data. However, the non-financial measures that matter to investors vary by industry and, within peer groups, from firm to firm.

Once again there was a high degree of agreement between analysts and fund managers on the kinds of measures they sought. Some are relatively 'soft', or perceptional, in nature. The ones they claim to value most are:

1 Strategy execution.
2 Management credibility.
3 Quality of strategy.
4 Innovativeness.
5 Ability to attract talented people.
6 Market share.

7 Management experience.
8 Quality of executive compensation.
9 Quality of major processes.
10 Research leadership.

The research also found that: 'When non-financial factors were taken into account, earnings forecasts were more accurate, thus reducing the risk to investors. If a firm's non-financial data are strong, this could facilitate its ability to raise capital. The message is clear: non-financial factors can be used as leading indicators of future financial performance.' They conclude, therefore, that if a firm does not strategically manage key non-financial measures, its operating performance and the value of its securities will suffer.

When the study was replicated in the UK three years later, an almost identical list of the top ten non-financial measures that matter (albeit in a slightly different order of priority) was gathered.[48] Indeed, the only significant difference was that quality of executive compensation was replaced in the list by global capability – which could be as much to do with 'Britishness', or even a movement in attitudes during the intervening period, as about real differences of opinion among the investment community in Europe.

Yet another study[49] of institutional investors and sell-side analysts globally – gathering survey data in the US, UK, the Netherlands, France, Germany, Italy, Switzerland, Sweden, Denmark, Australia, Japan, Hong Kong, Singapore and Taiwan – identified nine financial and non-financial measures that they consider particularly important in making their investment decisions. These are:

1 Earnings.
2 Cash flow.
3 Costs.
4 Capital expenditures.
5 R&D investment amounts.
6 Segment performance.
7 Statements of strategic goals.
8 New product development.
9 Market share.

Inevitably there are some industry-specific, as well as national, differences in the priorities that are given to individual measures by these professionals. Also, fund managers prioritize different measures than analysts.

On the whole, however, a large degree of agreement exists between institutional investors and equities analysts on both sides of the Atlantic and elsewhere as to what needs to be measured from their perspective. Financial measures are critical for their short-term evaluations, while non-financial measures are key to longer-term assessment. The latter though are more like a kind of jigsaw puzzle or 'future archaeology', piecing together scraps of information to try to make a coherent picture of what is going on and to make predictions. The implication then is that investor relations managers should use these factors as a checklist to see if they are measuring the right stuff within their organizations and whether they are giving out the right signals to their shareholders.

One indicator not mentioned in any of the surveys, but often tracked by private investors in particular (and which is regularly reported in the financial press) is the behaviour of company directors with respect to their own holdings of the company's shares. If directors are buying, it is generally taken as an indicator that they have confidence in the company's prospects and are prepared to 'put their money where their mouth is' – especially if several directors buy simultaneously. On the other hand, substantial director sales might signify the opposite (although smaller individual sales may signify their purchase of real estate or the settlement of divorce proceedings).

Managing Business Combinations and Alliances with Measures

Given that firms frequently use their equity – and debt – to acquire other companies in order to accelerate their rate of growth, this chapter would seem to be the most appropriate place to address the measurement of mergers and acquisitions too. Of course these affect many different stakeholders (employees, customers, suppliers and, increasingly, regulators) – but most of all they are targeted at investors' interests. M&A activity is directed primarily at shareholders because they seek growth. Growth is perceived as good since increased revenues *should* translate into higher profits – if not immediately, sometime in the not too distant future. M&A means rapid access to significant or even quantum leaps in volume of sales. Given the availability of money, it is fundamentally easier to buy an entity that exists than to grow it incrementally. Organic growth is virtuous, but it is also essentially medium to long term in nature and requires persistent diligence. While M&A growth is perceived as fast, bold and, frankly, heroic.

Given the shortening 'attention spans' of investors described previously, a series of daring acquisitions offers the potential of exponential growth. A further benefit can be that a takeover eliminates an established or emerging competitor. It is hardly any accident then that this form of growth appeals to the temperament of most chief executives too, whether it flatters their egos or fattens their wallets – or both. Today, there is pressure from institutional investors on CEOs to grow their companies rapidly and hence we have witnessed over the past decade what can rightly be described as a 'feeding frenzy' of corporate activity. Even in temporary periods of downturn, there have still been significant amounts of corporate M&A activity. In the name of increasing shareholder value, size matters.

The immense irony is that a whole bunch of research shows that most of these acquisitions do not end in enhanced shareholder value as evidenced in the company's share price nor even most other success criteria. Neither do strategic alliances offer better returns. At best, M&A deals offer a 50:50 chance of success. Some research indicates that it is worse odds than that. Indeed, failed mergers and acquisitions of the 1990s litter today's business landscape. Among the better known examples reported in the business press are AT&T, Quaker Oats, Mattel, Disney, Sony, Compaq, Bank of America, General Electric (*yes, GE*) plus BMW and, more recently, DaimlerChrysler. How come? There is some evidence to show that one of the primary reasons for this dismal outcome is that acquiring organizations tend to place the bulk of their effort into doing the deal(s) and not enough on planning their implementation. So-called 'bolt-on' acquisitions tend to work better than major acquisitions or mergers of equals (although seldom truly equal) because the acquirer can more easily dictate the level of integration or autonomy that the acquired company should have. They are, by definition, more manageable in scale too.

But mergers and acquisitions can go sour for many reasons, including poor strategic concepts or timing, executive egos, cultural differences, low morale and incompatible information systems. But probably the most ubiquitous cause is the failure to successfully integrate the two entities. After the ink dries on the contract unity proves elusive; instead of coming together, things fly apart. 'A whole consulting industry thrives by advising companies on post-merger integration, a salvage operation to recover something from the wreckage of impossible promises and ill-considered goals,' said *The Economist* (January, 1999), adding prescriptively, 'companies that agree on a clear strategy and management structure before they tie the knot stand a better chance of living happily ever after.'

Managing post-merger integration (PMI) differs from managing the enterprise on a day-to-day basis. Strategy has to be crystal clear and implementation razor sharp against tight deadlines. Each of the combining companies brings different processes and the best must be preserved. Difficult decisions are inevitable. What capabilities will we terminate, retain, transfer or build? The advantage of the Performance Prism framework is that it takes into account the critical strategies, processes and capabilities that business combinations need to achieve both short and longer term success. By drilling strategies down to processes and to capabilities, the Performance Prism achieves a wide-angle view that other performance measurement frameworks lack. It can track all the facets of post-merger integration at the appropriate level of detail. This comprehensiveness is particularly important in mergers, where integrating businesses often involves complex trade-offs and unique interdependencies.

Given that the evidence shows that it is likely to be an uphill struggle to implement any substantial acquisition or merger successfully, it is even more important that the right post-merger integration measures are identified and put in place. PMI can be complex, but managed well with the right measures the rewards can be significant. On the other hand, failure can mean that the new combined entity loses substantial stockmarket value and becomes the target and victim of a further takeover. For some practical considerations on the measurement and management of post-merger integration, see the box *Gauging the Success of PMI*.

Gauging the Success of PMI

The goal of mergers and acquisitions is to enhance shareholder value. Everything else is simply about damage limitation. Whether the anticipated benefits are higher revenues, lower costs, enhanced innovation, market dominance, or some combination of these, the ultimate goal is a higher stock price (or market capitalization). Yet top management often poorly articulates a merger's rationale to shareholders and its ability to create value for them. Rare indeed is the merger where management proclaims specific targets and accountability for reaching them. But a well-communicated strategy should enhance the credibility of the transaction with investors.

The architects of the Honeywell/Allied Signal merger in 1999 promised $500 million in cost reductions within three years, plus an 8–10 per cent annual growth rate and a 15 per cent gain in earnings per share. While the clarity of Honeywell's intentions is exemplary, this kind of approach is risky. Declared targets *do* have to be met. Any sign of backing-off from the target values is likely to provoke severe punishment by the stockmarket, as Honeywell experienced and which subsequently led to takeover bids from first United Technologies and then General Electric (subsequently disallowed by regulators).

The new entity's strategy will typically include such objectives as:

- Leverage the two companies' brands, products and services across the whole customer group.
- Strengthen market share or competitive positioning.
- Improve net cash flows through substantial cost savings.
- Deliver the benefits anticipated at the business unit level.
- Manage budgeted costs for the post-merger integration.

These objectives need grounding in a performance measurement system that monitors whether goals are being met so senior executives can quickly make informed judgements on the causes of performance variations and act accordingly.

Management will create projects at the operating strategy level to deliver on the promises made at the merger announcement. Special task forces recommend exactly where and how to extract value. They get budget allocations and delivery deadlines. Project performance needs close monitoring, with warning flags raised if the project will miss milestones. A popular technique is to track status with a red-yellow-green code.

The combined orgnization wants and needs things *from* its stakeholders too. Most importantly:

- A stronger investor profile.
- A positive response from securities analysts and the business media.
- Retained employees loyal to the new enterprise.
- No erosion of its combined customer base by opportunistic competitors.

Essential to realizing these aims is frequent communication with key stakeholders during this time of uncertainty. Companies that have weathered major mergers say it's almost impossible to communicate too much with the most affected stakeholders. With so much in flux, companies easily overlook communications or remain overly secretive. Creating a communication plan and monitoring its execution are essential. Executives should use feedback from briefing sessions to consider how well they are getting their message across to the key parties and to shape the agenda for further briefings.

All of the key business processes play a vital role in creating value – supporting revenue generation (through cross-selling) and cost reduction (through shrinking headcount and facilities). But attacking headcount and facilities alone can be a big mistake. Some of the largest cost savings often lie in purchasing and supply chain integration. Management must also decide which R&D investments to continue or curtail and which research initiatives will best leverage the collective capabilities of the new entity. This requires measuring, for example, the level of R&D spend by new or improved product, service or delivery channel over time (against each initiative's projected outcomes).

Capabilities that distinctively create value for stakeholders, and investors in particular, represent the fundamental building blocks of an integrating corporation's ability to compete and present many PMI issues. What is the right level of employee headcount and facilities? What are the critical skill-sets needed? What functions should move from one place to another? Which legacy information systems need immediate integration? Which are the unique product/process technologies and best operating practices of the merging orgnizations? How can the business combine them for optimum advantage?

We have considered what we would typically expect to be measured in a relatively large-scale acquisition or full merger situation. But what about less dramatic business combinations and alliances, such as smaller 'bolt-on' acquisitions, joint ventures and collaborations? For the 'bolt-on' type of acquisitions, the initial emphasis will typically be on retaining the acquired organization's key executives and integrating its financial reporting systems. In fact, many acquirers stop at that point or defer further integration for a period of time. However, they may miss a substantial opportunity if they fail to seek further synergies in cost savings (e.g. purchasing, marketing, sales force, distribution, R&D, etc.) and leveraging best practices, skill-sets, technologies and combined physical infrastructures.

We have noted earlier how business alliances rarely live up to their initial expectations too – just 39 per cent according to an Accenture study. They are also inherently more unstable, even when they are cemented with share cross-holdings. On the other hand, they do have the advantage of generally being less messy and traumatic than full mergers. In fact, many of the larger alliances frequently consist of a series of joint ventures. For example, the General Motors alliance with Fiat of Italy (involving a 20 per cent minority shareholding) announced in 2000 plans to benefit from pooling their purchasing, sharing technologies and exploring possible common platforms for volume cars. The companies expect to cut the mounting development costs for new models, while eradicating overlaps in research, component development and supply chain management. However, unlike a full merger, the individual partners apparently intend to retain their own separate manufacturing facilities (perpetrating the endemic over-capacity which exists within the industry), continue their own end-product distribution channels and actively compete against each other in certain markets.

This is an increasingly common phenomenon in today's business world, sometimes known as 'co-opetition'. In this scenario, there exists a spirit of co-operation to reduce costs but an ongoing competitive approach to winning and supplying customers. It is not difficult to imagine, therefore, how these kinds of relationships do generate difficult-to-manage tensions – especially in terms of how much information and performance measurement data is transferred between the two organizations – and how easy it can be for trust to evaporate and the joint venture become dysfunctional.

We shall return to this theme in Chapter 9.

So, recent research has trawled a considerable amount of evidence as to what it is the investment community thinks it wants and needs to be measured and reported. New and forthcoming regulations are likely to put greater pressures on companies to improve their performance reporting and forecasting. Today, however, execution in terms of satisfying these investors' wants and needs generally leaves much to be desired. Not only are the wrong performance measures often used, but also the wrong metrics for the right measures are sometimes applied – arguably, in a deliberately deceitful way. While one can sympathise with companies not wanting to release commercially sensitive information, there are far too many performance reporting gaps. Internally also, organizations need to improve the measures they use for managing improvement programmes; for managing the integration of mergers or acquisitions; and for managing the effectiveness of their various business alliances in order to ensure that they all deliver shareholder value. Figure 6.3 (p. 200) summarizes some of the key measurement issues associated with managing investor satisfaction and contribution.

The Investor Relationship Measures Design Process

The process whereby appropriate stakeholder relationship measures may be derived is, as we have described earlier, called 'success mapping'. It may be applied to each of the organization's key stakeholders. For investor relationships, it means addressing each facet of the Performance Prism framework by answering the following critical questions:

Fig 6.3 Sample Measures for Managing Investor Relations

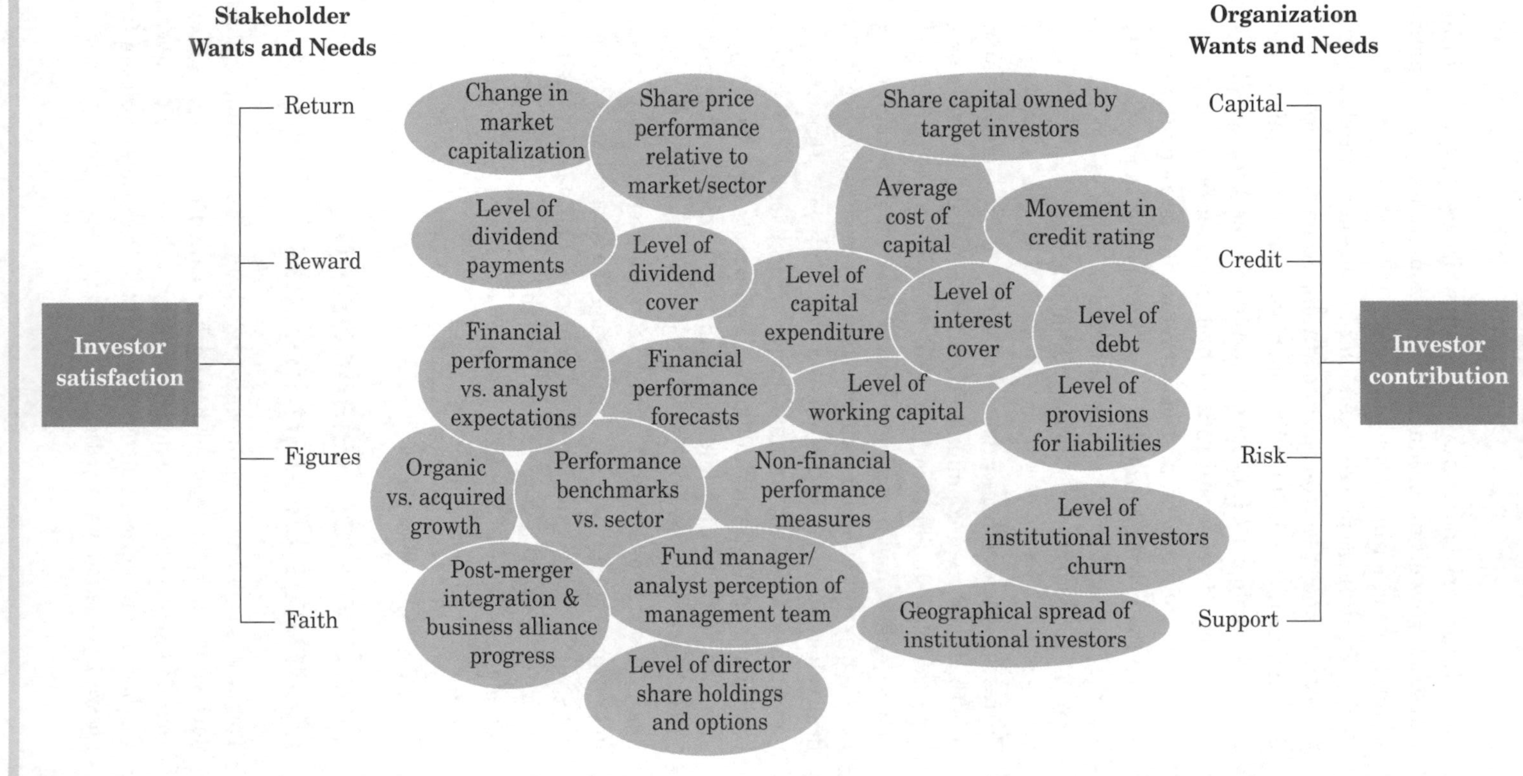

- What are the wants and needs of our key investors?
- And what does our organization want and need from these investors?
- What are our strategies for satisfying these sets of wants and needs?
- Which of our internal business processes will effectively and efficiently deliver them?
- Which particular capabilities do we need to establish and maintain in order to execute them?

Applying the Performance Prism – as conceptualized in Figure 6.4 – allows us to consider what the appropriate investor-centred measures should be for each individual organization.

Fig 6.4 Performance Prism Unfolded Schematic: Investors

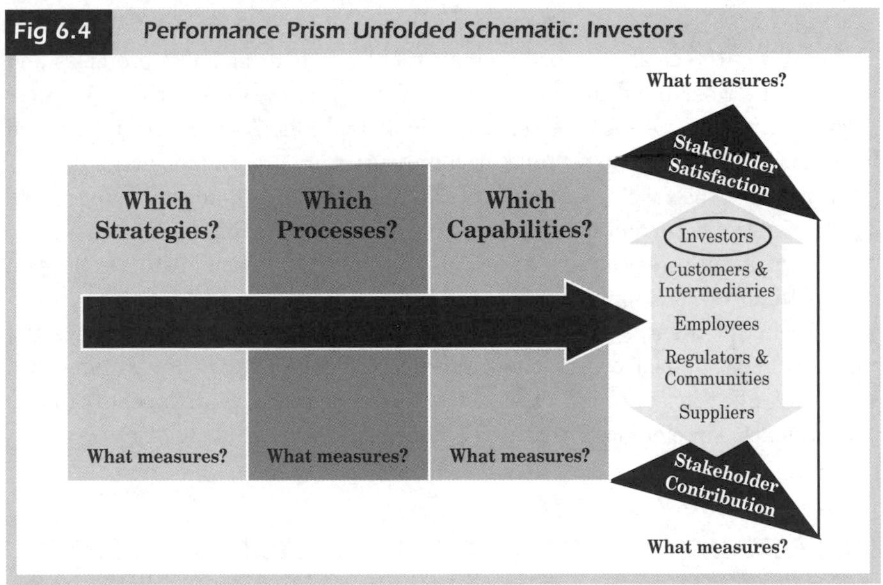

To make this more tangible, let us take the case example of a growing electronics company that wishes to attract and retain a greater institutional shareholder presence. It sees the route to achieving that aim as providing Total Shareholder Returns that are superior relative to the majority of other companies in its sector. It will deliver this through market capitalization growth, dividend and yield growth and, being a relatively small company still, optimizing its investor risk profile.

To achieve better market capitalization growth (i.e. share price outperformance versus its peer group), it believes that it will need to clearly communicate its strategic plans relating to improving its share of target industrial and geographic markets to these existing and potential investors. It will also need to demonstrate the strength and potential of its new product pipeline. It is actively seeking acquisition opportunities where there will be relevant synergies too. Strategic plans are fine, but it will also need to communicate the impact that these plans will have on its operating cash flow and how implementation of the plans will be financed. It will, therefore, also need to inform investors about the projected future state of its balance sheet and to what extent it believes that it will require further capital injections (and whether these are likely to be via debt or equity), especially if it were to make a substantial acquisition, or if perhaps two or three smaller 'bolt-on' ones happen to become available almost simultaneously.

So much for the future, but investors do not just want to know where the company's executives think it is going – they will also need a progress report on strategic initiatives planned previously and now in their implementation phase. They will want to be able to see if management is delivering on its promises and whether their assumptions about the financial impacts were correct. Are new product introductions ahead or behind budgeted targets? And are the anticipated benefits from the previously announced restructuring programme actually flowing through to the cash flow statement? Will they be enough to enable increased dividends? And is current debt interest now covered to a comfortable level?

The output of this process – at a high level and after some distillation – is a picture that may look something like that illustrated in Figure 6.5. From this picture, it should then be possible to identify the key performance metrics the company needs to measure, manage and report in relation to its investor-focused strategies. The Measurement Checklist, which is included as an appendix to this book, can also be referenced to help select the most appropriate metrics.

Post-merger Integration Measures Design

In a post-merger integration environment, a company's strategy towards creating investor satisfaction and retention is likely to be somewhat different. Here the emphasis will be entirely on strategy implementation and the delivery of the merger or acquisition benefits. These may come in terms of increased sales revenues or reduced operating costs, while the expenses involved in the integration process can be substantial and will need to be monitored carefully.

On the sales revenue side, it will likely be a case of leveraging the new entity's increased geographical coverage and distribution channels, cross-selling products and/or services to increase market penetration and optimizing margins through careful pricing management (given that competitors will probably try to undermine the benefits of the deal with customers). On the operating cost side, personnel

Fig 6.5 Generic Example of Investor Success Map

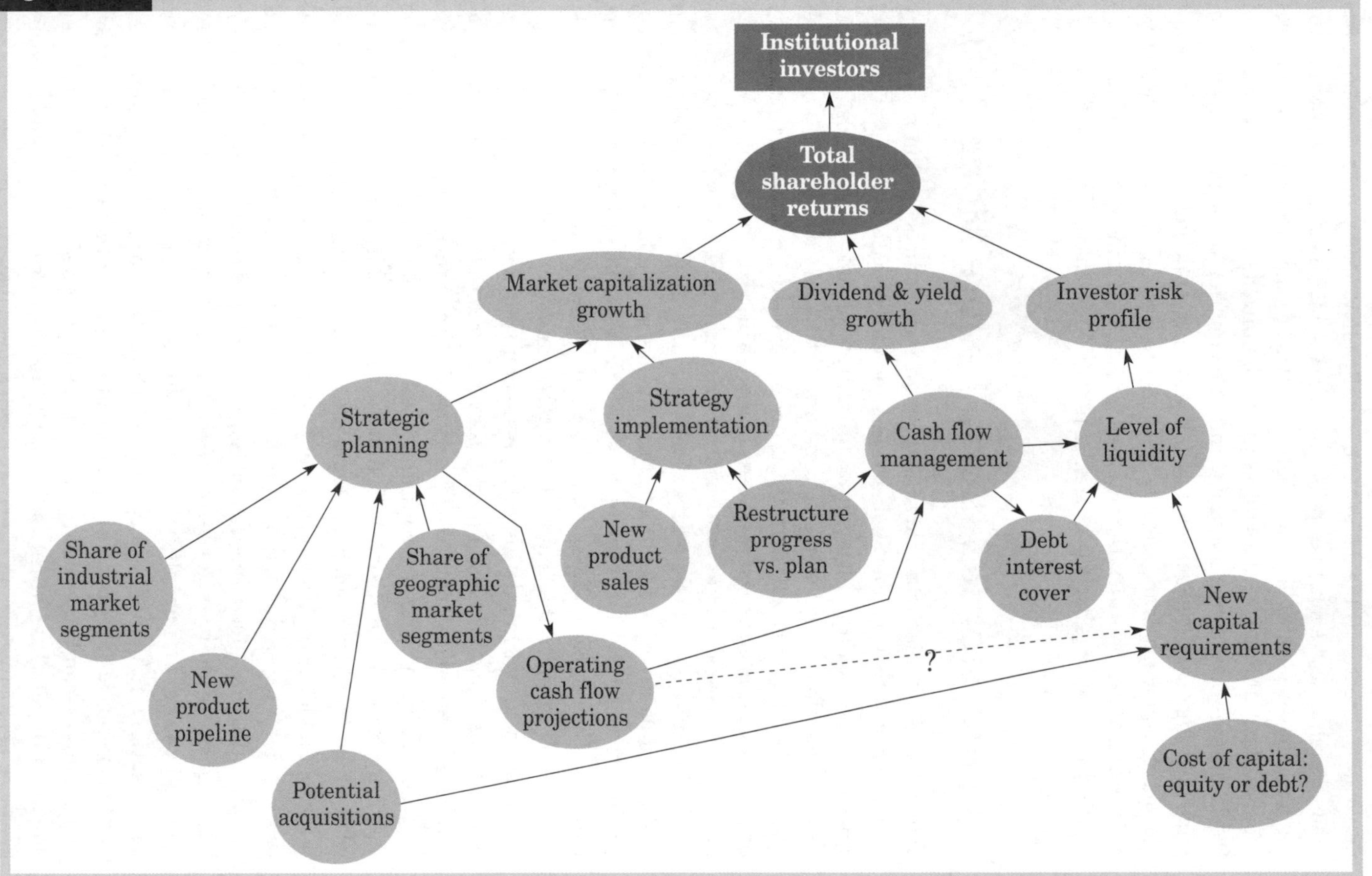

duplications created by the merger will usually allow headcount reductions to be made. Purchase costs must be optimized with the increased buying power of the combined businesses, while fixed assets may also become surplus to requirements – particularly if duplicated facilities are rationalized, as is typically the case. Working capital reduction may come into the equation too. Finally, the costs of implementing these changes must be taken into account, not least if significant personnel redundancies and facilities closures are planned. Given these somewhat different strategic priorities, the output of a post-merger integration success map relating to investors is likely to be similar to that illustrated in Figure 6.6.

The Investor Relations 'Failure Mode' Test

One of the great dilemmas that management faces is to be bold in its strategy – in order to satisfy its shareholders demands for growth – while at the same time exercising caution through its mitigation of risks. While this notion is usually well understood by major companies' treasury departments, who frequently need to hedge their firms' exposure to international currency fluctuations, it is often less well developed within executive suites. We know too from the research that professional investors tend to assess risk subjectively. In our view, this kind of 'suspension of reality' is not sustainable. In reality, companies at least cannot afford to take such a laissez-faire approach, while investors may have the opportunity to bail out. If things do go badly wrong for the company, the consequences can be catastrophic.

Marks & Spencer, the leading UK retailer and once doyen of best management practices within its industry, has seen sentiment towards its shares damaged by a long series of derogatory press articles and television programmes over many months. This very public scrutiny has ridiculed its merchandizing policies, its handling of supplier relationships (for which it was once famed) and its executive management skill-sets. The reverence with which M&S's management team had been held in the past ill-prepared it for its denouement. They never saw the warning signs – such as deteriorations in customer satisfaction and loyalty, declining employee morale and supplier dissent – focusing instead on reducing its costs to achieve record levels of profitability in order to increase short-term shareholder value, while at the same time whittling away the heart and soul of the company. The reaction of the media to this once hallowed organization accumulated further negative sentiment in the eyes of the general public, its customers and the investment community. Not surprisingly, its share price was eroded down to ten-year lows at the end of 2000. It has since shown signs of recovery after belatedly recognizing what needed to be done.

Fig 6.6 Generic Example of PMI Success Map

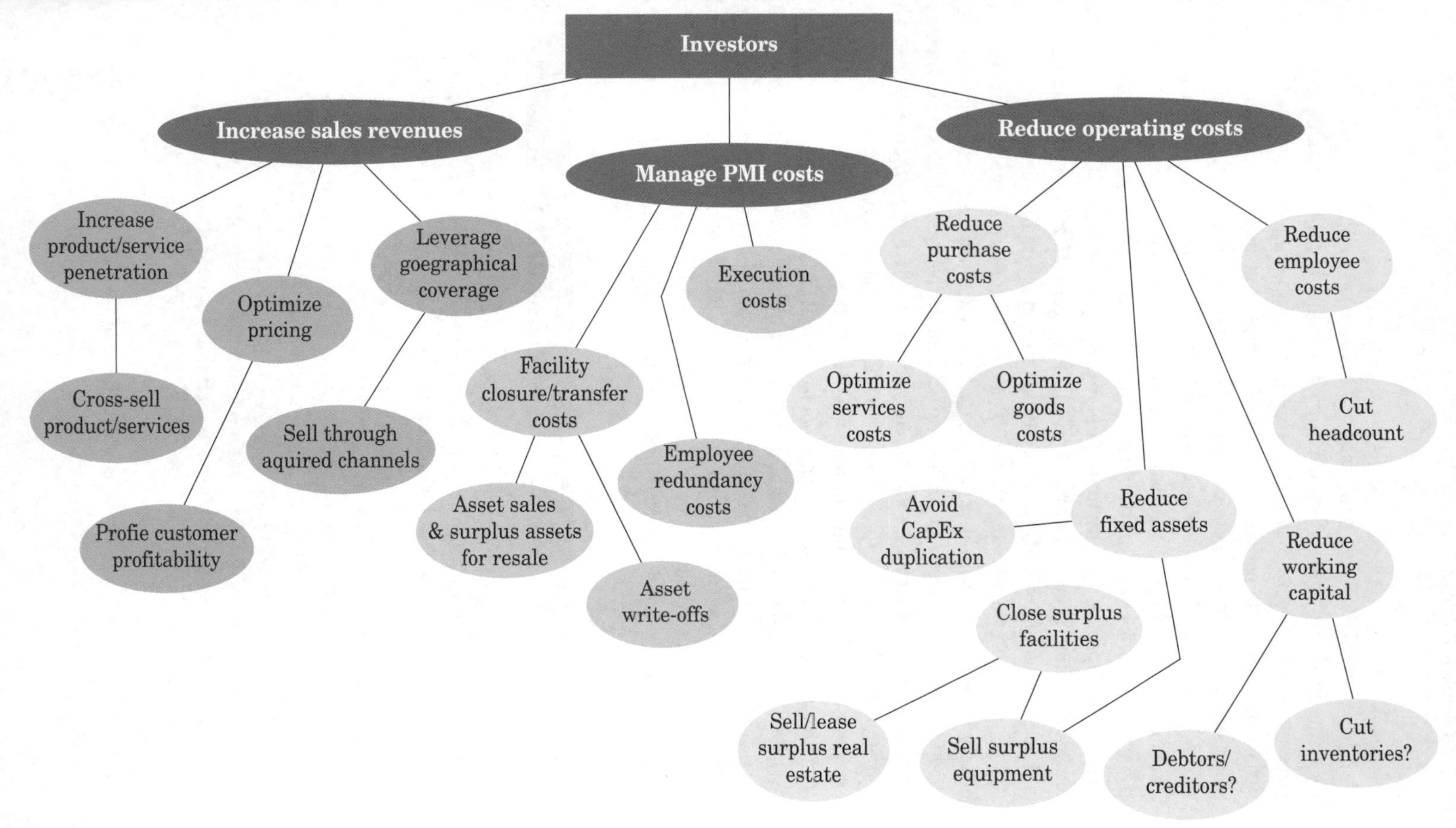

Barings, the UK investment bank that collapsed in March 1995, was bold in its strategy of creating and supporting an initially highly profitable market for derivatives trading in Singapore. However, its management was also singularly negligent in its policing of the level of risk to which Nick Leeson, the now infamous 'rogue trader' who eventually brought about the bank's demise, was exposing the firm. Leeson was recklessly extending his exposure to the Nikkei index in the vain hope that it would enable him to recuperate losses, hidden in the accounting system, on the highly geared derivative trades he made with little or no supervision. Unwinding his futures positions left Barings with a bill for £860 million. It could not pay and the business was sold to the Dutch financial services company ING for just £1 (but including its liabilities).

Clearly, this was an exceptional if not unprecedented event (Barings had nearly collapsed over a century before when speculation in Argentina precipitated a financial crisis in 1890 and it had to be rescued by the Bank of England). More normally, companies lose value when management loses the confidence of its investors simply by failing to deliver on its promises. Companies make informal 'contracts' with their institutional investors when they declare their ambition to achieve particular financial earnings growth targets. The problem comes when they can't quite make the numbers. Many then resort to cheating. In recent years, accounting has become more like marketing. It has shown an increasing propensity to be economical with the truth and cover up any bad news. It has also shown itself to be remarkably creative in the techniques employed to bolster revenues and profits (see the box *Making a Silk Purse from a Sow's Ear*).

Making a Silk Purse from a Sow's Ear

The suspension of reality involved in the reporting of 'proforma results' by employing aggressive accounting techniques has become so commonplace that it is scandalous. The results announced to shareholders and the general public can be selective in the extreme. And, what is more, to get to these selective 'glossy' figures there is a good chance that the company's management has increased the risk profile of the company along the way. Every possible means of projecting a sunny and optimistic picture to shareholders is explored when companies cannot quite make their forecast numbers. Only when the detailed accounts, prepared in compliance with generally accepted accounting principles, are distributed several weeks later does the true picture dawn. However, even then, it will only dawn to those investors and analysts who are prepared to scrutinize the accounts in some detail and to read the footnotes to the accounts. Some of the favourite tricks employed to perpetrate these deceits are:

- Excluding acquisition costs.
- Excluding payroll taxes on stock options.
- Excluding the losses of non-fully-owned subsidiaries.
- Including sales of undelivered products or contracts not yet complete.
- Excluding customer incentive rebates.
- Excluding the cost of lending money to cash-strapped customers.
- Excluding the cost of issuing share warrants given to customers.
- Excluding the results of loss-making new businesses.
- Excluding interest payments.
- Excluding restructuring costs.
- Including big losses in one bad year in order to report enhanced earnings in following years.
- Increasing depreciation and amortization periods.
- Hiding gains from pension fund contribution cut-backs.

It is not just dodgy internet and fledgling companies trying to put a glossy picture on their prospects in order to obtain additional survival funding who employ such techniques. Big companies do it too. They torture the accounting numbers until they confess good news that will be applauded by investors and analysts. Chief accountant of the US Securities and Exchange Commission (SEC), Lynn Turner, calls pro forma results 'EBS earnings' – for Everything but Bad Stuff. 'Way too often, they seem to be used to distract investors from the actual results,' she says.

We warned earlier in this chapter about the dangers of using EBITDA numbers, pro forma results and dubious (but not illegal) accounting practices are part of the same syndrome. It reinforces the notion that cash is fact, while accounting is opinion. Investor beware.

The flip side of investor relationship management is about the internal processes of managing business risks, managing investor communications and managing relations with the media. Here we need to consider what would cause investors to defect and the retention strategy to be unsuccessful. Using the failure mode method we have described earlier helps to ensure that the potential negative factors are identified and their associated measurements are appropriated (see Figure 6.7).

Fig 6.7 Investor Failure Mode Map – Example

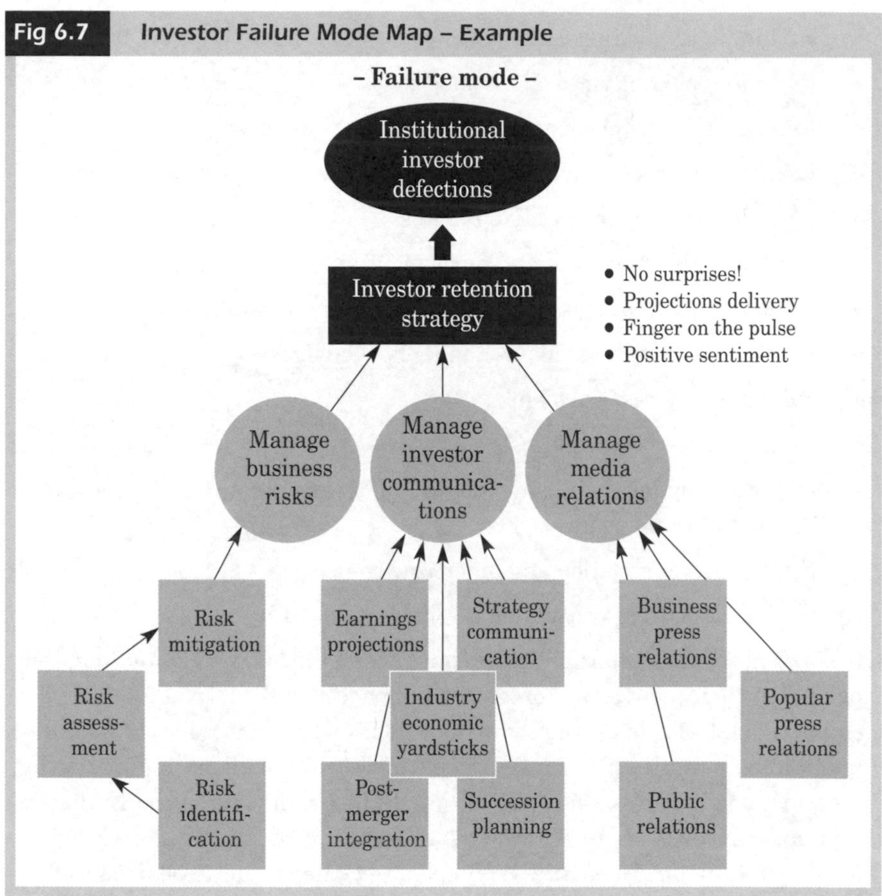

Management builds credibility over time by being perceived to have its finger on the pulse and by consistently delivering what it said it would do. It can easily lose that cumulative credibility by failing to identify a significant risk; by failing to keep investors in the picture; by mismanaging public reaction; and, most of all, by failing to deliver the expected results.

If an organization does not put in place the relevant measures that will lead to the effective (and efficient) management of predictable risks to the business, then it only has its executives to blame. When Murphy's Law comes into play and the things that could go wrong actually do go wrong, it is likely that they will be forced to 'fall on their swords' or be otherwise ousted. However, with the right measurement systems in place and the resultant 'nipping in the bud' of emergent problems, in most cases this course of action should not be necessary and executives can look forward to a longer length of tenure and the benefits that their position provides.

Finally, the investor relationship measures design process needs to be completed by the creation of a Performance Measure Record Sheet for each measure selected, as described in Chapter 3 (Figure 3.2 Measures Definition Template) and illustrated in Figure 6.8.

Fig 6.8 **Example of Investor-related Performance Measure Record Sheet**

Measure	Market share
Purpose	To determine the level of market penetration of the products (and services) offered by the business unit
Relates to	The Strategy of being the preferred supplier to the top 20 customers in the Eastern Region
Target	To achieve a regional market share of >50 per cent for the BU's three newest products (and services) within 18 months
Formula	Value of company sales of these products (and services) as a percentage of estimated total market
Frequency	Measured and reported monthly
Who measures	Business analyst compiles data (the data can be analyzed within one week of receipt)
Source of data	The data is collected from the sales ledger and industry market analysis reports (compiled by BBB associates)
Who acts on the data (owner)	Sales and marketing director
What do they do	Creates action plans to improve sales performance in below target performance districts of the region
Notes/comments	

Not many members of a company's payroll get out of bed every morning looking forward to another day of creating shareholder value. Developing products or services, generating demand for these and fulfilling orders for them, even planning and managing improvements, is intrinsically more appealing. It is nevertheless vital that managements communicate the importance of investor-centred performance measures to staff and ensure that they pervade the organization. They need to form part of a package of measures that is made widely available throughout organizations and which address all of the firm's key stakeholders.

Illustrative Investor-centred Measures

This checklist is not intended to be comprehensive, just indicative. There will inevitably be variability between industries and also in the relative maturity of companies (and their subsidiaries). The category within which each measure is represented may vary too. Some of the measures that firms typically adopt are:

Investor Satisfaction Measures

What do our investors want and need?

- Total Shareholder Return (market capitalization growth + dividends distributed)
- Market capitalization change relative to sector
- Earnings per share
- Corporate/Business Unit profitability
- Actual performance vs. Analyst forecasts
- Free Cash Flow/Cash-burn
- EBITDA relative to industry
- Value Added
- Sales revenues (by geography)
- Operating costs (by category)
- Margin/Return on sales
- Net asset value per share
- Return on assets/capital employed

Investor Contribution Measures

What do we want and need from our investors?

- Value of equity owned by institutional investors
- Level of institutional investor churn
- Investment analyst recommendation ratings
- Level of short-/long-term debt (vs. earnings)
- Level of liquidity (e.g. debt:equity ratio, current assets:liabilities ratio)
- Level of interest cover
- Level of dividend cover
- Level of provisions for liabilities and charges
- Working capital: debtor days and creditor days
- Inventory turns
- Credit agency debt ratings
- Investor performance improvement suggestions contributed/implemented

Investor-related Strategy Measures

What are our strategies for satisfying these sets of investor and organization wants and needs?

- Like-for-like/Organic/Acquired sales revenue and operating profit growth
- Market growth (by region)
- Market share growth
- Product (and product family) profitability
- Level of R&D expenditure
- Level of capital expenditure (e.g. capex:depreciation ratio)
- Relative level of employee productivity vs. competitors (e.g. sales per employee)
- Asset utilization (sales per $/£/€ of fixed assets, or per sq.ft. in retailing, per bedroom in hotels, per available seat mile in airlines etc.)
- Cost of capital (by source)

Investor-related Process Measures

Which of our internal business processes will effectively and efficiently deliver them?

- Sales from newly introduced products/services
- Sales from new markets and sectors
- Progress to internal financial management plans, budgets and forecasts
- Cost/Benefit impact of major process improvement programmes and projects
- Share price response to company announcements (relative to market)
- Cost of investor relations

Investor-related Capability Measures

Which particular capabilities do we need to establish and maintain to execute them?

- Number and potential sales value of products/services in development pipeline
- Valuation of brands
- Level of investments in core competencies
- Product SKU-level profitability (variety management)
- Product sales break-even level
- Post-merger integration progress to plan
- Restructuring/Re-engineering projects progress to plan

Summary

Who typically are this group of stakeholders?

- *Current shareholders* – Potential shareholders – Investment analysts – Banks – Venture capitalists [Charity donors and sponsors – Taxpayers].

What do investors typically want and need from your organization?

- *Return* – capital appreciation [or other tangible evidence of money well spent in not-for-profit sector].
- *Reward* – dividend distributions for loyal investors.
- *Figures* – data to review progress and to assess future prospects and risks.
- *Faith* – confidence in the management team to consistently deliver on its promises.

What does your organization typically want and need from its investors?

- *Capital* – so that it has enough working capital to operate and make value enhancing investments.
- *Credit* – access to adequate borrowing facilities, e.g. bank loans.
- *Risk* – to be taken by investors in exchange for providing capital or credit.
- *Support* – continued investor loyalty [and, where appropriate, relevant advice on direction].

What strategies typically address these wants and needs?

- *Organic growth* – creating growth within the existing business.
- *Mergers and acquisitions* – buying accelerated growth.
- *Cost reduction* – cutting back employees and/or bought costs.
- *Asset divestment* – selling businesses or capital assets.
- *Capital investment* – buying equipment, infrastructure or real estate.
- *Optimal cost of capital* – financing strategies at optimum cost [through equity or debt mechanisms].

Which processes typically relate to the execution of these strategies?

- *Develop new products and services* – for organic growth and to leverage benefits of M&A.
- *Generate demand* – for organic growth and to leverage benefits of M&A.
- *Fulfil demand* – to optimize operating costs while continuously improving product and service quality for organic growth [rationalization in M&A or restructuring situations].

- *Plan and manage the enterprise* – developing and maintaining strategic intents, plans, programmes and projects while mitigating significant implementation risks.

Which capabilities typically need to be developed and nurtured?

- New products/services pipeline.
- Market focus and positioning.
- Business Unit performance management.
- Brand management.
- Product/Service pricing management.
- Core competencies investment.
- Executive leadership.
- Investor relations.
- Financial controls.
- Risk management.
- Post-merger integration.
- Business alliance management.
- Social responsibility.

7 Managing Customer Relationships with Measures

You can't get to the future on time by running after your customers; you get there by running with your customers.

R. Wayland & P. Cole • *'Customer Connections'.*

Are our investors more important stakeholders than our customers? Or are the customers more important? This is a pointless (albeit frequent) and circular debate – you cannot have the one without the other. Organizations have to satisfy the wants and needs of both constituencies. However, historically, greater focus has been given to measuring from the investors' point of view, witnessed by the proliferation of financial performance measures in most traditional organizations. Indeed, the principal thrust of the balanced scorecard movement of the 1990s was to place measures of the customer point of view alongside those of investors.

The Components of Achieving Customer Satisfaction and Contribution

As we have seen in Chapter 4, most customers want high levels of 'fast, right, cheap and easy' or they are liable to take their business elsewhere. On the other hand, what do organizations want and need from their customers? The organization wants customers to trust it, to share information and opinions with it and, above all, to allow it to achieve profitable growth. The Customer Relationship model is summarized in Figure 7.1.

Fig 7.1 The Customer Relationship

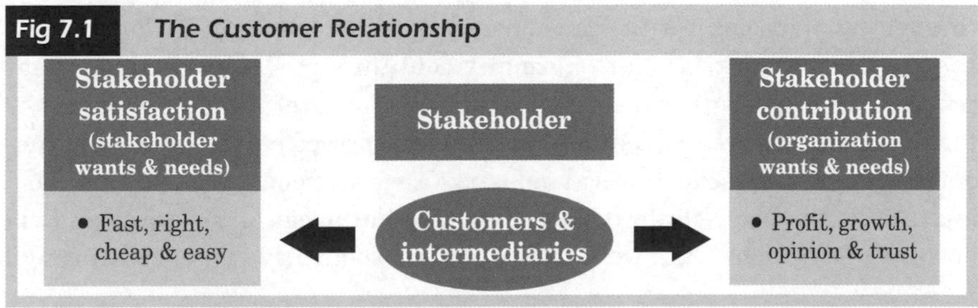

We have already indicated that in most industries the organization also needs customers to be, in the main, loyal – but is that all? Not at all. An organization needs several other contributions from customers to which we have so far only hinted. They need feedback from customers in terms of formal and informal survey inputs – what they like and hate about the organization, focus group participation in their product and services development initiatives, and process delivery improvement suggestions. In industrial businesses (business-to-business) the level of complexity can be significantly greater than in the consumer environment and more sophisticated data can typically be required in order to optimize the supply chain. Suppliers want their customers to give them forecasts of demand and, where applicable (for instance in retail environments), real-time data – through EPOS and similar systems – in order to help them optimize their production and logistics fulfilment processes. Obviously, this requires them to use the data in a secure and trustworthy manner and not let it be passed on to their customer's competitors, whom they may also supply.

Within the industrial sector too, customer-supplier relationships are becoming increasingly more 'intimate'. Although not an especially new concept, it is now becoming far more common for customers and suppliers to share marketing budgets, capital investment expenditures, and component design responsibilities. It goes without saying though that only the most trusted suppliers are allowed into the 'inner sanctum' of longer-term strategic initiatives. We shall discuss this theme in more detail in Chapter 9 since the same kinds of interrelationships exist between an organization and its customers as do between suppliers and the organization. In a supply chain, a customer has a supplier who is the customer of other suppliers, and so on.

Intermediaries

This raises a further issue: who exactly is the customer? Is it the end-user or the organization that buys and distributes the product? There is a difference. Many companies sell their products to end-users through a variety of intermediaries: retailers, wholesalers, brokers, agents, merchants, dealers and distributors. Food and other fast-moving consumer products are usually sold through retailers, but it is the consumers who either love or hate the products they buy. Cars and trucks are normally sold through dealers – some great products and a few 'lemons', but what are the after-sales services like? Financial services are frequently sold through approved brokers and independent agents. In the pharmaceutical industry, drugs are commonly sold through a mixture of over-the-counter (OTC) chemists/pharmacies/drug stores and via doctor prescriptions (Rx), the latter often subsequently dispensed through much the same (but more tightly controlled) distribution channel, but clearly the persons who actually take the chemical compound are the ones who will be affected by its relative efficacy. Doctors then are vitally important intermediaries for pharmaceutical companies, even though they neither buy nor take physical delivery of their products (see the box *Doctor Feelgood*).

Doctor Feelgood

A study of the European pharmaceutical industry found that marketing and sales play a crucial role in the financial success of drugs companies. These functions account for 70 per cent of the difference in the return on sales between the companies studied. The study identifies that three-quarters of the benefit can be realized by focusing on just two capabilities:

- Obtaining information about doctors' needs.
- Developing a good relationship with them.

Improving sales force effectiveness by linking rewards to performance and having a good mix of drugs to sell are secondary factors.

The report aims to help pharmaceutical companies spend their marketing budgets, which account for up to 45 per cent of costs, more effectively. The report says: 'Concentrating on a small number of key capabilities can massively enhance performance.'

Source: Accenture report, August 2001.

It is clearly the case that in industry after industry, the 'middle-men' are a critical success factor. The advent of e-commerce over the internet was supposed to dispense with the need for many of these intermediaries, but this has not happened in practice. Indeed, so far it has almost certainly served to create greater complexity of promotion and distribution through the introduction of so-called 'cyber-intermediaries' – essentially, new routes to market without elimination of established channels.

It may be fine to shift cars, electronic goods, books, CDs and all things tangible to be consumed at home or at work over the internet. Ebay, Amazon and their industrial equivalents do this every day. But of course some intermediaries, responsible for vast amounts of business, are simply irreplaceable by cyber-equivalents (see the box *Social Lubricants*).

Social Lubricants

Companies have traditionally directed their advertising at people who may influence consumer habits – for example, drug companies woo doctors, tour operators court travel agents and music labels cuddle up to radio disc jockeys. Jinro Ballentine's, a South Korean whisky company partly owned by Allied Domecq, also takes its principal intermediaries very seriously.

The company has targeted its marketing at senior hostesses – or madams – who attend to the needs of wealthy businessmen in South Korea's shady 'room salons'. It invited 150 of the women to sample Ballentine's scotch whisky at a Seoul hotel in the hope that they would then recommend the brand to their customers.

South Korea is the world's fifth largest whisky market and one of the fastest growing. Some estimates suggest that 80 per cent of its $1billion whisky sales are made in the 4,000 'room salons'.

Different customer and intermediary groups' various wants and needs are not necessarily homogeneous. If one fundamental question – who is the customer? – is not addressed at the outset, then the outcome will be that the wrong customer relationship performance measures get selected. And, given that you do get what you measure, then it's unlikely you'll get the result that you want. The questions that very obviously need to be addressed (but which are often overlooked) when considering customer-centred performance measures are: Who are the key customers? And what do they want and need?

This can pose some dilemmas. For example, a UK survey of schoolchildren (aged 8 to 16) and parents about school meals in 2000 found that parents wanted their children to have: fresh fruit, jacket potatoes, healthy meals, milk and yoghurt. But, on the other hand, the things that the children themselves wanted their school to provide were: squash or fizzy drinks, ice cream, pizza, crisps, cakes and biscuits. One of the trends from the previous survey (1998) was that demands from parents for schools to provide healthy food are increasing whereas children were showing a greater preference for snacks and fast food such as pizza, burgers and chips – roast dinners are no longer so popular. Who is the customer? Who are school caterers to please? And what are they to do about reconciling parents' and children's diverging demands?

In an industrial example, a bricks manufacturer has four key customer groups to consider – house owners (the end-users), architects, builders and builder's merchants. As illustrated in Figure 7.2, each group has distinctly different wants and needs. Which are the most important?

Fig 7.2 One Organization, Four Separate Customer Groups

	House owner	Architect	Builder	Builder's merchant
Fast	Important that whole house is finished on time.		Short lead time. Arrive when promised.	Short lead time. Arrive when promised.
Right	The bricks are lasting. Nice appearance.	Interesting appearance. Special effects.	Easy to lay. Undamaged. Consistent.	No returns.
Cheap	Cost is quite important.	Of little interest, but not prohibitively expensive.	Erected cost.	Margin of great importance.
Easy		Wide product range – brochures, samples.		Wide product range – brochures. Special promotions. Terms of payment.

Customer-focused Strategies, Processes and Capabilities

The means to achieving both sets of wants and needs (customer and organization) are essentially threefold: to win potentially profitable new customers, to ensure profitable existing customers do not defect and, you guessed, to win back profitable former customers who have already defected. Firms' generic strategies for achieving these aims may often be equally predictable; the organization must:

- Extend and renew the products and/or services it offers to its various customers.
- Attract those potentially profitable new (and lapsed) customers to buy the products and services offered.
- Ensure that existing customers are retained by satisfying their wants and needs very well.
- Grow the firm's share of the target market segments it has identified as being attractive.

The core business processes it will need to execute these strategic intents may seem obvious too but, as ever, the devil is in the detail of building the various capabilities that underpin them and – vitally – deciding which need to be merely adequate and which must be highly distinctive. We can trace these components at a generic level in Figure 7.3.

Fig 7.3 Mapping Customer Relationships through the Performance Prism facets

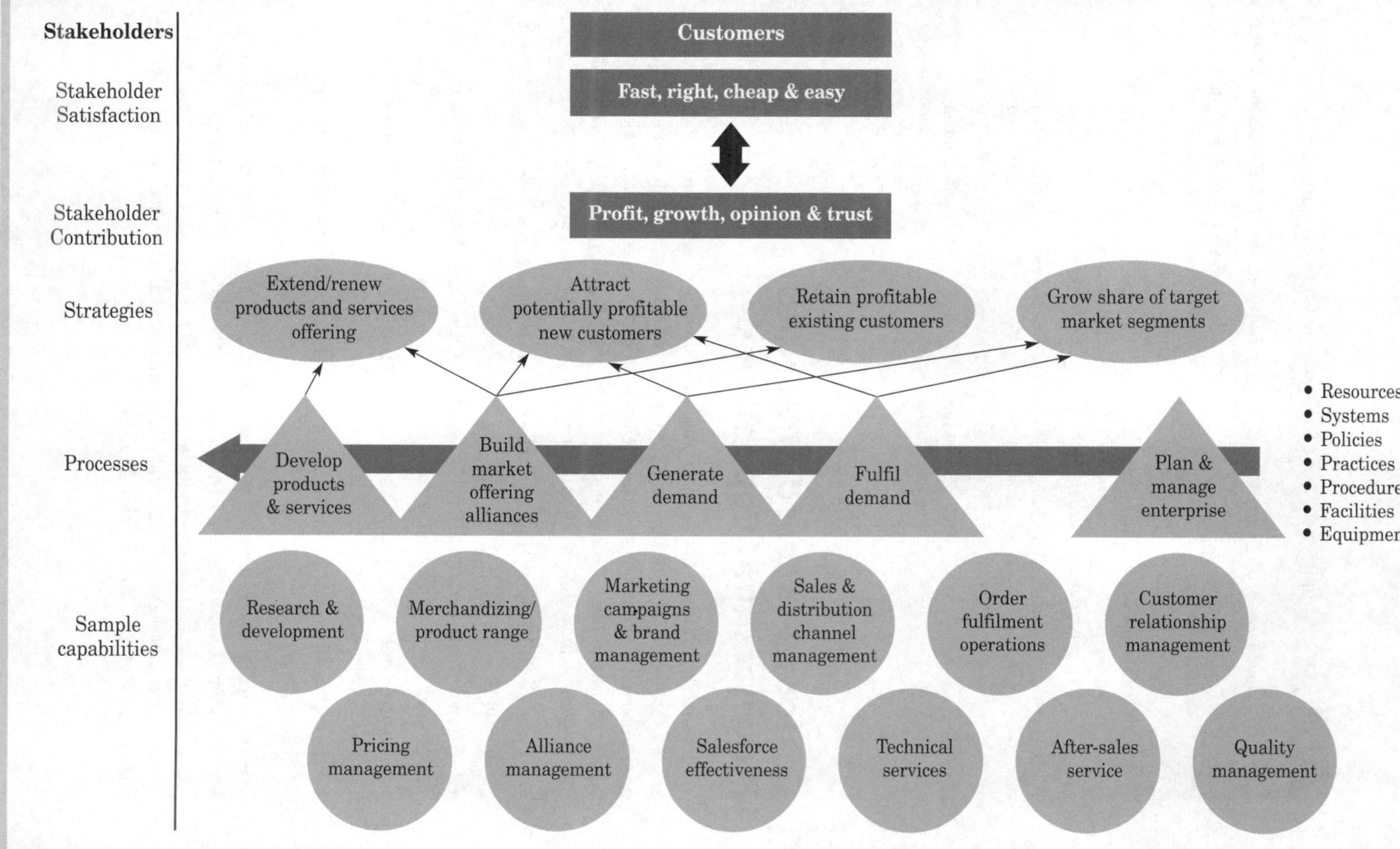

The first business process is to Develop Products and Services. Without this process it will not be possible to deliver on the first strategy of extending and/or renewing the product range. In manufacturing companies, this will typically require a strong research and development capability, while in retailing strong merchandizing skill-sets and information technology systems will be essential in order to ensure the right range of products is offered that will attract sufficient numbers of new, existing and former customers. These are traditional processes and there are a number of commonly applied quantitative and qualitative performance measures which assist executives in ensuring that this key process and its attendant capabilities are managed both effectively and efficiently.

The second business process is to Build Market Offering Alliances. For those firms who sell their products and services through various types of intermediary channels and for those who need to be part of a consortium in order to win certain categories of business, this will be a vital process. It will also be highly relevant to those businesses that have joint venture arrangements with third parties to develop new products and services. This process of course needs strong alliance management skills and practices. Measuring them will ensure that sufficient levels of the right skills are in place, that best practices for managing alliances are adopted and, above all, to ensure that the planned outcomes of alliances are achieved – they seldom are, but they are also seldom measured properly (see Chapter 6).

The third business process is to Generate Demand. This invariably requires the firms' marketing and sales resources to be highly effective (and perhaps efficient too). Generating demand for products or services is of course inextricably linked to developing – or merchandizing – the right products and services that customers want in the first place. (See the box *Marks & Spencer's Merchandizing Plan for Recovery* for an example.)

Marks & Spencer's Merchandising Plan for Recovery

Marks & Spencer, the troubled UK retailer that was once one of Britain's most admired companies, is trying to get its clothing sales back on track by overhauling its system for supplying merchandise to its 296 stores. Previously, stores were banded according to their retail footage and all stores of the same size were sent the same goods for sale. Now clothing is supplied to the store according to new profiles.

Under the new system, trialled at 31 outlets in early 2000, M&S's stores are grouped according to a series of criteria, including the demographics of customers, their lifestyle and working patterns. The new categories for stores were reached after detailed customer research – both with existing shoppers and those who prefer other stores. The company was also able to use data from its charge card records.

The store trials revealed that one-fifth of its clothes offering was wrong for the local market and out of line with what customers in that locality actually wanted. Those stores converted to the new merchandizing approach reported booming sales as a result – for example, one store reported a near-fivefold rise in sales of women's clothing and a less impressive but still significant 46 per cent increase in men's wear. Not only did sales rise year-on-year, the average value of a shopping basket of goods purchased at that store rose by 31 per cent. This means that not only was the store attracting more customers, it was also getting those new, returning and existing customers to spend more when they shop.

Luc Vandevelde, Marks & Spencer's Belgian executive chairman, claims that putting together a picture of customers in every store will give M&S a competitive edge over other retailers when it comes to generating sales. 'Very few retailers have the capability to do that today,' he says. The challenge then is to manage the additional complexity that this data-driven approach creates. Whether it will be able to do so and whether this system will prove to be the solution to M&S's problems remains to be seen.

The fourth process is that of Fulfil Demand. This is the process that former customers can describe with venom. This is the process that is most likely to despatch existing customers into the warm embrace of competitors. This is the process that new customers will observe most closely and decide whether doing business with your firm is a relatively good or bad experience. It tends to be highly operational in nature. It usually starts with a customer order and finishes when that customer has paid for the goods or services supplied (see the box *The Perfect Customer Order*). Different industries have different steps in between. However, it doesn't necessarily stop there, in some industries it is necessary to provide technical assistance or to perform other after-sales services, such as maintenance and breakdown repairs. It requires particular skill-sets (frequently specialized technical ones in the manufacturing sector, more inter-personal ones in services), appropriate use of information and process technologies, the application of best practices and, not least, the provision of often substantial and complex infrastructure. Fail to implement the right Fulfil Demand measures so that appropriate corrective actions can be taken and the firm is at significant risk.

The Perfect Customer Order

Milliken Europe, the European industrial textile division of a privately owned US parent company, endured a pioneering journey in the measurement of its demand fulfillment processes. Clive Jeanes, its former managing director, described how it sought to define the perfect customer order. It is worth repeating.

In the mid-1980s Milliken Europe's internal data proved that it had a near-perfect record for on-time delivery. Jeanes and his colleagues, however, listened to the management experts of the time, and decided that they were right when they said that it did not matter how good you thought you were, or even how good you knew you were. The only thing that mattered was how good your customers thought you were.

Grasping this message and acting on it required Milliken Europe explicitly to ask its customers how good they thought the company was. Milliken chose to do this through a customer survey conducted by an independent agency. The first survey took place in 1985 and the results were astounding. Milliken data showed that the company had a near-perfect delivery record, yet some 50 per cent of customers complained about products arriving late. An immediate investigation was launched and, after some searching, it became apparent that the reason for the discrepancy was that Milliken measured on-time delivery by checking whether the product had left its premises on time – whereas of course customers, reasonably, were interested in whether the product arrived at *their* premises on time.

Milliken then changed its definition of on time to: does the product arrive at the customer's premises on time? As expected, this harsher measure resulted in Milliken's near-perfect record of on-time delivery evaporating, so its staff was forced to work diligently to try and regain the peaks of performance they thought they had already scaled.

A year later the company commissioned another survey. Once again the results were astounding (and frustrating), for there was still a gap between how well Milliken knew it was performing and how well customers perceived it was performing. Another investigation ensued and this time it emerged that the internal measurement system recorded partly complete shipments as on time, whereas its customers were interested in on-time delivery of the full shipment. As a result management adopted a modified delivery performance measure: on time, in full. Not surprisingly this showed that Milliken's delivery performance was not as good as it should have been and once again it worked hard to try and rectify the situation. Its agency conducted yet another customer survey and once again found that a gap, albeit a smaller one, existed between actual performance and its customers' perceptions.

The story continues over several years. With each survey Milliken discovered something else that mattered to its customers but that the company was not measuring – whether the invoice was correct, whether the delivery date was a negotiated one or the one that the customer had originally requested, whether the product and packaging were error-free. Each of the customer surveys forced the management team to rethink what mattered to its customers and to challenge their own perceptions. Over a number of years, this approach enabled it to hone its order fulfillment process resulting in what it finally called the 'perfect order'. A perfect order is one where:

- The customer and Milliken's sales staff agree a delivery date at the time the order is placed and no subsequent attempt is made to renegotiate this date.
- The product is shipped on time.
- The product is delivered on time.
- The correct quantity of product arrives.
- The product is of the correct quantity when it arrives.
- The packaging is correct.
- The accompanying documentation is error-free.
- The accompanying documentation is mailed on time.
- The customer makes no other complaints.
- The invoice is paid on time.

The last item is interesting. Jeanes reports that the company experienced a reduction in debtor days outstanding following the introduction of the perfect order initiative. It positively impacts cash flow.

Source: Adapted from 'Measuring Business Performance' by Andy Neely. Published by *The Economist* (1998).

Finally, all these processes need to be supported by the Plan and Manage Enterprise process. This ensures, for example, that resources (e.g. recruitment) and systems are made available, that employees are trained in best practices, that policies are implemented and adhered to, and that facilities are built, upgraded and maintained. Without these basics, nothing works properly and customers either don't show up or walk away. The maxim used to focus on building customer-centric processes and capabilities is often to 'delight our customers'. The dolts who operate the majority of the world's fabulously efficient and woefully ineffective call centres would do well to include some of these factors into their planning and managing considerations. And the performance of their diabolical creations should be measured accordingly – *from the customers' point of view*. The increasingly common phenomenon of 'phone rage' is induced by delays in answering calls, being kept waiting for long periods, being cut-off in mid-conversation, and having to respond to or talk to a machine rather than a person. Inadequate resource scheduling, poor training, high employee turnover, inane policies and inappropriate performance measures all conspire against giving customers a decent service, never mind a delightful one.

Measures for Customer Relationship Management

In the early days (in the 1980s), we began by measuring customer complaints. This was done in the hope that by gauging the nature of these dissatisfied customers' problems something could then be done to prioritize improvement initiatives which would eliminate the root causes. For example, even today, UK retailer Marks & Spencer runs a central database where customer complaints are logged and from which they can feed information back to the relevant buyer and suppliers. This approach was fine in so far as it went, but of course not many people (even non-British people) take the trouble to complain to suppliers and to big companies, such as retailers, in particular. Why bother? The general perception is that they won't listen. And with some good reason. Even in today's cacophony of customer survey forms and complaints websites, often the silence of corporate response is still deafening. But receiving customer complaints is one thing, dealing with them is another. *The Economist* reported[50]: 'Compared with wresting an apology from American Airlines for a delayed flight or persuading AT&T that it really has overcharged you, returning a dead parrot to a pet shop seems like a doddle. Sadly – rather like the shopkeeper in the Monty Python sketch, who insists that the parrot is merely 'resting' – most firms in America are bad at dealing with complaints, if they deal with them at all.' The US is not alone of course in requiring better customer service.

Instead, consumer customers in particular tend to vote with their feet and take their business elsewhere, while showing a tendency to 'bad-mouth' the supplier to friends or colleagues. In the industrial landscape, the data can be almost impossible to collect since 'complaint-making' is seldom formalized until some massive issue has been exposed and court proceedings are imminent. More usually, it comes in the form of an ear-bashing from the customer's most senior production manager (or similar role) to his supplier and contains a variety of words we cannot include in this book, but the number and malevolence of them are very often extremely good indicators of the severity of the problem – sometimes known as the 'profanity quotient'.

So, if the documented level of customer complaints is a poor measure of customer satisfaction on its own, what should be done? The consumer products industries had pioneered customer satisfaction surveys early – *'Are you happy with your wash, Mrs Jones?'* – and these techniques were then taken up by a broad range of industries. Many organizations set out to discover whether their customers were happy with which aspects of the products and services they were providing. Some did this with annual 10-page, 84-question questionnaires; others got smarter and produced questionnaires with fewer questions, often in order to extract a higher response rate, and also conducted them more frequently in order to observe potentially meaningful trends for management action before it was too late. Brand awareness and brand value perceptions – and especially customers' so-called 'emotional attachment' towards them, in marketing-speak – became key issues too.

However, from the analysis of such data, originally carried out by pioneers such as Xerox, it emerged that customers who were satisfied with the products and services they received were not always loyal customers. Merely satisfied customers, it turned out, were often quite promiscuous in their buying habits. However, *very satisfied* customers appeared to be much more loyal and they also showed a greater tendency to recommend their favoured supplier to their friends and colleagues. So, organizations in the late 1990s tried to build much closer relationships with their customers through a variety of 'customer loyalty schemes' – for example, by offering regular customers special facilities (airlines) or money-back rebates (retailers and credit card providers). The measurement focus has now moved more towards customer churn trends, understanding customer behaviours and the effectiveness of initiatives aimed at improving retention; and, especially, towards customer profitability, understanding the financial impacts and costs involved.

There is now a substantial body of research, which is – or, at least, should be – common knowledge about customer behaviours and certain rules of thumb that seem to apply across multiple industry sectors with only minor statistical differences. The box *What Every Customer-facing Executive, Supervisor and Employee Needs To Know* summarizes many of the essential elements of this research effort gleaned from a wide range of different sources.

What Every Customer-facing Executive, Supervisor and Employee Needs to Know

1 It costs five or six times more to win a new customer than it does to maintain an existing one – in banking, apparently it can be as much as 11 times more expensive.

2 Between 94–96 per cent of dissatisfied customers don't complain – they simply walk away. It is reckoned that 91 per cent of them will never come back.

3 Of the customers who register a complaint, between 54 per cent and 70 per cent will do business with the company again if their complaints are resolved satisfactorily – this figure goes up to around 95 per cent if customers feel their complaints are resolved *quickly*.

4 A typical dissatisfied customer will tell eight to ten people about their problem. One in five will tell 20. The advent of the internet now makes it possible to tell several thousand. On the other hand, a satisfied complainer will on average tell five people about the problem and how it was resolved to their satisfaction.

5 It takes around 12 positive service encounters to make up for one negative incident.

6 Only about 5 per cent of customers who experience an out-of-stock situation return to make the purchase originally planned.

7 Around 68 per cent of customers stop doing business with suppliers because of an attitude of indifference towards them – only 14 per cent quit because they are dissatisfied with the product (so customers with a service problem are *five times* more likely to defect than customers with a product problem) and just 9 per cent leave for competitive reasons.

8 Between 80 per cent to 90 per cent of defecting customers say they are satisfied. But *very satisfied* customers are four (consumer products) to seven (industrial products) times more likely to repeat their purchase within the next 18 months than those customers who were merely satisfied.

9 A rise of as little as 5 per cent in customer retention can result in an 80 per cent to 100 per cent increase in profits.

10 Businesses with low service quality average only 1 per cent return on sales and lose market share at a rate of 2 per cent per annum. Businesses with high service quality average a 12 per cent return on sales, gain market share at the rate of 6 per cent per annum and charge significantly higher prices.

Using CRM Data

Given that the quality movement has been well-established in Western business culture for well over a decade and that its early focus was particularly in manufacturing businesses (service industries tended to embrace Total Quality Management programmes somewhat later), it is slightly surprising that a 1999 survey of 1,000 manufacturers found that 30 per cent of manufacturing companies do not measure customer satisfaction at all. Indeed, in 2000, our own joint Accenture/Cranfield School of Management survey found that 20 per cent of a mixture of both manufacturing and service companies do not measure customer satisfaction. But, significantly, we found that 100 per cent of those respondents who do not measure customer satisfaction today believe that they *should* measure it. Furthermore, we learned that two out of every three respondents do not measure customer contribution today, but over four out of five that do not measure it believe they should do so in future.

Many companies' data about their customers are still quite sketchy and/or flaky. For example, surveys indicate that 12 per cent of companies do not even know how many customers they have, let alone more sophisticated data such as why they lose customers (an amazing 43 per cent don't know why, by the way). No surprise then that specialist information systems development companies are selling more and more customer relationship management (CRM) software products. And many organizations seem to believe that is what CRM is – just plugging in some software that enables standardized customer interface processes and captures basic transactional data (plus installing a few computer terminals to distribute the information to 'the trenches'). Job done.

Of course this can be useful in itself and we do not mean to denigrate it (although we might ask, given its essential nature: what kept you?). But the key question that must be asked is how that information – and investment – will be *used* for creating additional sales revenues, the rapid resolution of customer problems, the retention of existing customers and, not least, customer profitability. If an analytics capability that assists these tasks is not included within, or added to, the software product then the system will not be fulfilling its full potential – it is just a prompting and logging device. The future of CRM software systems is in acting as a platform for gaining insights and making judgements on product and, particularly, service improvements that benefit a broad range of customers. This means capturing experiential data about problems and using them to enhance the levels of product and, again particularly, service delivery. At the same time, we must capture data about the relative profitability of customers and how this is influenced by the level of customers' perceptions about the virtues of the products and services they receive. This is a source of competitive advantage today, as few firms use CRM data in this way. Tomorrow, it will likely be a commodity. In our view, no firm – other than a monopoly – can afford to hold back on this investment. The ability to identify and prove the causal links is probably the imperative factor that will convince senior executives to invest in such systems.

Service Quality Data

Whereas product quality is critical to customers of manufacturing companies (and their suppliers), in our so-called 'post-industrial society' we are living in an era increasingly dominated by service industries – retailers, caterers, financial services, telecommunications, transportation, media and entertainment companies, and so on. The percentage of North American citizens employed in service industries, for example, is estimated to be well over 80 per cent with only around 15 per cent employed in manufacturing industries. And, indeed, the trend towards outsourcing has meant that manufacturers are required to provide greater levels of services to their customers too, otherwise they will be relegated to the lower, less profitable, levels of the 'food chain'. However, it is intrinsically more difficult to specify the wants and needs of customers in respect of their total service requirements, since much of it may be unspoken and exist in the 'soft area': the expectations of customers – a notoriously inhomogeneous thing.

Or so you might expect, but the evidence does not really support that presumption. Although perception will almost always need to be polled to get a real handle on service quality, the fundamentals of its delivery are often quite predictable. For example, readers will appreciate that although being ritualistically wished to 'Have a nice day' may be well-intentioned it simply doesn't cut the mustard. *Genuine* friendliness and a helpful attitude, on the other hand, can enhance our purchasing experience and our patronage of certain emporiums. Many retailers now employ so-called 'mystery shoppers' – independent researchers who pose as customers – to evaluate the performance of their employees in being pleasant and polite to customers. Trade Unions tend to regard this as spying on employees, but employers believe it is the only way that consistent standards of customer service can be maintained. Even in France, one of the great bastions of customer indifference and incivility, there is a revolution going on – that is joining the words 'customer' with 'service', an alien concept for the majority of Gallic shop assistants. Today, in many retail environments, a *client mystère* is likely to be checking their attentiveness, attitude, eye-contact and whether they obey what is known by the employee training acronym BSAM, or *bonjour*, *sourire*, *au revoir*, *merci* (hello, smile, goodbye, thank you).

The gulf between customer expectations of service and customer perceptions of the service delivered is sometimes referred to as the 'service quality gap'. Fortunately, its measurement has been extensively researched (for example, see the box *Measuring Service Quality*). While not all academics agree that the SERVQUAL methodology is necessarily the only or best approach to analyzing service quality (especially in respect to its questionnaire), in our view it is at least a reasonable starting point – especially given that, as we have seen, so many companies (over a decade later) have still not adopted its *fundamental principles*.

Measuring Service Quality

Groundbreaking research carried out in the US over a decade ago introduced what is known as SERVQUAL, a customer service quality gap model for measuring the five key dimensions of service quality – *Reliability, Responsiveness, Assurance, Empathy and Tangibles*.

Reliability is the ability to perform the promised service dependably and accurately. *Responsiveness* is defined as the willingness to help customers and provide prompt service. *Assurance* is the knowledge and courtesy of employees and their ability to convey trust and confidence. It consists of four component parts: competence, courtesy, credibility and security. *Empathy* is the caring, individualized attention the firm provides its customers. It has three sub-components: accessibility, communication and understanding the customer. Finally, *Tangibles* are the appearance of physical facilities, equipment, personnel and communication materials.

Furthermore, the researchers also found that the relative rankings of importance of the five dimensions of service quality differ only slightly between several different service industries. The number one concern of customers, regardless of type of service, is Reliability. The facet that matters least to customers is Tangibles (although they note that this may be more important to *potential* customers). Responsiveness, Assurance and Empathy have different importance levels in different industries but they are always relatively important – after Reliability.

The researchers also identified four critical gaps in delivering service quality:

- **Gap 1**: Insufficient Marketing Research – *the gap between what customers expect and what the organization thinks they expect.*
- **Gap 2**: The Wrong Service – Quality Standards – *the gap between internal perceptions of customer expectations and performance specifications for service delivery.*

- **Gap 3**: The Service Performance Gap – *the gap between service specifications and actuals.*
- **Gap 4**: When Promises Do Not Match Delivery – *the gap between promises and delivery caused by inadequate horizontal communications within the organization and the propensity to over-promise.*

More recently a fifth gap has been added:

Gap 5: when the organization has no real idea what its customers do want. An all too frequent occurrence!

Source: *Delivering Quality Service* by Valerie Zeithaml, A. Parasuraman and Leonard Berry (1990).

Brand Value and Impact Data

We have noted in Chapter 4 the importance of brands to consumer markets (and, increasingly, industrial markets too). Branding consultants, market research companies and advertising agencies have all developed specialized methodologies for assessing the value of brands and their impact on the public psyche. Indeed, many consumer products and services companies view their brands as a significant part of their intangible assets and would like to see this represented on their balance sheet. Such a balance sheet entry would go some way towards explaining the often substantial difference between the market value of the company and the book value of its assets and liabilities.

Whatever the claims by the peddlers of such methods, the fact remains though that there is no reliable and, perhaps more importantly, universally recognized way of valuing brands. It is a 'black art'. However, accounting aside, there will often be value for consumer-oriented companies to assess changes in the perception of their brands – provided that a consistent methodology is applied – to see whether they are adding more or less value to them, and whether competitive brands are getting relatively stronger or weaker than theirs.

The impact of advertising can be measured too. Where appropriate, such as in direct mail for example, consumer response levels to particular campaigns can easily be measured and insights gained. But other types of advertising tend to be more subtle. Until recently, advertising agencies tended to measure campaign success in terms of the target market's awareness of the brand, product or service being advertised. However, increasingly, consumer companies are demanding that awareness alone is not enough and that ultimately what they really want and need from advertising is *sales*. Indeed, some are even trying to tie their advertising agency spend directly to increases in brand sales revenues

– though payment by results is probably a more creative idea than the 'creatives' themselves want to hear.

But advertising is just one element of brand value building. The *customer experience* of the brand's delivery and use (as manifested in the product or service) is at least as much to do with the perception of the brand, if not more so, as the aura created by the marketing effort. And it doesn't necessarily stop at a product's delivery and use; its disposal after use can also represent significant branding and performance measurement issues (see the box *The Bottom Line*).

The Bottom Line

Nowhere is the notion of customer intimacy – knowing every last detail of customers' wants and needs – more apposite than in the toilet paper industry. But, in 2000, Procter & Gamble, the US consumer products group, was forced into an embarrassing U-turn in Britain over the 'flushability' of its newly launched Charmin toilet roll.

Charmin is the market leader is the US, where it has a one-third market share of American bottoms. However, for the UK, the product's wet strength was doubled after research found that the British tend to fold their toilet paper, while more US consumers scrunch it. 'This leads to a different dynamic in the product,' P&G said at the launch. 'Folding the paper means you need strength.' The company, therefore, marketed Charmin in the UK, in a £27 million campaign, promoting its outstanding 'temporary wet strength' properties.

However, the company has had to halve the 'temporary wet strength' after it was claimed that the product might block sewage pipes. This revelation invoked significant levels of media attention, causing 'negative coverage' of the brand. The Association of Makers of Soft Tissue Products subsequently agreed to harmonize toilet roll strengths across the industry to avoid 'large volumes of toilet tissue with transient wet strength' causing sewerage problems.

There is now a notion too, especially where the brand is the same as the company name, that everyone – from the boardroom to the shop-floor – must align, reflect and 'live' what the brand stands for, delivering the promises contained within the company's mission statement (its brand values) and the publicity blurb it distributes. And that's neither easy nor short-term. So, if continuous improvement is to occur, progress towards achievement of such ideals will need to be tracked, glitches identified, corrective actions taken, and the impact of these monitored. Consumer products and services companies need to be sure too that they have the processes and capabilities in place to deliver on their advertised promises. Customers can be extremely unforgiving when the hype does not match the reality.

Segmentation is very much at the fashionable end of customer relationship management these days. The received wisdom is that brands today need to be highly focused on particular micro-market segments. And that means gaining a deep understanding of those customer segments and positioning the brand accordingly. Susan Fournier, associate professor of marketing at Harvard Business School[51], says that if companies want to restore growth to their brands in the current business environment, they have to drop the 'one-size-fits-all' mass marketing approach. They need to discover how they can make their brands more relevant to different kinds of consumers. 'They tend to want to understand their brands, when what they really need to do is understand consumers' lives and fit their brands into them,' she says. Putting that right though requires lots of expensive market research that watches trends and 'street cultures' at a time when costs are being squeezed. But, in any case, she takes a pessimistic view of most companies' ability to do this, saying: 'They don't have the skills to do that because they are essentially pencil-pushing, balance sheet folks trying to make the quarterly results – and that's not what the game is any more.' But for those companies that do have the appropriate resources, here is an opportunity to really get those computers crunching the numbers.

Customer Segmentation and Behaviour Data

There are significant differences between consumer and industrial customer performance measurement and management environments too. In consumer industries, the emphasis tends to be on building knowledge about many hundreds of thousands, or even several millions, of customers. Whereas, in the industrial sector, the customer base of a single business unit can usually be numbered in the tens, hundreds or, at most, thousands. There is a huge scale difference. In the mass market industries, the tendency is to build software systems that capture large quantities of information about customer preferences, behaviours and trends, building so-called data warehouses so that this data can be mined and picked over by analysts, often using predetermined customer segmentation criteria, to help identify new opportunities. Customers can be sliced and diced into many different categories, some of the most common being age, gender, ethnic origin, income level, home location, social group, and so on.

The results can be idiosyncratic. One retailer discovered that in certain districts customers in their late twenties and early thirties who buy disposable nappies (diapers) on a Friday evening also tend to buy not only more baby food but also more bottled beers than other customers. The conclusion might be that less well-off consumers who have very young children may tend to go out less at weekends and, therefore, prefer to have a few drinks at home rather than going to the expense of hiring a baby-sitter. But how should the retailer react to this revelation? Should they position beers and nappies adjacent to one another in the store to aid customer convenience? Should they position them as far apart as possible so that this segment of customers may be tempted to spend the money they saved with the baby-sitter on spontaneous purchases? Or maybe they should mail special beer promotions to those customers with young families? The data may look useful, but what to do with it and how to react to it may not always be blindingly obvious.

In addition to using customer focus groups, Lloyds TSB, for example, carries out a quarterly survey, Life Index, which measures the 'mood of Britain' and estimates what it will be in the future. The views of 2,000 people are polled in each survey and the bank uses this information to improve its understanding of the influences on customers' – and potential customers' – lives. The goal is to build up a detailed profile of different social groups, based on their priorities and attitudes to work and life, and to take a strategic approach to both its customers and non-customers.

When Tesco launched its pet insurance service, it first pitched to customers whom it knew had recently bought dog food and cat litter at its stores and online. Some of the supermarkets are becoming very sophisticated in how they use these data. Having the right products available to sell to consumers when they want them is one of the central tenets of retailing. But forecasting demand is also one of the most difficult things to get right. J. Sainsbury, the UK retailer, has an in-house computer system that tracks sales of individual product lines, average ambient temperatures and hours of sunshine over a three-year period. It can then calculate what average sales have been in certain conditions and predict what stocks need to be ramped up when those conditions recur. For example, if the temperature should rise to 28°C, Sainsbury knows that it can expect to sell upwards of 18,000 bags of charcoal a week for barbecues versus a cooler summer norm (this is Britain) of 3,500 bags a week. Sainsbury's system is interesting also because it combines a mix of internally and externally generated data to help gain insights and make merchandising decisions. Most forecasting systems tend to use internally sourced sales and logistics data exclusively. It also benefits both the customers (fewer stock-outs) and the organization (higher sales and profits).

Website Behaviour Data

As we have seen, the internet provides many new opportunities to get to know customers better. In early 2000, Yahoo! was said to be collecting *four terabytes* of data each week about its users. From where did they log on? When? Where did they go? How long did they stay? And so on. The point is that this vast amount of data about customers' habits needs to be used extremely carefully and in a very focused way. But there are other real dangers too. First, if you ask customers, and particularly potential customers, for *too much* information about themselves, they are more than likely to come to the view that life is just too short and go elsewhere – remember, competitors are just a click or two away. The desire to profile customers more precisely has to be balanced with the need for a simple and user-friendly registration process.

In the run-up to Christmas 1999, Accenture conducted research into US consumer e-business performance. Of the 1,492 shoppers surveyed, 88 per cent reported problems. While that horrendous customer dissatisfaction level should have improved meanwhile, let's note the top ten things that irked them. They were:

1. Product was out of stock.
2. Item wasn't delivered on time.
3. Paid too much for delivery.
4. Connection trouble.
5. Didn't get a confirmation or status report.
6. Selections were limited.
7. Site was hard to navigate.
8. Site didn't provide enough information.
9. Prices weren't competitive.
10. Site didn't offer enough gift ideas.

This list gives us a lot of clues about what needs to be measured in a B2C environment and what particular customer service improvement initiatives need to be tracked. For further evidence as to what e-businesses are actually measuring and intend to measure about their customer interfaces (see the box *e-CRM*).

Furthermore, there are regulations in many countries, such as the UK's Data Protection Act, which determines what firms are and are not allowed to do with the data they obtain from customers. While these regulations are not exclusive to the internet, they are brought into stark relief by its particular digital attributes. Perhaps no one has suffered more from privacy's increased attention in the online world than DoubleClick, the leading US-based web marketing company. It became the prime target of regulatory probes, private

e-CRM

A company's website provides a unique opportunity to measure and monitor customer behaviours. It also has the potential to enable web customers to be segregated increasingly towards a one-to-one basis, creating the possibility to deliver dynamic web-pages based on their click behaviour.

A joint research survey conducted by Accenture's Managing With Measures team and Cranfield School of Management's Centre for Business Performance in 2000 sought to discover what e-businesses – both dot-coms and clicks-and-mortar firms – measure differently from other businesses. One of the many findings of this research was that 89 per cent of dot-coms surveyed measure click-stream patterns, 61 per cent track trends and predictions of click behaviour (website traversal forecasts), and 61 per cent also measure the level of website visits not resulting in a transaction. For each parameter, the vast majority of those dot-coms who do not measure it already expect to do so in the future. Clicks-and-mortar firms were less sophisticated (so far) in their use of the available data in this area, recording 63 per cent, 30 per cent and 56 per cent respectively. They too show a desire to collect and use this valuable customer data in the future.

Other crucial measurement issues were website maintenance costs, website downtime and the level of website security. A comparison with bricks-and-mortar companies showed that a surprisingly high percentage of traditional companies that do not use the internet for business transactions have web-specific measures in place. But even companies that have a website only for advertising and/or informational purposes need to be concerned about maintaining the site and making it user-friendly, constantly available and fundamentally secure.

The study also found that over 80 per cent of respondents – both dot-coms and clicks-and-mortar firms – claimed that they measured customer satisfaction, while 100 per cent of those who don't measure it thought that they should do so. However, customer contribution measures produced a much less consistent result. Some 89 per cent of dot-coms claim to measure customer contribution and 100 per cent of those that don't think that they should, while only 41 per cent of clicks-and-mortar firms measure it already and 75 per cent believe that they should do so.

While many of the dot-coms appeared to be ahead in the potential to gain customer insights through web-enabled performance measures, the clicks-and-mortar firms seemed to be ready to play 'catch-up' fast.

lawsuits and consumer watchdog campaigns. DoubleClick does two, individually innocent, things. First, it tracks surfers around the web through so-called 'cookies', which record what sites they visit and are downloaded to the users computer with their knowledge. Second, in 2000 DoubleClick bought Abacus, the largest US database of offline catalogue shoppers, which does contain names and addresses. The trouble was created due to the group's plan to integrate the two businesses, allowing it to identify the names, addresses, demographics, and purchase histories of particular internet users just from their cookies. While websites and advertisers would no doubt be willing to pay substantial premiums for such targeted data, privacy advocates were alarmed at the amount of personal information DoubleClick would potentially amass. Customer data needs to be managed both carefully and discretely.

Data Management

Where should all this data management activity take place? The recent proliferation of call centres, in particular (and where applicable), would seem to offer the greatest potential to capture much of the essential information and to analyze the data obtained. Néstle, for example, is testing an approach that allows it to handle everything from the creation of one-to-one customer communications through to both outgoing and incoming phone, fax, post and e-mail messages at a dedicated 'relationship centre'. There it hopes to create a different mind-set from the volume of flows needs that typically dominate call centre thinking. In other organizations it might be done at various similar forms of customer service centre. Wherever it is located, the nature of customer satisfaction and dissatisfaction with particular products or services needs to be collected, collated, analyzed and reported so that useful insights can be obtained and judgements made. However, this will seldom be the sole source of relevant data. The trick is to have the ability to match the data from several sources.

For example, a brown and/or white goods rental company can quickly get a measure of those individual products it installs which cause the most problems and technician call-outs from customer requests for after-sales service. But it should also be able to get a fix on the specific components within those products that fail most frequently from technician reports. This serves two purposes. Not only can service engineers or repair centres be equipped with the replacement parts that are most frequently needed (improving both customer service levels and spare parts inventory management), but it can also enter into a negotiation with the suppliers of these particular appliances about compensation with factual data to support the claim – or, at the minimum, plans (and targets) can be agreed as to how they will improve new models so that they will be more reliable in the future.

The ability to link the level of customer service quality failures to their attendant costs is another such example of data merging. Getting a handle on the cost of service failures gives management a better feel for the potential return on investment of implementing remedies through re-engineering processes or by continuous improvement initiatives. For instance, at one cable operator the following categories for the cost of poor service quality were identified:

- Complaint handling costs.
- Query handling costs.
- Invoice error correction costs.
- Cost of payment delays due to errors.
- Installation return visit costs.
- In-home equipment fault repair costs.
- Central set-top box repairs and return costs.
- Value of courtesy credits.
- Cost of avoidable customer churn:
  - lost revenues
  - termination costs
  - per cent of churn reparation team.

As we have seen in Chapter 2, with access to so much empirical data, the real danger for executives is of simply drowning in data. In general, organizations tend to use purposefully only a tiny proportion of the data they generate and have available to them. Nowhere is data overload more prevalent than in the consumer customer area. Nowhere is it more wanting than in the industrial customer area. Use it well and you gain a real competitive advantage, use it badly and you'll lose out to someone else. That is why the process of determining *what to measure* and selecting the appropriate customer-centric metrics is critical to business success. Figure 7.4 summarizes some of the key measurement issues associated with managing customer satisfaction and contribution.

The conduct of customer surveys is not necessarily as simple or easy as one might assume. Many companies fail to get the basic data they need in order to improve or they leave real opportunities to gain competitive advantage on the table. The box *Learning from 'Worst Practices' in Customer Satisfaction Measurement* illustrates many of these common glitches.

A couple of decades' worth of research and application has identified a considerable amount of evidence as to what it is that customers and intermediaries want and need, and consequently what needs to be measured and reported. The shame though is that so little appears to have been learned from it in terms of using the data to help improve products and services. Although there have been some notable successes that have tended to raise customer expectations of what

Fig 7.4 Sample Measures for Managing Customer Relations

Learning from 'Worst Practices' in Customer Satisfaction Measurement

Literally hundreds of books, articles, and consulting practices have sprung up from the seemingly straightforward idea that knowing whether a customer is satisfied with your offering is useful information. Researchers and practitioners now have more than a decade of experience with the concept and it is plain that measuring satisfaction correctly is far harder than it appears. We may not always know the best way to measure customer satisfaction, but we can avoid the following 'worst practices' to make sure we measure it much better:

Worst Practice #1: Survey only your current customers

Your current customers like you. That's why they are your current customers. If you only talk to current customers, you are likely to get an overly rosy picture. Unfortunately, in most organizations current customers are the path of least resistance for measurement. You know who they are and it's nicer to spend time talking with people who like you (ask anyone who has ever worked answering a customer complaint line). Seek out samples of competitors' customers and your former customers to counter that bias.

Worst Practice #2: Ask only about overall satisfaction

Companies that focus on broad satisfaction measures don't learn how to improve. Asking whether a customer is satisfied or dissatisfied overall is a useful first step because it gives a summary picture. If you stop there, however, you don't know what caused that picture. In any customer satisfaction survey, include items regarding the specific benefits and attributes that customers experience to gain a deeper understanding of what drives overall satisfaction.

Worst Practice #3: Ask only about your company

Customers choose among competing products and services. What drives their behaviour is their satisfaction relative to the competitive options available to them. Always ask about customers' satisfaction with competitors, and report satisfaction with your offerings in terms of relative satisfaction.

Worst Practice #4: Ask only about your product

Over time the basis of competition shifts from the core product offering to the accessories and services that companies offer. Indeed, evidence increasingly suggests that customer defection can be traced as much to service as product issues. Survey customers about their entire experience with the organization, from initial sales contact to post-sale installation, billing and use.

Worst Practice #5: Let your salespeople / dealers administer the survey

It may be the easy way to do it, but it's not the best way. The data will inevitably be either unintentionally distorted or deliberately manipulated. Headquarters staff or an external agency should perform customer satisfaction research.

Worst Practice #6: Don't ask about price

Price has a tremendous impact on most customer buying decisions. They may like your product better than competitors, but not if they have to spend 20 per cent more. Furthermore, customer satisfaction research can be criticized if it identifies areas for improvement without regard to the cost of improvement. Follow up with a small sample study that examines in detail the implications of greater added value vs. price.

Worst Practice #7: Don't segment the market

Customers and markets aren't homogeneous. Segmenting the market in various ways into smaller units provides far greater insights into a company's strengths and weaknesses.

Worst Practice #8: Focus on the mean satisfaction score

Don't aggregate 'satisfied' and 'very satisfied' customers into a single percentage in order to produce a gratifyingly large number. These different categories of customers behave in significantly different ways – the latter category will be much more economically valuable to the company than the former.

Source: Adapted from 'Worst Practices in Customer Satisfaction Measurement' by Dr Bruce Clark, Centre for Business Performance, Cranfield School of Management, published in *Performance Measurement Association Newsletter*, 1, 4, October 2001.

is possible, the general trend is not so impressive in many industry sectors. Even the dot-com start-ups replicated many of the customer service failures that traditional businesses had been making for years. While over-servicing customers is likely to adversely impact customer profitability unless the price is high, much can still be done in value markets to improve profitability. By providing decent reliable service that helps to attract and retain customers, and by eliminating the cost of fixing customer product/service glitches and complaints, profitability increases. Picking the right measures helps to identify where management action needs to be applied and how effective it has been so far. Much can be learned too about the behaviour of customers by selective analysis of the available data. The operative word here, however, is undoubtedly 'selective' – far too often the design process appears almost random.

The Customer Relationship Measures Design Process

The process whereby appropriate stakeholder relations measures may be derived is, as we have described earlier, called 'success mapping'. It may be applied to each of the organization's key stakeholders. For customer relations, it means addressing the following critical questions:

- Who are our key customer groups and what do they each want and need?
- And what does our organization want and need from these customers?
- What are our strategies for satisfying these sets of wants and needs?
- How will our internal business processes effectively and efficiently deliver them?
- Which particular capabilities do we need to build, maintain and improve in order to execute them?

This concept is shown schematically in Figure 7.5.

Fig 7.5 Performance Prism Unfolded Schematic: Customers and Intermediaries

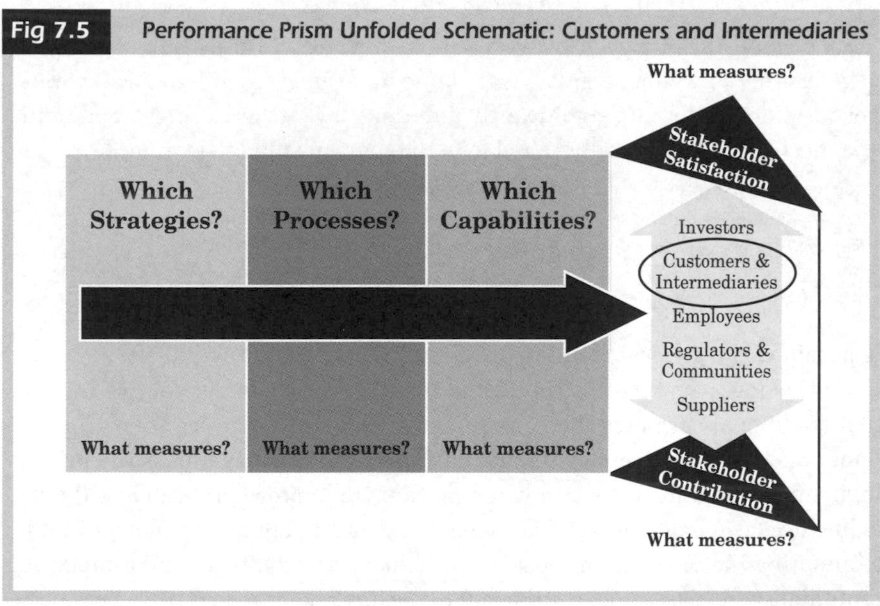

To make this more tangible, let us take as an example the logistics operations of a division of a European specialty chemicals company. While the division had enjoyed technological leadership in its field for some years, competitors were rapidly catching up with comparable products. Now there was a greater requirement for improved customer delivery service in order to retain market share. At the same time, the division – formerly an independent company – had recently been the subject of a rather expensive takeover and, consequently, there was considerable pressure from the new parent company to reduce its operating costs. The division owned subsidiaries in most European countries and a single manufacturing plant in the UK.

So, in this scenario, we have two critical stakeholders – its customers and its parent company – apparently making incompatible demands. Better service at lower cost. In fact, this is not an untypical dilemma for many companies and, with some focus and investment, both objectives can be achieved. In this case, by streamlining its order handling processes and by gaining better control of its central and subsidiary inventories, the division had realized that it could provide significantly better customer service at a considerably lower cost. Elcments of its physical distribution (transportation and warehousing) operations could also be improved, reducing costs substantially while at the minimum retaining existing service levels.

An analysis of customer types revealed that three major categories existed: the customers of subsidiary companies; selling agents who represent the company in geographical markets where it has no subsidiary; and customers who take direct shipments from the central factory warehouse (where there is no local subsidiary or agency) and those who buy product in bulk. Despite this segmentation, it emerged that all three groups had relatively homogeneous requirements. These were:

- Reliable on-time delivery (not necessarily fast, except in emergencies, but reliable – preferably on a definite weekly or twice-weekly delivery schedule).
- The right product specification (there being many technical grades of the same product lines, shipping errors sometimes occur).
- The complete order (i.e. no partial shipments and multiple invoices).
- A simple hassle-free ordering process.

The company's logistics management team identified just two principal things that it wanted *from* its customers (and, as it has many customers, it would want to focus these efforts on its major customers in each geographical area). These were:

- Customers' and agencies' short- and medium-term demand forecasts.
- Feedback on its efforts to improve services (by means of customer survey).

The parent company's wants and needs, not surprisingly, were transparently focused on achieving its desired cost reductions. They were:

- optimization of inventory holding costs.
- optimization of international shipping and domestic haulage costs.
- optimization of warehousing costs.
- minimization of the amount of repackaging and relabelling activity at the factory warehouse.

To make all this happen, the logistics management team simply needed sufficient budget – to upgrade the supply chain information systems in order to allow centralized planning and scheduling – and sufficient resources to implement the programme.

The strategy is already, so to speak, set in concrete – improve customer service *and* reduce distribution costs. The principal processes then are clearly around order handling, inventory management and physical distribution. The first and last of these processes demand capabilities both at its central location and within its local subsidiaries. While scheduling skills, best practices and, not least, the related information technologies would need to be assembled centrally (and removed from their existing location in the subsidiaries).

To help design the appropriate performance measures for the implementation of this supply chain strategy and process re-engineering project, a success map was drawn up in a schematic fashion. Using the primary elements of the Performance Prism helped to conceptualize the requirement. This is shown in Figure 7.6.

As this is in fact a hybrid example of more than one company's experience in this industry, we can talk about some of the specific measures that were actually selected without fear of breaching any confidentiality agreements. At the strategic level, typical examples included:

- Total distribution costs as a percentage of sales.
- Total sales value over distribution assets.
- Total stock days of cover.
- Value of lost supply opportunities.
- Pan-European on-time delivery performance.
- Benchmarked customer supply satisfaction index.

At the more detailed level, process and capability performance metrics typically included:

Fig 7.6 Supply Chain Success Map – Example

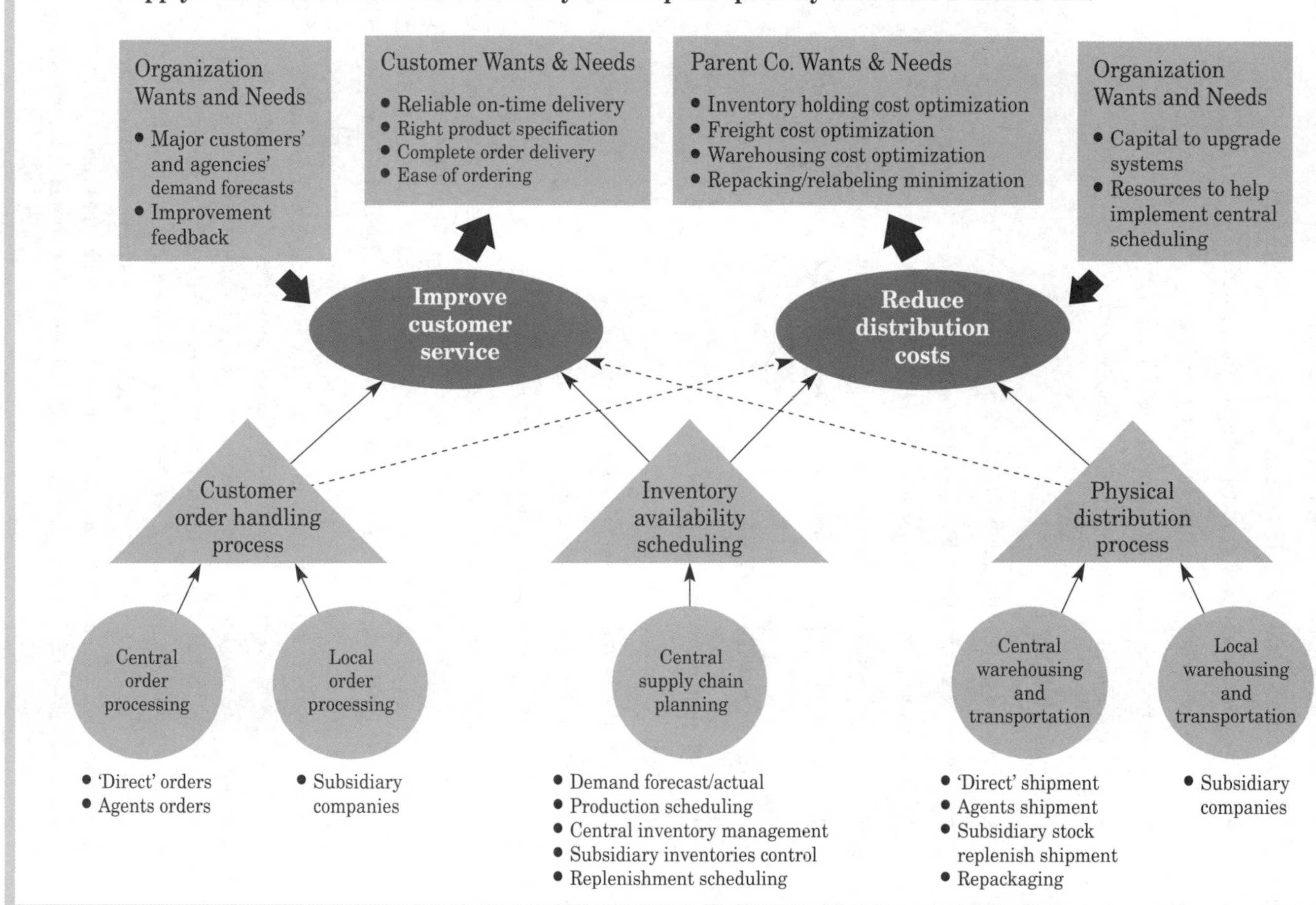

Supply Chain Planning

- Stock days of cover (by warehouse location).
- Inventory holding costs (cost of capital + warehousing).
- Stock age profile (by product category/by location).
- Stock accuracy (write-ups/downs by location).
- Sales forecast accuracy (by product/by country).
- Adherence to weekly production schedule.

Order Fulfilment

- Percentage of orders delivered to first promise (by location).
- Percentage of orders delivered to customer request (by location).
- Number of stock-outs per month (by product/by location).
- Level of distribution-related customer complaints (by category).
- Customer supply satisfaction level versus competitors (by country).

Physical Distribution

- Cost per tonne shipped (per destination).
- Tonnes shipped (per destination).
- Warehouse man hours per tonne shipped.
- Percentage packs repacked versus shipped.
- Percentage packs relabelled versus shipped.

This example also illustrates the need to cascade measures through the organization to the individual operating units. Some commentators advocate the implementation of just a very few critical performance measures. And indeed this may be fine and well for senior executive trend-watching and question–answering purposes. However, sooner or later, they are going to demand the detail from their sub-ordinates and a much greater degree of granularity will be required. And, in any case, many of these measures will be needed in order to manage effective and efficient operations at the local level. But there are two key tricks here. The first is to ensure that the measures (and, particularly, their metrics) are applied consistently across the organization and not in a localized ad hoc manner. The second is to create a hierarchy of measures so that all parts of the organization can understand how their operating measures relate to the organization's strategic objectives (in this case, of both improving customer service and reducing distribution costs), rather than in isolation. Simplification is not so much the key measurement issue today. It is more the integration of the measurement system through the organization to achieve the desired aims of the time.

A further example of this kind of approach – and a consumer-focused one this time – is provided by Telewest Communications, the second largest UK cable operator. Telewest used the Performance Prism's principles to gain a better understanding of its customers' experiences in an effort to drive higher levels of customer loyalty in order, in turn, to achieve improved levels of customer profitability (see the box *A Clearer Picture Now*).

A Clearer Picture Now

Cable company Telewest Communications provides television, telephone and internet services to several major conurbations in the UK. Its consumer division competes with alternative packaged services from satellite TV provider BSkyB, with digital terrestrial TV provider ONdigital (to be renamed ITV Digital), and with other providers of telephone and internet services. It has 1.7 million customers.

Telewest's Head of CRM Strategy, Clare Moore, admits that it has some way to go to achieve the levels of customer service performance it wishes to provide, but its 'Measuring for Customer Loyalty' programme is a good start. Its premise is that customer satisfaction is not only the driver of customer loyalty (i.e. gaining retention levels that more than cover the costs of acquiring, installing and providing standard services to them) but that it is also a key driver of customer extension (i.e. whether customers will be willing to buy additional or upgraded services) and also its chances of improving the level of customer expansion (i.e. signing up new customers). Word-of-mouth recommendations will be important to supporting its sales and marketing efforts too. If it can get its cost and pricing strategies right as well as its customer satisfaction ones, then customer retention, extension and expansion will result in improved customer profitability.

To help facilitate improved levels of customer satisfaction – and less churn – Telewest has developed what it calls its 'Customer Experience Monitor'. This identifies each of the key stages of its relationship with its customers and monitors performance within each one with a combination of external (survey) and internal (operations) measures.

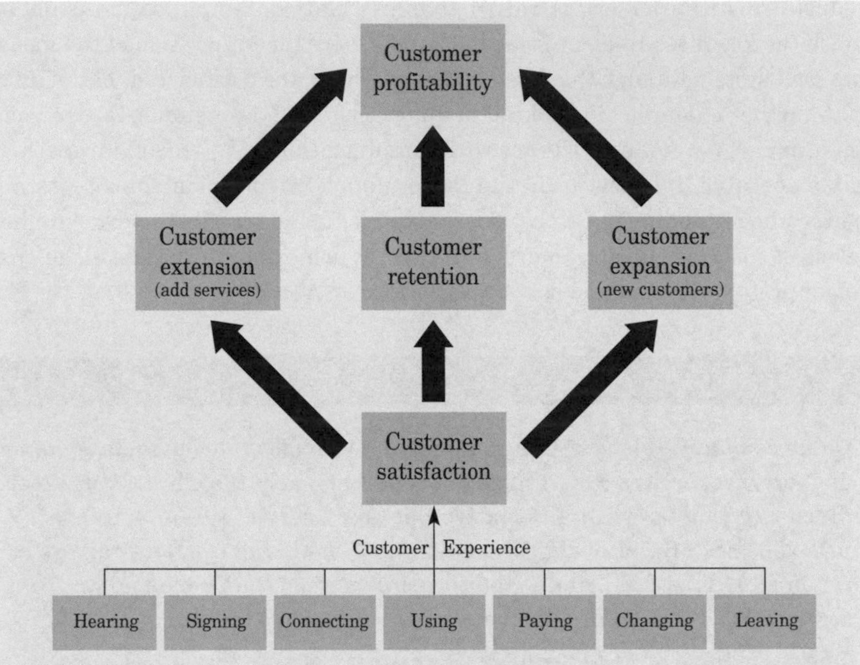

Applying the data it collects will enable Telewest to view its customer relationships 'in the round' and help it to take executive decisions that will:

- Increase the length of relationship and build loyalty.
- Increase the value of products sold per customer.
- Use profiles to target profitable prospect customers.
- Influence customer behaviour.
- Shape service design and optimize the cost of servicing.
- Reduce overhead costs associated with churn and complaints.

Source: Telewest Communications and Accenture.

The Customer Relationship Measures 'Failure Mode' Test

This test should, in our view, be put in place in order to validate the customer measures selected. It is simply too easy to be glib and pick the customer-related measures that are available, or the ones that are most familiar, rather than those that are really *needed* to manage the enterprise successfully. This test performs a 'sanity check' on the selected measures to ensure that important aspects of customer relationship measurement have not been overlooked. It is formulated by putting forward some sort of potential 'worst case scenario' and then tracking back to ensure that the right strategy, process and capability measures are in place to enable prevention of this 'failure mode' from severely affecting the business. It is, therefore, a means of helping to mitigate the most potentially serious customer-related risks.

The way to select the scenario or failure mode is to answer the question: *What would cause us to fail to meet our objectives in relation to customer satisfaction and contribution?* In this case, we have selected a high or increasing level of customer defections as a reasonably common failure mode, but others could be selected instead – for example, if they represent a greater risk to the business. The questions to ask then are:

- Are the strategies we have around customer retention right? And do we have the right measures?
- Are the processes that relate to customer retention right? And do we have the right measures?
- Are the capabilities that underpin those related processes right? And do we have the right measures?

In our experience, organizations have a tendency to put too 'glossy' an outlook on their customer-centred measures – especially during good times – and often fail to identify the critical risk factors that matter. 'Failure Mode Mapping' is a technique that helps to pinpoint these adverse factors. In the example shown in Figure 7.7 (p. 248), we have assumed that the principal reasons why customers might defect are: uncompetitive prices, poor product quality, poor delivery and other execution services, and an obsolete (or unfashionable) product range.

A practical application of Failure Mode Mapping is illustrated in the box *A Fine Line Between Success and Failure*.

By validating the selected measures (created through the 'customer success mapping' process) using the failure mode mapping technique, we believe that a robust set of customer-oriented measures will be created. The danger, as ever, is that too many measures will be created. Only the most critical measures need receive executive attention on a regular basis though, the rest can and should be delegated to lower ranks of management – but with 'red flags' delivered to the executive team as and when adverse trends are detected and decisions are demanded – and ownership for them assigned.

Fig 7.7 Customer Failure Mode Map – Example

As previously, when the measures selection activity is complete, we then need to finalize the design process by creating Performance Measure Record Sheets for each measure selected (see Figure 7.8, p. 250, for an example).

Even if most employees don't get out of bed every morning ready to satisfy the wants and needs of their employer's investors, a commitment to satisfying its customers' wants and needs should not be unreasonable to expect – provided of course that senior executives consistently make it clear that it is important to them too through the measures that they apply and regularly review. Customer-centric measures, in particular, should pervade the whole organization.

A Fine Line Between Success and Failure

Before the semiconductor downturn in 2001, ASML, the world's largest maker of machines that etch incredibly minute semiconductor circuits, wanted to implement relevant performance measures within its Goods Flow (supply chain) operations. With hundreds of different parts and sub-assemblies, not least the highly specialized optical lenses, needed to assemble a single lithography system machine that can cost as much as €10 million, any late deliveries are not only a blow to its demanding customers but also to the Dutch company's investors. The lack of a critical component can have a disproportionate effect on the company's performance. With technology development moving rapidly in the sector, overstocking of such components is not a viable solution either.

To validate measures selection for both its overall supply chain performance and its operational effectiveness and efficiency measures for managing its purchasing, manufacturing and planning activities, a reverse success mapping (failure mode map) technique was applied. The map identifies all the critical 'pinch-points' where failures to have the right materials, the right resources or the right information could easily cause delivery delays – and hence unhappy customers and shareholders.

ASML goods flow 'failure map' schematic

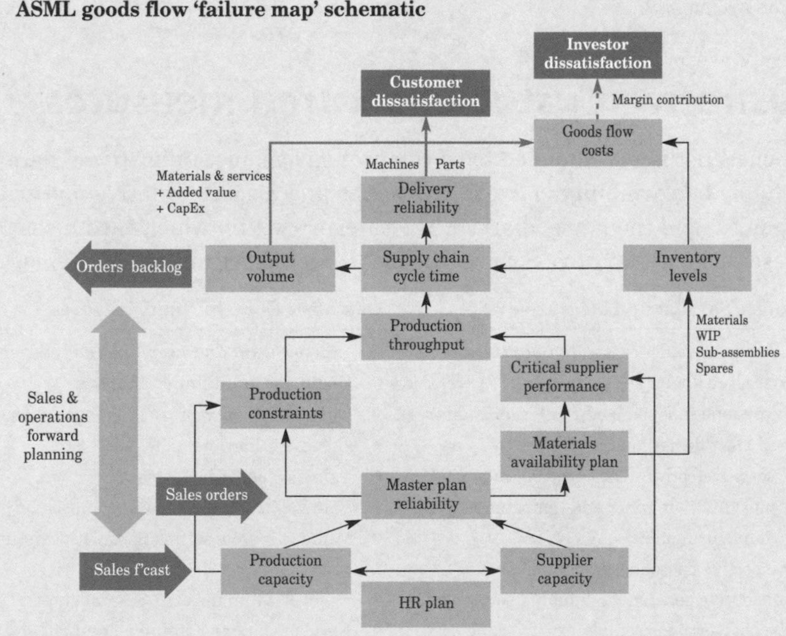

Source: ASML and Accenture

Fig 7.8 Example of Customer-related Performance Measure Record Sheet

Measure	**Customer Satisfaction Index**
Purpose	To determine the level of customer satisfaction with the products and services provided by the organization
Relates to	The strategy of being the preferred supplier with the top 10 customers
Target	To achieve a score of 4 out of 5 for the 6 most important indicators used within 12 months, from a baseline of 2 out of 10 and with competitors A and B currently dominating this position
Formula	A questionnaire sent to each of the top 20 customers, asking them to rate us in 12 key areas
Frequency	Measured and reported once every two months, the data can be analyzed within one week of receipt
Who measures	Business Analyst compiles data
Source of data	The data is collected from the customers [the data should be chased up by the account managers so that it is as full as possible and timely]
Who acts on the data (owner)	Customer service manager
What do they do	Creates action plans to improve areas of performance on which the customers do not rate the business highly
Notes/comments	

Illustrative Customer-centred measures

This checklist is not intended to be comprehensive, just indicative. There will inevitably be variability between industries and also the relative maturity of companies (and their subsidiaries). The category within which each measure is represented may vary too. Some of the measures that firms typically adopt are:

Customer Satisfaction Measures

What do our customers want and need?

- Existing customer satisfaction level (perception surveys and independent or internal audits):
  - product design/quality/reliability in use
  - services (convenience/speed/ease of use/ punctuality/manner and competence of staff)
  - value-for-money
- Prospective customer perception survey
- Competitive benchmarks (quality/service/value)
- Level of customer complaints (by category)
- Level of product warranty claims
- Level of faulty product returns
- Level of customer savings achieved

Customer Contribution Measures

What do we want and need from our customers?

- Customer profitability analysis
- Customer loyalty/churn [by reason category?]
- Customer lifetime value
- Value of repeat business
- Value of lost business [per competitor?]
- Value of increased business with existing customers [intermediaries/end-users]
- Level of willingness to recommend
- Level of customer improvement suggestions contributed/implemented
- Accuracy of forecast demand [B2B]
- Level of on-time/late payments/credit risk

Customer-related strategy measures

What are our strategies for satisfying these sets of wants and needs?

- Number of customers
- Level of new/existing product sales trend
- Level of new/repeat business trend
- Market share (by market – product/segment/geography)
- Customer profitability (by market – product/segment/geography)

Customer-related process measures

Which of our internal business processes will effectively and efficiently deliver them?

- On-time delivery-to-promise performance
- Level of requested delivery date/time refusals
- Average delivery lead time/order cycle time
- Level of inventory stock-outs (and inventory records accuracy)
- Level of shipping/delivery/installation/billing errors [by type]
- Cost of poor quality (e.g. scrap and rework, complaints handling, inventory, etc.)
- Advertising/Promotion response rates [by source]
- Level of proposals/quotations/pitches/website visits leading to sales (and repeat business)
- Level of investment in new/improved products and services development

Customer-related capability measures

Which particular capabilities do we need to establish and maintain in order to execute them?

- Level of demand versus capacity
- Customer segmentation and profiling
- Brand awareness, perceptions and positioning
- Comparative selling price benchmarking
- Revenues per sales channel/sales representative
- Cost of attracting new customers versus retaining existing ones [and breakeven level?]

Summary

Who typically are this group of stakeholders?

- *Current, potential and former customers (end-users)*, plus key intermediaries such as retailers, wholesalers, brokers, agents, merchants, dealers and distributors.

What do customers typically want and need from your organization?

- *Fast* – rapid and reliable delivery of products and services offered
- *Right* – high quality products and services
- *Cheap* – reasonably priced products and services (that offer value for money)
- *Easy* – low-hassle transactions (easy to do business with)

What does your organization typically want and need from its customers?

- *Profit* – reasonable margins (to reinvest in improved products and services)
- *Growth* – increase in sales volumes over time
- *Opinion* – feedback on performance and suggestions as to ways of improving products and services
- *Trust* – access to key information in order to aid supply chain efficiencies and to establish longer-term collaborative ventures

What strategies typically address these wants and needs?

- *Extend/renew products and services offering* – create offerings that target customers want/need
- *Attract potentially profitable new/lapsed customers* – bring in new business at the right price
- *Retain profitable existing customers* – keep key current customers very satisfied and loyal
- *Grow share of target market segments* – through leveraging core processes and capabilities

Which processes typically relate to the execution of these strategies?

- *Develop new products and services* – create innovative target market offerings
- *Generate demand* – leverage brands, products and services in target markets
- *Fulfil demand* – execute in accordance with market segmentation standards and specifications
- *Plan and manage the enterprise* – provide resources, systems, training, policies, facilities, etc.

Which capabilities typically need to be developed and nurtured?

- Market research
- Product/service development
- Merchandizing/product range
- Pricing management
- Marketing campaigns and brand management
- Sales and distribution channel management
- Alliance management
- Salesforce effectiveness
- Order fulfilment operations
- Technical services
- After-sales service
- Customer relationship management
- Quality management

8 Managing Employee Relationships with Measures

The investor and the employee are in the same position, but sometimes the employee is more important, because he will be there a long time whereas an investor will often get in and out on a whim in order to make a profit. The worker's mission is to contribute to the company's welfare, and his own, every day.

Akio Morita • *co-founder of Sony, 'Made In Japan'.*

Employees are the lifeblood of every corporation. They are involved in enacting corporate strategies (and they really should help to develop them as well); they operate and interact with the organization's essential business processes; and they represent a significant component of its capabilities development too. Technology can help to improve productivity significantly, but it cannot replace employees entirely. Indeed, firms often find that there are shortages of people with the particular skills they need. But employees also represent a substantial part of most organizations' operating costs, often the most easily dispensable part. While many executives pay lip-service to their employees' vital contribution, few actually treat them as much more than 'passing ships in the night'.

The Components of Achieving Employee Satisfaction and Contribution

As we have seen in Chapter 4, companies have been going out of their way to attract and retain the talent they need throughout most of the last decade. Employee satisfaction and motivation has become a key business issue because it was recognized that it was expensive and sometimes difficult to replace employees who defect. It was also found that disaffected employees lose interest in their employer's objectives and behave accordingly in terms of their contribution. This, in turn, tends to negatively impact customers who have choices as to where they buy their goods and services. Bad morale is bad for business. Furthermore – surprise, surprise! – employees (and executives) behave in ways that reflect the way they are incentivized. Inappropriately incentivized employees tend to adopt dysfunctional behaviours. And so, the right employee relationship measures are needed in order to achieve the desired outcomes.

Employee Wants and Needs

What are the things that employees want and need from their employers? We have tried to summarize this in just four short words: *purpose*, *care*, *skills* and *pay*. By expanding on these four words we shall be able to get an idea of what is important to employees and the measures to apply in relation to monitoring their satisfaction.

Purpose

Employees seek interesting work or, at the minimum, work that they can take pride in accomplishing. They would also like their job to be designed in a way which encompasses sufficient variety for it not to be boring or tedious, but at the same time not to be so pressurized, overworked or subject to abusiveness that employment becomes unacceptably consuming or stressful. A 'good job' also needs to be properly supported with systems that enable employees to be productive and gives access to the space, equipment and information that employees need to do their work. So, if the work isn't well designed and supported, all the HRM programmes in the world are probably not going to make much difference. We, therefore, need to get a fundamental understanding of what employees think about their jobs and whether they perceive it to be getting better or worse.

Care

Employees wish to be cared for in a variety of different ways. They want to be treated with respect; they want to be treated fairly (regardless of gender, race or creed); they want to work in a pleasant, safe and comfortable environment with a practical and ergonomic layout. They want to work for an organization that espouses certain humanistic values. They want to work with colleagues and bosses that they can get along with. They want to work for an organization that has a fundamentally caring attitude towards its employees, where morale is generally good and where prospects are positive (both for the organization and for the individual). They also want to be treated decently if they are genuinely ill, have a birth or bereavement in their immediate family, or some other sort of domestic crisis demanding time off work. Keeping a finger on the pulse of an organization's mood is vital since it can rapidly change with, for example, adverse publicity, organizational changes, or as a result of M&A activity (and the consequent threat of job losses).

Skills

Of course, while desirable, it is not always possible for companies to provide employment security. Mass downsizing exercises of the 1990s tore up the implicit job contract between workers and their employers whereby job security was exchanged for commitment and loyalty. Employees today have given up on the 'job-for-life' mentality of their forebears (even in Japan), but they do want to pick up the transferable skills that will be useful to them in enhancing their careers. If a firm is unable to offer long-term employment, it should at least be able to offer long-term employability. Employees want portable skills that they can take with them if they were to be made redundant in the future – they are their entry ticket on their curriculum vitae to other alternative jobs. So, the availability and quality of the training made available by their current employer may be of considerable importance to them. They will also value access to advice and information about aspects of their jobs which they are, from time-to-time, uncertain what to do – appropriate support mechanisms need to be available to them. Employees working in specialist areas will want to keep their skill-sets up to date on the latest trends in their field – and so access to advanced courses, seminars, journals and books will be vital to enable them to do this. In short, measures of internal service quality relating to essential skills development are needed here.

Pay

The compensation package offered by organizations is important to potential employees seeking recruitment opportunities; to ambitious incumbent employees who may be tempted to take their skill-sets elsewhere (where better packages are offered); and also to those more 'long in the tooth' employees who intend to retire with a decent pension provided and contributed to by their former employer. The 'compensation package' can include a multitude of components, from company cars to healthcare, to equity share options, and, as we have seen in Chapter 4, to a whole range of other benefits and taxation-defying 'perks'. There is also the thorny issue of bonuses. Linking a substantial proportion of pay to the performance of the company as a whole; to particular business units within it; to particular teams; and to individuals' contribution (as measured via the firm's employee appraisal system) has become commonplace. We make no claim whatsoever to be employee compensation experts; however, we do know that the effects of linked compensation – and bonus systems in particular – have on the broader measurement systems which a company tries to apply in good faith can be devastating. Probably more balanced scorecard initiatives have failed because of incongruently linked reward systems than any other single reason. Also, cheating and gaming the few measures that are linked to the rewards is not uncommon. Money talks, and it tends to dominate both employee and management behaviours. Nevertheless, benchmarking the compensation packages offered by industry counterparts and other local employers for approximately equivalent jobs is an essential element of employee recruitment and retention today.

Employer's Wants and Needs

The flipside of employee satisfaction is employee contribution. What are the things that employers want and need from their employees? Again, we have tried to encapsulate the essence of what the organization requires from its employees into four short words: *hands*, *hearts*, *minds and voices*.

Hands

The term hands here relates to the number of people an enterprise employs. Obviously, an organization seeks to hire and retain the relevant skills it requires in the sufficient quantities it needs them in the places it wishes to deploy them. However, few firms maintain an inventory of the skill-sets they possess. If a firm's employees are truly its greatest asset, as is so often declared, where is the asset definition list? And without such a tool, how can managers effectively plan the human resources that they will require in the future? Employee and employee-related costs typically represent a substantial proportion of a company's operating costs. They, therefore, have a very direct effect on the profit margins of the business. Corporations typically adjust the number of staff they employ approximately in accordance with the level of demand for its products and/or services. When things are going well, they recruit more employees than they lose; when things are going badly, recruitment is curtailed and sometimes the number of employees reduced through early retirement programmes or, in a severe downturn of demand, through redundancies. Alternatively, given that some regard continued employment even more highly than pay, compensation packages might sometimes be adjusted downwards. Businesses continuously seek productivity improvements too – doing more with less resources. A company, therefore, needs to track its headcount closely to ensure that the appropriate levels of productivity are maintained. To overcome the need to constantly adjust its employee register where demand fluctuates seasonally or cyclically, firms frequently achieve the flexibility they need by retaining a variable balance of temporary personnel to supplement their so-called permanent staff. However, while expedient for flexibility, temporary employees – not surprisingly – are likely to be far less committed to the interests of the organization than their permanent work colleagues. Clearly then, the ability to be flexible in terms of the employee skill-sets available to fulfil variable demand needs to be tracked. Typically, the current and expected order-book quantity per employee (or employee-related costs) is matched to historical patterns of sales per employee (or their inflation adjusted cost).

Hearts

Employers generally want to retain loyal and committed employees. They are the nucleus of the firm, who possess a bank of knowledge about the company – its history (successes and failures), its people, its processes, its products and services, its customers and its competitors in the industry in which it does business. It can be argued though that this can become too incestuous a relationship and subject to 'group think' or lack of innovation. And so a mix of a few senior 'outsiders' blended with the core long-term management team is generally regarded as being healthy, although this can create destructive factions too (see Employee Loyalty on p.258). Where firms allow morale to deteriorate too far, it is invariably the best people who will either be headhunted or use their network of contacts to find employment elsewhere. This of course is unhealthy for the organization and, as we have noted earlier, it is often expensive to fully replace such people. Measures of employee loyalty and other predictive 'tell-tale' signs of commitment and morale then are important to most organizations. Unusual levels of employee turnover or absenteeism would be examples of problem indicators.

Minds

Until relatively recently it seemed as though most firms were quite content just to have the hands and hearts of its employees. Ideas for improvement to working practices would come from managers, not their employees. Perhaps a legacy of Frederick Taylor's doctrines, employees were simply required to attend and to do what they were told. More recently, however, firms increasingly do not want their workers to leave their brains behind when they come to work. The late 1980s and early 1990s saw a marked increase in the number of formal employee contribution initiatives, such as suggestion schemes and quality circles. Some worked brilliantly, while others were poorly implemented and rapidly withered. Today, these tend to be less formalized initiatives with a greater emphasis on team-based projects. They typically involve employees from a broad range of disciplines to help resolve systemic problems within the organization's business processes and implement the solutions. Meanwhile too, the very nature of work is rapidly changing with more service-based industries and fewer manufacturing jobs carried out in high wage earning countries. Now it is the so-called 'knowledge workers' that are in greatest demand and these are the specialist skills shortages that employers complain most about not being able to fill. A measure of the educational qualifications of an organization's employees is commonly applied, especially for its recruitment intake.

Voices

As we have seen, the role of the employee used to be to 'put up and shut up'. Increasingly today, employers look for articulate people who demonstrate a positive and constructive attitude; who communicate well with other employees and their bosses; who work well in a team environment; who will advocate the firm as a good employer; who are friendly towards customers and other important stakeholders. As organizations become increasingly global in the scope of their business and more open in their internal cultures, they typically seek greater diversity in their employee mix too. Procter & Gamble, for example, has a vast variety of customers and wants its workforce to reflect that fact. Their chief executive, Alan Lafley, told the company that: 'Our success depends entirely on our ability to understand these diverse customers' needs. A diverse organization will out-think, out-innovate and out-perform a homogeneous organization every single time. I am putting particular importance on increasing the representation of women and minorities in leadership positions at all levels.'The implication, then, is that not only will measures of individual employee contribution towards team efforts be needed, but also the diversity representation of the organization as a whole (perhaps even at a regional level too) will need to be captured in order to monitor implementation of these policies. The Employee Relationship model is summarized in Figure 8.1.

Fig 8.1 The Employee Relationship

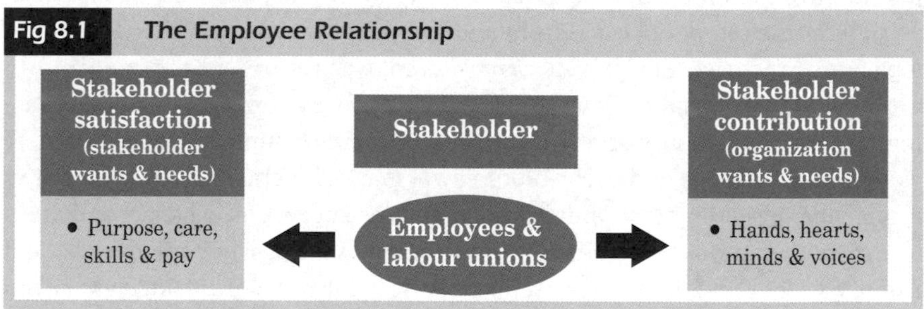

Employee Loyalty

It may be a somewhat unfashionable concept these days but, in the main, employers want their employees to be loyal to the organization. After all, they go to the trouble of hiring them, training them and enabling them to gain experience and expertise. If they leave, not only has all that investment walked out of the door, a replacement – assuming the work remains – will have to be found either from within the organization or from outside. That replacement will take time to 'learn the ropes' and will not normally be in a position to contribute as much as the departed employee for some time – the 'wet behind the ears' effect.

We have seen in the previous chapter the importance that customer loyalty has to achieving customer profitability, given that the costs of winning new customers are significantly higher than retaining existing ones. Some commentators suggest that the same rule applies to employee profitability (or productivity). For example, Frederick Reichheld, author of *The Loyalty Effect* and *Loyalty Rules! – How today's leaders build lasting relationships*, says: 'I have yet to encounter a company that has achieved extremely high customer loyalty without fostering similarly high loyalty among employees.'

Others though think that labour turnover is a healthy thing – bringing new ideas, experiences and attitudes to the prevailing inward-looking corporate culture. A balance of the two approaches may seem to be theoretically ideal. In practice, however, the two people-sets – the 'internals' and the 'externals' – can often have such a different view of life, the universe and everything that they can hardly communicate with each other. Managerial 'camps' or factions, who oppose each other's ideas and proposals almost on principle, tend to form and little other than heat is generated or achieved. On balance, employee loyalty is significantly underrated and organizations only have themselves to blame if they inbreed a myopic culture. In general, the drivers of employee loyalty need to be managed and, therefore, measured.

However, while achieving acceptable levels of employee loyalty and contribution through a broad mix of initiatives is an important factor to the majority of organizations, loyalty itself is not necessarily the 'be-all and end-all' of employee relationship management, particularly where high attrition levels are endemic (see the box *Employee Motivation in an Inherently High Staff Turnover Business*).

Employee Motivation in an Inherently High Staff Turnover Business

Pret A Manger, the privately-owned UK sandwich and coffee bar organization that recently opened an outlet in New York's Wall Street district and has sold a 33 per cent stake in its business to McDonald's, has – you would imagine – an enormous staff turnover problem. It runs at about 70 per cent per annum. Yet it was voted as one of the UK's top ten employers in "The Sunday Times 50 Best Companies To Work For – 2001". It employs over 2300 people in its 108 sandwich-making outlets. Nearly half are women, the average age is 26 and nearly 60 per cent are not British.

Launched in 1986, Pret A Manger feeds London's (and other cities') hungry office workers with £77 million worth of fresh, healthy, high quality, take-away or eat-in lunches. Others have tried to capture a substantial slice of this market with regular sandwich shops, baked-potato outfits and other fast-food concepts. But none have succeeded like Pret in this segment. Its secret? – employee relationships. It provides London's itinerant workforce of young students and English learners with a source of income that's better than most and, above all, it treats them with respect. It also teaches them its own brand of customer service ethic.

For example, quality and service are core values that it is passionate about. Team members are required to serve every customer within 90 seconds in a friendly and individual way. On the other hand, employees are helped with setting up a bank account; weekly pay and cash bonuses are other incentives. Staff salaries are increased by £0.75 an hour if a store reaches 90 per cent on good customer service. Team members can win a £50 bonus if they are named by one of the "mystery shoppers" hired to monitor performance. There are also prizes of up to £1,000 for good ideas. Pret spends £250,000 on two huge parties in the summer and at Christmas, and subsidizes Friday night drinks at trendy nightclubs too. Not surprising then that foreign students recommend Pret A Manger to friends and relations back home who will be seeking employment in London in the future.

Given that it has a young workforce, its maternity/paternity package is also generous and appreciated. New mothers have 10 weeks on full pay, 10 weeks on £100 and another 20 weeks unpaid. During pregnancy they are given £20 for a new pair of jeans. They get flowers at the birth, and a voucher for a month of nursery care. Fathers, on the other hand, are given a pager for the last two weeks of pregnancy and a week off at full pay, while adoptive parents have four weeks at full pay and £100 in Baby Gap vouchers.

However, employees who don't tow the line are warned that disciplinary action will result for those who are repeatedly late, thereby "disrespecting" their colleagues. For those who last the distance and want to stay, there is a clear career path from team member to coffee-maker and then into management. Although Pret invests a considerable sum of money in training, which arguably is rapidly wasted if staff turnover is high, it does clearly set out the standards it expects its employees to provide to its customers. It considers that this investment is worth it in order to achieve the levels of product quality and customer service that differentiates it in the marketplace. It is a strategy that defines the outcomes of the Fulfil Demand process that is so important to its success through a particularly people and practices focused business capability.

As this example shows, staff loyalty isn't necessarily the holy grail of successful HRM programmes. Pret A Manger illustrates that, while it might be desirable, it is possible to live very healthily without it. The key is for a company's HRM systems to collectively spell-out and communicate not only what its values are, but also to treat its employees in a way that reinforces its commitment to those values. It then needs to monitor whether the components of its programme are collectively achieving the desired results. It is just astonishing how many companies do the first bit, but then dismally neglect the second and third parts of the puzzle.

HR Strategies, Processes and Capabilities

Having established – in a very generic sense, we stress – what employees typically want and need and what the organization usually wants and needs from them, we should next consider how firms satisfy these demands through their strategies, processes and capabilities. The four most common strategic intents relating to employee relationships are probably to:

- Increase workforce flexibility.
- Attract and recruit best people.
- Retain existing key people.
- Reinforce the desired culture.

Culture change is notoriously hard to do and potentially even harder to measure, but it can be done. Employee attitude surveys sometimes get a bad press because they often end up with results so homogenized that they defy interpretation or action. However, when designed to track specific changes in attitude, they can become valuable tools for monitoring success and will provide the insights necessary to manage cultural revitalization effectively. A firm's people policies are inextricably entwined with its culture and how it performs versus its competitors (see the box *Corporate Cultures and High-Performance Organizations*).

Corporate Cultures and High-Performance Organizations

In a follow-up to their pioneering work on corporate cultures, "The New Corporate Cultures", Terence Deal and Allan Kennedy explore the relationship between business cultures and superior financial results. They say that: "Creating a high-performance organization requires building a strong and cohesive culture supportive in every way of efforts required to produce exceptional results." They then propose that companies, which aspire to be high-performers with strong cultures, should ask themselves the following questions about their people policies:

- Can you write down on a sheet of paper in 20 words or less the unique characteristics of people who "belong" in your company's culture? If not, why not?
- How explicit are your recruiting standards? Are they always applied?
- How much senior management time goes into recruiting new members of your culture?
- When you are promoting people, do you apply the same standards you use in recruiting new people? If not, why not?
- How many promotions and rewards doled out in your company reinforce cultural standards?
- How well do your pay policies work in reinforcing a common culture?
- Are your executive compensation plans consistent with what is required to build a shared sense of purpose in the company?
- How often do you move people around in the company? How easy do you find it to make such moves?
- Do you orchestrate career moves to achieve cultural objectives, such as building different parts of the company closer together?
- How often do you challenge your people to really excel? How well do they respond?
- Do you have hands-on involvement in special projects?
- Do people who take on special projects receive appropriate rewards, short and long term?
- Do you keep score? Do your people know you do? How well do they respond?

With regard to processes, there is essentially only a single – but key – business process in play: Manage Human Resources. That is not to say, however, that it is the sole property of a single organizational entity (i.e. the personnel or human resources department). On the contrary, the burden of managing employees must be carried across the whole organization, especially at the management and supervisory levels. While central personnel departments may typically be responsible for establishing the appropriate training curriculum, they are also likely to be accountable for formulating HR-related policies that are important to the firm's success and reputation, and for policing their implementation. But it is the local operations managers that have to 'walk and talk' those policies with the employees that report to them. Without that support, it will almost always become just another well-intentioned initiative that failed to get off the ground. As with all business processes, it will be important to measure both the efficiency and effectiveness of the Manage Human Resources process execution. A good Manage Human Resources process will typically be supported by a wide-ranging set of capabilities, many of which will be highly influential in differentiating the company from its competitors. Some examples of these are illustrated in the diagram shown in Figure 8.2 (p. 264).

Lynda Gratton, associate professor of organizational behaviour at London Business School, argues that it is people, rather than finance or technology, that are the route to sustained competitive advantage.[52] Too many companies say they value their people, yet treat them as interchangeable parts of a machine. It is hardly surprising then if they find themselves relying on mistrustful employees, who are inflexible and resistant to change. 'It may be fashionable to speak about how organizations have changed overnight, of how a poorly performing company was turned around by a charismatic and dynamic chief executive, but the longitudinal research from the Leading Edge Research Consortium [which Prof Gratton founded at LBS in 1992] gives no hint of sudden transformation,' she says. For her, there are three central tenets: people's behaviour is influenced by the past and by their beliefs about what will happen in the future; they strive to understand their role and to interpret the messages, both overt and tacit, given out by the organization; and their emotions play a part in their working life – they can feel committed and inspired (or not) and in turn can choose to give or withhold their knowledge. More often than not, culture change is a long journey.

Given that context then, selecting the right employee measures is vital – but it will seldom be very easy. For years, head hunters and personnel departments have used various 'psychometric' personality tests as part of the recruitment process, allegedly to introduce some science into checking whether candidates are really like they say they are and to gauge whether they have the right psychological traits for the job. Other popular questionnaire-based tests – such as the Belbin Self-Perception Inventory and the Margerison-McCann Personal Profile – assist people to identify their preferred teamworking roles.[53] While these measures may be interesting at the level of the individual, we are more interested here in gaining a better understanding of the perceptional and behavioural dynamics of the whole workforce and of key component groups of employees within the organization.

Fig 8.2 Mapping Employee Relationships through the Performance Prism facets

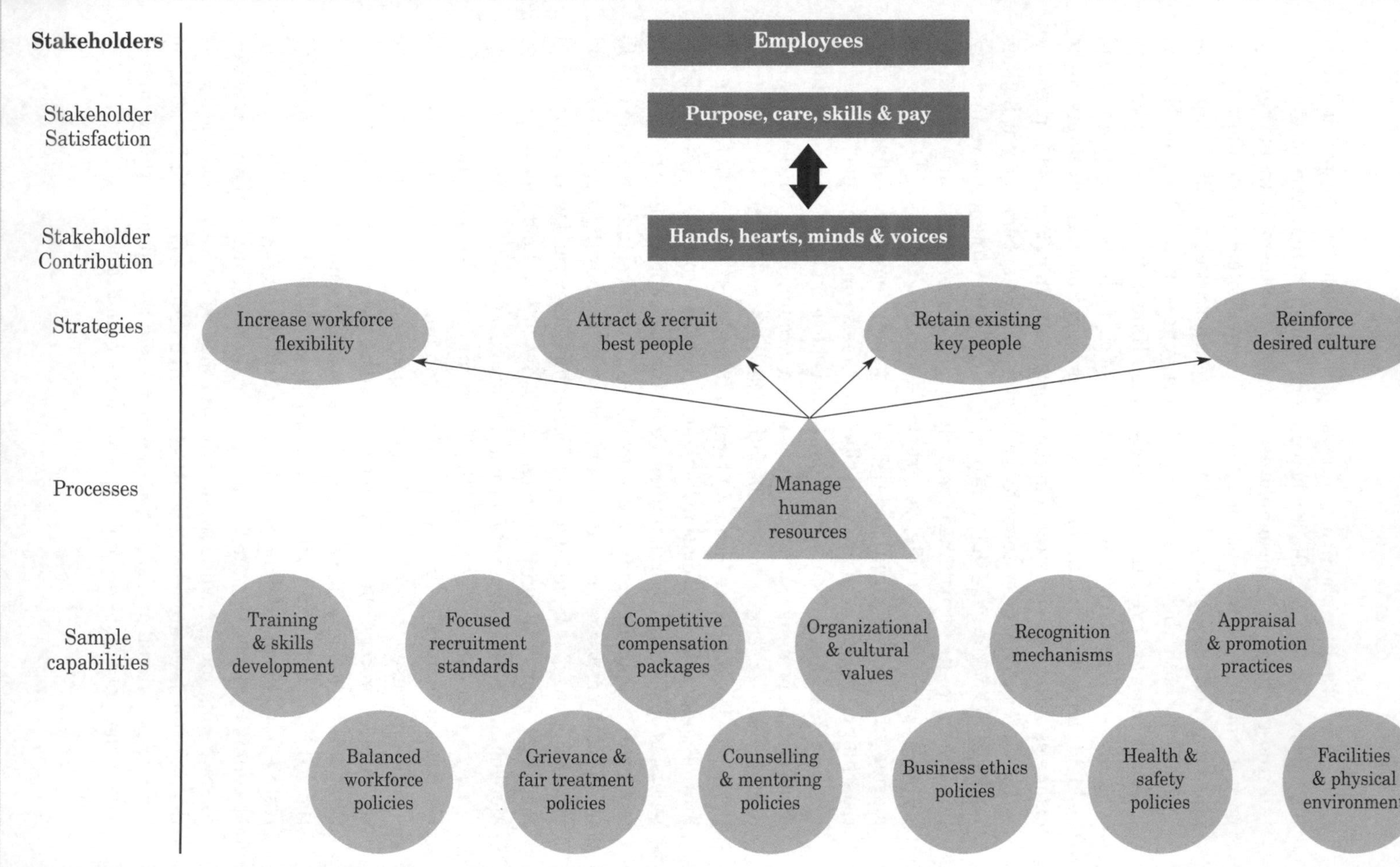

Measures for Employee Relationship Management

Relatively recent research has enabled a better understanding of the role of employee satisfaction to be gained. A study carried out by Harvard Business School's service-management interest group[54] on the series of links contained in what they call the 'Service-Profit Chain' addresses this issue. This service industry research links the level of *internal* service quality (workplace and job design, tools, training, recognition and rewards, etc.) to the levels of employee satisfaction, retention and productivity to *external* service quality. External service quality is the outcome of the internal process, the results experienced by the service organization's customers. This in turn is directly linked in the chain to the levels of customer satisfaction, customer loyalty and, therefore, revenue growth and profitability. To complete the virtuous cycle, the latter then needs to be reinvested in improving internal service quality, and so on. The essence of what they propose is summarized in Figure 8.3 (p. 266).

However, we have already dealt with the downstream links in the chain – those between customer satisfaction and loyalty to company financial performance – in the previous chapter. Here we need to focus on the upstream components and employee factors which drive customer satisfaction.

Employee satisfaction, retention and productivity are each very closely linked. A US example is at Southwest Airlines, which is consistently ranked in the Top 10 of Fortune's 'The 100 Best Companies To Work For'. While it is unionized, Southwest experiences the highest rate of employee retention in the airline industry. Satisfaction levels are so high that at some of its 70 operating locations, employee turnover rates are below 5 per cent a year (although its average is 7 per cent). In 1999/2000, it received 144,500 job applications for its 3,300 vacancies, 1,300 of which were new jobs. Productivity is good too. Around two-thirds of its flights are disembarked and reloaded in less than 15 minutes. Southwest is reported to have roughly 40 per cent more pilot and aircraft utilization than its competitors. It also regularly achieves the highest level of on-time arrivals, the lowest number of complaints, and the fewest lost-baggage claims per 1,000 passengers in performance measures published by the Federal Aviation Administration. Perhaps it helps that 218 active employees have become dollar millionaires?

The authors of the Service-Profit Chain propose an audit format for readers to check where they believe they are in terms of identifying the links in the chain within their own organizations and, therefore, what drives their firm's sustainable profitability. The audit questions they ask in relation to the employee-specific component are highly relevant to managing employee relations with measures and we think worthy of reproduction here as food for thought (see the box *Upstream in the Service-Profit Audit*).

Fig 8.3 The Links in the Service-Profit Chain

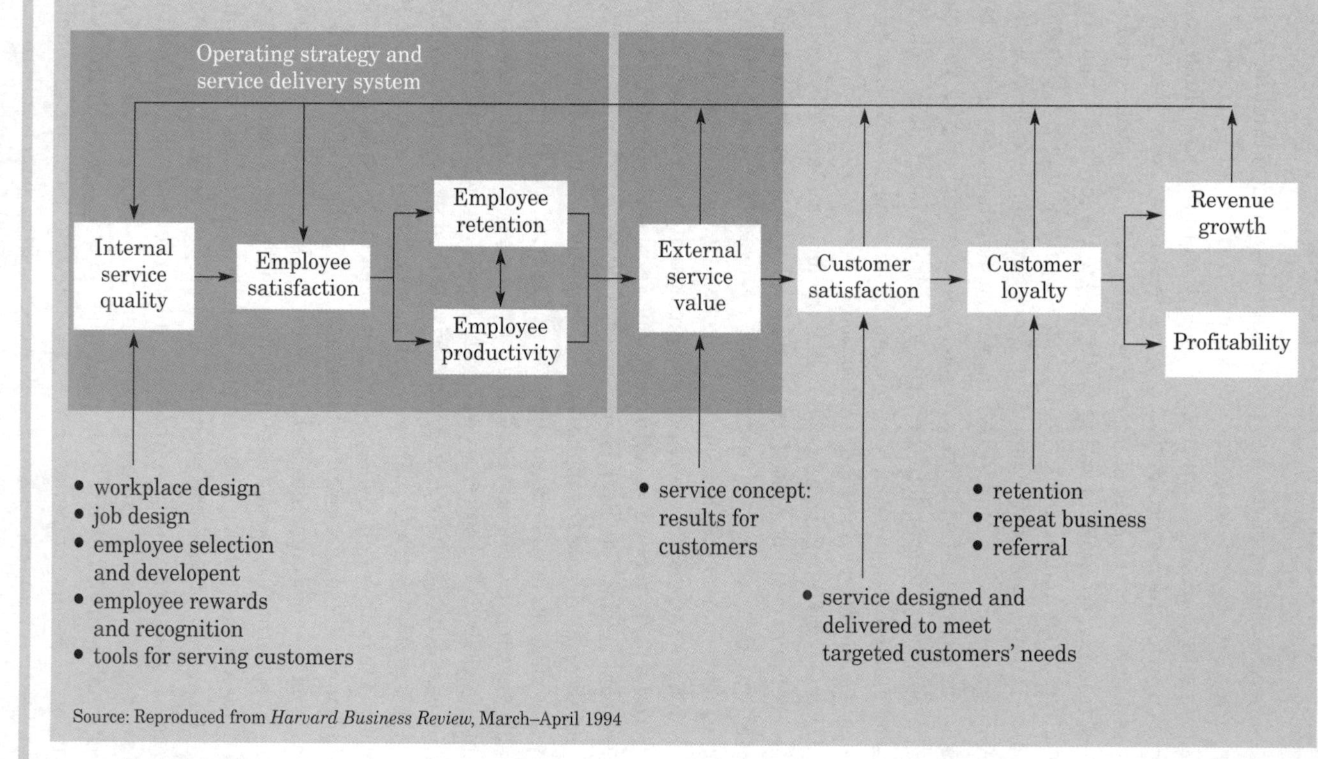

Source: Reproduced from *Harvard Business Review*, March–April 1994

Upstream in the Service-Profit Audit

Internal Service Quality

- Do employees know who their customers are?
- Are employees satisfied with the technological and personal support they receive on the job?

Employee Satisfaction

- Is employee satisfaction measured in ways that can be linked to similar measures of customer satisfaction with sufficient frequency and consistency to establish trends for management use?
- Are employee selection criteria and methods geared to what customers, as well as managers, believe are important?
- To what extent are measures of customer satisfaction, customer loyalty or the quality and quantity of service output used in recognizing and rewarding employees?

Employee Retention

- How do you create employee loyalty?
- Have we made an effort to determine the right level of employee retention?

Employee Productivity

- How do you measure employee productivity?
- To what extent do measures of productivity identify changes in the quality as well as the quantity of service produced per unit of input?

Source: Reproduced from *Harvard Business Review*, March–April 1994

A further study, the results of which were published four years later, addresses the approach taken by Sears, Roebuck, the department store chain and No. 2 retailers in the US, as it tried to sustain its transformation following recovery from a series of poor financial results – it lost a staggering $2.4 billion in 1992. The Sears case is interesting in that it went a stage further than the earlier work by attempting to *quantify* the strength of the linkages.

Sears' executives, then led by Arthur Martinez, created a model of the key links within their organization as having three essential dimensions that were central to its strategy. These were that it must be:

- A compelling place to work.
- A compelling place to shop.
- A compelling place to invest.

The latter, it should be made clear, was evaluated in terms of the company's financial performance – such as return on assets, operating margin and revenue growth – rather than in terms of its share price performance relative to its sector or its distribution of dividends (but, as we have already noted, that is as much to do with the vagaries of stockmarket sentiment as about company performance). Its compellingness as a place to shop was measured in terms of customer retention, customer satisfaction, and whether customers' needs were met. As a place to work, it initially implemented new measures to evaluate personal growth and development plus empowered teams, but these were subsequently modified. In 1995, these measures for its Employee–Customer–Profit model collectively became the Sears Total Performance Indicators (or TPI).

As the executives say in an article subsequently published by the *Harvard Business Review*[55]: 'We wanted to go beyond the usual balanced scorecard, commonly just a set of untested assumptions, and nail down the drivers of future financial performance with statistical rigour. We wanted to assemble the company's vast body of interview and research data – some of it from the task forces, much of it collected routinely over the course of years but never used strategically – then analyze it, draw connections across the data sets, and construct a model to show pathways of actual causation all the way from employee attitude to profits.' To do this they employed a firm of econometric statisticians to carry out the analysis of data from its 800+ stores, applying a technique called causal pathway modelling (which was perceived as more appropriate than regression analysis as the latter examines data and makes correlations without establishing causation).

One of the 'discoveries' from this analysis was that an employee's ability to see the connection between his or her work and the company's strategic objectives was a driver of positive behaviour. They also found that two dimensions of employee satisfaction – attitude towards the job and towards the company – had a greater effect on employee loyalty and behaviour towards customers than all the other dimensions put together. They discovered too that responses to ten particular questions of their 70-question employee survey had a higher impact on employee behaviour (and, therefore, on customer satisfaction) than the measures that they initially devised for being a compelling place to work. So, in the revised version of the Employee-Customer-Profit model, for which see Figure 8.4, the following ten questions about the job (6) and the company (4) were substituted:

Fig 8.4 Sears, Roebuck's Employee–Customer–Profit Chain

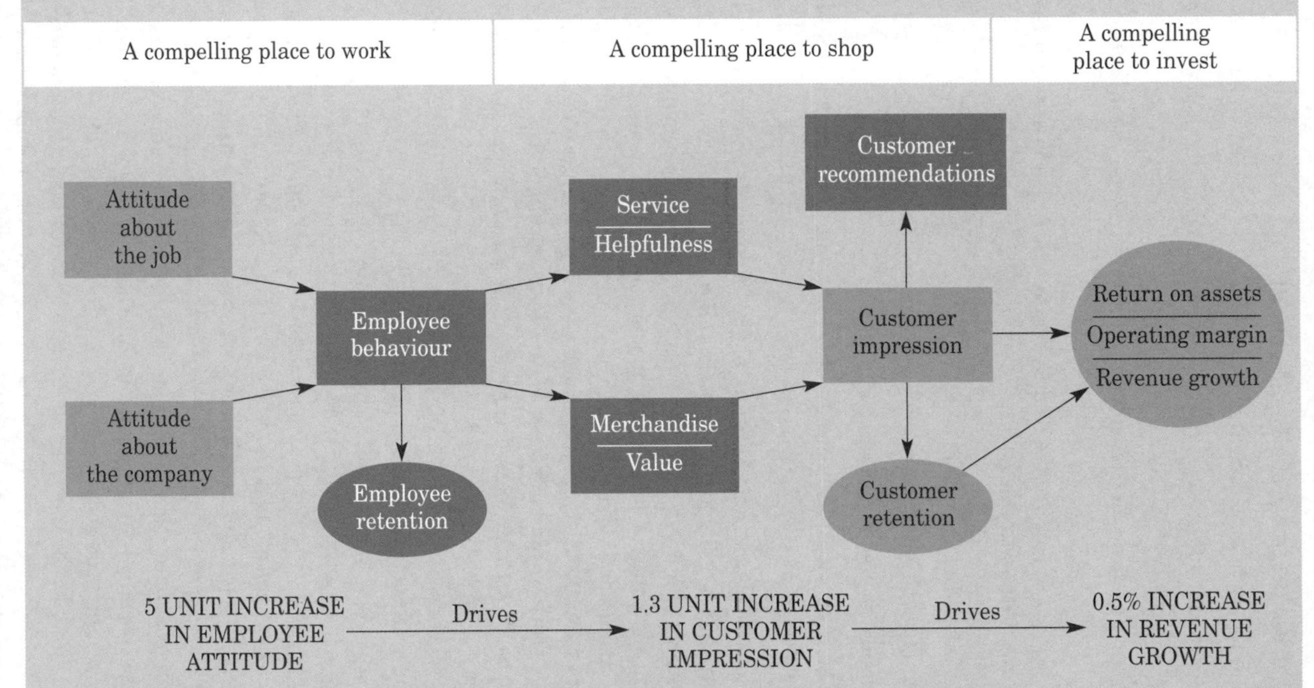

Rectangles represent survey information, the ovals hard data. The measures marked in dark lettering are those collected and distributed in the form of 'Sears Total Performance Indicators'.

Source: Reproduced and adapted from *Harvard Business Review*, January–February 1998.

- I like the kind of work I do.
- My work gives me a sense of accomplishment.
- I am proud to say I work at Sears.
- How does the amount of work you are expected to do influence your *overall attitude* to your job?
- How do your physical working conditions influence your *overall attitude* to your job?
- How does the way you are treated by those who supervise you influence your *overall attitude* to your job?

- I feel good about the future of the company.
- Sears is making the changes necessary to compete effectively.
- I understand our business strategy.
- Do you see a connection between the work you do and the company's strategic objectives?

The executives also claim that: 'Our model shows that a 5-point improvement in employee attitudes will drive a 1.3 point improvement in customer satisfaction, which in turn will drive a 0.5 per cent improvement in revenue growth. If we knew nothing about a local store except that employee attitudes had improved by 5 points on our survey scale, we could predict with confidence that if revenue growth in the district as a whole were 5 per cent, revenue growth at this particular store would be 5.5 per cent. These numbers are as rigorous as any others we work with at Sears. Every year, our accounting firm audits them as closely as it audits our financials.'

Has Sears prospered as a result of this initiative? Initially it did, but some would point to its subsequent financial performance. In the third quarter of 1999, it was forced to issue a profits warning: its earnings failed to meet analysts' forecasts and even its previous year's performance for the same period. Consequently, and not surprisingly, its share price plummeted. Same-store sales were growing at a rate of just 0.1 per cent against industry norms of 5–6 per cent. While sales of 'hardware', such as tools, paints and kitchenware were growing strongly; apparel (a significant proportion of revenues) was bursting at the seams. Sears' core customers were migrating to other retailers like Target, Kohl's and even Wal-Mart. Competition is especially tough in retailing. Anecdotal evidence suggests that the quality of its clothing goods was perceived as inferior by a significant number of customers. Presumably, therefore, it cannot have been taking enough notice – and actions on – the feedback it was receiving from its 'customer impressions' data. Making the wrong decisions on merchandising policies may have wasted all the effort it put into linking employee feedback to customer perceptions. Sears now has a new CEO to steer that decision-making process.

While this is a salutary lesson (that essential data is only as good as the people who use it), other studies conclude that Sears was on the right track with its employee measures. An investigation conducted at a leading UK retail business by the Institute for Employment Studies presents further objective evidence[56]. Based on data from 65,000 staff and 25,000 customers in almost 100 of the company's stores, the study conducted a robust statistical survey of employee commitment and customer satisfaction in order to establish a direct and strong link to sales increases at store level. The resulting model was able to predict which aspects of employee and customer satisfaction need to be improved to increase sales. The researchers claim that for this retailer a one-point increase in employee commitment led to a monthly increase of £200,000 per store. They say: 'Human resources management in the retail sector has a significant part to play in making the service-profit chain work. Keys to success include a positive organization culture, good quality line management, committed employees and low rates of sickness ... However, most UK retail sector businesses do not collect or analyze the necessary data. Few collect adequate information on employee satisfaction and commitment ... Products, prices and loyalty bonuses are easy to copy; companies should take employee satisfaction measurement more seriously. Relying on financial information alone to monitor business performance is like driving a car while looking in the rear view mirror. Employee satisfaction measures help predict hazards ahead.' Again the evidence seems to be clear – good people management policies and practices result in tangible business benefits when appropriately applied.

Just to stress that this is not a retailing phenomenon, research carried out by Mark Huselid of Rutgers, the state university of New Jersey, found that an analysis of 968 American firms with more than 100 workers led him to conclude that the appropriate use of specified people management practices was associated with increased profits of nearly $4,000 per worker per year. While Jeffrey Pfeffer, author of *The Human Equation*, identifies seven practices that 'seem to characterize most, if not all, the systems producing profits through people.' These practices are:

- Emphasizing employment security.
- Investing heavily in recruiting the right people.
- Making extensive use of self-managed teams and decentralization.
- Paying high wages, linked to the organization's performance.
- Spending generously on training.
- Reducing status differentials.
- Sharing information.

But here, perhaps not surprisingly, not all the academics are in agreement about what the components of human resource management are, which of them are most effective, and whether effectiveness should be measured by component or by the whole integrated system. Some also hold doubts about the validity of the methodologies used to prove the links between HRM practices and profitability – for example, aren't more profitable companies inherently more likely to experiment with fashionable management practices and have the resources available to implement them? So, do the practices drive the profits, or the profits the practices?

Whereas Pfeffer has identified seven key components, other authors identify almost any number between six and eighteen HR policies and practices that may be instrumental in determining business performance. Some, like Dave Ulrich and Dale Lake (authors of *Organizational Capability – Competing from the Inside Out*, 1990), argue the case for the inclusion of effective appraisal systems and also some of the broader impacts of organization design – the process by which responsibility is allocated, roles are defined, control and accountability are established, and decision-making authority is delegated – beyond that inferred by self-managed teams and decentralization. They draw attention too to the role of shared mindsets within organizations and how this is influenced by what they call generating competencies (employee selection and development), reinforcing competencies (appraisal and rewards), and sustaining competencies (organization design and communication). On the other hand, David Guest of Birkbeck College, University of London, points to the importance of gaining an understanding of how HR practices impact on employee attitudes and behaviour.[57] He advocates the inclusion of these factors into further research in order to improve the research methodologies used that link HRM with performance. He says: 'We should begin to build in measures of employee commitment, employee quality and employee flexibility to improve our ability to explain the [HRM – Performance] link and consequently focus policy and practice more effectively.'

However, doing yet more research to gain a better understanding of the influence of individual components of HRM approaches (or High Performance Work Systems, as they are sometimes called) might be a misplaced effort. In the US, Brian Becker and Mark Huselid have researched the impacts of 'complete HR systems' and have identified what they call *Powerful Connections* and *Deadly Combinations*. Powerful Connections reflect the presence of complementary or synergistic effects by implementing complete HRM systems rather than isolated policies and practices. They say: 'In empirical work in over 1500 companies we have found that combining above-market pay policies with comprehensive performance management systems has a 50 per cent larger effect on firm performance than the effects of the two policies considered in isolation. This finding reflects the synergistic gains of a better applicant pool, more talented hires, and an HRM system that is able to recognize and reward these more talented employees for their superior performance.' Deadly Combinations can arise though when firms adopt HRM policies that seem to make sense in isolation but when considered within the context of their other HRM practices are a recipe for disaster. They cite examples such as firms that invest in sophisticated performance management systems only to adopt compensation policies that provide little meaningful distinction between the pay of high- and low-performing employees; or firms that encourage employees to work together in teams, but then provide pay rises based on individual contributions[58].

In their book, *The HR Scorecard – Linking People, Strategy, and Performance*, Becker, Huselid and Ulrich offer some examples of High Performance Work System measures. They suggest that these should include:

- How many *exceptional* candidates do we recruit for each *strategic* job opening?
- What proportion of all new hires have been selected based primarily on *validated* selection methods?
- To what extent has your firm adopted a professionally developed and validated competency model as the basis for hiring, developing, managing and rewarding employees?
- How many hours of training does a new employee receive each year?
- What percentage of the workforce is regularly assessed via a formal performance appraisal?
- What proportion of the workforce receives formal feedback on job performance from multiple sources?
- What proportion of merit pay is determined by a formal performance appraisal?
- If the market rate for total compensation would be the fiftieth percentile, what is your firm's current percentile ranking on total compensation?
- What percentage of your exempt and non-exempt employees is eligible for annual cash or deferred incentive plans, or profit sharing?
- What percentage of the total compensation of your exempt and non-exempt employees is represented by variable pay?
- What is the likely *differential* in merit pay awards between high-performing and low-performing employees?

A recent transatlantic research study adopted a 'people-factor' framework to gather data about the relative impacts of organizations' HRM policies. This scorecard aims to mix traditional HR criteria with more progressive, so-called 'intrapreneurship', factors (see the box *The People Factor*).

The People Factor

A study by the US Department of Commerce and Boston Consulting Group analyzed companies in the US and Germany using a 'people factor scorecard', which contained a combination of traditional HR and 'intrapreneurship' factors:

People factor scorecard	
HUMAN RESOURCE CRITERIA	INTRAPRENEURSHIP CRITERIA
Staff training and education ☐ • Spending/days per employee • Career-long training opportunities • Employee-driven curricula **Loyality of the employee** ☐ • Lay-offs compared with industry • Outplacement efforts • Worker-friendly work reductions **Corporate recognition of employees** ☐ • Breadth, frequency and consistency **Quality of HR policies** ☐ • Recruiting incentives • Benefits • Detailed performance evaluation and feedback • Promotion within/career development **Job satisfaction indicators** ☐ • Employee sick days taken • Employee turnover	**Flexibility of work structure** ☐ • Flexibility in structuring work content • Flexible hours/scheduling **Organizational structure** ☐ • Fewer levels of hierarchy • Prevalence of team structures • Decentralized decision making **Versatility of employee** ☐ • Lateral transfers within company • Cross-functional exposure and training **Entrepreneurial opportunities** ☐ • Recognition of innovation and contribution (awards, bonuses, etc.) • Profit-sharing opportunities at business, team unit or product level • Linkage of compensation to individual performance
HUMAN RESOURCE SCORE ☐	INTRAPRENEURSHIP SCORE ☐

The survey produced two main findings. First, investing in people-factor criteria strongly increased job satisfaction and employee loyalty. Overall, 34 per cent of US workers and 35 per cent of German workers described themselves as satisfied with their jobs. But among workers within companies that offered greater people-factor benefits, job satisfaction was much higher – 58 per cent and 63 per cent respectively.

The factors that increased job satisfaction most were: allowing people to influence decisions that affect their work life; training; and performance-linked pay. Similar factors increased employee loyalty. The happiest and most loyal respondents were those who enjoyed both traditional HR benefits (especially training) and intrapreneurship.

The second finding was that there is a huge gap between what companies thought they provided and what workers perceived that they received. Most companies claimed to offer training, performance evaluation and employee involvement in decision making. Yet only one-third of employees said they enjoyed such benefits. Furthermore, the largest gap was in those attributes that employees believed were most important.

Those companies that scored highest had a better total shareholder return than lower-scoring companies too. However, the people-factor benefits take time to emerge – only over four years and longer does a pattern of competitive advantage become clear.

Source: Adapted from *The People Factor* by Linda Bilmes (FT Prentice Hall, 2002).

On the other hand, Jac Fitz-enz – founder of the Saratoga Institute in California, which provides benchmark data on employee productivity, retention and effective HR practices in twenty countries – advocates the application of a simple 'human capital scorecard'[59]. This consists of four quadrants, each devoted to the measurement of one of the basic human capital management activities: acquiring, maintaining, developing and retaining employees. He also offers a sample of its application with example metrics in Figure 8.5.

There are dangers nevertheless in prescribing a fixed set of best practices that can be fairly easily benchmarked and copied – without distinctiveness they will soon fail to provide any competitive advantage. Becker and Huselid argue, rightly in our view, that 'HRM systems only have a systematic impact on the bottom line when they are embedded in the management infrastructure and help the firm achieve important business priorities such as shortening product development cycle times, increasing customer service, lowering turnover among high-quality employees, etc. The particular form of these problems, and more importantly the appropriate design and alignment of the HRM system with business priorities, is highly firm-specific.' And this is one of the reasons why we have included a 'people' component within the Capabilities facet of the Performance Prism framework so that a broader context of HR management can and should be included within each stakeholder dimension of business performance measurement and management.

Fig 8.5 Human Capital Scorecard

Acquisition	Maintenance
• Cost per hire • Time to fill jobs • Number of new hires • Number of replacements • Quality of new hires	• Total labour cost as percentage of operating expense (including contingent labour cost) • Average pay per employee • Benefits cost as percentage of payroll • Average performance score compared with revenue per FTE
Retention	**Development**
• Total separation rate • Percentage of voluntary separations: exempt and non-exempt employees • Exempt separations by service length • Percentage of exempt separations among top-level performers • Cost of turnover	• Training cost as percentage of payroll • Total training hours provided • Average number of hours of training per employee • Training hours by function • Training hours by job group • Training ROI

Job Satisfaction	Employee Morale

The implication for performance measurement systems then is that there are no 'cookbook recipes' here either, but it will be important that the HR-related measures selected are not only linked but also *aligned* both to each other and to measures of the specific business issues the firm wishes to resolve or improve. All the research evidence points to the fact that, while there are tangible links between company success and the attitudes of its employees to their work and their employer, it is the detailed practices which firms adopt that need to be both holistic in satisfying employees' wants and specific in addressing the organization's needs. The measures to implement then must be those that address both sets of requirements (for examples, see Figure 8.6).

The Employee Relationship Measures Design Process

Before we develop this section further, we should probably issue a 'health warning' right from the start. Many things *can* be measured about an organization's relationship with its employees, but the trick is to identify the essential things that *must* be measured. Using the success mapping technique

Fig 8.6 Sample Measures for Managing Employee Relationships

Typical measurement issues for satisfying employee and organization wants and needs:

in conjunction with a measures catalogue can help to pick the most appropriate ones. The danger with the catalogue approach though is that there is a tendency for users to try to short-cut the process of really understanding the key employee relationship issues. Creating a 'pick-and-mix' selection of employee stakeholder measures from a catalogue can appear to provide a necessary and sufficient set, perhaps even a comprehensive one, but such an approach is unlikely to be focused on the organization's particular business issues and priorities. Success mapping, or some similar process, is therefore essential to focusing the selection process *in tandem with* the application of a measures catalogue or checklist.

The success mapping process for employee relations means addressing the following critical questions:

- Who are our key employee groups and what do they each want and need?
- And what does our organization want and need from those employees?
- What are our strategies for satisfying these sets of wants and needs?
- How will our internal business processes effectively and efficiently deliver them?
- Which particular capabilities do we need to build, maintain and improve in order to execute them?

Applying the Performance Prism in this way – as per the schematic shown in Figure 8.7 – helps us to select the right employee-related performance measures.

Fig 8.7 Performance Prism Unfolded Schematic: Employees

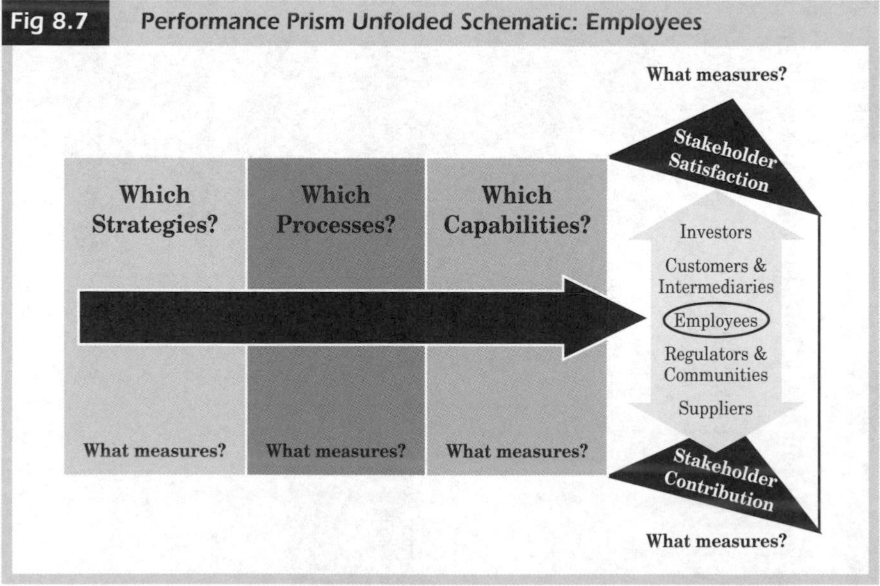

The first decision is to determine whether employee wants and needs are sufficiently homogeneous to count them as a single body of people, or whether there are enough differences between different groups – for example, between different levels of seniority, different nationalities, different business units or between different functional specialisms – for segmentation to be necessary. Where a segmentation route is required, then the separate wants and needs of each group should be captured. A template similar to the one we applied in Chapter 7 for different customer categories can be used to capture the differences (see Figure 8.8).

Fig 8.8 Employee Segmentation Analysis

Employee satisfaction	All employees (high priority SWANs)	Employee Group 1 only	Employee Group 2 only	Employee Group 3 only
Purpose Care Skills Pay				
Employee contribution	**All employees** (high priority OWANs)	**Employee Group 1 only**	**Employee Group 2 only**	**Employee Group 3 only**
Heads Hearts Minds Voices				

SWANs = Stakeholder Wants & Needs.
OWANs = Organization Wants & Needs.

Because of the additional complexity it introduces, we would not especially advocate the use of segmentation unless it is really essential. However, some interesting paradoxes can be exposed in this way. For example, senior executives may be substantially rewarded through stock options in their company's shares and, therefore, their primary want and need is likely to be to execute strategies that enhance short-term share price growth so that they can exercise their options at an optimum level. Salaried employees, on the other hand, may be more concerned with the longer-term success of the company so that the purpose of their employment (e.g. product development, customer service, production, etc.) is maintained, job security is improved and the prosperity of the firm is enhanced in a more sustainable way. By answering the critical questions and drawing links between the cause-and-effect elements, the perceived problems are more fully defined and the actions needed to resolve them highlighted.

For instance, in employee contribution, this process is quite likely to identify that there are shortages of particular kinds of skill-sets that the firm wants and needs to accumulate. If the organization has not already done so, this technique can help to articulate the strategies, processes and capabilities it needs to build and the initiatives in which it needs to invest its capital in order to ensure that the right resources do become available. The 'success mapping' technique helps to identify the relevant issues; (see Figure 8.9, p. 282).

Another typical consideration would be, for example, in an M&A situation where – as we have noted earlier – the preservation of executive and employee morale among retained employees is imperative to achieving the benefits of the deal in the post-merger integration (PMI) phase. Here effective communications between management and staff will be critical to achieving that objective. So, a 'success map' that flushes out the key performance measurement and management issues for this application might look something similar to that shown in Figure 8.10 (p. 283).

The success mapping technique is highly flexible to different circumstances, in this case in relation to satisfying the essential wants and needs of employees and the organization's wants and needs of its employees. It allows the key business issues to be identified and the strategies, processes and capabilities that the organization either has now or, more importantly, needs to create or enhance in the future. The relevant performance measures can then be identified and implemented. For an actual example of its application (see the box *Aligning the Human Element of Cable Services*).

Aligning the Human Element of Cable Services

The previous chapter described the predominantly process-focused approach taken by Telewest Communications, the second largest UK cable operator, towards designing its customer relationship measures and applying the principles of the Performance Prism framework. This is a business characterized by high levels of customer interactions through several key operational functions, including marketing, sales, field operations, contact centres and credit services. It has high levels of customer churn which it is trying to address through its Measuring for Customer Loyalty programme. It also experiences high levels of employee attrition – a not uncommon problem in this industry, but a significant burden none the less.

When Telewest came – subsequent to its customer relationship measures selection effort – to design its employee measurement system, a very similar approach was taken. It again applied the Performance Prism as a framework to assist the process. Telewest first recognized that it needed a combination of both employee satisfaction and employee contribution measures. Satisfaction measures were clearly needed in order to address the causes of the relatively high levels of employee attrition and to check the effectiveness of improvement initiatives implemented in this area; contribution measures would be needed in order to check employee alignment with its newly-introduced brand values and its relative productivity levels versus similar operations both internally and externally. It also planned to implement bonus payments based on an employee competence development accreditation scheme.

Telewest had already identified the five primary components of its HR strategy – the '5Rs'. These refer to Recruitment, Retention, Remuneration, Relationships and Renewal. What was needed was to identify the essential measures that would relate to its strategic intents from both an employee satisfaction and an employee contribution point of view. It was agreed that a sequence of measures which tracked the Employee Experience Lifecycle processes from recruitment to leaving – in a very similar way to the Customer Experience lifecycle described earlier – would fit the bill. Ulf Larsson, Telewest's HR Head, had tracked the development of the customer loyalty measures and liked the idea. The employee relationship measures design process began and the consequence was a model that is shown in Figure 8.11 (p. 284).

Although Telewest had already recently introduced an annual MORI survey of employee opinions and attitudes, it was clear that an implementation programme of employee relationship measures enhancement was required. While not all measures could be practically implemented immediately, a relevant measures hierarchy was drawn up in order that a deployment plan could be prioritized and agreed – including increasing survey frequency.

Source: Telewest Communications and Accenture.

Frequency of measurement can be a critical issue, particularly for getting feedback from employees through satisfaction surveys. Many (mostly large) companies conduct annual employee perception surveys, which can provide useful data and – after a while – trends, but are hardly frequent enough to gauge the movement in employee attitudes in turbulent times. They also tend to ask far too many questions. Response rates, unsurprisingly, can be poor too. We subscribe to the 'focused, frequent and few' school of thought to getting feedback from employees (and customers too). This means developing focused questionnaires that are issued frequently – or conducted via short telephone interviews, for example – not to everyone in the organization, but to a cross-section of a relatively few, but enough for statistical robustness purposes, of its members. Different questions can be asked of different members of the same department. For the following month's or quarter's questionnaire, ask them another question; that way they won't get bored constantly answering the same question repeatedly. Keeping it short helps to improve response rates too.

Fig 8.9 Employee Success Map – Example

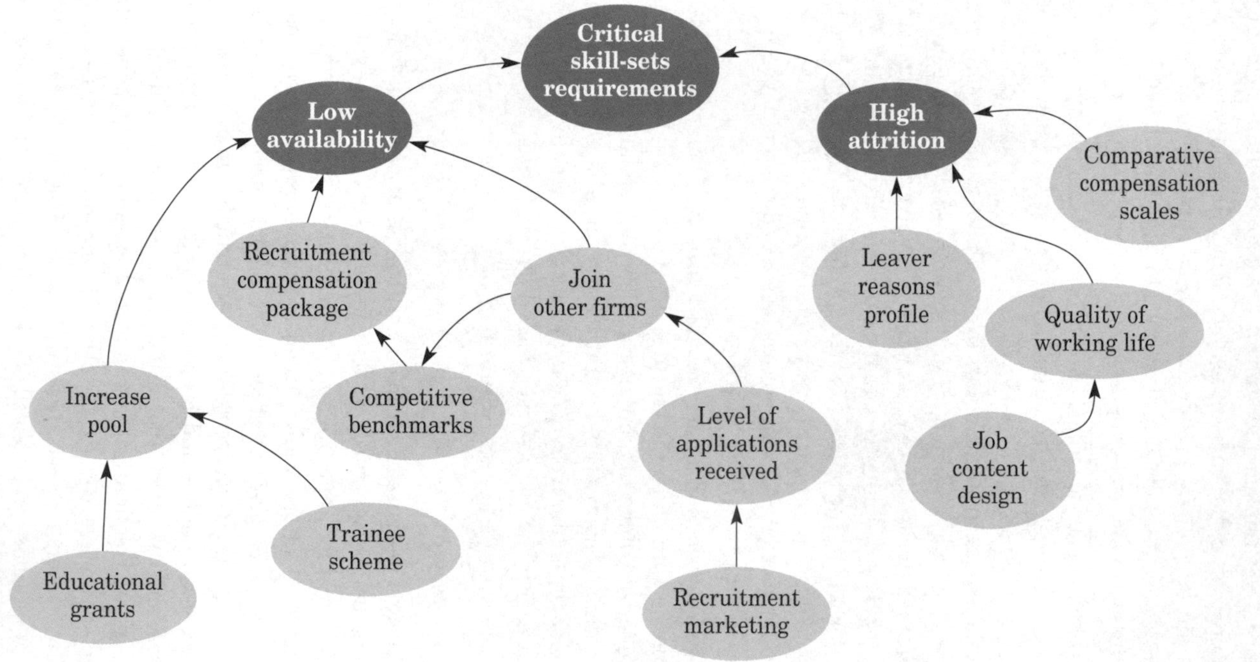

Critical skill-sets requirements
Low availability
High attrition
Comparative compensation scales
Recruitment compensation package
Join other firms
Leaver reasons profile
Quality of working life
Increase pool
Competitive benchmarks
Level of applications received
Job content design
Trainee scheme
Educational grants
Recruitment marketing

Fig 8.10 Employee Success Map – PMI Example

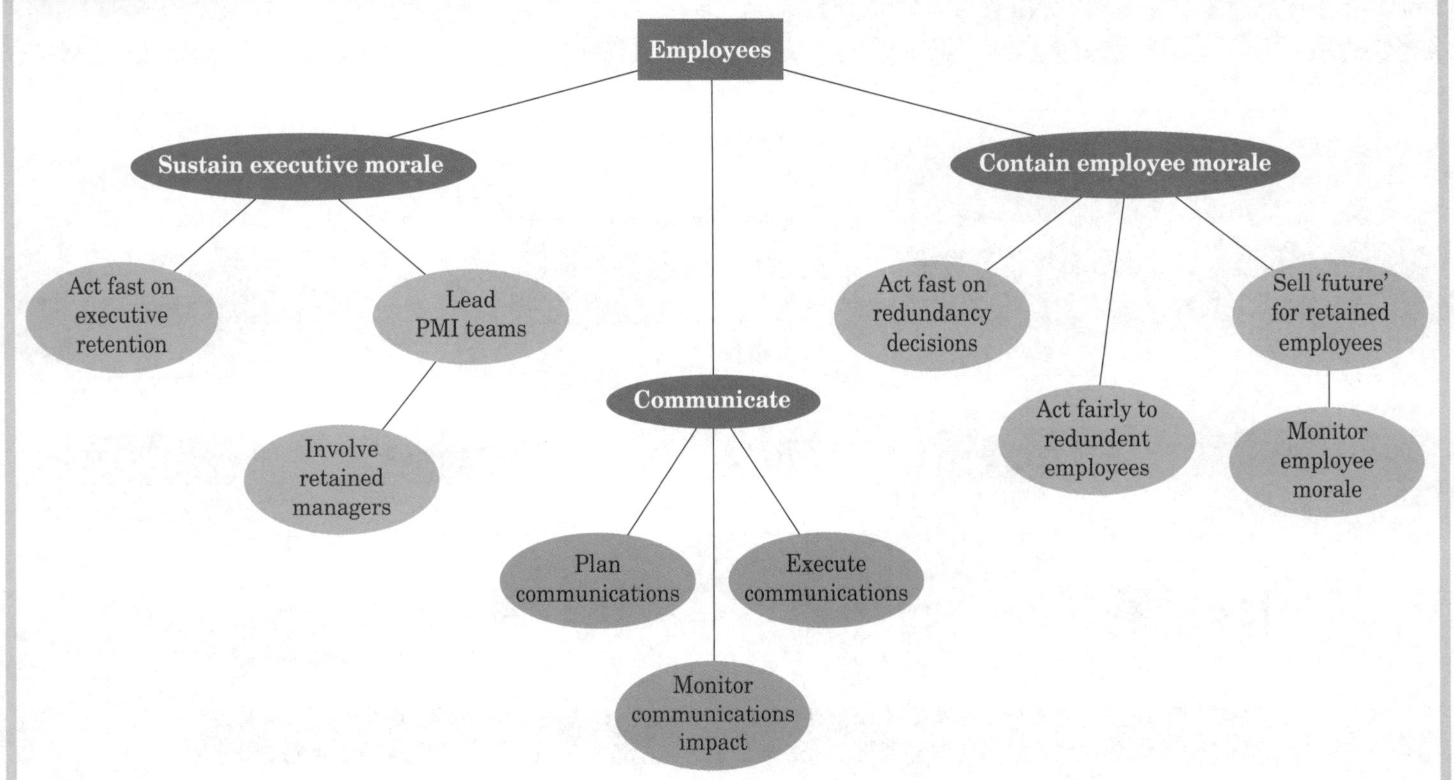

Employees

Sustain executive morale

Act fast on executive retention

Lead PMI teams

Involve retained managers

Communicate

Plan communications

Execute communications

Monitor communications impact

Contain employee morale

Act fast on redundancy decisions

Act fairly to redundent employees

Sell 'future' for retained employees

Monitor employee morale

Fig 8.11 Employee Relationship Measures – Telewest

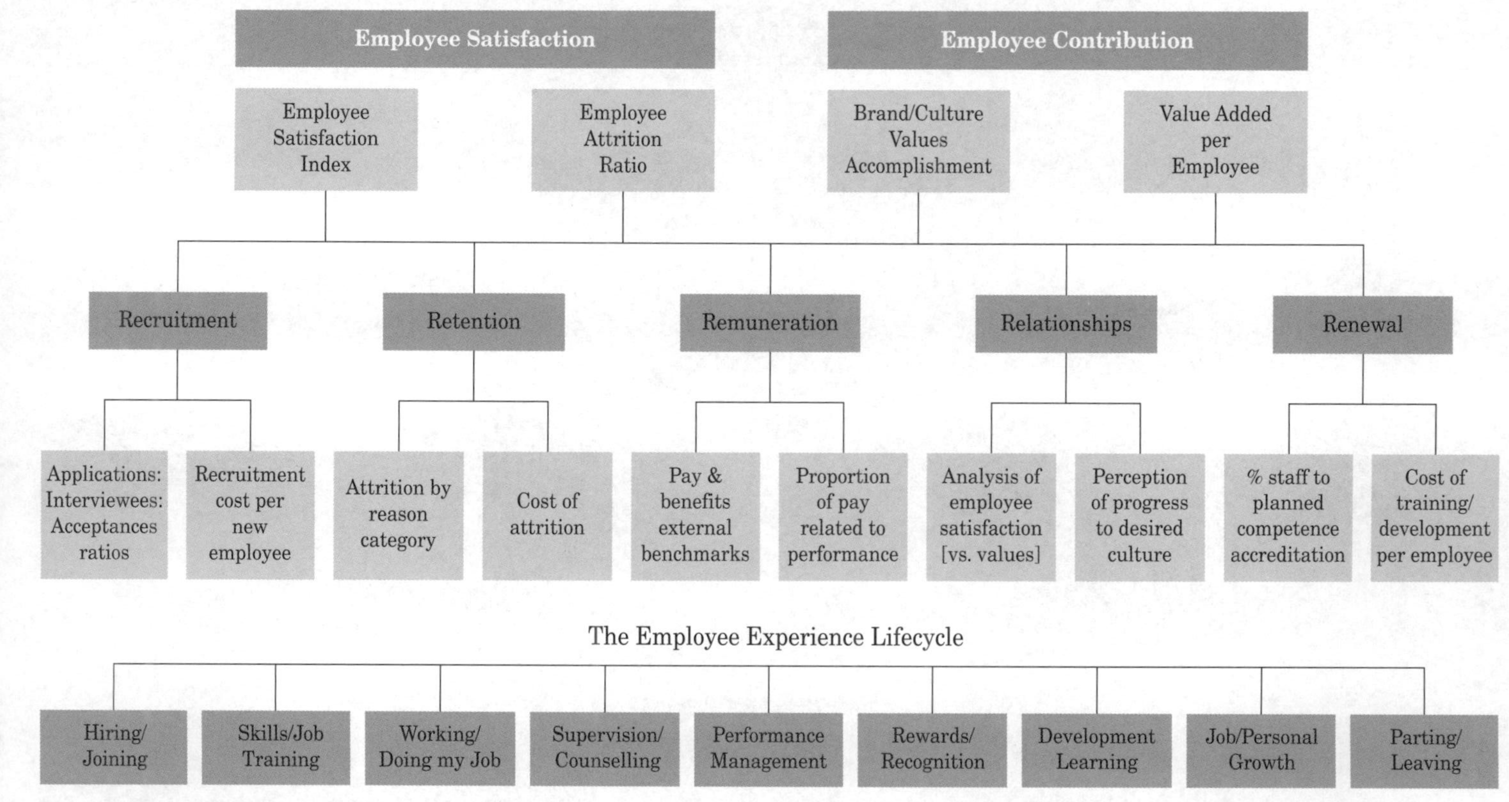

Source: Telewest Communications and Accenture

Senior managers used to a regular financial measurement regime and facing the addition of a barrage of non-financial measures, for which they must now also be accountable, often ask us how many measures their organization should have in any particular category. And perhaps nowhere is this more prevalent than in the employee one. The answer, of course, is however many it takes to manage employee relations both effectively and efficiently so that the desired outcomes are achieved. This is not necessarily the answer they are looking for though: it still seems like it might be a lot. However, the fact is that senior executives do not need to own every single measure the organization uses. Lower orders of management (or supervision) can be made responsible for the ownership of particular employee-related measures – provided that they are in a position to influence the performance factors that determine them – on condition that they 'red-flag' to executives performance levels that show a negative trend or consistently fall outside the control limits set. For example, the board's members, or even a single member of the board, might keep watch over an overall employee satisfaction index. Operational and/or Human Resources managers might be responsible for owning the specific component elements (which, incidentally, might also be weighted for importance) of the index.

There are cost implications too. Few companies stop to consider or evaluate the cost of measurement. However, clearly (unless there is some regulatory requirement to capture the metric), the sum of the tangible and intangible benefits of measuring aspects of the organization's relationship with its employees needs to outweigh the costs of collecting, collating, analyzing and reporting the data. It is possible to create a sizeable bureaucracy in this area and, obviously, this must not be allowed to happen. However, as is usually the case, targeted investment can pay significant dividends.

On its own, no framework can resolve the measures selection problem. However, if it helps to ask the right questions and to verify the outputs, then the framework does add significant value to the selection process. It does so by channelling executive thinking in the right directions – in this case, around the employee relationship issues – to allow capture of the critical success factors and the relevant measures to deploy.

The Employee Relationship Measures 'Failure Mode' Test

At the end of the above process we should think that all the important measures for managing and achieving employee satisfaction and contribution have been captured. But have we really done so? What are the risks that we might have overlooked? This needs to be tested.

Let's say that key employee retention has been identified as one of the critical success factors for achieving the corporation's aims. In order to conduct an 'acid test' as to whether we have captured all the relevant measures we need in order to manage employee retention effectively, we should address the failure mode: key employee departures. Our strategy then would be to retain them and the business process that will provide it is still to manage human resources. Which of our internal capabilities will make a difference to increasing retention rates? The most likely suspects are perhaps: the firm's recognition and reward policies; the ability to obtain promotion; the perceived biases in dealing with diversity in gender and race; and its internal culture as promulgated by the incumbent executive management team. So, the 'failure mode test' might be illustrated in Figure 8.12.

Fig 8.12 Employee Retention Failure Mode Map – Example

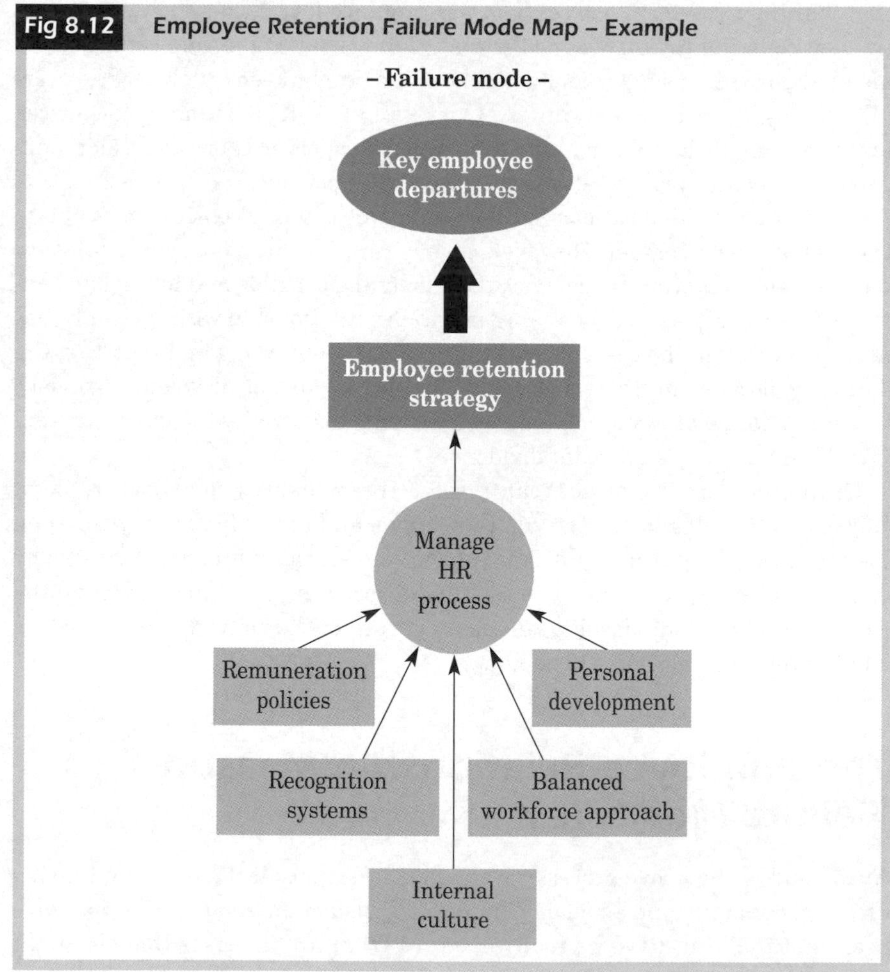

These suppositions may or may not be correct – and, if possible, they should be tested (for example, through leaver interviews) – but, if they are perceived by the management team to be significant factors in determining the desired outcome, then appropriate measures should be installed to capture them *if they have not already been identified and selected*. Clearly, other critical failure modes might be identified – such as the inducement of dysfunctional behaviours through obsolete recognition and reward systems, for example – but this is illustrative of the kind of rigorous and iterative process that needs to be conducted in order to ensure that the right employee-related measures are put in place and are actively managed.

Employee relationship measures selection is not a process that should be conducted lightly, nor should it be conducted *in camera* within HR and Personnel departments. Inputs from operational managers and senior executives will be imperative to achieving a balanced and validated outcome that everyone – or at least the vast majority of employees – buys into. Without that support, it is almost certain to fall into disrepute despite the best of intentions.

Having decided what needs to be measured, the spotlight must now be turned to how to measure it and how to manage with it. As previously, we advocate the use of a Performance Measure Record Sheet to collect the essential information about each measure (as described in more detail in Chapter 3), such as frequency, formula, data source and measure owner. An example of an employee relationship measure – from the contribution side – would be the level of employee performance improvement suggestions. So, a completed record sheet might look something like that shown in Figure 8.13 (p. 288).

Most of the employees that get out of bed every morning to help to create shareholder value and to satisfy the wants and needs of their employer's customers, don't do it just for the fun of it. They do it for themselves and their loved ones. But they are more likely to do it diligently and with good grace if they enjoy what they are doing; if they have the information, training and support they need to do their job; if their efforts and contributions are appreciated; if they have decent facilities to work in; if they are treated without prejudice; if they are gaining skills that will be useful to them whatever the future holds for their employer; and if they get relatively well paid for it. Simple!

Fig 8.13 Example of Employee-related Performance Measure Record Sheet

Measure	Employee performance improvement suggestions
Purpose	To measure the level of operating performance improvement suggestions made by employees using the "suggestion line" telephone service
Relates to	Operating cost reduction goals for FY XXXX/XX
Target	> 100 suggestions per month
Formula	Number of calls logged per month by "suggestion line" service
Frequency	Weekly report
Who measures	Outsourced provider of "suggestion line" service
Source of data	Calls logged by service provider
Who acts on the data (owner)	Executive team (led by operations director)
What do they do	Responds to all employees who leave their name within ten working days Creates action teams and plans based on selected improvement suggestions (weekly meeting)
Notes /comments	Level of improvement suggestions implemented also measured

Illustrative Employee-centred Measures

This checklist is not intended to be comprehensive, just indicative. There will inevitably be some variability between industries and also the relative maturity of companies (and their subsidiaries). The category within which each measure is represented may vary too. Some of the measures that firms typically adopt are:

Employee Satisfaction Measures

What do our employees want and need?

- Employee satisfaction level (perception survey)
  - Job satisfaction rating
  - Working life rating
  - Working environment rating
  - Immediate boss rating
  - Policy implementation rating
  - Training provided rating
  - Remuneration package rating
- Employee turnover/attrition trend
- Leaver reasons profile (exit interviews)
- Level of employee grievances (by category)
- Relevance/Quality of each training course

Employee Contribution Measures

What do we want and need from our employees?

- Sales/Value-added per employee
- Output per employee (i.e. productivity)
- Average length of service
- Absenteeism rate
- Feedback in relation to sufficiency and necessity of training programmes offered / required
- Employee performance improvement suggestions contributed / implemented
- Willingness of employees to develop additional skills
- Willingness of employees to recommend firm as an employer

Employee-related Strategy Measures

What are our strategies for satisfying these sets of wants and needs?

- Headcount vs. plan [+ level of permanent vs. temporary workers]
- Recruitment vs. plan
- Skills inventory vs. plan
- Manager:Worker ratio
- Senior employee attrition rate (unplanned)
- Level of variable pay / incentives awarded
- Actual employee and employee-related costs vs. plan
- Employee redundancy and redundancy-related costs vs. plan [where applicable]
- Gender/Race equality policy achievement vs. declared goals

Employee-related Process Measures

Which of our internal business processes will effectively and efficiently deliver them?

- Level of employee awareness of company strategies
- Level of employee awareness of company policies
- Recruitment cycle time
- Job offer acceptance rate
- Availability/Take-up of training offered
- Level of employee evaluations completed
- Internal feedback as to effectiveness and efficiency of HR services provided
- HR personnel per employee benchmarks [vs. other comparable organizations]

Employee-related Capability Measures

Which particular capabilities do we need to establish and maintain in order to execute them?

- Total employee cost per employee trend [industry benchmarks]
- Level of job applications received
- Quality of recruits vs. standards / targets set
- Level of training hours per employee per annum
- Pay and benefits benchmarks
- Best Practice HR policy benchmarks [vs. other employers]
- Level of business ethics infringements
- Level of safety incidents / Lost work days due to safety incidents

Summary

Who typically are this group of stakeholders?

- *The organization's employees* (of each gender, and every race and creed) at all seniority levels, in all countries, from all business units, and within all functional disciplines.

What do employees typically want and need from your organization?

- *Purpose* – work interest, job design, pride of accomplishment, essential support elements

- *Care* – respect, fair and decent treatment, physical environment, policies, morale and prospects
- *Skills* – portable skills, availability and quality of training, access to knowledge and advice
- *Pay* – total comparative compensation package for joiners, incumbents and leavers.

What does your organization typically want and need from its employees?

- *Hands* – headcount, skill-sets inventory, productivity, flexibility
- *Hearts* – loyalty, commitment, experience, morale
- *Minds* – qualifications, knowledge workers, project teams
- *Voices* – suggestions, team contribution, diversity, culture.

What strategies typically address these wants and needs?

- Increase workforce flexibility
- Attract and recruit best people
- Retain existing key people
- Reinforce desired culture

Which processes typically relate to the execution of these strategies?

- Plan and manage the enterprise – manage human resources

Which capabilities typically need to be developed and nurtured?

- Training and skills development
- Focused recruitment standards
- Competitive compensation packages
- Organizational and cultural values
- Recognition mechanisms
- Appraisal and promotion practices
- Balanced workforce policies
- Grievance and fair treatment policies
- Counselling and mentoring policies
- Business ethics policies
- Health and safety policies
- Facilities and physical environment

9 Managing Supplier and Alliance Partner Relationships with Measures

As buyer–supplier relations move forward towards 'partnerships' – a phrase used more often by the assemblers [the customers] than by the suppliers – more and more of the suppliers' internal operations are likely to come under the scrutiny of their customers.

'The Japanization of British Industry' by Nick Oliver and Barry Wilkinson.

For most organizations, especially in manufacturing and retailing for example, bought goods and services represent a substantial part of their operating costs – often the largest part. Given that suppliers are so important to achieving success and that evidently they should be an obvious focus of performance measurement activity, it is perhaps odd that they fail to figure in most performance measurement frameworks. Kaplan and Norton's balanced scorecard, first published in the January–February 1992 edition of the *Harvard Business Review*, does not have a supplier perspective (but then it doesn't have an employee one either – unless, as some practitioners have done, the Innovation & Learning perspective is modified to an Employee one). The European Foundation for Quality Management's widely acclaimed business excellence model, introduced in 1992 for the European Quality Award, did not have a supplier component to its nine 'enablers and results' dimensions (until recently modified to include 'partnerships'). Neither do the performance excellence criteria for the Malcolm Baldrige Award, created in 1987, specifically address supplier management issues.

The reason is threefold. First, in each case, supplier management seems to be subsumed into an amorphous category of 'internal business processes'. Second, the concept of building closer relationships with major suppliers in order to improve efficiency and effectiveness throughout the supply chain, in preference to maintaining essentially adversarial relationships with direct suppliers, is a relatively recent trend. Third, the importance of supplier management has escalated rapidly in parallel with the fad for strategic outsourcing partnerships during the past decade. The measurement models simply haven't caught up with the pace of change. Without the aid of a contemporary performance management framework, such as the Performance Prism, it is easy to get confused and to overlook the issue of vital supplier relationship measures.

The Components of Achieving Supplier/Alliance Partner Satisfaction and Contribution

Our own research (Cranfield/Accenture) shows that 52 per cent of firms measure supplier contribution today but, of those that don't already measure it, 83 per cent believe that they should. Just 30 per cent of survey respondents claim to measure supplier satisfaction but, 77 per cent of those that don't, believe they should measure it. So, even where companies have taken account of measures for supplier relationship management, there is a tendency for such metrics to have a particularly self-serving bias towards their own interests alone – for example: pricing benchmarks, on-time delivery, quality and service performance, etc. Little mention is usually made of whether suppliers get paid on time, the amount of business done with each supplier, or the benefits of mutual co-operative initiatives. A better balance of supplier-related performance measures is needed and the survey evidence would suggest that there is some recognition that there is a need to improve.

Wants and Needs

The nature of the relationship between the organization and its suppliers is the reverse of the one the organization has with its own customers. However, in supplier relationship management, there is a tendency for the organization's wants and needs from its suppliers (i.e. contribution) to predominate over its suppliers' wants and needs. That is not to say this is the way it should be but, to be pragmatic, that's the way it usually is. The organization wants its suppliers to provide products and/or services on a 'fast, right, cheap and easy (to do business with)' basis. Exactly what its own customers want of it.

Business alliances, though, tend to have more complex raisons d'être, where the organization's wants and needs are more likely to be specific capabilities such as, for example, particular skill-sets and leading technologies, or access to established sales networks and distribution channels. Essentially, these are things that are difficult to acquire, too expensive to build or would take too long to develop internally.

Both suppliers and joint ventures need feedback in terms of opinions about how well they are doing so that they can improve (and, dare say, they would like their own opinions to be heard within the organization too), they want to be trusted by the other party and often to share vital proprietary information mutually. Not least, they want the relationship to work in a way that allows them to be profitable and enables their business to grow – for example, through expanding the scope of the relationship, making capital investments, or by developing new products and services.

The Supplier Relationship model is summarized in Figure 9.1.

Fig 9.1 The Supplier Relationship

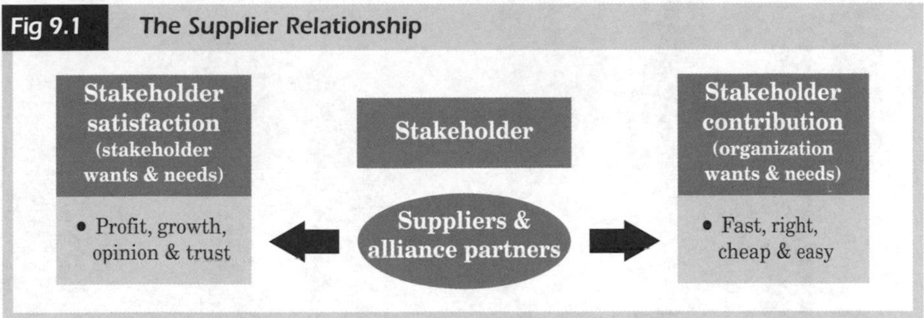

Supply Chain Strategies, Processes and Capabilities

Some of the generic strategies that commonly apply to supplier and alliance partner relationship management are, most typically, to:

- *Improve supplier performance* – by establishing service level agreements (with associated penalties and/or rewards), monitoring quality/service delivery performance, and establishing formal accreditation or audit practices.
- *Optimize procurement costs* – by tracking total acquisition cost savings achievements accomplished through capability development initiatives, such as implementing internet exchange auctions, vendor managed inventories, self-billing systems, or outsourcing, as well as regular purchasing negotiations.
- *Establish alliance or joint venture partnerships* – whereby forecast and demand data are shared with suppliers (via electronic data interchange or collaborative planning systems) and the modus operandi of joint ventures is defined.
- *Accomplish desired outcome objectives* – by measuring the progress towards and the achievements accomplished of whatever the specific defined objectives of the alliance or merger may be.

Figure 9.2 illustrates the key components of this vital and sometimes complex relationship.

Fig 9.2 Mapping Supplier Relationships through the Performance Prism Facets

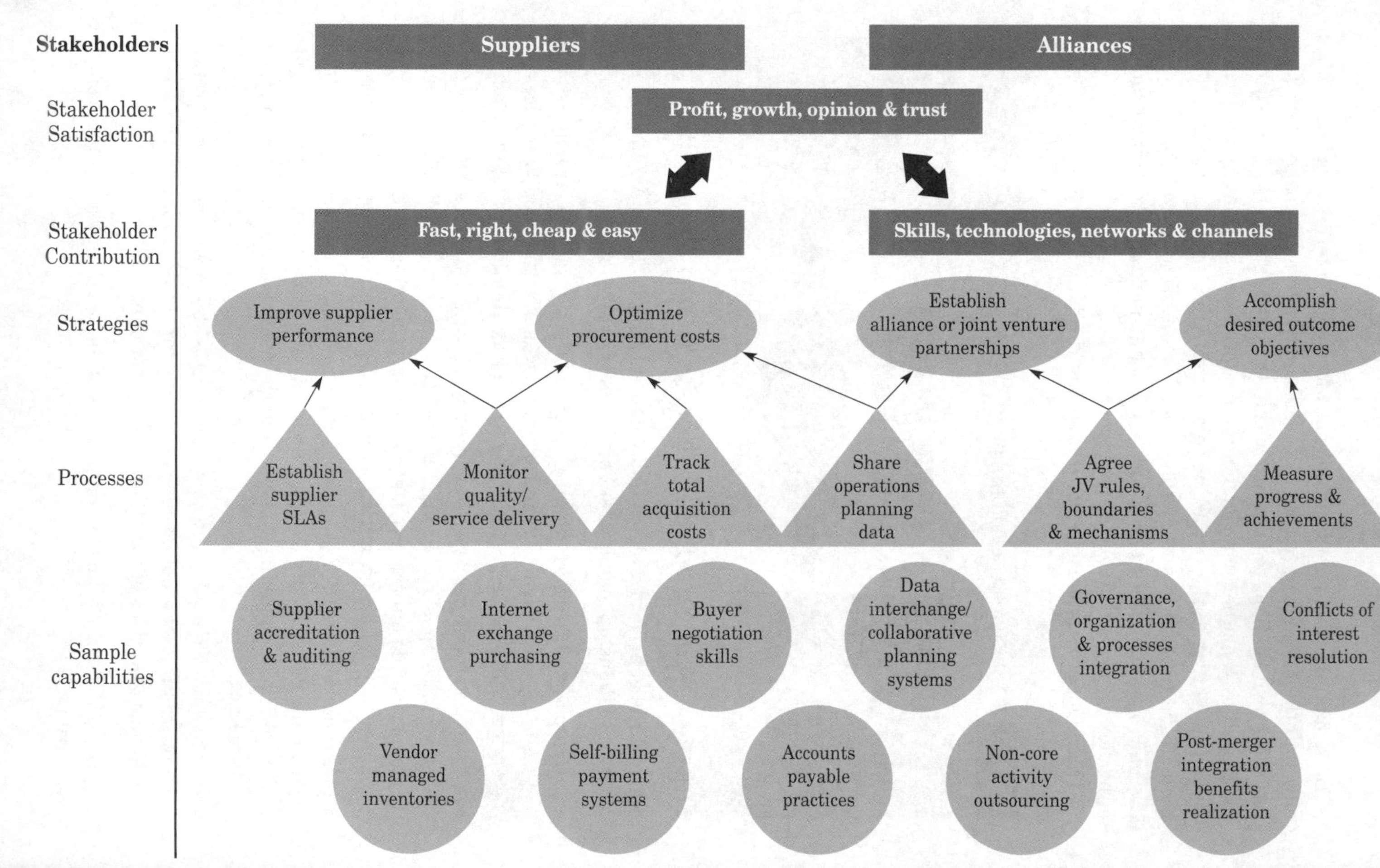

The purchasing departments of many large organizations, although by no means all, do create supplier-related measures to monitor performance at the rolled-up strategic intent level. But, in our experience, few are quite self-critical enough. We believe that most really do need to delve deeper and monitor their performance at the process and capability levels. We think that they need to be more sophisticated in their use of measures in this area and, if continuous improvement is to be achieved, then there is value in doing so. If a culture of managing with measures, applying a broad spectrum of metrics at the operational level, is not created then the traditional focus of purchasing departments on pricing to the exclusion of almost everything else will inevitably prevail – and to the longer-term detriment of the enterprise.

For example, the process of establishing Service Level Agreements, as shown in Figure 9.2, would suggest the need to measure the proportion of suppliers – probably by category – with whom SLAs have been established. Monitoring Quality/Service Delivery infers that some measures of individual supplier performance in keeping the promises to which they have signed-up in SLAs will be necessary. Where manufactured components are involved, for instance, this should also extend to their reliability in use by end-users as well as in production. We discuss elsewhere in this chapter some of the relevant factors that can contribute to 'total acquisition cost', but clearly these might also further extend to supplier maintenance costs, such as the 'knock-on' costs of settling their invoices or the purchasing team's costs associated with dealing with a particular group of suppliers. Sharing operations planning data also implies measuring the quality of the information that is shared and checking suppliers' perceptions of its worth. We have already indicated too that purchasing departments should benchmark themselves against best practices to evaluate their efficiency and effectiveness. Not many bother to do so.

Purchasing is, in our view, a good example of the type of under-measurement that exists within company functional departments that are critical to organizational success. Cascading the performance measurement ethic through the organization in order not only to achieve strategic intents, but also to improve vital business processes and to ensure the development of important capabilities is an imperative that many organizations overlook.

Measures for Supplier and Alliance Partner Relationship Management

Total acquisition cost will normally be high on the priority list of measures from a supplier contribution point of view. It is not enough to simply compare the negotiated unit price of commodities purchased from across the globe. The costs of shipping (or airfreight), duties payable, handling fees, demurrage costs, inland freight, insurance premiums and inventory holding costs may need to be included in the equation in order to make like-with-like comparisons with local suppliers. Moreover, where supply prices are volatile, the fluctuations and trends will need to be tracked and reported, since these may have a highly direct impact on sales pricing.

As noted above, service level agreement achievement is also another common supplier contribution requirement. Product quality, delivery performance and other service elements, such as documentation completeness and accuracy, will usually need to be taken into account. In manufacturing industries especially, companies might also need to track the consequential impact costs (such as scrap, rework, warranties, etc.) of poor supplier quality control. And those consequences can sometimes be dire (see the box *Latches Close Car Plant Doors*).

Latches Close Car Plant Doors

Sourcing parts from a single supplier offers big cost savings. But when that supplier has problems and fails to deliver, single sourcing in a Just-In-Time environment bites hard. When Ford's supplier of door and boot latches defaulted, plants in Dagenham and Cologne came to a halt. At a stroke, output of nearly 3,000 cars a day was lost, and more than 10,000 workers were either sent home or diverted to plant maintenance.

What you might imagine was not one of the most critical components that Ford's procurement experts should lose sleep worrying about had, in fact, caused logistics chaos.

The level of business with preferred and/or accredited suppliers would generally be a fair indicator of progress achieved within a strategic purchasing initiative implementation. Also, the trend in the value of business per supplier might be a useful measure of the overall deployment of supplier relationship policies and practices. In terms of satisfying suppliers' wants and needs, some companies (predominantly those with relatively advanced attitudes towards managing supplier relations) conduct periodic supplier perception surveys in order to ascertain their views about the current relationship and how it might be improved in the future. The voice of key suppliers and alliance partners may be as important to hear as the voice of other critical stakeholders – such as investors, customers and employees – in helping to make vital strategic decisions. For example, one revelation early in Ford's programme was that some suppliers were reluctant to share their newest technology with the company for fear that they would not be adequately rewarded for their co-operation.

Unfortunately, many company procurement executives are too insular (or at least think they know best) to listen to such viewpoints. Where these views are obtained through surveys, invariably it will be necessary to ensure that they are collected anonymously (especially at first, when it is a new programme) if they are to be truly reflective of what suppliers really think, and not just kow-towing to provide what are perceived to be the 'right answers'. Engrained behavioural suspicions tend to die hard. Where suppliers and/or alliance partners make specific suggestions for improvements, then clearly the level of their implementation should be monitored too.

What we should be looking for are measurement methodologies in the arena of supply chain management that allow the satisfaction of both organizations (as customers and suppliers) to be tracked. Some such methodologies do exist. First Point Assessment, for example, have developed a supplier evaluation methodology for the petrochemical industry. This consists of three linked reports. The first, supplier performance, reports on the supplier's performance during the delivery of goods and/or services to its customers. The second, product performance in service, reports on the ongoing service performance of a supplier's product and/or equipment after it has been operating for a period of time. The third, purchaser performance, is the unusual one and reports on how the purchasers (the customers) support the supplier during the provision of their products and/or services. This report explores issues such as: the clarity of the specification, the efficiency of the tender process, the effectiveness of communication, and so on (see Figure 9.3, p. 298). In so doing it explicitly addresses the question: 'Is the customer a good customer for the supplier?' This, of course, is a question that customers would want to ask of themselves if they really were committed to a relationship with their suppliers.

For improving collaboration with suppliers, relevant performance indicators might also include the level of plan/schedule stability, the level of demand visibility given to suppliers, and the level of supplier involvement in product/service design. The trend in the proportion of long-term supply contracts might also be a measure of commitment. Getting their invoices paid on time is always a bugbear for suppliers in terms of managing their cash flow (and potentially their borrowing requirements). So, an organization should know what the level of its creditor days outstanding is and it should also be able to compare this with its debtor days outstanding. Financial controllers may seek to extend creditor payments – often way beyond that of the firm's debtors – for as long as they can get away with, since it benefits the company financially. However, it is an underhand practice if organizations use the power of their size to delay payment beyond the terms that have been

Fig 9.3 First Point Assessment: Purchaser Performance Report

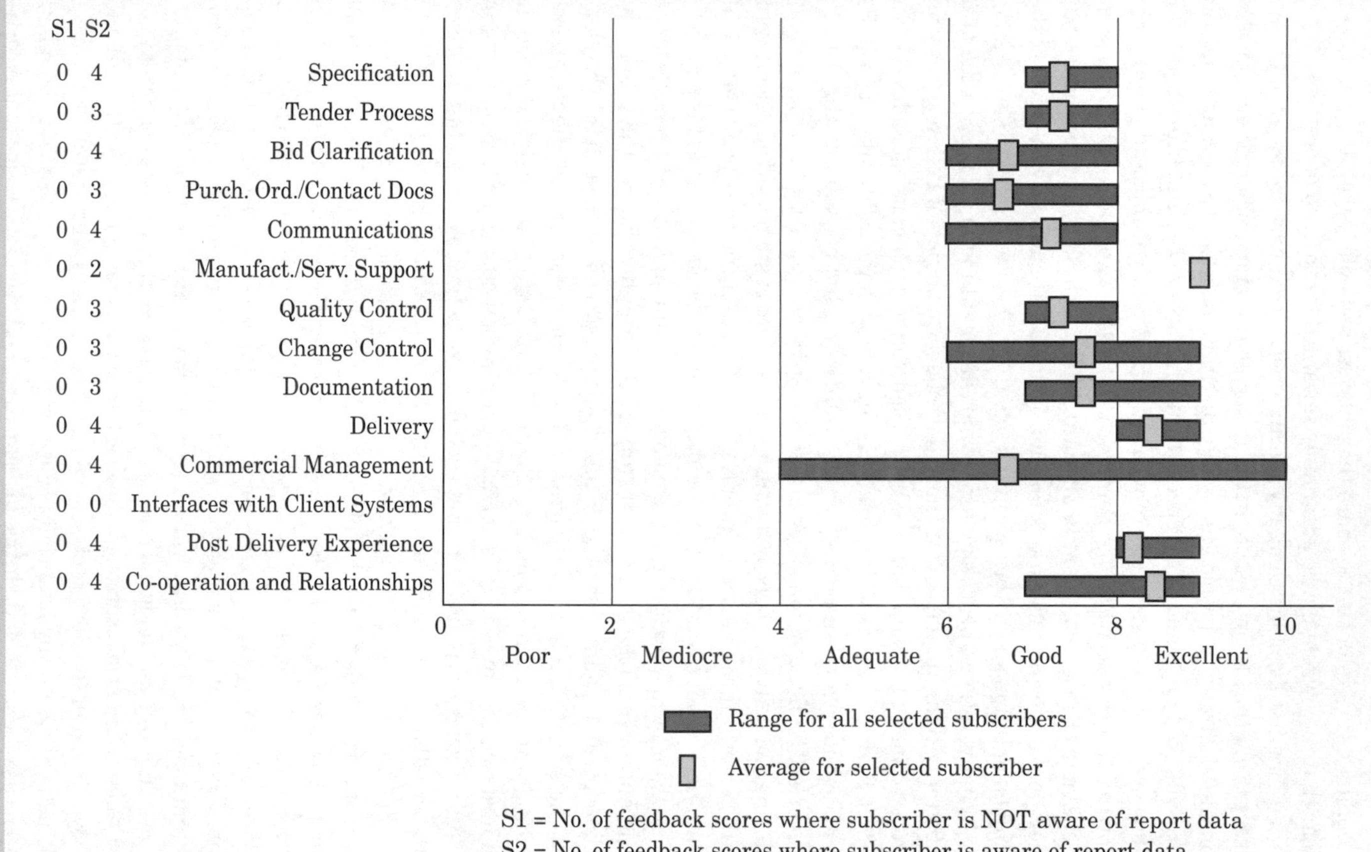

agreed, and purchasing executives should ensure that such abuses are not allowed to occur. Even though the concept is more than 25 years old, best practice is probably still represented by those companies that apply 'self-billing' methods, which avoid the requirement for processing thousands of supplier invoices (and, importantly, their associated queries). They simply prepare a statement from internal data reports and credit suppliers' bank accounts monthly.

Inventory levels are another working capital issue that is highly relevant to supplier relations. However, passing the burden of holding inventories down to the next link in the chain – as some 'Just-In-Time' initiatives have done – does not make for a more efficient supply chain. It just passes the holding cost onto someone else's ownership. To recount the views of the embittered managing director of one automotive industry supplier[60]:

> JIT has been used as a myth on which to hang the transfer of the responsibility for stockholding to another point in the supply chain as long as it isn't the blooming car companies ... Basically most people who have achieved it have done it by switching it to some other poor sod.

An understanding of where inventory is kept in the whole supply chain is needed in order to find a solution and to build an end-to-end demand fulfilment channel that is highly efficient, effective and difficult to copy. Supplier leadtimes of high-value materials can have a significant impact on inventory holding levels (because of the need to hold 'buffer' stocks) and so, where this is a significant issue, there may be a need to track improvements in supplier leadtimes in order that stock levels can be adjusted accordingly. As we have noted earlier, inventories of some categories of materials can be self-managed by the supplier; where appropriate, therefore, the proportion of vendor-managed inventories (VMI) and the achievement of related cost saving projections may well be pertinent measures.

Not forgetting Nike's (and other 'third world' supplier users') public perception problem relating to its supplier management policies and practices discussed in Chapter 4, the trends in conformance to defined working practice standards may need to be audited independently. The overall trends can be tracked but, for executive action purposes, it will need to be reported on an individual factory basis so that specific remedial actions can be taken with recalcitrant supplier managements who continue to abuse their workers.

For a purchasing department, the value of purchase cost savings achieved can be an important metric. But, as we have discussed above, these need to be reflective of genuine cost savings, not just the outcome of unit price negotiations. Another purchasing office consideration could be the risk of a critical supplier defaulting due to liquidity problems. Some purchasers believe, therefore, that it is prudent to monitor (and set limits on) the share of each supplier's turnover that their business represents. Leading purchasing departments also measure their own efficiency against the best in the world through benchmarking practices.

The decision whether to outsource aspects of current production and internal services to other parties, or to continue to keep them in-house, is not necessarily an easy one. There may be a 'strategic logic' to outsourcing those activities that are non-core and which distract management attention from the most important parts of the business, but will it make economic sense and what are the ramifications? Certainly, good measurement data will be required in order to help make the decision and, after the decision is made, measures will be needed in order to ensure that the benefits are actually being realized. Some of the key strategic issues and pertinent data requirements are described in the box *Twenty Critical Questions for Outsourcing Decisions*.

Twenty Critical Questions for Outsourcing Decisions

Strategic considerations

- Is this activity core to deploying our business strategy, and how does it affect our future ability to compete effectively?
- Could outsourcing this activity negatively impact our most important customers or market perceptions?
- What confidentiality risks are implied by outsourcing this activity, and can proprietary concerns be satisfactorily overcome?
- What investment would we need to make in order to produce the product or provide the service to best practice benchmark standards ourselves?

Cost comparison

- What is the (direct) cost of making/doing this activity internally?
- What additional overheads are attracted by this activity?
- What would be the impact of outsourcing on remaining overhead cost allocation?
- Can a supplier/contractor (outsourcer) provide the product/service, to the required standards, more cheaply?

Suppliers

- What are the *sources* of an outsourcer's ability to provide the product/service more cheaply (and still make a profit)?
- Do potential outsourcers possess skills/assets that can enhance the product/service provided (e.g. quality improvement, process improvement, R&D, back-up resources)?

- Are potential outsourcers flexible enough to cope with probable demand and timing fluctuations and, therefore, will a single outsourcer be sufficient?
- What additional costs will be incurred internally as a consequence of outsourcing (e.g. administration, quality assurance, transportation, storage, duties, etc.)?

Employees

- Would outsourcing this activity involve the creation of redundancies, and if so, what are the risks of a serious industrial dispute?
- What is the cashflow effect of redundancies versus anticipated benefits over time?
- Would existing employees need to be transferred to the prospective outsourcer?
- What are the implications (e.g. employment law) of transferring employees to the outsourcer?

Contract management

- Are the resources available to effectively initiate and then manage the relationship with the outsourcer?
- What guarantees should be incorporated within the outsourcing arrangement to ensure that the benefits can be sustained over the longer term?
- Is protection needed against the outsourcer becoming a potential competitor?
- If needs be, would the outsourcing arrangement be practically reversible in the future?

Source: Chris Adams, *Outsourcing/Insourcing Decision Criteria*, 1997.

Measuring Business Alliances

In partnerships, alliances and joint ventures, the appropriate measures are likely to be centred around the progress made towards their principal objectives. We have discussed earlier how business alliances rarely live up to their initial expectations. They are also generally more unstable, even when cemented with cross-shareholdings. A particular characteristic of alliances, which rarely applies to mergers and acquisitions for example, is that there is a tendency to assume that the joint venture activity does not need to be separately measured in its own right. The assumption is that the benefits will, through some miracle, automatically flow through to the partners and the benefits will be identifiable there. Nothing could be further from the reality of course. Indeed, Accenture's Alliance Survey exposed the fact that only 51 per cent of alliances use formal performance measures and, of those that do, just 20 per cent of executives believe the measures to be sufficient. All told, barely 10 per cent of alliances have meaningful performance measures. It is hardly surprising then that so many fail to live up to their expectations.

The implications for performance measurement are, first, that business alliances tend to have different governance structures, with representation from both parties who may have separate underlying agendas. It is, therefore, *doubly* important – contrary to common practice – to agree appropriate performance measures at the outset of each joint venture component of the alliance. Second, for each key measure selected it is important to agree a realistic performance target – and, where appropriate, interim milestones – so that progress towards the alliance's aims and goals can be tracked. In addition, the individual parties may wish to set themselves private targets for the benefits they seek from the alliance so that executives can make judgements on whether it is providing the anticipated benefits or not, and take actions accordingly. Third, the management team should agree ways in which it will audit the cohesiveness of the alliance – if appropriate, by means of confidential perception surveys – as it matures. Such audits should be conducted within multiple levels of the allied organization so that both top-down and bottom-up views are obtained.

Finally, we fully endorse a measure suggested by Accenture's Charles Kalmbach Jr. and Charles Roussel in their article 'Dispelling the Myths of Alliances'.[61] They recommended that a useful measure of the harmony of an alliance is to introduce a metric that tracks the trend in the number of times that decisions – which the alliance's management team would reasonably be empowered to make – are referred back to bosses within the individual corporations or a more senior group. They call these the level of 'pass-ups'. The benefit of this measure is illustrated by the example of an alliance that introduced such a metric. The companies found that the level of 'pass-ups' dropped from over 100 in the first month to fewer than ten after six months with the result that the alliance was significantly faster to market.

All that assumes, of course, that the joint venture gets off the ground in the first place. If the right level of basic quantitative and qualitative due diligence is not done, then catastrophe can only be expected (see, for example, the box *Mission and Mammon Collide*).

Mission and Mammon Collide

Bank of Scotland found itself embroiled in a public relations disaster of epic proportions in 1999. It was forced to apologize for its aborted joint venture scheme to start a direct bank with Pat Robertson, the US television evangelist.

What was the source of this regret? Pat Robertson had made a TV broadcast in which he described Scotland as a 'dark land' excessively tolerant of homosexuals. He said the moral message of John Knox no longer existed and Scotland 'could go right back to the darkness very easily'. 'In Scotland, you cannot believe how strong the homosexuals are.' The outcome was massive unwanted media attention to the deal.

When at first about 500 indignant Scots closed their account and a few protesters chained themselves to the railings outside its head office over the announcement of the deal, the bank was not too concerned and believed it might ride out the storm. But then the Trades Union Congress threatened to pull out of a credit card contract; charities began to express concerns and ethical investment funds began looking at moving their deposits elsewhere; West Lothian Council, whose £250 million a year income is channelled through the bank, said that it proposed to vote to move its business to another bank; and the new Scottish parliament's £55 million account seemed to be in jeopardy too. The problem was not going away as hoped, and then came newspaper reports of that broadcast – a bombshell. The bank now had no option but to pull the deal.

Robertson, the founder of the Virginia-based Christian Broadcasting Network (on which he 'heals' people in a television show) and the lobbying group Christian Coalition, had done a $3 billion telebanking venture deal with Bank of Scotland in which he would take a 25 per cent stake. From Bank of Scotland's point of view, here was an opportunity to sell its financial services to the 55 million born-again Christian viewers of his broadcasts – equal to the entire population of Britain – with negligible start-up costs. If it worked, some analysts reckoned it could double its 5 million customer-base in four years.

However, it is a source of some astonishment that a highly conservative organization like the Bank of Scotland was unable to recognize that Robertson was not exactly a controversy-free character. As journalist Libby Purves observed (*The Times*, 8 June 1999), it was a shade incautious in that 'a bank rooted in Scotland might have taken an interest in his referring to "Episcopalians and Presbyterians and so on" as "the spirit of the Antichrist" for not being born again; a land in the middle of democratic devolution might have balked at getting involved with someone who condemned the introduction of one man, one vote in South Africa as dangerous to the white minority; who has said that atheists cannot be considered citizens of "a Christian nation" and sends out fundraising letters explaining that feminism encourages women to "leave their husbands, kill their children, practice witchcraft, destroy capitalism and become lesbians" [and who refers to] all non-Christians as "termites" requiring "a godly fumigation".' That's one thing, but calling the men in kilts gay was just too much.

The words 'loose' and 'cannon' come to mind. Indeed, it is hard to imagine how much more clearly Robertson could have warned them of the inevitable gaffe that was to come. Reports at the time suggested that Bank of Scotland would have to pay up to £30 million in compensation to Robertson for pulling out of the deal and millions more were wiped off its market capitalization. One imagines that the bank will vet any new joint venture partners very carefully indeed.

A further consideration for business alliances is that it is becoming increasingly common for joint ventures to be focused towards developing, and generating demand for, products and services, thereby *avoiding* costs rather than proactively reducing them. The prevalence of this practice varies considerably from industry to industry. Companies in the pharmaceutical industry, for example, are often very willing to form alliances for selling drugs, but are highly protective and secretive about their product development patents (although even they are finding that they need joint ventures with biotech and other specialist new technology firms). Automotive industry companies, on the other hand, are often keen to share product and major component development, but vigorously protect their sales channels. Nevertheless, whichever the case, measures for these two business processes – such as time to market and revenues from new products/services – and, from a strategic viewpoint, measures of its brands, products and services strategic intents – such as market share and sales channel performance – are likely to be far more predominant than, for example, in the case of post-merger integration (PMI) measurement.

Conversely, in other sub-types of business alliances, it is also becoming increasingly commonplace in a wide variety of industries to outsource many 'plan and manage enterprise' processes, such as accounting and personnel functions. While other companies elect to give up or reduce their 'fulfil demand' processes, such as component manufacturing, product distribution and document processing. Although the justification normally runs along the lines of these companies needing to focus on their core competencies, the primary motivation here is invariably to achieve present cost reductions and/or to avoid future cost expenditure. The measures that will be predominant in these cases, therefore, will be cost saving accomplishment ones.

Purchasing Power in Post-merger Integration

In major mergers and acquisitions, where the emphasis of post-merger integration is often on headcount reduction and facilities rationalization, the opportunities for leveraging scale in purchasing power is often overlooked – or at least deferred until much later in the integration process. However, the opportunity to optimize bought costs should, in most cases, be grasped at the earliest possible moment. When seeking PMI purchase cost savings, data will be essential. First, it is advisable to break down the rolled-up spending of the combined organization into spend categories. This data will then need some detailed analysis in order to gain a better understanding of the opportunities. However, note that it is highly likely that the biggest cost savings opportunities will be found in the integrating organization's purchases that are common across multiple business units and geographical regions. Figure 9.4 (p. 306) may help to identify the most common principal categories of spend.

Once the biggest spend categories have been identified, the next stage is to analyse the number of suppliers used to provide the same – or very similar – goods and services. Company procurement policies differ as to whether it is best to optimize scale and build long-term partnerships with sole suppliers, or to retain two or three suppliers in order to maintain a rivalry that will keep each vendor sharp on pricing and to ensure that back-up is always available in the event of one of the suppliers failing to meet their obligations. Nevertheless, it is not untypical to find situations where there are many tens (and even hundreds) of suppliers for some categories of purchase. This is normally a very good sign that there is going to be a high opportunity for cost savings because procurement has previously been done on an ad hoc basis with no consideration given to inter-divisional and inter-regional scale.

It can be argued of course that this is not particular to a PMI situation. This is true, but in a PMI situation it is exacerbated because two entirely separate purchasing policies, practices, processes and people are suddenly brought together. It is *inevitable* that their respective purchases will not have been co-ordinated and that multiple supplier overlaps will be compounded. The combined purchase analysis helps to identify which categories of purchase a

Fig 9.4 Key Target Areas for Post-merger Integration Purchase Cost Savings

Scope	Services bought	Goods bought
Global	Travel services Banking services Advertising services Consulting services International distribution services	Raw materials – commodity categories (mfg.) Capital equipment (particularly mfg.) Equipment spare parts & consumables Computer hardware (& peripherals) Computer software
Regional/national/local	Utilities services (electricity, water, etc.) Telecommunications services Catering and hospitality services Cleaning services Waste disposal services Site maintenance services Computing maintenance services Payroll administration services Domestic/Regional distribution services Printing services Real estate services Construction services Company car administration services Temporary labour	Packaging materials – incl. pallets (mfg.) Transportation equipment (mfg.) Field service vehicles & equipment Stationery Publications Office furnishings & equipment
Head Office – central	Accounts auditing services Share registration services Pension administration services Insurance services Treasury services	

PMI team should be responsible for attacking and which are better left to other local, regional and head office staff to resolve. Note, however, that the data needed for this analysis may not be so straightforward to obtain. Information systems may not yet have been integrated and two sets of data may need to be formatted and brought together. Or, indeed, it is possible sometimes that the level of detail required (e.g. vendor data) may only exist within multiple regional and/or business unit databases. Consider the data collection and collation requirements carefully before identifying the PMI team resourcing needs.

Once the initial analysis is available, PMI teams should seek to target savings in two particular areas. The first of these is where there is *a combination of* high values of goods and services bought, pan-divisional and/or pan-regional spend and multiple suppliers. The action here will be to identify those suppliers that can provide the goods or services needed at the required level of scale and obtain quotations from them for the greater volume and scope of business. Note that preferred suppliers will need to be vetted to ensure that they have the necessary capabilities to provide the right quality of goods and – particularly – services required. The biggest companies may not always be the best from a service delivery perspective. The second major area in which to watch for purchase cost savings is where the two organizations have previously purchased high values of goods or services from the *same* supplier. Doubling, or even just substantially increasing, the volume of business with that supplier opens up price negotiation opportunities. Very often, these can prove to be 'quick wins' from the initial analysis.

In terms of measuring the benefits that the PMI team have realized, a record should be maintained of the anticipated annual spend – say, over the next three years – for each of the categories of purchase identified for special PMI action and the impact of newly negotiated cost savings achieved over the period.

Suppliers and alliance partners can be vital to the success of a corporation. Picking the right measures will be a critical part of that success in a range of different supplier and alliance interrelationship situations. Different sets of measures gain different levels of importance in different situations. Simple procurement, partnerships, outsourcing, joint ventures, mergers and acquisitions all present their own challenges and measurement needs. Selecting and implementing the right measures will be crucial to the outcomes. Once again, there won't be a single recipe for success. However, common supplier relationship considerations will normally include many of the factors that are illustrated in Figure 9.5.

Fig 9.5 Sample Measures for Managing Supplier Relationships

The Supplier/Alliance Partner Relationship Measures Design Process

Once again, the 'success mapping' process for measures design is likely to be the best approach for selecting the appropriate measures. For supplier relationships, the key questions to be asked should be along the lines of, for example:

- What do we want and need from our suppliers?
- What do our suppliers want and need from us?
- What are our strategies for satisfying these separate sets of wants and needs?
- Which processes need to be efficient and effective to support these strategies?
- What specific capabilities do we need to develop for each of these processes?

Applying the Performance Prism in this way – as per the schematic shown in Figure 9.6 – helps us to select the right supplier-related performance measures.

Fig 9.6 Performance Prism Unfolded Schematic: Suppliers

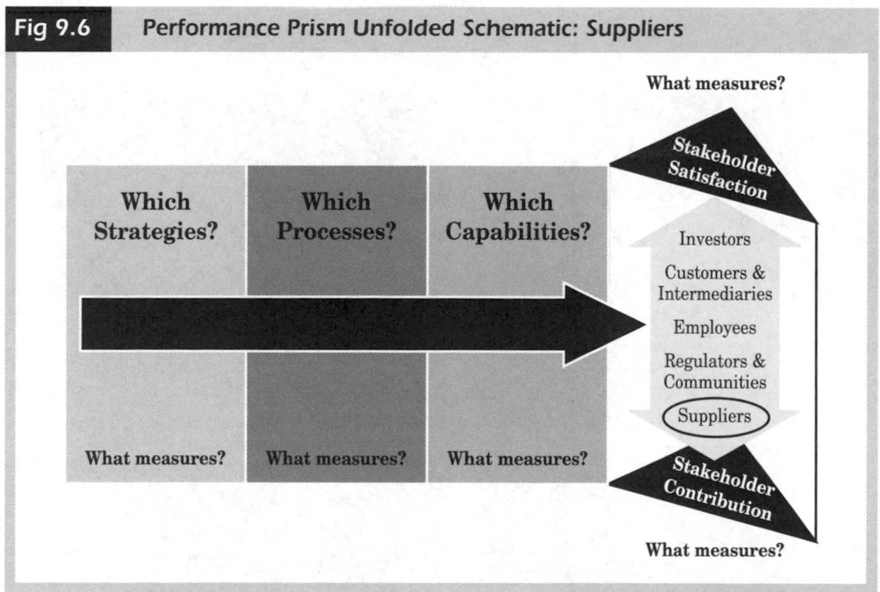

The first step is usually to segment suppliers into categories which will help to determine the nature of the organization's relationship with its various suppliers – it is unlikely to be homogeneous. (The *Dangerous Liaisons* box in Chapter 4 provided one such segmentation example.) Once these categories have been established, then the organization's wants and needs of its suppliers and the supplier's wants and needs of the organization (in this stakeholder's case, usually in that order) can be identified, defined and prioritized. A few outcome measures can then be identified which capture the essential essence of each point of view.

The next step is to review the purchasing strategy. This document should usually define how supplier relationships will work in terms of procurement objectives and policies. Does it? Or does it need to be made more explicit? And how well are these strategies being implemented? The process component might then, for example, review measures relevant to new supplier selection, existing supplier management, demand forecasting and accounts payable. The final step then is to review the measures of capability development in terms of putting in place relevant resources and skill-sets, best practices adoption, and the information systems needed in order to track and share relevant data.

The diagram shown in Figure 9.7 provides an illustration of the line of enquiry that needs to be followed in relation to this effort in order to identify what needs to be measured.

Fig 9.7 Example of the Supplier Measures Selection Process

The Supplier/Alliance Partner Relationship Measures 'Failure Mode' Test

We would recommend applying the same sort of measures selection verification process, applying one or more critical risk scenarios, as has been adopted in the previous chapters on managing investor, customer and employee relationships with measures. However, there are some particular issues we need to highlight here.

Supplier Failure Modes

In this case, let us assume that the critical 'failure mode' is a worsening detected trend in the level of reported faults for a supplied component when in use by the organization's customers (see Figure 9.8, p. 312).

Obviously once more, there is no single right answer or prescription. In this illustration, the failure mode analysis challenges whether the product quality strategy is sufficiently complete. It considers whether it addresses the key elements of having processes in place for managing business risks (in this case, in relation to components supplied to make end-products), managing supplier quality, and managing end-product warranties. In the first process, significant product risk identification, assessment and mitigation practices will be demanded. The second contains the supplier accreditation and process audit capabilities that we have mooted earlier in this chapter. However, there is also a supplier design review capability and best practice procedure to ensure that the two companies' engineers agree that the component design is sufficiently robust for its application in the climate and conditions it will be used.

The consequences of these engineers collectively getting this call wrong can be catastrophic. For example, in January 1985, the space shuttle Challenger exploded seconds after lift-off, killing its crew of seven, when a relatively simple component – an o-ring – failed and created a 'major malfunction'. The problem later transpired to be that NASA engineers, reluctant not to have a further launch delay, allegedly pressurized its o-ring supplier, Morton Thiokol, to approve clearance for the safety of its o-rings in the unusual sub-zero temperatures that prevailed in Florida that day. Some of Thiokol's senior engineers at the time have subsequently testified that they were deeply reluctant to give such clearance since the o-rings had not been designed or tested for use within that unexpected launch temperature range.

The third process is that of end-product warranty management. This requires capabilities not only in product rectification and, in extreme cases, product recall but also in handling warranty claims and, more rarely but

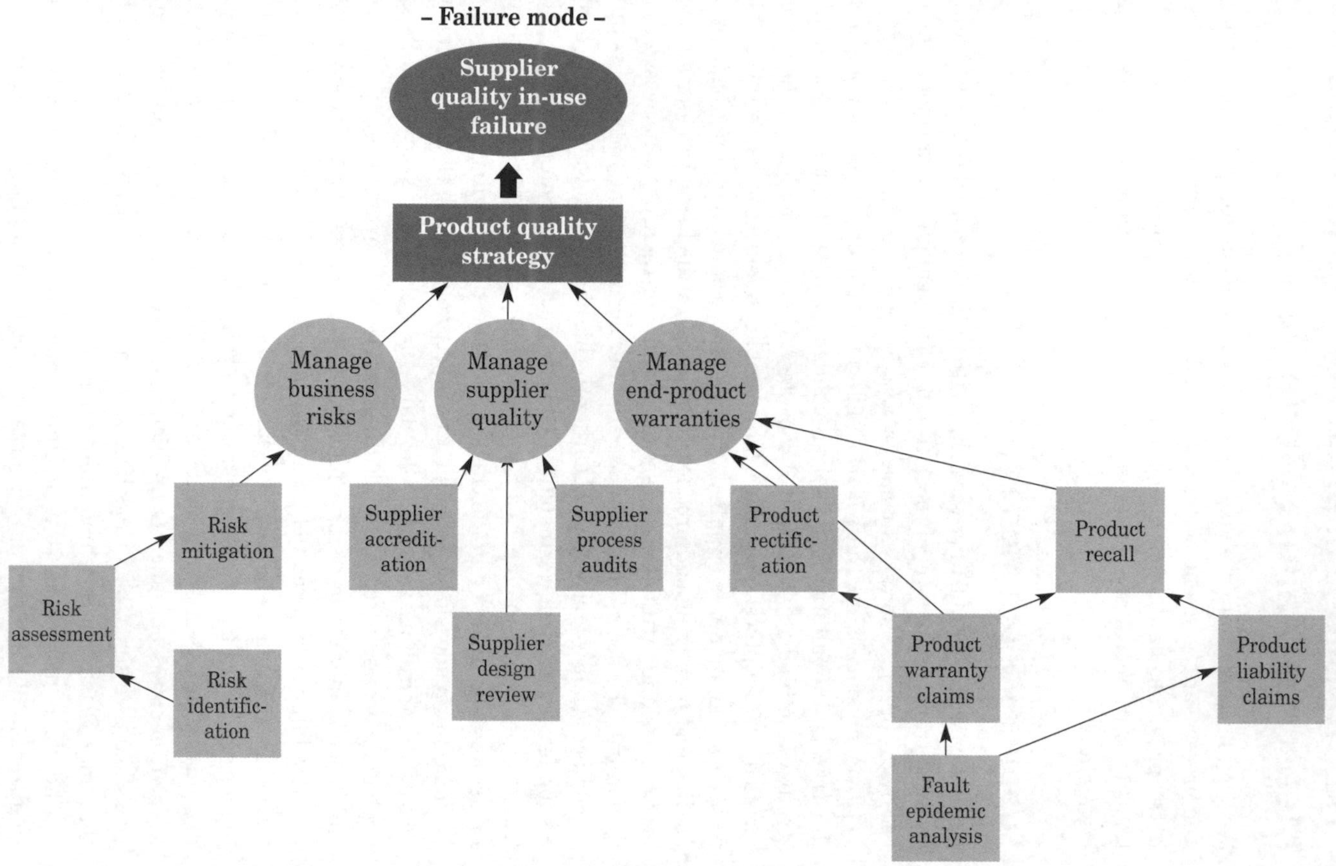

Fig 9.8 Supplier Component Quality In-use Failure Mode Map – Example

increasingly common, product liability claims. Rapid response to each of these potentially significant additional cost and corporate reputation threats requires first of all a capability to quickly identify fault epidemics and assess their potential severity (see the box *Ford and Firestone's Fatal Flaws*).

Ford and Firestone's Fatal Flaws

In August 2000, Bridgestone/Firestone ordered the recall of 6.5 million tyres, following fatalities involving a large number of US and Venezuelan motorists – variously reported to be between 174 and 203 deaths plus many more injuries. These were caused by tread separation on Firestone tyres fitted to Ford Explorer sports utility vehicles, many of which were involved in rollover accidents.

The ensuing spat between Bridgestone and Ford as to who was to blame became extremely public. Ford maintained that it was solely a defective tyre issue, while Bridgestone/Firestone contended that the carmaker's recommended tyre pressure and overall design of the Explorer – specifically, its weight distribution on the rear axle – contributed to the problem. Ford fiercely denied this, claiming that competitive-make tyres had performed almost flawlessly. As one industry analyst noted: 'Bridgestone is really walking a thin line in its relationship with Ford, trying to allocate some of the blame while at the same time keeping one of its major clients in line.'

The consequences were that Ford has suffered considerable embarrassment, image damage, and took an estimated recall-related cost charge of $500 million. Whether that includes the not inconsiderable cost of mobilizing its full publicity and damage limitation machine to help mitigate its role in the scandal isn't disclosed. Firestone, meanwhile, set aside $350 million to cover losses arising from the recall and, subsequently, a $750 million charge to cover legal fees and potential damages claims. Several of its senior executives subsequently 'elected to retire', its sales in the lucrative replacement market sunk 40 per cent after the recall, and its share price slumped.

While Firestone promised it would put new quality control measures in place to restore consumer confidence, including the formation of an enhanced 'early warning' safety system, several questions remain (and may never be disclosed) about the nature of its relationship with Ford. The first is: Why did Ford not notice the faults earlier? It says it relied on Firestone to monitor tyre performance because it had a separate warranty and claimed it virtually had to 'pry' data from the tyremaker's hands when it became concerned about the problem. But certainly the bigger question is: Why did so many deaths have to occur before either party did anything about the problem when industry safety data must surely have been available that pointed to the fact that there was a serious problem unfolding? A fault epidemic appears not to have been detected by either party early enough or, if they did, both remained 'in denial' about it for much too long. It is not unreasonable to speculate that at the very least one hundred or so people's lives could have been saved, and many more injuries avoided, if the interrelationship between customer and supplier had been working properly.

But that is not quite the end of the story. Ford subsequently announced, in May 2001, the massive recall of a further 13 million tyres on its Explorer vehicles, which the carmaker estimates will cost a further $3 billion. That same week, Firestone announced the severance of its 95-year relationship with Ford – Harvey Firestone first started doing business with Henry Ford in 1906. It is unlikely that the story will end there either; it could easily become a long, messy and expensive divorce.

Managing critical supplier risk is a fundamental business issue. For example, a US electronics manufacturer identified that a component essential to its key product was purchased exclusively from a German supplier that built the component at only one of its plants. It, therefore, faced a significant level of risk if something should happen to prevent that plant from supplying the particular component. When the company quantified the risk, it realized that it could be out of business for at least six months if something happened to the supplier. To deal with the risk in the short-term, it bought insurance to cover losses if its supply were interrupted. To create a longer-term solution, it began looking for alternative suppliers. Certainly, the risks of single-sourcing need to be weighed versus the several advantages that can be gained.

Alliance Partner Failure Modes

For an alliance partnership, the failure mode technique can also be applied to help ensure that joint ventures do not fail as a result of poor planning. When the key components of what would be most likely to cause the venture to fail are identified, then appropriate action planning – and relevant progress measures – can be put in place to ensure that these critical success factors do not get overlooked. A highly simplified example is illustrated in Figure 9.9.

Fig 9.9 Joint Venture Failure Mode Map – Example

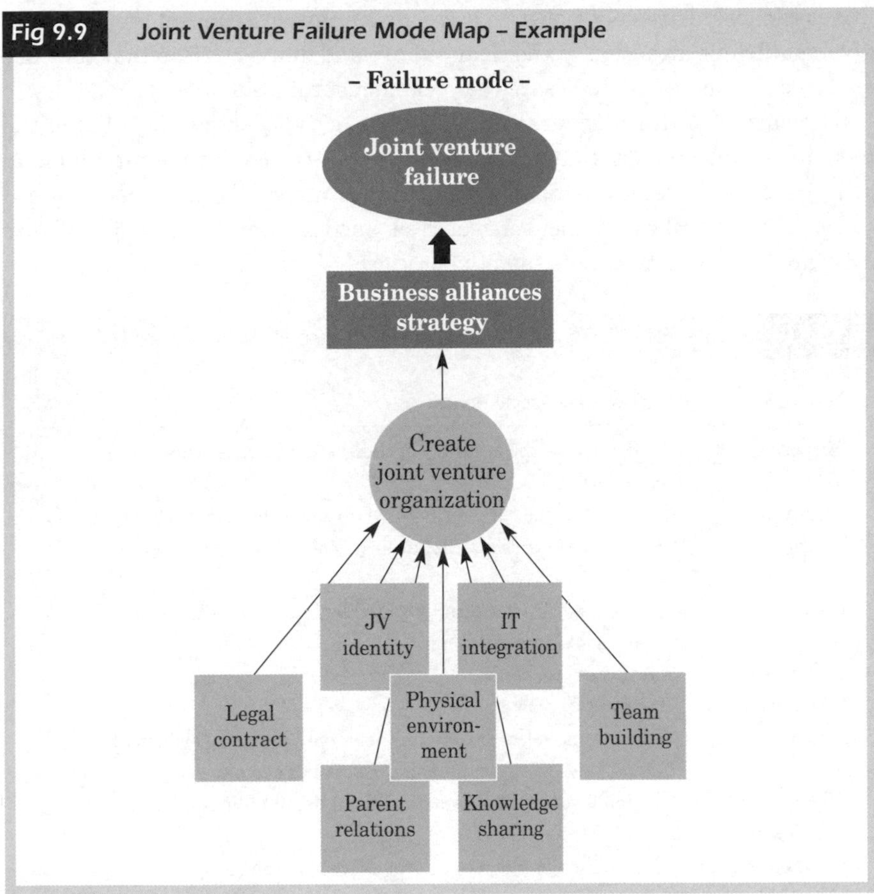

By taking this kind of reverse approach to validating the selection of measures for managing supplier and alliance partner relationships, it is highly likely that we will have uncovered key areas of risk and essential capabilities – which will almost certainly demand performance measurement attention – that would not otherwise have been readily identified through the success map routine. The failure mode mind-set again helps us to flush out these critical issues and measurement needs. And, indeed, other potentially critical supply failure scenarios (e.g. supplier on-time delivery failure) might need to be investigated as well – witness the consequences of the car door latches example mentioned earlier in this chapter. This type of assessment will not always be needed, but it should be applied wherever significant product or service supply and partnership implementation risks abound. While this design step may seem to add an extra level of complexity to pertinent measures selection, executives can look extremely foolish in *post mortem* investigations if they have not given sufficient attention to the clear supply and delivery risks that they are expected to manage. As they say, what gets measured gets managed.

The output of this measurement selection activity should be a list of the measures and metrics that matter in relation to managing supplier and alliance partner relationships. A set of Performance Measurement Record Sheets that describe each measure selected, such as that illustrated in Figure 9.10, are the primary outputs from the process:

Fig 9.10 Example of Supplier-related Performance Measure Records Sheet

Measure	**Sales forecast accuracy**
Purpose	To determine the accuracy of the system forecast versus the actual sales
Relates to	The need of the supplier to have an accurate demand forecast
Target	To achieve a sales forecast accuracy of 90% on the top 80% of products
Formula	Actual sales by stock unit divided by forecasted sales by stock unit expressed as a percentage
Frequency	Measured weekly
Who Measures	Demand forecaster
Source of data	The data is collected from online supply planning system and actual sales from company transactional system
Who acts on the data (owner)	Regional supply chain manager and demand forecaster
What do they do	Creates action plans to improve forecast accuracy
Notes/comments	

Suppliers are more important than they are given credit for. While that may be an appalling pun, we hope the point has been made about suppliers' relevance to achieving corporate success in a broad spectrum of industries. Most other performance management frameworks probably aren't going to help you much in this area – the Performance Prism asks the important questions not only about what the organization wants and needs from its suppliers (the usually predominant element of the relationship), but also what suppliers want and need from the organization. Managing relationships with suppliers, and more elaborate arrangements with alliance partners, demands the selection of relevant measures so that performance can be tracked, data analyzed, insights gained and management actions taken to initiate improvements.

Illustrative Supplier and Partner-centred Measures

This checklist is not intended to be comprehensive, just indicative. There will inevitably be variability between industries and also the relative maturity of companies (and their subsidiaries). The category within which each measure is represented may vary too. Some of the measures that firms typically adopt are:

Supplier/Alliance Partner Satisfaction Measures

What do our suppliers / partners want and need?

- Supplier/Alliance partner satisfaction level
- Average spend per supplier trend (by spend category)
- Average supplier retention (length of service)
- Percentage of value purchased through single-source supplier arrangements
- Percentage of suppliers to whom demand visibility provided
- Level of demand forecast accuracy
- Level of specification changes
- Level of supplier payments overdue
- Level of supplier billing errors (e.g. day purchases outstanding)
- Impact of currency exchange rate movements and other cost base changes not within control

Supplier/Alliance Partner Contribution Measures

What do we want and need from our suppliers / partners?

- Alliance Partner contribution to revenues / contribution to cost savings
- Level of complaints about supplier performance
- Level of product quality non-conformances
- Level of late deliveries (to promise / to request)
- Level of after-sales product/service problems
- Level of customer warranty / liability claims attributed to supplier failures
- Level of supplier-generated improvement suggestions contributed / implemented
- Perceived value-for-money of supplier contribution

Supplier/Alliance Partner-related Strategy Measures

What are our strategies for satisfying these sets of wants and needs?

- Progress towards purchasing strategies
- Progress towards joint venture objectives
- Total acquisition cost of purchases vs. plan
- Trend in percentage of cash outflows outsourced

Supplier/Alliance Partner-related Process Measures

Which of our internal business processes will effectively and efficiently deliver them?

- Number of suppliers
- Purchase value by spend category
- Percentage spend with accredited suppliers
- Supplier audits completed vs. plan
- Number of supplier invoices processed
- Number of alliance partner disputes outstanding
- Number of alliance partner decision pass-ups
- Purchasing function productivity benchmarks (e.g. comparative spend, or number of suppliers, per buyer)

Supplier/Alliance Partner-related Capability Measures

Which particular capabilities do we need to establish and maintain in order to execute them?

- Value of discounts negotiated
- Level of inventory in supply chain (by category)
- Level and impact of stock-outs
- Level of supplier financial stability (each critical supplier)
- Percentage spend via internet exchange(s)
- Post-merger integration purchase cost savings
- Accounts payable cost

Summary

Who typically are this group of stakeholders?

Suppliers of goods and services, alliance and joint venture partners

What do suppliers/alliance partners typically want and need from your organization?

- *Profit* – reasonable margins (to reinvest in improved products and services)
- *Growth* – increase in sales volumes over time
- *Opinion* – feedback on performance and suggestions as to ways of improving products and services
- *Trust* – access to key information in order to aid supply chain efficiencies and to establish longer-term collaborative ventures

What does your organization typically want and need from its suppliers?

- *Fast* – rapid and reliable delivery of products and services offered
- *Right* – high quality products and services
- *Cheap* – reasonably priced products and services (that offer value for money)
- *Easy* – low-hassle transactions (easy to do business with)

What does your organization typically want and need from its alliance partners?

- *Skills* – access to specialist skill-sets and expertise not easily recruited internally
- *Technologies* – access to leading product, process or information technologies
- *Networks* – access to customers via successful sales networks (contacts, mailing lists, websites, etc.)
- *Channels* – access to vital large-scale distribution channels too costly to replicate

What strategies typically address these wants and needs?

- *Improve supplier performance* – quality, delivery, service
- *Optimize procurement costs* – total acquisition costs
- *Establish alliance or joint venture partnerships* – integrating shared interests
- *Accomplish desired outcome objectives* – achieving the intended benefits

Which processes typically relate to the execution of these strategies?

- Establish supplier service level agreements
- Monitor quality/service delivery
- Track total acquisition costs
- Share forecast and demand data
- Agree joint venture rules, boundaries and mechanisms
- Measure progress and achievements

Which capabilities typically need to be developed and nurtured?

- Supplier accreditation and auditing
- Vendor managed inventories
- Internet exchange purchasing
- Self-billing payment system
- Buyer negotiation skills
- Data interchange/collaborative planning systems
- Accounts payable practices
- Non-core activity outsourcing
- JV governance, organization and processes integration
- JV conflicts of interest resolution
- Procurement post-merger integration benefits realization
- Purchasing function efficiency and effectiveness benchmarking

10 Managing Regulator and Community Relationships with Measures

You learn it on the first day of your first economics class: Smart businesspersons seek monopolies. Because as Willie Sutton said about banks, that's where the money is. (Which is why smart governments try to keep smart businesspersons from achieving monopolies.)

Tom Peters • *in his book 'Liberation Management'.*

As we have noted earlier, apart from the Performance Prism, there is nothing in any other commonly used measurement framework we have come across that directly addresses satisfying regulatory requirements. It is clearly a significant strategic business issue, so surely any valid measurement framework needs to address this factor? All organizations are subject to regulatory requirements, although some will clearly tend to apply more to larger companies. So, here is a major stakeholder that can have a significant impact on business success, but around which there is generally no representation in any other popular measurement framework that is likely to help us to address the pertinent issues. Given the prevalence of regulatory influence and its increasingly strategic implications, that really is a substantial and extraordinary anomaly.

Yes, we would acknowledge that the EFQM's Business Excellence Model does contain a 'society results' box as one of its nine elements – which it says, 'relates to the organization's performance as a responsible citizen, its involvement in the community in which it operates, and any recognition it might have received.' While this is obviously an improvement on the balanced scorecard, which goes nowhere near the subject, this element sounds similar to some aspects of regulatory concerns but it is not quite the same thing – and is hardly explicit.

That apart, we have found in practice that the essentially more explicit language of 'regulators and communities' is better accepted by most business people than the fundamentally looser concept of 'society'. This may be playing at semantics to a degree, but there is the important aspect of gaining acceptance for the principles involved with hard-nosed business executives who want to know 'how this stuff impacts the bottom line'.

The Components of Achieving Regulator/ Community Satisfaction and Contribution

Regulators are taking an increasingly important role in business today. They have significantly more powers to control how corporations and their executives behave. Why so? Corporations have shown an apparently increasing preponderance towards abusing their powers by behaving in ways that flout broader considerations beyond those of their shareholders and their own short-term executive rewards. A growing number of cases, which have resulted in fines and even custodial sentences for executives, have highlighted a problem which has been largely 'swept under the carpet' for too long – negligence, misrepresentation, connivance, denial of responsibility and inordinate greed are just some of the corporate sins that have been exposed (see Chapter 4). If corporate executives don't take note of this movement, they are not only deluding themselves, they are also gambling with their company's hard-won reputation.

A further reason for the increase in regulatory activity is the worldwide trend towards privatising formerly government owned utilities and other assets. Governments no longer want the burden of managing these businesses but need to maintain some degree of control over their former monopolies. Hence the formation of specific regulatory bodies that monitor consumer complaints and police monopolistic abuses using a combination of performance measures and pricing constraints.

Beyond regulatory compliance, corporations increasingly need to consider the impact of their behaviour on the broader community. Communities are tending to take a greater interest in the impact that corporations have on them and many are seeking to impose new laws to protect their interests. If corporations, in the interests of serving their shareholders, simply milk the handouts that communities offer in order to attract them, but then proceed to put nothing back into the community by, for example, avoiding the payment of local taxes, then they should not really be surprised if there is a backlash. Other, perhaps more serious, abuses involve polluting the local environment with hazardous chemicals, obnoxious odours, noise, traffic and visual obscenities. When large-scale employee redundancies occur too, these can have a highly adverse effect on local communities and many think that corporations should bear the responsibility of finding alternative employment for the people that they have disenfranchised.

The actions of pressure groups have lately received considerable publicity in both the business and general press. While some executives initially buried their heads in the sand, the persistence and communicating ability of these non-governmental organizations that keep watch over perceived corporate abuses has surprised many. Again, the corporation's reputation may be at stake. As we have also noted in Chapter 4, several companies have underestimated the power of this movement to their cost. The issues they raise are consequently receiving increased executive attention. Those executives then often need more factual information in order to enter into a dialogue with these groups.

The overriding message seems to be that it is fine to make profits for your investors but not at any price. It has to be done in an honest, fair and sustainable way.

While there are some overlaps, the wants and needs of regulators and communities, and what the organization wants and needs from them, are not homogeneous. We shall address the priorities of each separately here.

Regulator Satisfaction

What are the things that regulators want and need from organizations? We think that this can be encapsulated in shorthand again using just four short words: *legal*, *fair*, *safe* and *true*. This means that regulatory bodies exist essentially in order to police the activities or organizations so that they conform to the laws of the lands in which they reside and other generally accepted codes of practice; they do not abuse principles of fair competition or fair treatment; they do not expose their customers, their employees or the local communities in which they operate to undue health and safety risks; and they report information that truly reflects their actual activities and resources. By expanding on these four words we shall be able to get a good idea of regulatory wants and needs and, therefore, the kinds of measures that need to be applied in order to satisfy these requirements.

Legal

Senior executives have a governance responsibility to ensure that their organizations comply with the legal requirements not only of the country in which they are registered but also those of the countries, regions and districts in which they operate. Given the trend towards 'globalization', this becomes an increasingly complex task and onerous responsibility as corporations expand their reach. Corporate headquarters' personnel will typically be familiar with the laws that apply in their homeland, but may not be fully aware of local constraints (or the lack of them) in far-flung parts of their business. Therefore they must be confident – and have a responsibility to ensure – that the executives who run their operations abroad are aware of the nuances of local requirements (even more especially if these executives were not recruited locally). For example, employment and data protection laws can be significantly different in different countries. In general, some kind of compliance auditing system may be required according to the level of potential risk involved.

Fair

Companies, and particularly companies with a large market share in a particular geographical domain, must also operate in a way that retains fair competition. In other words, dominant companies cannot employ practices that actively pursue exclusion of competition. For example, mergers and acquisitions offer companies the opportunity to control certain markets in particular countries. Regulators take a view as to whether sufficient competition will exist after the deal or arrangement is completed in order to protect consumer/customer interests. Companies may very well need to 'take the temperature of the water' with the relevant regulatory bodies before jumping in. Regulators may also investigate a company's particular pricing and supply chain practices as a result of complaints from competitors or consumer/customer associations. Companies – particularly dominant ones – need to be vigilant to ensure that they do not over-step the mark of what constitutes fair competition throughout their operating subsidiaries and divisions. As we have seen, the penalties and the implied costs of delays in implementing their strategies can be highly significant. Furthermore, in many countries today, companies need to comply with regulations relating to the equality of treatment relating to gender, race, creed and physical disabilities. Investors too are now protected in some countries through fair disclosure regulations.

Safe

Companies must ensure that their employees work in safe environments and that the products and services they provide do not jeopardize the safety of customers and intermediaries. They must also, for example, protect the communities in which they operate from pollutants. Implementing practices that comply with these regulations will largely be the responsibility of local managers at individual sites but under the direction of corporate policies. The scope of complying with this requirement may vary from industry to industry of course, however, the importance of complying with it remains constant. All companies and operating sites need to have auditing systems that regularly and frequently monitor health, safety and environmental risks.

True

Companies must do what they say that they do, and they must provide products and services that do what they say they will do as well. For example, their financial statements must not be misleading. At an operational level, quality manuals and procedures must reflect what is actually done – and not what management may think is, or should be, done – if compliance with quality accreditation standards is to be maintained. This type of regulation also accounts for the vast amounts of small print to be found in contractual agreements and marketing materials, which are supposed to define and clarify what is included, and what is not, but which invariably only serve to confuse us even more. In most countries, advertising is strictly regulated not only to ensure that certain moral standards are upheld but to prevent false claims being made about products or services too. Not all 'truth-related regulations' are imposed on organizations by external regulators. For instance, some are imposed by customers as 'qualifiers' for doing business with them (such as the ISO 9000 international quality standard), or some companies may volunteer to have standards imposed upon them in order to enhance their image and reputation. Either way, independent compliance auditors will judge whether systems and practices are sufficient and whether policies and procedures are adhered to in accordance with written documents and manuals.

Regulator Contribution

Inevitably, the primary focus of corporate attention in relation to regulators must be in conforming to their multiple requirements. What companies want and need from their regulators is a much more difficult area and is certainly one which is usually more difficult to obtain. Nevertheless, particularly where new or amended regulations are to be developed and introduced, best practice leaders in a particular field can be highly influential in framing the content of regulatory requirements and ensuring that they are worded in a satisfactory way. However, the fundamental requirements of organizations from regulators are that their rules should be devised with good reason and that they should be crystal clear as to what the requirements are. Time spent clarifying, or even contesting, opaque rules is essentially money wasted.

A further and more practical want or need though might be the provision of sound advice on how to implement the rules. Regulators' employees, some of whom seem to be of a different species of human being, do have the virtue of getting to meet and see inside a number of different companies. They, therefore, often have contacts who have already implemented or are in the process of implementing the regulations they create and/or are responsible for monitoring. They may also form views on and have insights into the best way to go about doing whatever it is that has to be done. And so they can be a very useful advisory resource from an organization's perspective. It will normally be sensible for corporations to set aside appropriate budgets for all such regulatory contribution activities.

The Regulator Relationship model is summarized in Figure 10.1.

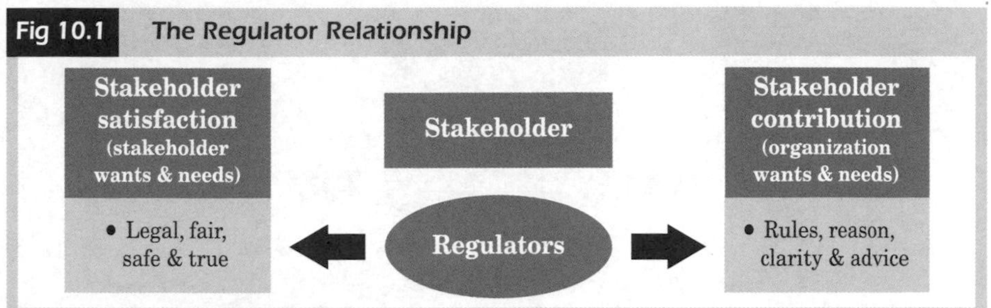

Community Satisfaction and Contribution

What do communities want and need from organizations? Our shorthand this time is: *jobs*, *fidelity*, *integrity and wealth*. This means that communities are dependent on organizations – and especially major corporations – to provide local employment; to remain loyal to the geographical region or site and preferably grow there too (not just close down as soon as the grant aid runs out or the first economic downturn comes along); to behave in a way which is open, honest, responsible and charitable; and, most of all, to help create sustainable wealth for the country, town or district in which the firm is located.

In return, what organizations want and need from the communities within which they reside and wish to prosper is in essence: *image*, *skills*, *services and support*. In other words, they want to have a good reputation through the local media and community word-of-mouth so that customers will want to buy from them, people will want to work for them, and suppliers will want to provide them with goods and services; they need availability of particular skill-sets appropriate to their business needs (as we have noted earlier, many companies today bemoan local skill shortages but do little to help alleviate it); likewise, they want local suppliers with the right capabilities to provide the services they need and they will require supplies of electricity, gas or oil, water and sewerage from the local utilities; and, lastly, they will seek the support of the local community to help them achieve whatever their vision for the region, country, district or site might be (which will necessarily be highly individual) – this may take the form of grants, subsidies, tax breaks, permissions, infrastructure development, and so on.

The Community Relationship model is summarized in Figure 10.2 (p. 326).

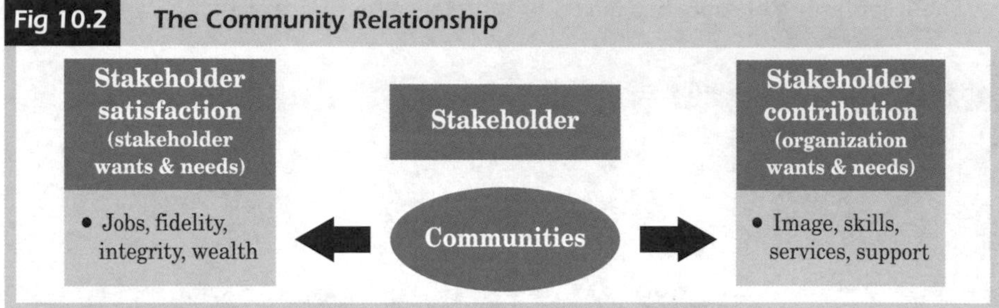

Fig 10.2 The Community Relationship

Strategies, Processes and Capabilities

Generic strategies, in this context, tend to advocate the requirement for regulatory compliance (the minimum); the desire for responsible care and the raising of standards; and the vision of how the geographic unit or specific site will develop and grow in the future.

Typically, the related business processes which apply will be, on the one hand, those that focus on developing and implementing policies; on managing compliance programmes; and on preparing for future regulation. And, on the other hand, there will be those that relate to establishing local community relations and planning future needs, especially in relation to infrastructure/resource requirements. Once again, these processes need to be supported by all the essential related capabilities that make the processes work towards delivering the organization's strategic intents in this area. Some examples of these are illustrated in the diagram shown in Figure 10.3.

Unlike most other stakeholders, regulators do (usually at least) specify – often in more detail than you would like – what it is that they want you to do. All you have to do is comply. Simple. Or not so simple? Usually it will be a good deal more difficult to implement because the right processes and capabilities need to be put in place to make it happen and to ensure that it continues to happen. They may also need to be deployed throughout the firm, or one or more of its organizational units.

It is generally a good idea to be 'ahead of the game' in anticipating the imposition of new regulatory requirements too, rather than struggling to keep up with them once they have been introduced. Otherwise, the firm's hard-won reputation is likely to be discredited in increasingly common non-compliance citations, which can lead to negative publicity, fines and even jail sentences. While the threat from communities only features the first of these three punishments, it is a risk that is enough to be taken very seriously. Good relations with

Fig 10.3 Mapping Regulator and Community Relationships through the Performance Prism Facets

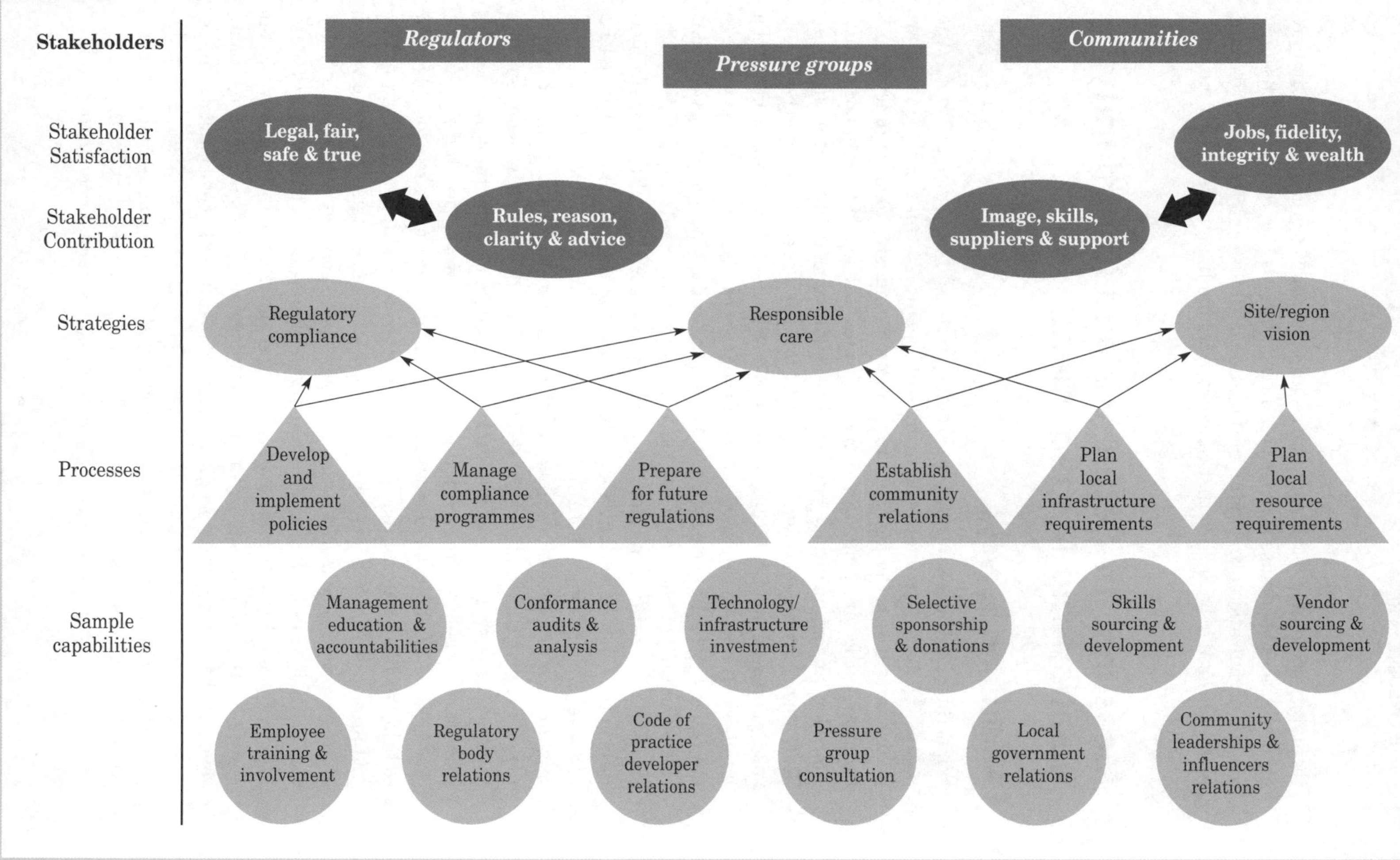

regulatory bodies and local communities are important to organizations, but are easily overlooked because of other pressures. To ensure that employees throughout the organization are mindful of their responsibilities in this area, relevant measures need to be applied that constantly remind them of its importance.

Measures for Regulator and Community Relationship Management

Audits and Surveys

What then are the essential measurement factors? The principal – but by no means the only – tools for measuring performance in this field are familiar: audits and surveys. Conformance to regulations, industry codes of practice and internal policies are commonly checked through the use of compliance audits. Indeed, many organizations have internal audit departments (often affectionately known as 'the Gestapo') that carry out such checks, while others rely solely on independent external auditors. Whichever is the case, the trend in the number of seriousness-graded non-conformances can be tracked to see whether managers have got to grips with implementing and maintaining practices that really work. Where new regulations, codes of practice or internal policies are in the process of being introduced, it may be necessary to monitor the effectiveness of the communications about these through internal surveys that check the level of awareness about their content. A further sensible measure then might be the proportion of employees that have received education and training on the particular topic in question. You might also ask them whether they thought these programmes were useful and clear, and whether they understand how it applies to the work that they do or the workplace that they use.

While the employees and suppliers of most organizations are probably used to being audited, it is not really a viable method for dealing with communities and pressure groups for example. The types of 'radar systems' we have talked about may need to be more subtle. Companies often conduct surveys of community attitudes to specific issues through research agencies that conduct these kinds of polls. Industry associations can sometimes help themselves, and spread the research costs too, by commissioning surveys about emerging public concerns that are pertinent to their members in different geographical regions.

Perceptions are important. It is easy to be dismissive of them, especially where insiders think they already know 'the truth', but they are – reality or not – what the world thinks the situation is. Today's 'spin society' is becoming increasingly cynical though. Scientists, who have much factual data about their field of expertise at their disposal, are particularly prone to dismissing public opinion as ill-informed. Yet, for example, a recent UK survey[62] has shown that the public no longer believes reassurances from government, the media or industry about the safety of new technologies. Almost half of over 1,000 people questioned (46 per cent) said that they thought government had something to hide when it offered reassurances about the safety of vaccines, mobile phones or genetically modified food. Only 40 per cent trusted product safety information from the mobile phone industry, and only 36 per cent believe what the food industry tells them about GM foods. Less surprisingly perhaps, only 22 per cent claim they believe what they hear or read in the media. More shocking though is the loss of respect for scientists. The fact is that only around a half (49 per cent) of those surveyed now trust the information that scientists provide.

Benchmarking

Benchmarking is popularly used to compare the performance of similar organizations. The UK's water industry, for example, is regulated by Ofwat (the Office of Water Services). When the Water Regulator and his team completed a price review in 1999 they decided to link the prices companies could charge to the level of service they delivered. They developed an Overall Performance Assessment (OPA) methodology that defined service in terms of four performance areas – water supply, customer service, sewerage service and environmental performance (see Figure 10.4, p. 330).[63] The individual companies were then ranked against these criteria and a league table produced. Those at the top of the table were allowed to increase their prices by 0.5 per cent. Those at the bottom were forced to reduce their prices by either 0.5 per cent or 1.0 per cent. The regulator and his team are now in the process of reviewing this methodology. They have no intention of scrapping the link between service levels and price. Instead, they are looking at the validity of the specific measures they have decided to use.

Other Performance Measures and Reports

Audits, surveys and benchmarks are all well and good, but are there not any more concrete indicators? Sometimes. Counting the level of positive and negative press mentions is one way of monitoring public perceptions about the firm, but relying on these alone would be ill-advised. By the time some adverse report hits the press, it is likely to be already too late to do much about the problem other than try to limit the damage. However, where applicable, it is perfectly possible to measure the total level of capital expenditure that has been invested in providing improved environmental standards. In manufactur-

Fig 10.4 The Overall Performance Assessment Methodology for the Water Companies

Performance dimension	Sub-measures
Water supply	Water pressure, interruptions to supply, hosepipe bans and drinking water quality.
Customer service	Written complaints, billing contacts, meter reading, telephone answering, telephone access, services to customers with special needs, meter options, supply pipe repairs, debt and disconnection policies, complaint handling, compensation, payment options and customer information.
Sewerage service	Sewer flooding incidents caused by hydraulic incapacity and risk of flooding.
Environmental impact	Leakage, bathing water quality, sewerage sludge disposal, sewerage treatment works, combined sewer outflows, pollution incidents and sea outfalls.

ing industries, the actual level of offending chemical emissions, effluent discharges, uncontrolled spills and other such incidents – and their trend – should be a known quantity too. On the community side, measures of the level of sponsorship and donations to various categories of local community efforts can be quantified quite easily also. And indeed, in each of these cases, it may well be advantageous for companies to make the figures publicly available through press releases in order to demonstrate their recognition of and commitment to the community as a stakeholder.

Some companies at the forefront of this movement even go to the trouble of producing separate detailed annual reports which are also externally audited. The UK's Co-operative Bank, for example, has published 'The Partnership Report' since 1998 and has its social responsibility effort independently audited. However, some have taken issue with what costs and savings are included in the category and the objectivity of the auditing (it claims in its latest report that 18 per cent of profit is 'reasonably' attributable to its ethical policies). Shell UK also first produced its Report to Society in 1998, which refers to 'the 'triple bottom line' of social, environmental and economical measurement' (see the box *Shell UK's Report to Society* for an extract from its chairman's statement).

Shell UK's Report to Society (1998) – The Chairman's Statement

'The Shell UK Report to Society is published at a time when society's demands of the business world have never been greater, and complements the recent publication of the Royal Dutch/Shell Group report, *Profits and Principles – Does There Have to be a Choice?* The Shell UK Report explains how principles and practices followed by Group companies worldwide are embedded in our daily operations.

'The days when individual companies were judged solely in terms of economic performance and wealth creation have long disappeared. Today, companies have far wider responsibilities to the community, to the environment and to improving the quality of life for all. We have a duty to innovate, to support research and development, and to apply new technology responsibly. We must respond openly, quickly and effectively to the diverse concerns of shareholders, customers and employees. In a free society, other stakeholder groups such as the media and pressure groups have legitimate and important roles to raise difficult questions and to debate seriously issues of genuine public concern. We acknowledge that the reputation of Shell UK can also be influenced by perceptions of the activities of other Shell companies around the world.

'Society's changing expectations are having a profound impact on the way in which we, and others, do business ... From ethical investments to rising demand for "green" products, from concern over employment conditions in the developing world to consumer boycotts, the evidence of a more committed public is all around us. The public demands from us the highest standards of ethical and environmental responsibility. They expect us to take a long-term interest in the economic and social well being of the wider community ...

'At Shell UK we do not believe that there is such a thing as a "black and white" issue. We have to face daily the practical challenge of juggling competing interests, of balancing conflicting demands, and of satisfying the needs of different stakeholder groups. This report reflects these social, environmental and economic realities.'

Source: Chris Fay, Chairman and Chief Executive, Shell UK Limited, May 1998.

And, fair play to Shell, it is prepared to admit that not everyone trusts its motives. Its 2000 report includes an abrasive e-mail sent to its Tell Shell website, which says: 'This is the most obvious Greenwash I have yet to see – well done Shell, you've sunk to new levels. It appears your PR agency have successfully managed to convince you that the bulk of the population are morons.' Which goes to show you can't please everyone by publishing measures of performance in this area, but it is a good idea to be open about it and to acknowledge diversity of opinions. So, you may well be damned if you do, but you risk being damned much more and much worse if you don't.

The practical need for measurement in order to identify problems and monitor improvement progress will be partially determined by the organizational scope of the regulation or requirement. For instance, compliance with fair disclosure regulations is normally in the hands of a very few executives. An organization-wide measurement system is, therefore, very unlikely to be needed, but perhaps non-executive directors might take greater interest in forming external communications policies in this area and monitoring their exception. On the other hand, equal opportunities and supplier management issues are clearly departmental in nature, but extend across the whole enterprise. Health and safety regulations though have a major impact and usually need to involve the whole organization. Every site and every department will probably need to be monitored or required to have effective self-monitoring processes in place.

An additional complication is that regulations can differ from region to region, from nation to nation, and from district to district. This can be a regulatory nightmare with little in the way of common standards. Indeed, the standards with which multinational companies are required to be compliant are almost infinitely variable at the local level and are, therefore, quite difficult to police from a corporate centre standpoint. Most large companies try to solve the problem by devising fundamental 'good practice' principles, leaving local management to interpret them and put them into effect within their local regulatory regimes. The problem then is that while head office is preaching principles and business ethics that may seem fine in New York, London, Geneva or Tokyo, they are likely to be perceived as being almost irrelevant to doing business in Bucharest, Jakarta, Lagos or Bogotá. Indeed, they could easily put the company's local business at a significant competitive disadvantage if it were to comply with these corporate edicts. But, as Shell has found (near Lagos, in fact), corporate behaviour and management practices enacted in some remote outpost of a corporation's empire can severely impact its reputation worldwide. The internet, and in fact most other media too, loves a story – especially a corporately embarrassing one.

Some leading multinational groups are trying to combat this problem through improving the training programmes they provide on the subject of corporate governance in different countries. Some of the practical problems are relatively obvious (and we have already contrasted typical corporate centres with their business units in remoter parts of the world). Yet the practical regulatory and governance problems of just managing subsidiaries in different European countries are not an insubstantial challenge (see the box *A Journey Through the Global – and Europe's – Corporate Maze*). We would recommend measuring the reception and impact of such training courses.

A Journey Through the Global – and Europe's – Corporate Maze

Reuters is doing its bit for corporate governance in a complicated world. The electronic information group, which has 245 subsidiary companies worldwide, is one of the UK's most proactive multinationals in training its directors to fulfil their responsibilities in different countries and territories around the globe.

In its European operations alone, Reuters directors work in 36 different legal jurisdictions. This means they not only have to know what is expected of them as company directors, as distinct from company managers, they also need to know their rights and duties within different and often conflicting legal environments. In response, the company has developed a specific training programme together with the Institute of Directors.

So far, Reuters has focused on training its directors in the "greater European area" (the European Union, central and eastern Europe, and the Middle East), but intends to spread the programme globally. Plans are in place to run similar executive training with local partners in Asia and North America. The requirements placed on directors in both these regions are different to what is required of them in Europe.

Source: Reported in *Financial Times* supplement, 30 March 2001.

While this may be one of the most difficult areas in which to determine the selection of appropriate measures, it is important that corporations do find the right solutions. It is a topic that is receiving increased attention today particularly through media exposure, because of both past and present abuses. While the media may have a short attention span, it also has the memory of an elephant. It never forgives or forgets, constantly referring back to past misdemeanours. It is, therefore, in companies' best interests to identify the right measures and put the associated management practices in place. The consequences of failing to do so are of course not inconsequential. Figures 10.5 and 10.6 illustrate some of the measures that organizations typically adopt.

Fig 10.5 Sample Measures for Managing Regulator Relationships

Typical measurement issues for satisfying regulator and organization wants and needs:

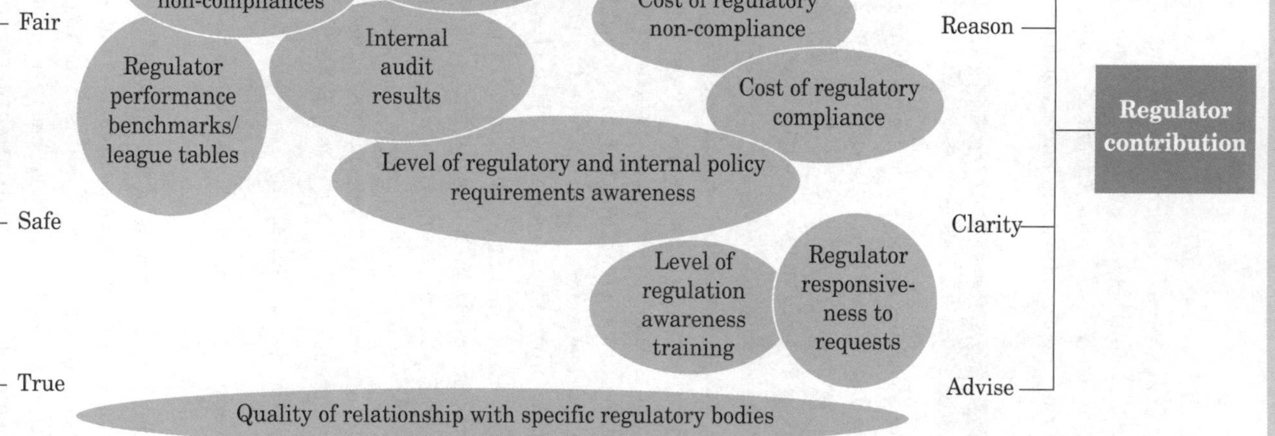

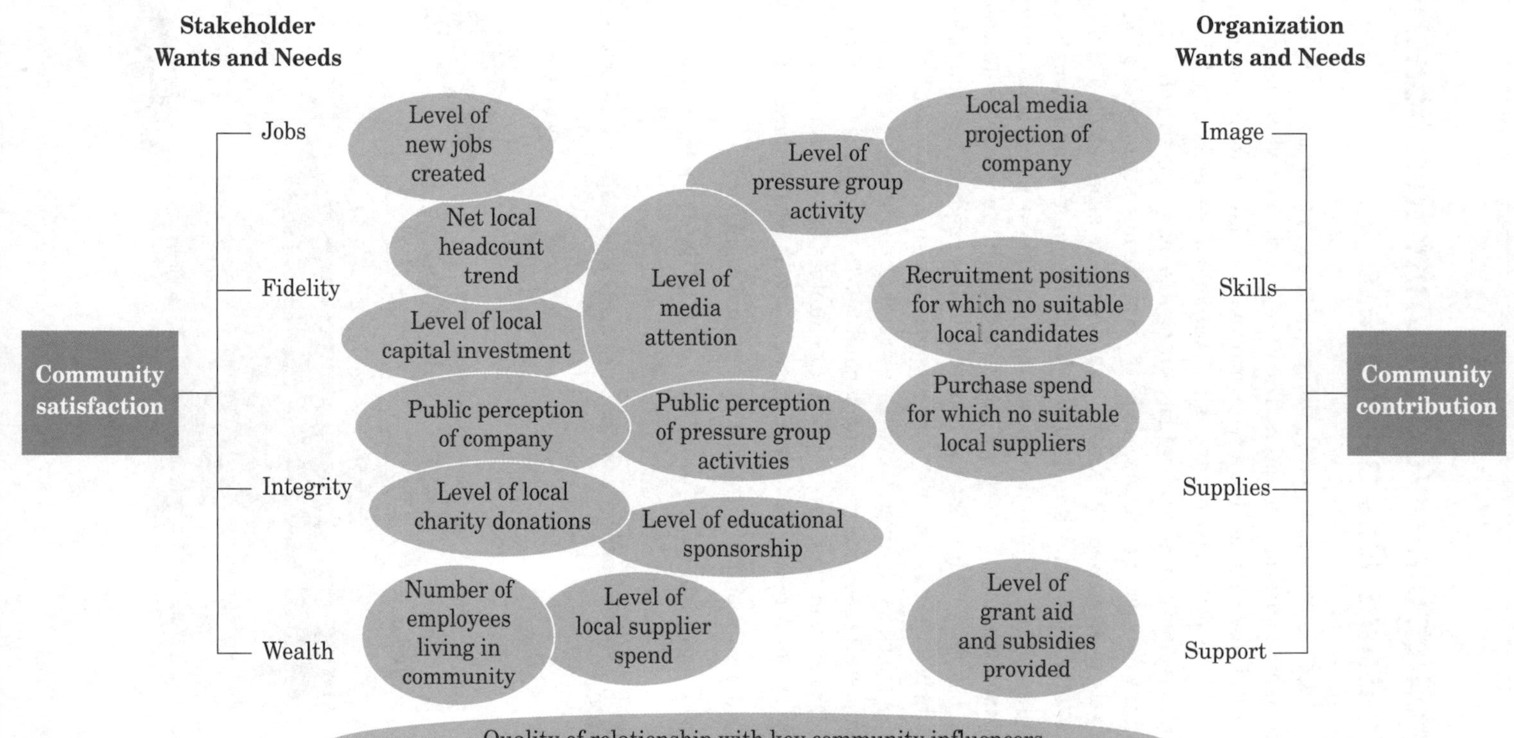

Fig 10.6 Sample Measures for Managing Community Relationships

The Regulator/Community Relationship Measures Design Process

This chapter advocates a slightly different approach to measures design than that applied in the previous chapters. The reason is obvious when you come to think about it. Those chapters have been principally about designing measures associated with creating opportunities, albeit with a few elements of risk included. This chapter is almost entirely about measuring and managing threats.

In the four prior chapters, we have recommended the use of a 'failure mode analysis' to ensure that the right measures have been selected and the critical risks have not been overlooked as a kind of validation and completeness test. In this chapter, potential risks are the primary area of focus, rather than a checkpoint, and therefore we suggest that the measures selection process should start by addressing the potential failure modes. Here the risks of failing to comply with regulations, to avoid disasters, to circumvent liabilities and to assess the risks of adverse publicity are paramount. Risk mitigation requires specific strategies, processes and capabilities to be in place (see Figure 10.7).

So, as a turnaround from previous chapters, let us first consider what the categories of threat – the failure modes – are. Typically, these might include:

- Failure to comply with existing external regulations.
- Failure to prepare for compliance with forthcoming regulations.

Fig 10.7 Performance Prism Unfolded Schematic: Regulators and Communities

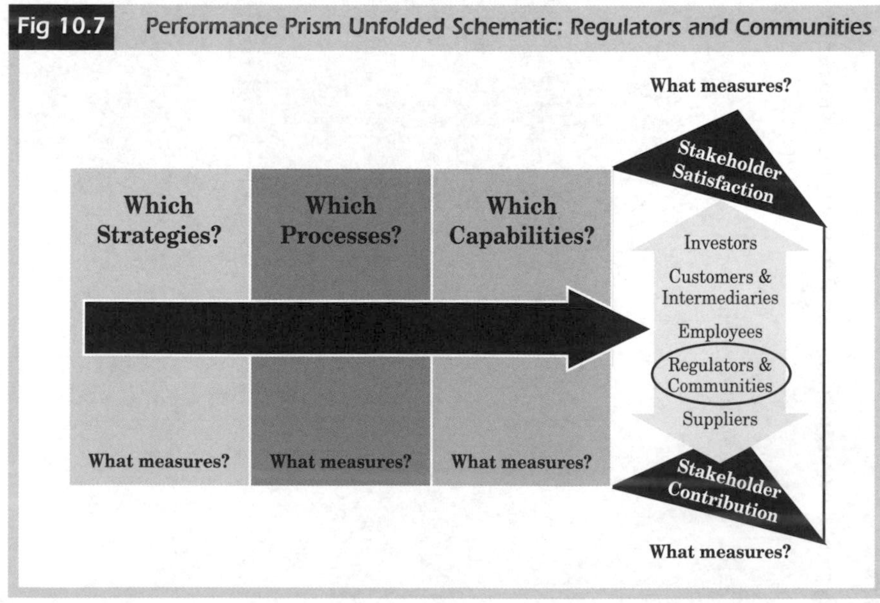

- Failure to comply with internal risk-related policies.
- Failure to improve compliance performance over time.
- Failure to maintain image and reputation.
- Failure to influence regulatory development.
- Failure to influence community/public opinion.

Failure mapping is a valid technique to apply in this case and, if we are considering the measures across the entire spectrum of a corporation (rather than an organizational unit within it), then it will be necessary to address each of the generic business processes and how they are exposed to regulatory compliance or other liability risks. The output from this process may be illustrated (in a somewhat simplified way) by the example shown in Figure 10.8 (p. 338).

This first output is likely to contain a relatively complex-looking 'vulnerability map' of where the organization is most exposed to threats. Whereas complexity is not necessarily the word that executives want to hear, it will not be an unhealthy thing if this process does expose the key elements of where their organization is vulnerable. It is extraordinary just how few firms bother to get a real understanding of this. Indeed, some of those that have done so have found that they are significantly underinsured.

Some would argue that a company, or even a business unit, can only manage a relatively small number of risks at any one time. This is much the same argument as that an organization can only manage a certain number of measures. It is also an equally futile – and in this case, frankly, irresponsible – argument. The secret once more is effective delegation of responsibilities and accountabilities together with very clear definition of policies. Clearly, senior executives have a responsibility to manage strategically important factors and drive appropriate actions. Other risks and their attendant performance measures may be delegated to lower levels of management, which senior executives may need to *oversee* and ensure that policies are being followed but not actually manage and control on a day-to-day basis. What matters is that the pertinent risks are identified; that appropriate measures are identified and selected to manage them; that the frequency of each measure is determined; that accountable measurement owners are identified; and that the agreed measures are reviewed at both an operating and a governance level.

To document the identification of risks and the measures selected in response to each of them, we would recommend that a table should be drawn up similar to the example illustrated in Figure 10.9 (p. 339).

Fig 10.8 Failure Mode Map for Regulatory and Internal Policy Non-compliance

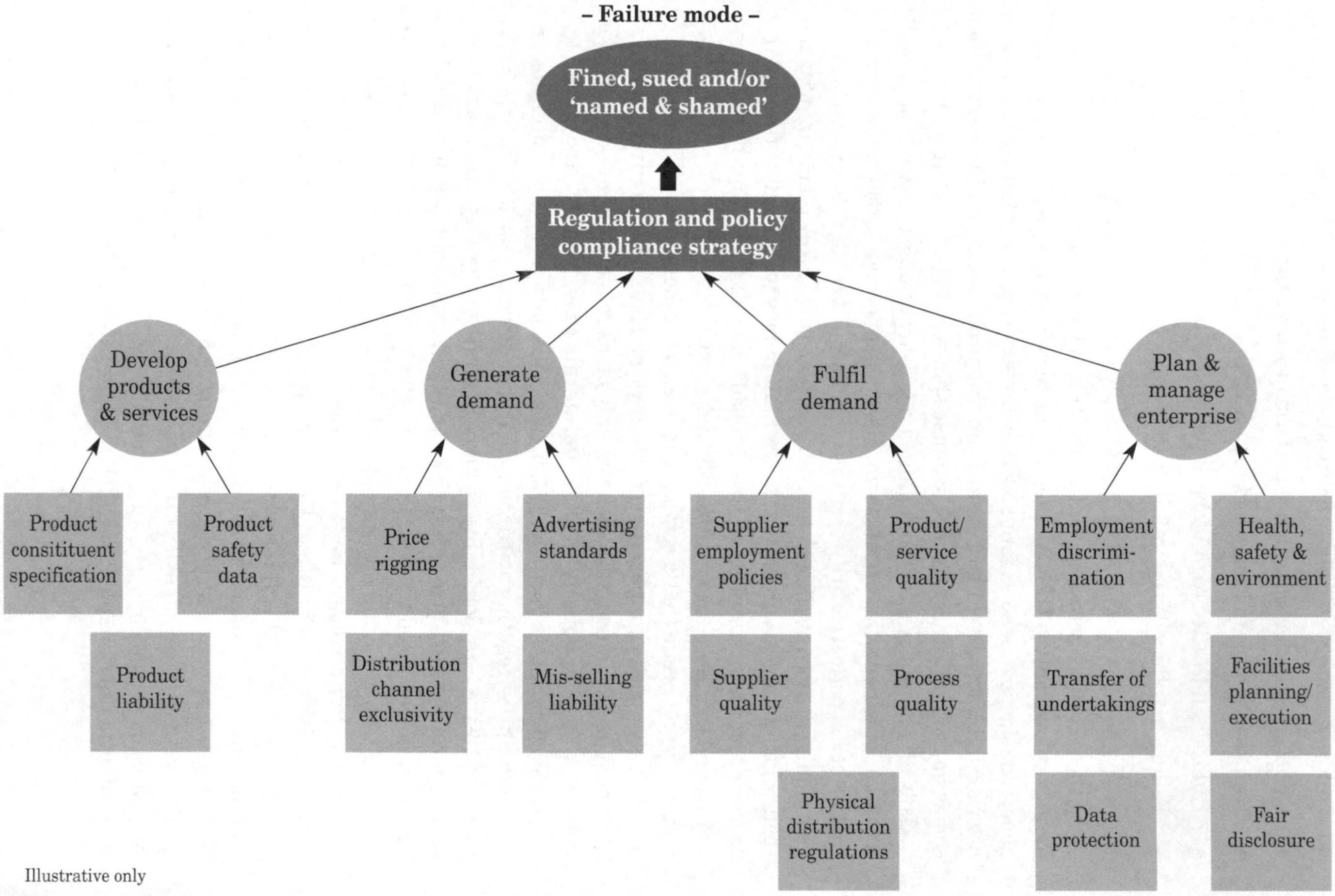

Illustrative only

Fig 10.9 Measuring Business Risks – Example

Stakeholder categories	Exposure category SWANs/OWANs	Likely consequences	Potential impacts	Hi-Med-Lo	Ownership	Performance measure
Regulators						
– Legal	Health & safety data sheets	Customers' employees at risk	Law suits/fines	H	Prod. Devel.	External/internal compliance audit results
– Fair	Environmental discharges	Local community at risk	Fines/reputation	H	Mfg./ Dist.	Volume of unplanned discharges by type
– Safe	Product contamination	Public health risks	Product recall/ adverse publicity	H	Mfg./ QC	Product quality tests Consumer complaints
– True	Restrictive distribution	Competitor complaints & regulatory investigation	Fines/reprimand	M	Mktg/ Sales	Internal compliance audit results
	Price-rigging cartels	Competitor complaints & regulatory investigation	Company/personal fines/jail sentence	M	Sales	Internal compliance audit results
	- etc -	- etc -	- etc -		- etc -	- etc -
Communities & pressure groups	Supplier employee abuses	Adverse publicity & potential boycotts	Reputation & loss of sales	H	Purch.	External/internal compliance audit results
– Image *– Skills*	Key skill shortages	Inability to satisfy demand	Loss of business	M	HR	Positions for which no suitable local candidates
– Suppliers *– Support*	Inadequate local supplier capabilities	Importation costs	Profit margin/ selling price	M	Purch.	Total acquisition costs of purchases for which no suitable local supplier
	Planning permission for expansion	Delay in plant build/ product launch	Loss of sales	H	Fac.	No. of planning committee members canvassed

In addition to these internal process-focused measures, it is likely that individual business units will also need measures to ensure that declared internal policies and practices are being enacted at the capability level – an example would be the percentage of compliance audits completed on time to plan. While this may seem bureaucratic, if it isn't measured will it get done? Once this measures selection activity has been completed, the measurement frequency, measures owners and the management review process (plus any other relevant details about the data, its source and its interpretation) can then be dealt with through completing the regular Performance Measure Record Sheet routine, which we have illustrated in earlier chapters.

Although organizations have been at risk for many centuries, arguably they have never been so at risk. Certainly, mainstream performance measurement remains an emerging theme in this area. However, simply waiting until there is a crisis and then patching it up after the damage is done is hardly a great way to mitigate risks through performance measures. It is not a viable option. While learning from the experience of some of the pioneers can be valuable, it is likely that most organizations will need to bite the bullet and do some pioneering of their own. Only they know where they are most vulnerable.

Illustrative Regulator and Community-centred measures

This checklist is not intended to be comprehensive, just indicative. There will inevitably be variability between industries and also the relative maturity of companies (and their subsidiaries). The category within which each measure is represented may vary too. Some of the measures that firms typically adopt are:

Regulator/Community Satisfaction Measures

What do our regulators and local communities want and need?

- Level of repeated regulatory non-compliances
- Regulatory performance benchmarks (e.g. published league tables)
- Level of support given to local communities
- Value of charitable donations made
- Level of pressure group activity

Regulator/Community Contribution Measures

What do we want and need from our regulators and local communities?

- No. existing/new regulations requiring compliance
- No. of existing regulation revisions
- Level of responsiveness to organization's requests for information / clarification / permission / advice
- Level of regulator improvement suggestions contributed / implemented

- Public perception of firm as an open, honest and responsible organization
- Public perception of community / pressure group concerns
- Level of local infrastructure investment made
- Level of new jobs created (directly / indirectly)
- Level of community improvement suggestions contributed / implemented
- Level of development grants provided
- Recruitment positions for which no suitable local candidates
- Purchase value for which no suitable local suppliers

Regulator/Community-related Strategy Measures

What are our strategies for satisfying these sets of wants and needs?

- Level of regulatory non-compliances by cause category (e.g. lack of knowledge, policies, owners, etc.)
- Level of internal policy non-compliances by cause category
- Cost and impact of regulatory non-compliances
- Cost and impact of internal policy non-compliances
- Progress towards site / region development vision

Regulator/Community-related Process Measures

Which of our internal business processes will effectively and efficiently deliver them?

- Level of new and existing regulation awareness
- Level of internal policies awareness
- Level of internal audits completed vs. plan
- Cost of individual regulation compliance (employee costs + bought costs + capital investment)

Regulator/Community-related Capability Measures

Which particular capabilities do we need to establish and maintain in order to execute them?

- Level of employee awareness education and compliance training provided
- Trends of internal policy compliance audit findings
- Quality of relationship with regulatory and other influential bodies
- Percentage of redundant employees found alternative employment [where applicable]

Summary

Who typically are this group of stakeholders?

International, national, local and industry-specific regulators. Local communities. Pressure groups.

What do regulators typically want and need from your organization?

- *Legal* – companies must comply with the laws of the legal jurisdiction in which they reside
- *Fair* – companies must not behave in ways that are monopolistic or anti-competitive
- *Safe* – companies must not allow their customers, employees or the local community to be endangered

- *True* – companies must say what they do and do what they say they do (and so must their products)

What do communities typically want and need from your organization?

- *Jobs* – communities need employment for the people who reside in the geographical area
- *Fidelity* – they want companies to sustain and preferably grow their employment with local people
- *Integrity* – they want companies to behave in an open, honest, responsible and charitable manner
- *Wealth* – they want firms to contribute towards making their community a healthy and prosperous one

What does your organization typically want and need from its regulators?

- *Rules* – companies want rules to be applied that ensure they will not be competitively disadvantaged
- *Reason* – companies want rules that have a sound purpose and which are reasonable to implement
- *Clarity* – companies want unambiguous rules that cannot be misconstrued by competitors/authorities
- *Advice* – companies want advice from regulators about implementing new and existing rules

What does your organization typically want and need from its communities?

- *Image* – companies want to have a strong and positive image within the communities they reside
- *Skills* – companies want availability of the specialist skill-sets they need within the local community
- *Suppliers* – companies want availability of local vendors with the particular capabilities they need
- *Support* – companies want the community in which they reside to be supportive of their aims

What strategies typically address these wants and needs?

- Regulatory compliance
- Responsible care
- Site/Region vision

Which processes typically relate to the execution of these strategies?

- Develop and implement policies
- Manage compliance programmes
- Prepare for future regulation
- Establish community relations
- Plan local infrastructure requirements
- Plan local resource requirements

Which capabilities typically need to be developed and nurtured?

- Management education and accountability
- Employee training and involvement
- Conformance audits and analysis
- Technology/Infrastructure investment
- Regulatory body relations
- Code of practice developer relations
- Pressure group consultation
- Local government relations
- Community leader and influencer relations
- Selective sponsorship and donations
- Skills sourcing and development
- Vendor sourcing and development

11 The Performance Prism in Practice

Effective management always means asking the right questions.

Robert Heller • *business writer and editor.*

Chapters 5 to 10 have described in detail the Performance Prism framework, majoring on the distinctions between stakeholder satisfaction and stakeholder contribution plus the vital role of strategies, processes and capabilities. Between them, these chapters have covered vast swathes of theory and practice, ranging from the drivers of shareholder value through to the detailed application of service level agreements. But how do we pull all of this material together? How can the Performance Prism be applied in practice? And what insights will this practical application provide?

Earlier in this book – in Chapter 3 – we argued that there are four fundamental processes that underlie the successful development and deployment of a performance measurement system:

- **Design**: select measures, define metrics.
- **Plan and Build**: develop systems and practices, communicate intentions.
- **Implement and Operate**: apply systems and practices, manage with measures.
- **Refresh**: refine application, review relevance.

Let us use the content provided by these four fundamental processes to explore how the Performance Prism was applied in DHL.[64]

The DHL Experience

DHL is one of the world's most successful international express courier companies. Founded by Adrian Dalsey, Larry Hillblom and Robert Lynn (D, H and L) in 1969, the business was originally set up as a door-to-door express service between San Francisco and Honolulu. Today, the company is reported to hold 34 per cent of the world's international express market and worldwide its 69,000 employees serve over one million customers in more than 220 countries and territories on a daily basis. Its UK subsidiary, DHL UK, began implementation of the Performance Prism in late 1999, when sales for the division were in excess of £300m and the business employed almost 4,000 people, across 50 locations.

Back in 1999, DHL UK's Managing Director, David Coles, and the company's Business Process Director, Drew Morris, had a concern that the division's performance reviews were in danger of becoming too tactical in orientation. The UK's executive team would meet on a monthly basis to review the division's performance. They would examine the UK operation in terms of its ability to achieve 'notional result', DHL's internal measure of profitability. They would also review the division's operational performance. One of the problems with the latter was that the number of definitions of operational performance was vast. For DHL, operations can be reviewed in terms of packages shipped (either by weight or number), packages delivered (on time, to the right destination, in one piece), packages collected (before a specified time or from a specified location), latest cut-off times, earliest delivery times, and so on. The volume and variety of transactions within DHL meant that the UK executive team could easily get engrossed into incredibly detailed reviews of the division's operational performance at their monthly meetings. While interesting in themselves, such detailed reviews might overlook the strategic content.

The UK executive clearly recognized this issue and began to question whether the structure and focus of their performance reviews was appropriate for their business. They began to ask themselves: How should we structure and co-ordinate performance reviews in a business of DHL's size and complexity in the 21st century? Far too often organizations seem to allow performance reviews to evolve haphazardly. Because specific measures are available, they are put on the agenda. When a particular problem occurs, a new performance measure is developed, implemented and added to the agenda. Fifteen years later that measure is still on the agenda, even though the original problem is lost in the mists of time and the root causes of it have long ago been eliminated.

So it was with DHL UK. The performance reviews had begun to lose their structure and purpose. They provoked interesting discussions among the executive team, but often the same discussion took place month after month. Parodying this, the Business Process Director commented how the performance review process would encourage him and his colleagues to bring massive spreadsheets to the meetings. They would be copied onto acetates and then individuals would apparently pick individual cells on the spreadsheet at random to talk about during their respective presentations. Often their opening statements would be prefaced with comments such as, 'Oh, look at this. This is interesting. It is up 15 per cent from last month.' The executive team would then spend 15 minutes debating why the number in cell C72 was up by 15 per cent, before the director concerned would spot another interesting number in another interesting cell on the spreadsheet and so provoke another highly therapeutic, but ultimately futile discussion.

The point was the performance reviews were losing their purpose and clarity. The executive team was getting so dragged into the minutiae of the data that they were in danger of losing sight of the big picture. Why so? It was not the fault of the people, as such. It was actually the fault of the process. The aims and objectives of the performance review process were not clearly articulated or widely understood. Without clear structure and purpose, the performance review had drifted and evolved into a process that simply encouraged the executive team to debate the minutiae.

Once the executive team recognized that the structure of their performance reviews was driving this behaviour, they began to explore how they could and should restructure them. They started by making them longer and less frequent, moving from a monthly one-day event, to a quarterly two-day performance review, which was explicitly described as strategic in orientation. Clearly, operational reviews still took place on a regular basis, but these were deliberately separated from the executive team's strategic reviews. In effect, the operational reviews became functional in nature with the quarterly performance review providing a forum for strategic debate. Next, the executive team began to consider how they should structure their quarterly performance reviews and what they should discuss. It was at this point that the Performance Prism framework was introduced to them as a way of thinking through this issue.

Applying the Performance Prism: The Design Process

During the design phase, the executive team at DHL UK participated in a series of workshops in which they explored their shared understanding of the organization's strategy and plans for the future. The first round of workshops were structured so that the executive team identified the wants and needs of their stakeholders (and their contribution to the business). The outputs from this first round of workshops were taken as the inputs to the second, where the executive team were asked to identify the strategies, processes and capabilities the organization would need to have in place in order to satisfy the wants and needs of each of its stakeholders.

Take, for example, customers as a stakeholder. As we described in Chapter 7, DHL had to begin by recognizing that the organization had several different kinds of customers. Broadly speaking, they categorized their customers into three separate segments – Advantage, Regular and Ad Hoc – based on customer needs. Specific strategies, processes and capabilities relevant to each of these customer segments were then identified, giving rise to the outline success map shown in Figure 11.1.

Fig 11.1 Extract from DHL UK Success Map

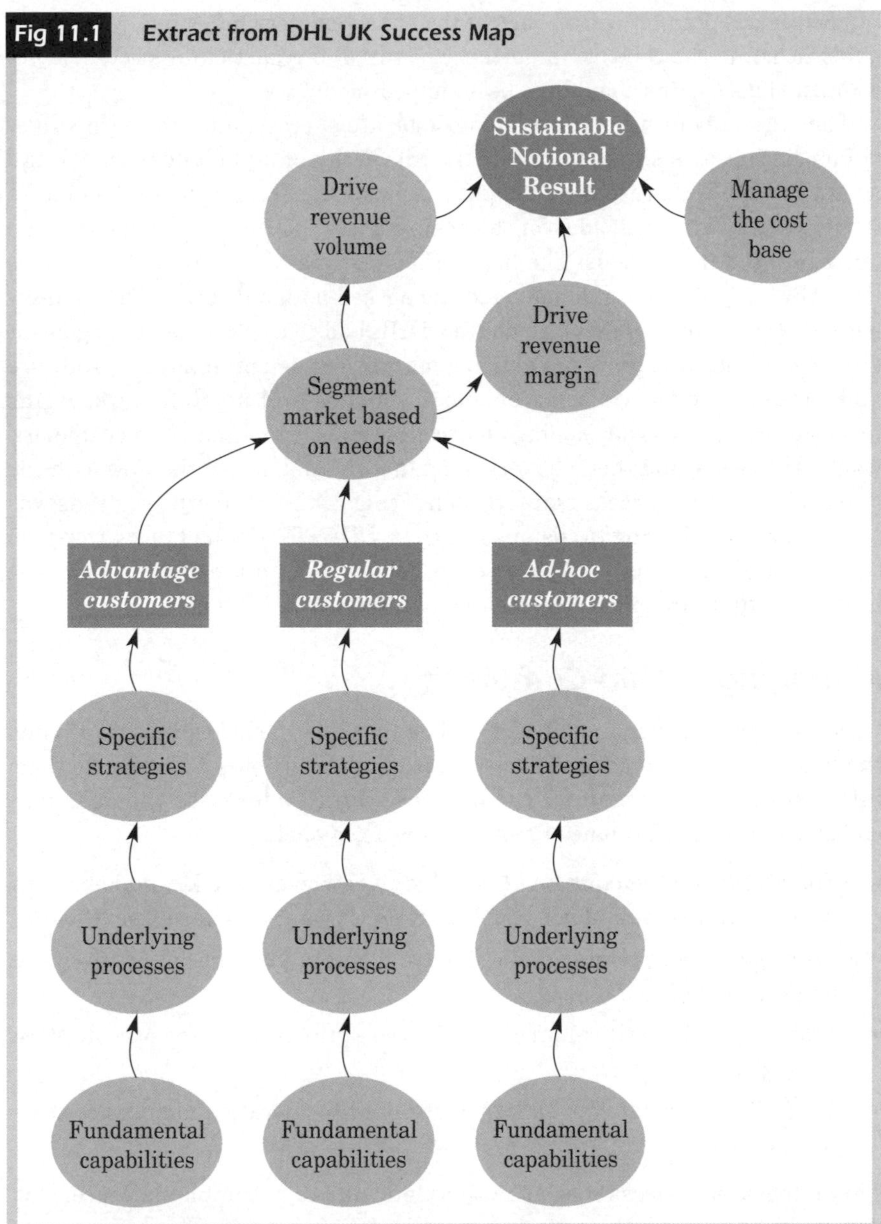

One of the most practical ways of developing the success map is to continue to iterate through this process of identifying the appropriate strategies, processes and capabilities for each stakeholder – and distinct stakeholder subsets, such as the customer segments described above – in turn. Clearly, there can be some repetition within each of the subset success maps but, provided it helps to define the relative importance of satisfying particular stakeholders' wants and needs, this should not be an impediment.

The other advantage of developing separate success maps for each stakeholder is that this starts to reveal the hierarchy of stakeholder wants and needs. In DHL UK's case, for example, it became apparent early in the process that a significant stakeholder for the business was the European regional head office, located in Brussels. The head office's primary requirement was that DHL UK hit its budget and delivered the agreed notional result (DHL's internal measure of profitability). To do this, DHL had to execute its strategies for growing business volumes, maximizing margins while optimizing expenditure and working capital. Growing business volumes and maximizing margins involved the business developing an excellent understanding of its customers' wants and needs, and then delivering against these – hence the link with the customer segment success maps. So delivering to the head offices' needs was not just about delivering to customer's needs. DHL UK also had to seek ways of continually improving its operating efficiency, by enhancing its business processes, often through the application of information technology.

Managing within Complexity

Once the separate success maps for each stakeholder have been developed and the links between them identified, then it is relatively easy to integrate them into a single success map for the business, which addresses the questions embodied in the Performance Prism framework, namely:

- *Stakeholder Satisfaction and Contribution* – who are the key stakeholders, what do they want and need, and what do we want and need from them?
- *Strategies* – what strategies do we have to put in place to satisfy these sets of wants and needs?
- *Processes* – what critical processes do we require if we are to execute these strategies?
- *Capabilities* – what capabilities do we need to operate and enhance these processes?

This integrated success map inevitably ends up as a complex picture. But, despite its complexity, the picture is meaningful to those who were involved in developing it and, perhaps even more importantly, the picture actually illustrates graphically the complexity of the business environment that the executives concerned have to cope with and operate within.

In DHL UK's case, the success map that the executive team developed had over 100 'bubbles' on it (see Figure 11.2). For the first time, it brought together

Fig 11.2 DHL UK Success Map (in detail) – *Illustrative Purposes Only*

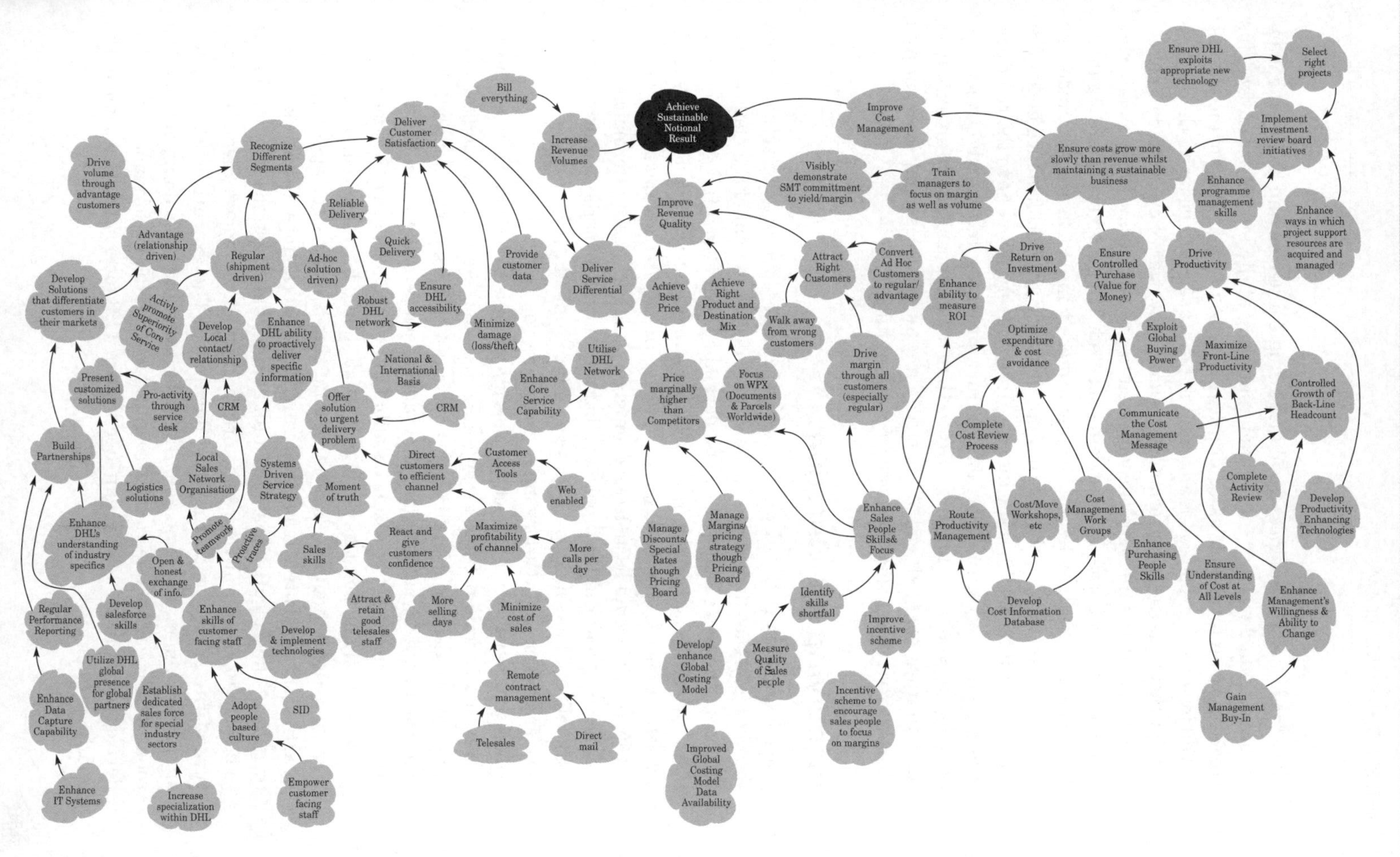

all of the issues the business faced into a single diagram and helped the management team develop a shared understanding of the business context. This proved to be an invaluable asset for progressing to the next stage of the process.

Obviously the executive team could not discuss *every* issue on the success map at their quarterly performance reviews. However, they wanted to understand whether the linkages encompassed in the business's success map were valid and, if so, whether it were being enacted. This is where many organizations go wrong, for they tend to leap immediately into measurement under the misguided assumption that, if they specify the right performance measures, then they will be able to track their progress. Surely, if you have the right performance measures, you'll be able to track progress; but which elements of progress do you want to track? Given that it is impossible for an executive team to track every strand of activity in a typical success map, how can you narrow down the strands to the most meaningful few?

Identifying the Questions

The trick used in DHL UK was to encourage the executive team to think about the questions that they wanted to be able to answer in light of the material contained on the success map they had developed. Fundamentally the executive team was being asked: *what is it that you as an executive team need to know in order to decide whether the business is moving in the direction you want it to?*

Clearly, this could be addressed simply by asking: what performance measures do you need? But the problem is that measures are merely a source of data. They tell you how many packages you have shipped. Or how many packages have arrived on time. Or how many customers you have lost. Or how many customers you have won. But each of these statements is narrow. As an executive in a business, I do not necessarily want to know the minutiae of how many packages we delivered on time. Or how many new customers we have won. I don't want data. I want information. I want answers to questions. The measures are merely a means of accessing data that allows me to answer questions.

So, the starting point has to be not what should be measured, but instead, what questions should we be asking? And this is exactly the approach taken by DHL UK's executive team. The third set of workshops, therefore, focused on getting the executive team to think about what questions they would like to be able to answer at their quarterly performance reviews, given the structure of the success map they had developed. The executive team spent a significant amount of time debating this issue and in so doing developed a robust framework of questions, structured around the Performance Prism, but derived from their success map. See Figure 11.3 for a sample of some of the questions identified.

Fig 11.3 A Sample of DHL's Questions

	Today ...	←	Tomorrow ...	→
Stakeholders	**Stakeholder satisfaction**	**Strategies**	**Processes**	**Capabilities**
External customers	What are our customers doing? What are our competitors doing?	Are we positioned well in the market? Is our revenue quality strategy working? Is our revenue volume strategy working? Is our customer relationship management strategy working?	Do we have the processes in place to support our revenue quality, revenue volume and customer relationship management strategies in the long term?	Do we have the money needed to sustain market leadership? Do we have the human resources to drive differentiation and segmentation? Do we have the right product offering? Do we have the information to manage these processes?
Internal customers (DHL network)	Are we delivering service against network expectations?	Is our network service strategy working?	Are the processes in place to support our network service strategy?	Do we have the capacity in place to satisfy forward network demand?
Brussels (Regional head office)	Are we going to deliver Notional Result target for the year? Will the shape of the Notional Result be in line with GCC expectations? Are we generating cash flow in line with targets?	Does the combination of cost, revenue, people & service strategies meet the long-term requirements of GCC in terms of Notional Result?	Are the processes we have in place supporting our cost management strategy? Are receivables in line to cover investments? Are we achieving ROI on our investment decisions?	Will we have the capabilities in place to: – Exploit technology? – Review & refine processes? – Continue to innovate and change?

Selecting the Measures

Once the right questions have been identified, it becomes relatively straightforward to think about what should be measured. Hence the fourth and final set of workshops for DHL UK focused on what measures are required, and thus what data is needed, to answer the questions identified by the executive team. These workshops involved the business's performance analysts, as well as members of the executive team. In DHL UK, each member of the executive team has one or more performance analysts reporting to him/her. The role of these analysts is to provide insights into business performance for the executive team – hence their engagement in the process of deciding what and how to measure at this early stage.

The selection and design of the measures followed the process described in Chapter 3. The Measures Design Template and the Ten Tests of a good measure, as described in that chapter, were also applied. The end result was a set of measures that mapped onto the specific questions that the executive team had identified. Figure 11.4 shows an extract from this. This maps appropriate measures against the questions identified under the heading 'External customers' in Figure 11.3. For commercial reasons, this is illustrative rather than comprehensive.

Applying the Performance Prism: The Plan and Build Process

Once the measures had been selected and defined, DHL entered the Plan and Build phase of the process. The organization was fortunate in that it already had in place much of the data capture infrastructure, so there was only a limited need to develop reporting capabilities (not always the case elsewhere). DHL did, however, invest a significant amount in education and process facilitation – and, with the benefit of hindsight, it is clear that this investment was fundamental to the success of the implementation programme.

The first investment DHL made was in the use of an external facilitator for the process, supported by an internal facilitator who was also the business's Improvement Programmes Manager. The external facilitator was a recognized expert in the field of performance measurement and brought with him the credibility to drive specific changes through. The internal facilitator played an invaluable support role and was able to keep the momentum behind the process and address any concerns that members of the senior management team might have, but not be willing to express in a public forum. These two facilitators, with the support of the Managing and Business Process Directors, plus the improvement programme manager's team, were able to shift the mindset of the executive team away from detailed operational reviews and

Fig 11.4 Measures Used to Answer Questions About External Customer in DHL UK

	Today ...	←	Tomorrow ...	→
Stakeholders	**Stakeholder satisfaction**	**Strategies**	**Processes**	**Capabilities**
External customers	How are our customers feeling and what are they doing? What are our competitors doing?	Are we positioned well in the market? Is our revenue quality strategy working?	Do we have the processes in place to support our long-term strategies (sustainability): 1. Revenue volume 2. Revenue quality 3. CRM (including customer interface)	Do we have the money needed to sustain market leadership? Do we have the human resources to drive differentiation? Do we have the right product offering? Do we have the information to manage these processes?
Key measures	Complaints / feedback	Customer research (satisfaction)		AP&P spend
	Loyalty/retention analysis	Market share	Pipeline Call rate	System availability – IT
	Market share	Customer mix Product mix Year-on-Year revenue volume growth	Sales account planning	

onto more strategic debates. The process was a subtle and, in fact, somewhat elongated one. But this is often the right approach, given that the process architects are effectively trying to enable an organizational culture change. Essentially, all the process involved was constant reinforcement of the key messages underpinning the Performance Prism framework. Focus on stakeholders. Align strategies, processes and capabilities. Ensure measures are used to answer questions, not simply as an end in themselves.

The Role of the Process Manager

We have mentioned the various enablers that encouraged this culture change – the Managing Director, the Business Process Director, the external facilitator, the internal facilitator and the performance analysts. One of these, the internal facilitator, deserves special mention because her role was crucial. In addition to acting as an internal facilitator, she also acted as performance manager. Not in the sense of taking responsibility for the business' performance, as this was definitively left to the senior management team. But, instead, in the sense of managing the performance management process, she would regularly call groups together to reflect on the process itself. She would always, at the end of each quarterly performance review, facilitate a discussion among the senior management team, asking them to reflect on what had worked well and what had not worked well during the performance review. And she was also influential in helping establish a community of performance analysts in the business that was encouraged to share thoughts and ideas.

Essentially, the internal facilitator was deliberately building into the performance review process the fourth fundamental process of successfully designing and deploying a performance measurement system that we identified in Chapter 3, namely the Refresh process. She was acting as a Performance Process Manager – a role that rarely exists in most organizations but, in our view, is fundamental to the success of most performance measurement initiatives.

The Role of the Performance Analyst

The second major investment that DHL UK made during the Plan and Build process was to enhance the skills of the business's performance analysts. DHL had deliberately – and, again, somewhat unusually – adopted a structure where each member of the senior team (effectively the UK board) had one or more performance analyst reporting to him/her.

One of the key roles of each of these performance analysts was to brief the board member, prior to the quarterly performance review, on the business issues that they felt needed to be raised (especially controversial ones) and to prepare any accompanying documentation for the board member. Clearly, if the structure of the quarterly performance reviews was to be modified in line with the Performance Prism framework, then this would have implications for the briefings prepared by the performance analysts. To prepare the analysts for this, a training course followed by discussion workshops was put in place. The aim of the training course was to explain to the performance analysts the latest thinking in business performance measurement and to set the Performance Prism in context with this. The follow-up discussion workshops were designed to reinforce the messages delivered during the training course and emphasise to the performance analysts a key analogy that we frequently use – that of the detective.

If a detective is investigating a crime or constructing a case, he/she does not rely on a single piece of data. Instead he/she gathers all of the available evidence and tries to piece together the story or sequence of events. So it should be with performance analysts. When the analysts in DHL are constructing a case they should pull together all of the available data and use it to present a coherent answer to a specific question. Only then will they enable the board to have the right level of discussion. As we have already mentioned, to facilitate this process, DHL deliberately established an analyst community. Not only did this provide a forum for analysts to meet and share ideas and best practices, but it also provided an opportunity for them to share their respective analyses prior to the board meeting and frequently allowed cross-functional issues to be identified and highlighted.

Applying the Performance Prism: The Implement and Operate Process

The two key investments made by DHL UK during the Plan and Build process proved to be fundamental during the Implement and Operate process. The starting point for the Implement and Operate process was to restructure the agenda for the business's quarterly performance reviews, so that the discussions that would take place would reflect the key questions that the executive team had decided they should be addressing.

The new structure was introduced during the June 2000 quarterly performance review and evolved over the next 12 months. The first morning of the June 2001 quarterly performance review agenda, for example, was structured as shown in the *QPR Agenda* box.

Note the similarity here with the original set of questions identified by the executive team, following their review of the success map. Some 12 months after the launch of the process, and following regular appraisals prompted by the performance manager, the executive team were still convinced that they were now focusing on the right questions during their quarterly performance reviews.

So what was the outcome for DHL? What do the members of the senior management team think of their new performance reporting and review process? What new insights has the process resulted in? And would DHL recommend this approach to others? We can't speak on behalf of DHL on this matter and some insights obviously must remain confidential; all we can do is report some of their views and experiences with the Performance Prism that they were willing to share with us.

QPR Agenda – 28/29 June 2001 – Visitors Suite, HLB

Day One

0900 **Setting the scene – top line NR results and forecast** **Financial Analyst**

GCC NR & Cost – Are we going to deliver NR target for the year?

0930 **Customers** **Commercial Overview**

– How are our customers feeling and what are they doing?
– What are our competitors doing?
– Are we positioned well in the market?
– Is our revenue quality strategy working?
– Is our revenue volume strategy working?
– Is the CRM strategy working?
– Do we have the processes to support our strategies for CRM?
– Do we have the £s to sustain market leadership?
– Do we have the HR resource to drive differentiation?
– Do we have the right product offering?
– Do we have the information to manage these processes?

1000 *Questions – Commercial Overview*

Tea/coffee

1025 **Customers** **Customer Interface**

– How are our customers feeling and what are they doing?

1055 *Questions – Customer Interface*

1105 **Customers** **Strategic Business Unit**

– What are our customers doing?
– Is our revenue quality strategy working?
– Is our revenue volume strategy working?
– Do we have the processes to support our long-term strategies?

1135 *Questions – SBU*

1145 **Customers** **Relationship Business Unit**

– What are our customers doing?
– Is our revenue quality strategy working?

– Is our revenue volume strategy working?
– Do we have the processes to support our long-term strategies?

1215 *Questions – RBU*

1225 **Customers** **Direct Business Unit**

– What are our customers doing?
– Is our revenue quality strategy working?
– Is our revenue volume strategy working?
– Do we have the processes to support our long-term strategies?

1255 *Questions – DBU*

1305 **Lunch**

1345 **Review of issues and resulting actions for Customers** **ALL**

Covering commercial and business units

The initial QPR, the first one in the new format, took place in June 2000. Following it, the HR director, the business process director and the managing director made the comments shown in the *June 2000 QPR* box.

June 2000 QPR

'The June QPR was the best board meeting I have ever attended, in this or any other company' – *DHL UK, HR Director*.

'We have moved *from* scrutinizing lots of numbers that told us very little *to* asking pertinent questions about how we are doing and where we are going.' – *DHL UK, Business Process Director*.

'This approach encourages us to work together on the key business issues rather than emphasizing individual functional responsibilities.' – *DHL UK, Managing Director*.

By June 2001, a year later, the business had evolved its QPR process much further. At this time, the managing director wrote to the performance analysts saying:

> Thank you for your excellent input to last week's QPR. The overall focused content and clear communication of issues contributed enormously to us spending quality time on key issues. Having established these, we are committed to following up through driving improvement on the top issues agreed.
>
> We thought our early QPR meetings were good, with your help we are practising what we are preaching in achieving continuous improvement in the QPR process itself.

Applying the Performance Prism: The Refresh Process

The process for DHL did not end with the implementation of the Performance Prism and the new quarterly performance review meeting structure. Instead, DHL have continued to evolve their measurement system and review processes throughout the last 18 months, and will continue to do so in the future. At the time of writing, they are in the process of cascading the performance review process down through the organization and have already reached the stage of all operations and sales managers structuring their local performance reviews in the same way.

During the course of such a journey, some significant lessons will have been learned. Key among these for DHL UK are:

- *The Role of the Board*
  The role of the board members in the performance review process has changed significantly, in the last 18 months. Now the business's performance analysts play a far greater role in the performance reviews than they ever did before. Instead of preparing material for board members to present, the performance analysts are expected to present their own analysis and effectively face a cross-examination from the board, which focuses on two issues:

  1. The quality and comprehensiveness of the analysis.
  2. The implications for the business and the actions that are required.

  Involving the performance analysts more fully in the process has been an extremely important development for DHL because it has enabled the board to act as a board, rather than individual functional directors acting as departmental representatives for their functions. For example, in the days when the director responsible for compliance had to do the presentation on 'How well are we meeting regulations?', he naturally tried to present data that showed his function in a good light. Now, the compliance director is simply another member of the board. Everyone in the business plays a role in ensuring that the business meets the regulator's requirements, so it is essential that the board understands the currant situation, based on an open and honest appraisal, and it jointly decides what the business has to do next.

Importantly too, DHL have recognized the power that this structure devolves to the performance analysts. Effectively, the analysts are the ones who are setting the agenda for the board's discussion because it is they who decide what to and what not to present, albeit with guidance. One additional safety check that DHL have built into the process is to define, for every key performance indicator, exception reporting targets. If performance ever falls below one of these targets, then the analyst has to raise it with the board. This ensures that the board is able to devolve appropriate responsibility to the performance analyst, without ceding control of the business-critical issues.

- *Focus on action, not measurement*

  In addition to more fully involving the performance analysts in the performance review process, DHL have also devoted significant effort in shifting the focus of performance reviews towards worrying about closing the performance gap, rather than justifying the current position. Far too often in organizations the debate around performance data centres on a justification of why the business is where it is. Why the business is where it is is an irrelevance (other than as a learning exercise). What really matters is what the business has to do now to get it to where it wants to be.

  To encourage this shift of emphasis, DHL have adopted new performance visualisations, such as the one shown in Figure 11.5 (p. 360), which explicitly puts more emphasis on action. Such visualizations encourage the board to decide what they are going to do, given the information they have received.

  Because this process is deemed to have been so successful at board level, the process – focusing on measures associated with the key questions, rather than on measures in isolation – is now being rolled out across the entire UK operation. Every branch, every region is being asked to establish their own version of the quarterly review process, addressing the same key questions for the business. During these reviews the focus is always on: what do we need to do differently in light of the new insights we have gained into how the business is performing?

Fig 11.5 Action Oriented Visualization

Strategy: Is our customer strategy working?

What are our customers doing?

Dec 2001 - QPR RBU
Service centre : CBG/IPW

ACTION

More SPD from active accounts

- SPD increase in Aug–Oct
- Oct +XX%
- Sept +XX%
- Aug +XX%

Balance Sheet Index (BSI) < XX%

- 3 months to Oct 01 BSI = XX%

Numbers of active accounts continue to increase:

- Numbers now approaching XX per month
- Oct = XX +XX% year on year
- Sept = XX +XX% year on year
- Aug = XX +XX% year on year

- *Prioritizing Actions*

  The third significant change that DHL have made to their performance review process is to be much more explicit about which of the potential actions they have identified will have the greatest pay-off. They conduct this analysis in a number of ways. First, they evaluate the impact of the proposed action on the customer through their HDIATC programme. HDIATC – How Does It Affect The Customer? – requires the board to consider the impact of each specific action they are proposing on DHL's customers. Second, they prioritize actions based on importance and required focus (see Figure 11.6). Third, they consider a variety of other issues, including:
  - Cause and effect.
  - Cost versus benefit.
  - Capability and resource.

Fig 11.6 Importance/Focus Prioritization Process

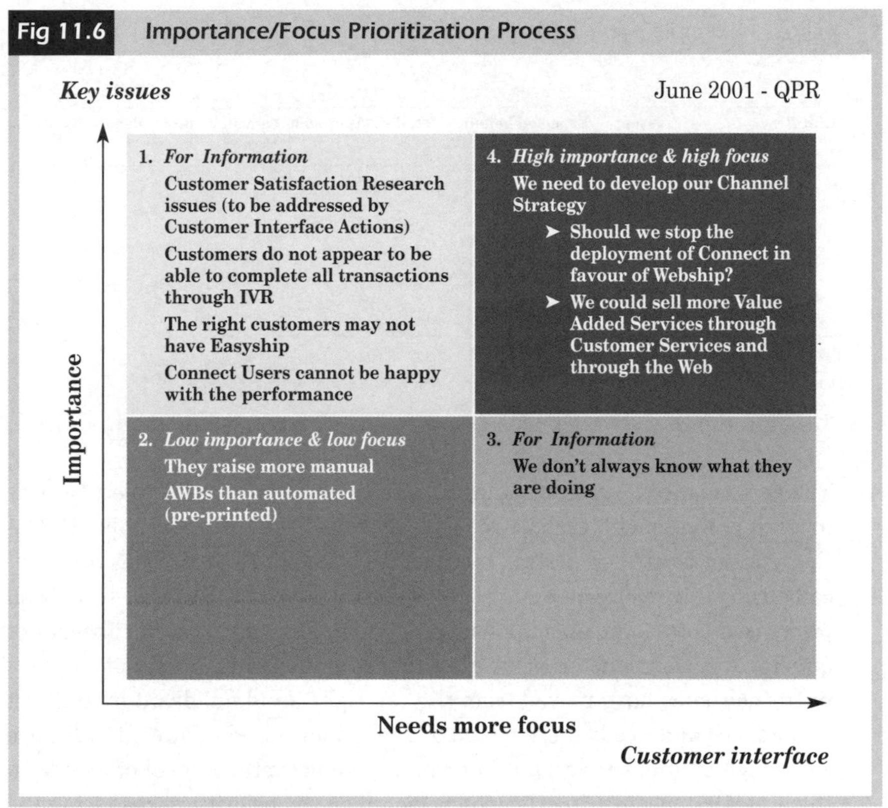

This approach allows the board to take input from the performance analysts which might, for example, enable them to 'understand how the business's customers are feeling' and to 'identify *why* the customers are feeling as they are'. The board then decides as a team what actions the business could take to address any concerns that the customers might have. Inevitably, the board is able to generate more suggestions and potential solutions than the business is able to impliment, so the HDIATC and importance/focus categorization process is one of the ways used to prioritize the initiatives.

- *Driving Accountability through the Issue Management Process*
  Once initiatives have been categorized they then enter the issue management process if they fall into the top right hand quadrant of Figure 11.6 (high on importance and needs more focus). For each of these initiatives, formal project records that track the issue, action and progress are developed (see Figure 11.7).

Fig 11.7 Example Issue Plan

Issue:				Sponsor:	
Brief	**Next steps**	**Expected benefit & target**	**Method/Approach/team make-up**	**Resp.**	**By**

Progress update

Date	Actions taken	Progress towards expected benefit

The performance processes manager and her team use these project records to track progress with each issue on an ongoing basis, using a simple RAG – Red, Amber, Green – reporting mechanism (see Figure 11.8). They are basically using this to ensure that progress is made on the issues that have been prioritized both on an ongoing basis and more formally at each subsequent quarterly performance review. This tracking mechanism is kept in place until the issues have moved from the top right hand quadrant of (high on importance and needs more focus) to the top left hand quadrant of Figure 11.6 (high on importance, but is receiving an acceptable level of focus). In this way, DHL is ensuring the loop is closed on the priority issues facing the business and creating very explicit individual accountability, not simply for delivery performance figures but for actually driving improvements in underlying performance.

- *The Analyst Community*

  We have already commented on how important the performance analysts were in the implementation process. Clearly, they had to start to think differently about how they analyzed and presented data, given the focus in the business on the key questions. More recently, the analysts have begun to form a community in their own right. They are now meeting prior to the board's quarterly performance reviews to screen each other's presentations and to look for overlaps and points of commonality.

  For example, if the answer to the question 'How are our employees feeling?' is negative, then this could have an impact on the quality of service delivered – and hence the answer to the question 'How are our customers feeling?'

Fig 11.8 Project Record Tracking Chart

Issue	Brief specified	Targets agreed	Timings agreed	Monitoring in place	Milestones reached	Review	Changes
Commercial							
Others (JW)						CRB	☺
Lead generation (JW)						CRB	😐
Lead management (JW)						CRB	😐
SRA Process (TH)						CRB	☺
SBU SRA management (JJ)						QPR	😐
TDD (JW)						QPR	😐
Operations							
Management tools in field (TS) – RF						CRB	☺
Review of central/local audit (RF) – TS						CRB	☺
People							
GPM; Flying Start (MB)						QPR	😐
Team Briefing (MB)						CRB	😐
Systems							
Data Centre Quality of Service (MC)						QPR	☺
Ops Systems Data Process (MC) – RF						CRB	☺

Far too often these links are not sought in organizations. Those responsible for reviewing the employee satisfaction data do so independently of those responsible for reviewing the customer satisfaction data, with the obvious result – namely, that the links between employee and customer satisfaction are not explored fully or robustly. In DHL, the meetings and discussions that the analyst community are having are rectifying this situation and ensuring that an integrated view of the organization's performance is presented to and discussed by the board.

DHL UK understands that it is involved in a journey of discovery. Naturally, its executives will not now let their performance measurements and management process stagnate. Instead, they will continue to evolve the practices they have adopted so that their effectiveness as management tools will be constantly enhanced. The role of the Performance Prism in this journey has been a vital one in that it has provided a logical and coherent structure for the board to shape their performance measurement and management system.

While DHL UK is by no means the only organization that has benefited from using the Performance Prism's principles to improve its measurement process and management practices (see Acknowledgments), it was among the first to do so. Consequently, we hope you agree that it has an interesting story to tell about its application, implementation and evolution. We are, therefore, extremely grateful to the DHL executive team for allowing us to co-operate with them and to summarize this practical case example in some detail here. As David Coles, managing director, says, 'We could have reached that same state of measurement maturity without the structure provided by the Performance Prism, but we would never have got there so fast or so completely.'

12 Getting Started on the Journey

Information may be accumulated in files, but it must be retrieved to be of use in decision-making.

Kenneth J. Arrow • *US Economist, 'The Limits of Organization'.*

We have described how the need for broader perspectives of performance measurement has advanced in the last decade or so. We have described how this new complexity is not effectively and efficiently satisfied in most organizations today, principally because of a lack of attention to the right facets of management – especially the organisation's stakeholders. We have also described too how this can lead to crises that can severely dent both corporate and executive reputations. We have described too how performance *management* needs to be addressed alongside performance *measurement*. We have described as well, in some detail, how our second-generation performance measurement and management framework can help to address the very real problems that organisations face. And lastly, we have described a case example of how the Performance Prism framework can be applied in practice. This final chapter tells, very briefly, what we think you should do next if this book has inspired you to improve the performance measurement and management systems within your own organization – an objective that we set in the preface to this book.

We suggest that the following ten steps should be considered:

1 Examine your existing performance measures and management systems. Use the four key questions we pose (see Figure 3.12, p. 77) as the basis of a diagnostic tool to evaluate them.

2 Think about the 'stakeholder web' (see Figure 4.1, p. 84) and consider whether your organization's performance measures and management systems sufficiently address all the key stakeholders and their essential wants and needs. And do they also sufficiently address the organization's wants and needs *from* its stakeholders? If you think there might be some holes in your stakeholder relationship management systems, there are a couple of associated techniques to help you evaluate the substance of the problem.

3 Use these 'success mapping' and 'failure mapping' techniques to help expose where there are weaknesses in your existing systems, especially in

relation to each stakeholder. Explore the application of these in terms of your organization's strategies, processes and capabilities, and how these respond to satisfying each stakeholder's wants and needs, i.e. applying the principles of, and the five key questions posed by, the Performance Prism framework (see Figure 5.1, p. 161).

4 Create a unique high-level business performance model that synthesises and links each of the key performance management elements (stakeholder satisfaction and contribution, strategies, processes and capabilities). This model should simplify the outputs of the mapping processes and provide an integrated diagram that you can readily explain to each and every employee within your organisation.

5 Now apply the maps and model, derived from the Performance Prism framework, as vital context for selecting the appropriate questions and, subsequently, the measures that you will use to manage your business (reference the DHL case, the sample measures illustrated in Chapters 6 to 10, and also the measures catalogue provided as an appendix to this book, as aids).

6 Define each measure in detail using the performance measure record sheet template (see Figure 3.2, p. 35) – including the purpose, formula, frequency, data source(s) and, vitally, who exactly will be the owner of each measure. And then apply the Ten Tests (see Figure 3.4, p. 45) to validate the suitability of each of the measures you have selected.

7 Identify which existing measures are surplus to requirements and might be eliminated, then confirm their obsolescence and remove them (if needs be, ritually exorcize them!).

8 To implement the new measures and measurement system, use the second and third elements of the Four Fundamental Processes model (see Figure 3.1, p. 33). This will ensure that, beyond measures design, the new systems are planned and built – including relevant visualizations of the data and, critically, communication with and training of affected staff. And then all plans must be implemented and systems operated.

9 Apply the Data to Decisions Cycle model (see Figure 3.10, p. 66) to optimize the benefits of overhauling your measures and measurement system. Effective analysis of data to gain 'cause-and-effect' insights, and the application of 'double-loop' learning to track the effects of decisions taken, helps to deliver best practice performance levels. Consistently applied, this will enable a sustainable competitive advantage, based on empirical knowledge capital, to be achieved.

10 Finally, applying the fourth element of the Four Fundamental Processes model, regularly review and refresh both the measures and the measurement systems. This will ensure that they remain relevant and useful to the

organization's ongoing management needs. Reflect on the barriers to and enablers of measures evolution (see Figure 3.11, p. 74). Wherever data analysis is conclusive, replace past assumptions with factual models. Consider too whether stakeholder wants and needs have changed significantly since they were last reviewed. In other words, return to steps one and two, and then begin the implementation of a continuous improvement process.

Figure 12.1 summarizes this 'to-do' list.

Fig 12.1 Ten Steps Towards Excellence in Managing With Measures

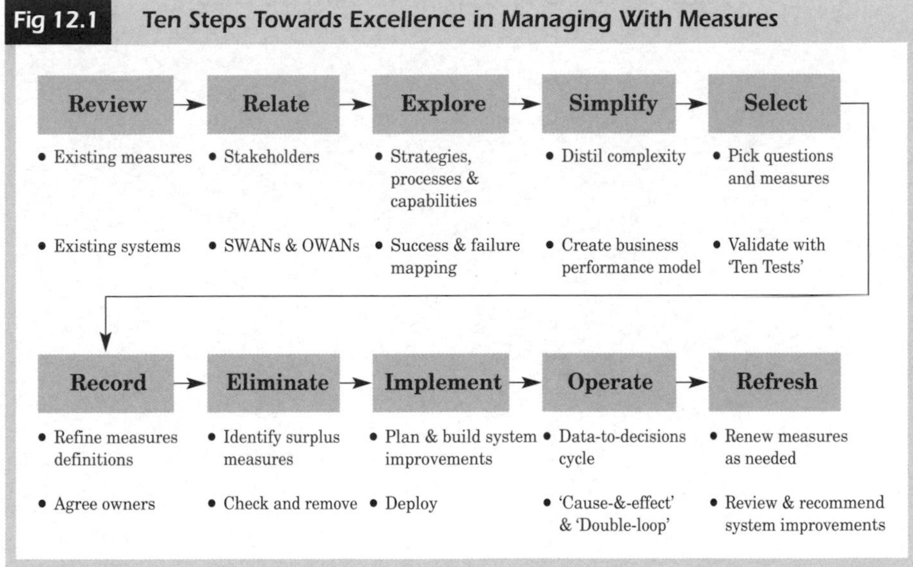

That may sound kind of easy and straightforward, but it certainly isn't likely to be so. Although it will require a lot of focus and support, and a sustained effort and dedication over time, it can be done – and, we would argue, *has* to be done. Managing With Measures is not the latest 'flavour-of-the-month' management initiative that will emerge and then evaporate into the mists of history; it is an enduring facet of business life. All organizations need performance measures and performance management systems which address the things that matter to their businesses at all times: good times and hard times. Clearly, the focus of attention towards specific measurements will vary over time, but the need to measure and manage the right things should not waver. The Performance Prism is the best tool and approach we know of to help get you to that position and keep you there. We wish you luck on this journey, for that is exactly what it is.

Bon chance and *bon voyage*.

APPENDIX

Performance Measurement & Management Self-Assessment Checklist

Twenty-five Pertinent Questions

Common problems with scorecard implementation	Very true	Partially true	Slightly true	Not applicable
1 Your organization doesn't have a balanced scorecard because its senior executives believe that the financial measures are all that matter; and that, after all, is what they get rewarded for …				
2 Your organization has an eclectic collection of measures which you call a "balanced scorecard" – but, in truth, it's a fairly random set (mostly data that is easy to collect rather than what is vital to managing the business) and many of the measures are really not complementary to the business's short- or long-term priorities …				
3 Your organization pays "lip-service" to using a balanced scorecard, but in reality it's no such thing. It's just the same old monthly financial report with a couple of other infrequently collected measures (such as the aggregated results of customer and employee surveys) tacked onto it – so this part of the report hardly ever gets reviewed …				
4 You've got a balanced scorecard (of sorts) that's been in place for some time – but you'd agree that the business environment you operate in has moved on quite a bit since you created it, and so you are not very confident that it really meets today's needs …				
5 The set of measures you use today was created before many of the management team were appointed to their current roles. You (and a few colleagues) feel pretty frustrated that you haven't had an opportunity to influence what you believe ought to be discussed at your regular performance review meetings …				

Common problems with scorecard implementation	Very true	Partially true	Slightly true	Not applicable
6 In your view, your organization's measures are almost entirely inward-looking – they address neither how your organization looks to the outside world nor how the outside world looks to your organization …				
7 You work in an enterprise where some of the key stakeholders that you need to take into account – because they are intrinsic to its success (such as employees, alliance partners and suppliers, or regulators, or a particular community group) – are not even mentioned in the performance reports that management review …				
8 Your strategic measures just monitor downstream outcomes and do not allow you to check how well your organization's strategy is being implemented …				
9 Your measures do not allow you to effectively communicate to employees how their efforts contribute to making the organization's strategy happen …				
10 Your measures do not allow you to challenge the assumptions inherent within the strategy (so that a constructive debate can be had – using the analyzed data – as to whether the right strategy is being implemented) …				
11 Your organization's measures and measurement system do not enable executives to effectively identify where there is a significant exposure to critical business risks …				

Common problems with scorecard implementation	Very true	Partially true	Slightly true	Not applicable
12 Your internal process measures are almost entirely departmental and fail to capture the key end-to-end cross-functional processes (such as, for example: order-to-cash or concept-to-launch) …				
13 The measures you have in place do not help you to both nurture and protect your organization's core/distinctive capabilities – those that give it a real competitive advantage (which are embodied in your people skill-sets, your business practices, your leading technologies, and your physical infrastructure) …				
14 The measures that your organization uses are almost entirely short-term in nature. Data are not used to help create medium- and longer-term plans for capability development and to monitor their implementation …				
15 Your organization is relatively good at measuring what matters at the aggregate level but, when it comes down to monitoring the progress and contribution of particular improvement programmes and projects, it falls apart …				
16 Other functions and departments within your organization (on which you are partially reliant) have measured objectives and targets which clearly conflict with the set of measured objectives and targets that you are accountable for …				
17 Your organization seems to measure just about everything that moves, and yet you still don't have the essential information you need to help you make the right decisions …				

Common problems with scorecard implementation	Very true	Partially true	Slightly true	Not applicable
18 The measures applied by your organization act predominantly as a "stick to beat people with' – there is little incentive, therefore, to co-operate with others to resolve and implement systemic solutions to problems …				
19 The measures your organization adopts as part of its executive or employee recognition and reward mechanisms (e.g. performance bonuses) often encourage dys-functional behaviours that are not in the best interests of the organization's other key stakeholders …				
20 The measures used by your organization are sometimes deliberately gamed by managers to produce "the right answer" (e.g. to hit budget or forecast figures, etc.), in order to avoid criticism, irrespective of whether doing so (probably not) is in the best interests of the organization or its principal stakeholders …				
21 The information you receive (that you need in order to manage) is so out of date by the time you get it that it is practically useless for tactical decision-making / action-taking purposes …				
22 You receive stacks of data, but therein lies the problem – it's just raw data. What you really want is applied analysis, trends, comparisons, performance against targets, and so on …				
23 Your organization is inundated with data, but you only use a tiny proportion of what is available. You simply don't have the capacity to have it analyzed and so draw the meaningful insights that you potentially could do …				

Common problems with scorecard implementation	Very true	Partially true	Slightly true	Not applicable
24 Even if you were to define the fundamental measures that you really need in order to manage the part of the business you are responsible for, the data capture systems you have in your organization are simply not sophisticated enough to collect and collate the essential information that you need …				
25 Your information systems are reliant on separate databases which do not allow efficient or effective cross-analysis of the data that is actually available in them (if only it could be tapped, you could achieve so much more) …				
TOTAL				

Note: High marks for 'Very True'; 'Partially True' answers should lead you to question whether the measurement systems and practices you have in place today – or are planning to implement – are really adequate.

Notes

Introduction

1. This is an alpha version of the measures catalogue. A revised, updated version is available from www.cranfield.ac.uk/som/cbp.

Chapter 1

1. Quoted in article 'Stakeholders Revolt' by Shari Caudron in *Business Finance* magazine, January 2001 (p. 57).

2. Vidal, J. 'McLibel Two Savour a Partial Victory as Appeal Court Cuts Damages', *Guardian*, UK, 1 April 1999; Vidal, J. and Bellos, A. 'David and Goliath 315 Day Libel Case Leaves Burger Giant Tainted', *Guardian*, UK, 20 June 1997.

3. *Financial Times*, 20 September 2000.

4. The 21st Century Annual Report, The Institute of Chartered Accountants in England and Wales, November 1998.

5. *Modern Company Law*, Department of Trade and Industry, UK. 2001.

6. Kaplan, R.S. and Norton, D.P. 'The Balanced Scorecard: The Measures That Drive Performance', *Harvard Business Review*, January–February 1992, 71–79.

Chapter 2

7. Economic Value Added (EVA) is a registered trademark of Stern Stewart.

8. Frigo, M.L. and Krumwiede, K.R. 'Balanced Scorecards: A Rising Trend in Strategic Performance Measurement', *Journal of Strategic Performance Measurement*, 3, 1, 1999, 42–44.

9. Downing, L. 'The Global Balanced Scorecard Community: A Special Report on Implementation Experiences from Scorecard Users Worldwide', BSC European Summit, Nice, May 2001.

10. Frigo, M.L. and Krumwiede, K.R. 'Balanced Scorecards: A Rising Trend in Strategic Performance Measurement', *Journal of Strategic Performance Measurement*, 3, 1, 1999, 42–44.

11. Anonymous. 'Managing Corporate Performance: Today and Tomorrow', PriceWaterhouseCoopers, 1999.

12. Anonymous. 'Managing Corporate Performance: Today and Tomorrow', PriceWaterhouseCoopers, 1999.

13. Hayes, R.H. and Abernathy, W.J. 'Managing Our Way to Economic Decline', *Harvard Business Review*, July 1980: 67–77.

14. Kaplan, R.S. 'Yesterday's Accounting Undermines Production', *Harvard Business Review*, 62, 1984,: 95–101.

15. Womack, J., Jones, D. and Roos, D. *The Machine That Changed The World*, Rawson Associates, New York, 1995.

16. With thanks to Mark Wade, Head of the Sustainable Development Group at Shell International Ltd.

17. Osterland, A. 'Knowledge Capital Scorecard: Treasures Revealed', CFO.com, *CFO Magazine*, 1 April 2001, based on work by Professor Baruch Lev of New York University.

18. Osterland, A. 'Knowledge Capital Scorecard: Treasures Revealed', CFO.com, *CFO Magazine*, 1 April 2001, based on work by Professor Baruch Lev of New York University.

19. And various other terms for practically the same thing, after Stern Stewart copyrighted this term and acronym.

Chapter 3

20. With thanks to Professor Bob Johnston of Warwick Business School; who provided the original inspiration for several of the items contained in this list.

21. Source: Accenture and Telewest Communications. Mock-up contains fictitious data.

22. Many of these insights have been adapted from Accenture's *Managing With Measures Implementation Guide* written by Chris Adams and Neil McTiffin.

23. Peter Senge – *The Fifth Discipline: The Art and Practice of the Learning Organization*. 1990.

24. Adapted from research carried out by Dr. Mike Kennerley at Cranfield School of Management's Centre for Business Performance with EPSRC funding and additional inputs provided by Chris Adams (then head of Accenture's 'Managing With Measures' development initiative).

Chapter 4

25. *Financial Times* 'Mastering Management' supplement, 16 October 2000.

26. Taylor, A. 'UK Water Companies Struggle in Wake of Regulator's Price Cuts', *Financial Times*, 17 April, 2000, p.3.

27. See, for example: *Cannibals with Forks: The Triple Bottom Line of 21st Century Business* by J. Elkington. Capstone Publishing, 1997, and *The Stakeholder Corporation: THE BODY SHOP Blueprint for Maximizing Stakeholder Value* by D. Wheeler and M. Sillanpää. Pitman Publishing, 1997.

28. 'Shareholders of the World: Sue!' by Geoffrey Colvin. *Fortune* 19 March 2001.

29. *Financial Times*, 10 January 2001.

30. 'When Capital Gets Antsy', *Business Week*, 20 September 1999.

31. *Sunday Times*, 7 January 2001.

32. *Sunday Times*, 4 February 2001.

33. *Milton Keynes Citizen*, 21 February 1999.

34. The term was coined in *Business Week* – 23 October 2000.

35. This improvement has not been sustained. ACSI data published in August 2001 shows that the index is again on a downward trend as companies look for ways to cut costs and service quality is again undermined.

36. 'A Strategic Role for Purchasing' by Robin Cammish and Mark Keough. *McKinsey Quarterly* 1991 Number 3, 23.

37. Statistics quoted in the *The Machine That Changed The World* by J. Womack, D. Jones and D. Roos (1990), 155–56.

38. 'Harder than the Hype' by Robyn Meredith in *Forbes Global*, 16 April 2001.

39. Conducted by Cap Gemini Ernst & Young. Published May 2001.

40. British Chambers of Commerce report. May 2001.

Chapter 5

41. Kaplan, R.S. and Norton, D.P. (2001) *The Strategy-Focused Organization: How Balanced Scorecard Companies Thrive in the New Business Environment*, Harvard Business School Press, Boston, MA.

Chapter 6

42. In a published letter to the *Financial Times*, 11 January 2001.

43. 'Customer Intimacy and Other Value Disciplines' by Michael Treacy and Fred Wiersema, *Harvard Business Review*, Jan–Feb 1993.

44. 'The Secret of Picking Tech Winners', *Investors Chronicle*, 16 February 2001.

45. Reported in UK edition of *Business* 2.0, March 2001.

46. Dr Richard Barker, 1998, and reported in Jim Kelly's column in the *Financial Times* 2/7/98 and 9/7/98.

47. Bierbusse, P. and Siesfeld, T. (1997) 'Measures that Matter', *Journal of Strategic Performance Measurement*, 1, 2, pp.6–11.

48. Anon (2000) 'Measures that Matter: an outside-in perspective on shareholder recognition', Ernst and Young, UK Study.

49. Conducted by PricewaterhouseCoopers in 1997–98.

Chapter 7

50. *The Economist*, 5 August 2000.

51. Quoted in *Financial Times* 'No Logo' article, 7 August 2001.

Chapter 8

52. *Living Strategy – Putting people at the heart of corporate purpose,* Lynda Gratton. Prentice Hall, 2000.

53. Cranfield School of Management's Human Resource Research Centre (in association with the Crane Davies Consultancy) has developed a Team Competency Model, which addresses the *collective* competences required for teams to operate effectively.

54. 'Putting the Service-Profit Chain to Work', James L. Heskett, Thomas O. Jones, Gary W. Loveman, W. Earl Sasser Jr., and Leonard A. Schlesinger. *Harvard Business Review*, March–April 1994.

55. 'The Employee-Customer-Profit Chain at Sears' by Anthony J. Rucci, Stephen P. Kirn and Richard T. Quinn. *Harvard Business Review*, January–February 1998.

56. 'From People To Profits' by Steven Bevan and Linda Barber. Institute of Employment Studies at Sussex University, UK. 1999. Also referenced *Financial Times* 24/6/99: 'The benefits of service with a smile' by the study's authors.

57. 'Getting Inside the HRM – Performance Relationship' by David Guest, Jonathan Michie, Maura Sheehan and Neil Conway. Research paper.

58. 'HR as a Source of Shareholder Value: Research and Recommendations' by Brian E. Becker, Mark A. Huselid, Peter S. Pickus, and Michael F. Spratt. *Human Resource Management*, Spring 1997. Vol. 36, No. 1.

59. *The ROI of Human Capital – Measuring the Economic Value of Employee Performance*, by Jac Fitz-enz (2000).

Chapter 9

60. Quoted by Nick Oliver and Barry Wilkinson in *The Japanization of British Industry – New Developments in the 1990s* (1992).

61. *Outlook* Special Edition, Accenture, October 1999.

Chapter 10

62. Conducted by Taylor Nelson Sofres in March 2001.

63. Anon, 'Linking Service Levels to Prices: A Consultation Paper'.

Chapter 11

64. With thanks to our colleague, Dr Yasar Jarrar, formerly of Cranfield's Centre for Business Performance, who provided valuable material for this chapter.

Index

Copyright notice

Disclaimer

Pearson Education Limited Terms and Conditions for Performance Prism Single User CD-ROM Licence

IMPORTANT – READ CAREFULLY

This is a legal agreement between you, ('the Licensee') (either an individual or a legal entity such as a corporation) and Pearson Education Limited ('the Publishers').

1. GENERAL

a) These terms and conditions ('the Agreement'), shall exclusively govern the Licensee's purchase of the Product and the grant of a non-exclusive licence to the Licensee by the Publishers for the use of the Product. For the purposes of this Agreement: **'the Product'** means the contents of The Performance Prism CD-ROM ordered by the Licensee, the software which enables search and retrieval of information contained on the CD-ROM and the accompanying manuals;

b) The Licensee may not assign or sub-license any of its rights or obligations under this Agreement without the prior written consent of the Publishers.

c) This Agreement is governed by the law of England and the parties accept the exclusive jurisdiction of the English courts.

2. GRANT OF LICENCE

Single Computer Use This Agreement permits the Licensee to use one copy of the Product on a single computer for search and retrieval purposes only. Once the Licensee has run that portion of the Product which set-up or installs the Product on the Licensee's computer, the Licensee may only use the Product on a different computer if the files installed by the set-up or installation program from the first computer (if any) are first deleted. The Licensee may not copy the contents or any part of the Product from the Product to a computer hard disk or any other permanent electronic storage device (except as occurs when the Licensee runs the set-up/install program or uses other features of the Product on a single computer).

For the avoidance of doubt, the Product shall remain the exclusive property of the Publishers at all times.

Purchase of the book entitles the purchaser to a single user licence for the CD of The Performance Prism. To purchase additional licences contact Dr Mike Kennerley at the Centre of Business Performance, Cranfield School of Management, e-mail: m.kennerley@cranfield.ac.uk

3. PROPRIETARY RIGHTS IN THE PRODUCT

Copyright and all intellectual property rights in the Product including in any images, photographs, animation, videos, audio, music, software and text incorporated in the Product is owned by the Publishers or their suppliers and is protected by United Kingdom copyright laws and international treaty provisions and the Licensee acknowledges that it has no rights therein except as set out in this Agreement.

4. OTHER RESTRICTIONS

The Licensee may not:

i) pass free of charge, or sell, name and address information from the Product to any third party;

ii) duplicate, transfer, sell, rent, lease or commercially exploit the Product or information contained therein.

iii) alter, merge, or adapt the Product or any part thereof in any way including dissembling or decompiling except as permitted by law.

5. WARRANTY

The Publishers warrant that the Product will substantially conform to the applicable user documentation accompanying the Product and also that the CD-ROM media on which the Product is distributed is free from defects in materials and workmanship. The Publishers will replace defective media at no charge, provided that the Licensee returns the Product with dated proof of payment to the Publishers at Pearson Education Distribution Centre, Magna Park, Coventry Road, Lutterworth, Leicestershire, LE17 4XH within 30 days of receipt. These are the Licensee's sole remedies for any breach of these warranties.

Although the information contained in the Product has been prepared with reasonable care the Publishers do not warrant the accuracy or completeness of the Product or the results to be obtained therefrom. The Publishers do not warrant that the Licensee's use of the product will be uninterrupted or error free. Any implied warranties on the Product are limited to 30 days from the date of receipt.

While the Publishers have used all reasonable endeavours to ensure that the software they have written is Year 2000 compliant it is not possible to ensure that software and systems supplied by third parties are Year 2000 compliant and accordingly no guarantees are given in that respect and all warranties, whether express or implied (whether arising statutorily or otherwise), are hereby excluded to the maximum extent permitted by law.

EXCEPT AS EXPRESSLY PROVIDED IN THIS AGREEMENT the Publishers disclaim all other warranties either express or implied including but not limited to implied warranties of satisfactory quality or fitness for a particular purpose with respect to the Product, accompanying materials and any accompanying literature to the maximum extent permitted by law.

6. LIMITATION OF LIABILITY

a) The Publishers entire liability and the Licensee's exclusive remedy shall be, at the Publishers' option, either (i) termination of this Agreement and return of the fee paid for the Product upon return of the Product and all copies thereof; or (ii) repair or replacement of the Product. Any replacement will be warranted for 30 days from the date of receipt of the replacement by the Licensee.

b) To the maximum extent permitted by law, in no event shall the Publishers or its suppliers be liable for any damages whatsoever including without limitation special, indirect or consequential loss, damages for loss of business, lost profits, business interruption or other pecuniary loss arising from the use or inability to use the Product, even if advised of the possibility of such damages. In no case shall the Publishers' liability exceed the fee paid by the Licensee save that nothing in clauses 5 or 6 of this Agreement affects any rights the Licensee may have against the Publishers for death or personal injury caused by the Publishers' negligence.

7. TERMINATION

This Agreement may be terminated by either party if the other is in material breach of this Agreement and has failed to rectify such breach within 30 days of receipt notice of the same.

If you agree to abide by the Pearson Education Limited Terms and Conditions for The Performance Prism License please click here. If you do not agree to the terms of this agreement promptly return the CD-ROM with its packaging and accompanying items (including written materials) to the place you obtained them for a full refund.

8. WRITTEN CONFIRMATION

The Publishers reserve the right to demand, not more than once per annum, written confirmation, signed by an officer of your organisation, that your organisation has fully complied with the terms of this Agreement at all times during the period from the date when the last confirmation was provided or the start of this Agreement if no such confirmation has yet been provided.

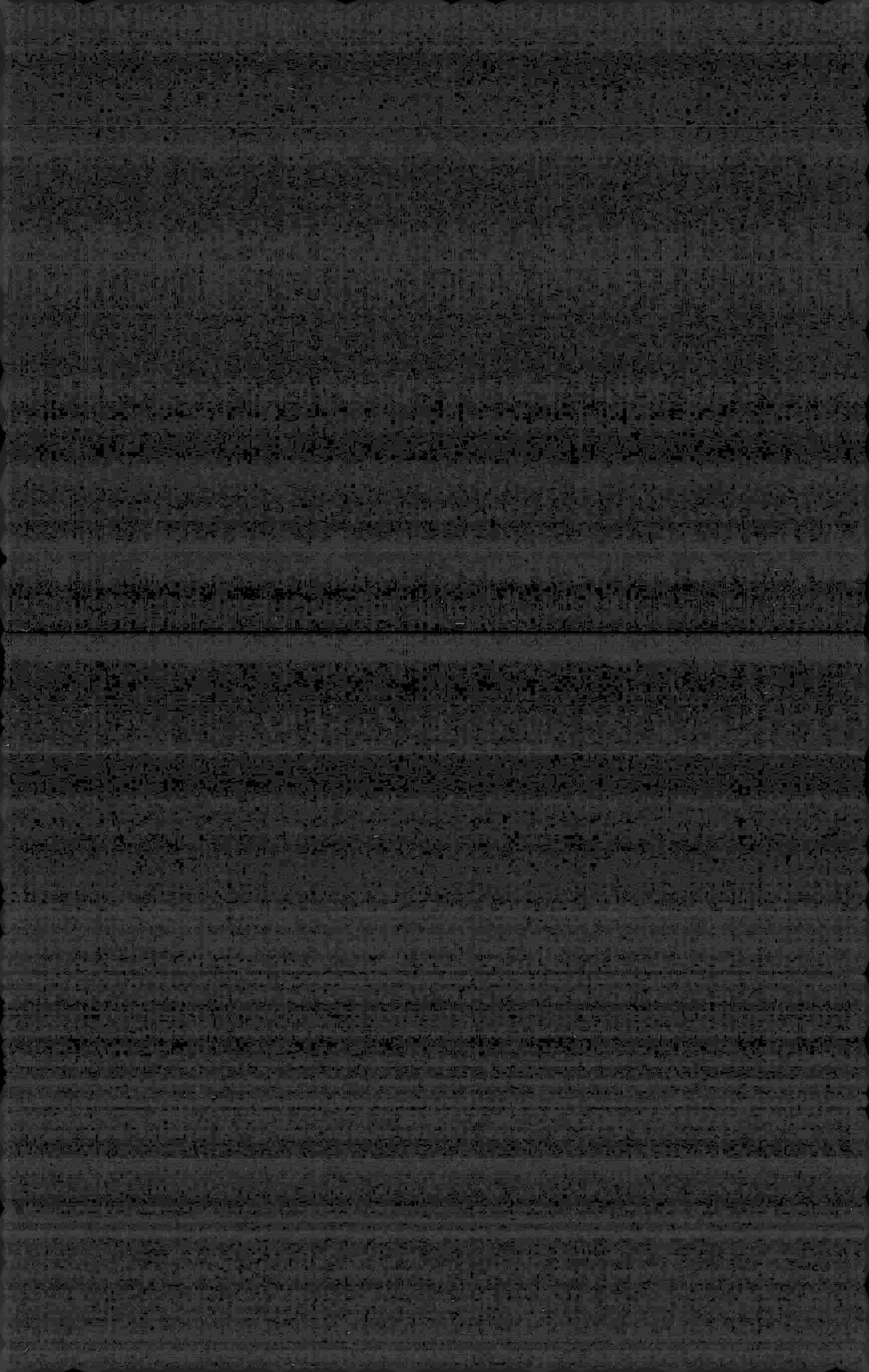